Post-Quantum Cryptography and IoT Communications for Sustainable Urban Development

Baghavathi Priya S.
https://orcid.org/0000-0001-9168-7810
Amrita Vishwa Vidyapeetham, India

Subha S.
https://orcid.org/0000-0001-8123-5941
SRM Institute of Science and Technology, India

Sountharrajan S.
Amrita Vishwa Vidyapeetham, India

Balamurugan Balusamy
Manipal Academy of Higher Education, Dubai, UAE

Suganya E.
Sri Sivasubramaniya Nadar College of Engineering, India

IGI Global
Scientific Publishing
Publishing Tomorrow's Research Today

Vice President of Editorial — Melissa Wagner
Director of Acquisitions — Mikaela Felty
Director of Book Development — Jocelynn Hessler
Production Manager — Mike Brehm
Cover Design — Jose Rosado

Published in the United States of America by
IGI Global Scientific Publishing
701 East Chocolate Avenue
Hershey, PA, 17033, USA
Tel: 717-533-8845 | Fax: 717-533-7115
Website: https://www.igi-global.com E-mail: cust@igi-global.com

Library of Congress Cataloging-in-Publication Data

Names: S., Baghavathi Priya, 1978- editor | S., Subha, 1980- editor | S., Sountharrajan, 1982- editor | Balusamy, Balamurugan editor | E, Suganya, 1991- editor
Title: Post-quantum cryptography and IoT communications for sustainable urban development / edited by Baghavathi Priya S., Subha S., Sountharrajan S., Balamurugan Balusamy, Suganya E.
Description: Hershey, PA : IGI Global Scientific Publishing, [2026] | Includes bibliographical references and index. | Summary: "This book aims to address the urgent need for secure IoT communications in smart city infrastructures by exploring quantum cryptographic solutions"-- Provided by publisher.
Identifiers: LCCN 2025031494 (print) | LCCN 2025031495 (ebook) | ISBN 9798337331669 hardcover | ISBN 9798337331676 paperback | ISBN 9798337331683 ebook
Subjects: LCSH: Smart cities | Internet of things--Security measures | Quantum cryptography | Sustainable urban development--Technological innovations
Classification: LCC TD159.4 .P67 2026 (print) | LCC TD159.4 (ebook)
LC record available at https://lccn.loc.gov/2025031494
LC ebook record available at https://lccn.loc.gov/2025031495

British Cataloguing in Publication Data
A Cataloguing in Publication record for this book is available from the British Library.

Table of Contents

Detailed Table of Contents

The growth of Internet of Things (IoT) devices has driven the evolution of smart cities that enable enhanced efficiency, sustainability, and citizen well-being. This chapter provides an in-depth strategy for the development and integration of lightweight post-quantum cryptography (PQC)-based protocols, especially for IoT devices within secure city infrastructures. The suggested architecture combines lattice-based key exchange (CRYSTALS-Kyber), lattice-based digital signatures (CRYSTALS-Dilithium), Grover-resistant symmetric encryption, and AI-powered intrusion detection. Key compression, signature aggregation, and adaptive security configurations are the added protocol improvements. This approach involves risk analysis, modeling, and performance evaluation (latency, energy, bandwidth, packet loss) and is significantly advanced over legacy RSA/ECC models, offering quantum-resilient security with efficiency for large-scale IoT networks.

The use of IoT in the building of Smart cities has transformed how urban areas are managed, as people cannot only monitor in real-time but also automate and make decisions that rely on the data they gather. The post-quantum cryptography (PQC) adoption is a very urgent need as the current classical encryption techniques like RSA and ECC can be broken with quantum computers. The chapter discusses PQC usage in the real world, specifically, in terms of smart urban ecosystems and major areas. It includes real-life case studies of PQC pilotage or proposals in quantum-vulnerable settings to make them more resilient. Moreover, the chapter explains the cryptographic algorithms standardized by NIST, assesses their applicability to constrained IoT use, and proposes a Proof of Concept (PoC) architecture of a PQC-enabled smart city. The chapter is an interim between theory and practice and is a part of the overarching topic of quantum-safe and sustainable urban development, and it provides a practical plan to urban planners, technologists, and cybersecurity professionals.

Krithikha Sanju S., Sri Sivasubramaniya Nadar College of Engineering, India
Madhu Annam R., Sri Sivasubramaniya Nadar College of Engineering, India

The development of quantum computing represents an evolutionary change to commonly used forms of public encryption, such as RSA that is designed to protect certain municipal systems which will create further vulnerabilities. Post-quantum cryptography (PQC) can provide a further level of encryption. This chapter discusses how post-quantum techniques can be used to secure the smart infrastructures that support an overall long-range planning process and possibly improve a city's resilience to respond to shocks. This chapter also demonstrates examples from practice, references implications for the original research, and makes recommendations for incorporating quantum resilient cryptography into the urban development agenda through systems thinking.

M. Nalini, S.A. Engineering College, India
B. Yamini, School of Computing, SRM Institute of Science and Technology, India
Monica G. K., R.M.K. College of Engineering and Technology, India
R. Kennady, Rajalakshmi Institute of Technology, India

The emergence of quantum computing poses significant threats to classical cryptographic systems, particularly in smart urban environments powered by the internet of things (IoT). This chapter explores the sustainability aspects and future prospects of integrating post-quantum cryptography (PQC) into IoT-based infrastructures. It examines various PQC algorithms, their deployment challenges

Quantum algorithms have emerged as powerful computational tools that leverage the principles of quantum mechanics to address complex problems beyond the scope of classical computing. This chapter explores the foundational concepts, classifications, implementation challenges, and future prospects of quantum algorithms. Key breakthroughs such as Grover's and Shor's algorithms are explored alongside recent developments in quantum machine learning and optimization. The chapter also compares quantum and classical algorithmic complexity, highlighting areas of potential speedup. Practical limitations including hardware constraints, error correction, and resource estimation are critically analyzed. Finally, the chapter outlines emerging research directions and ethical considerations essential for responsible quantum computing development.

As quantum computing advances, existing cryptographic techniques used in smart city infrastructures face increasing vulnerability, especially within internet of things (IoT) networks. This chapter explores the critical role of post-quantum cryptography (PQC) in securing urban IoT ecosystems against quantum threats while addressing sustainability challenges. It covers PQC principles, algorithm families, integration with IoT communication protocols, and the protection of critical sectors such as energy, healthcare, and transportation. The chapter also explores quantum-specific network attacks, supply chain vulnerabilities, and the role of green cryptography and AI-assisted security. Emphasis is placed on balancing quantum resilience with energy efficiency to ensure secure, scalable, and sustainable smart cities. The chapter concludes by identifying future research directions to guide the transition toward quantum-safe and eco-conscious urban infrastructure.

Preface

In the last decade, two major developments have converged to bring security to the forefront of urban development: the rise of smart cities and the threat of quantum computing. First, the increasing reliance of urban infrastructures on interconnected Internet of Things (IoT) systems has made them critical for everything from traffic management and energy grids to public safety and resource management. These systems are essential for achieving the efficiency and sustainability goals of modern cities. Second, the rapid advancement of quantum computing threatens to undermine the very security protocols that protect these critical infrastructures. Whereas, in the past, data could be secured using classical cryptographic methods like RSA and Elliptic Curve Cryptography (ECC), quantum computers, armed with algorithms like Shor's (1994), can break these systems, leaving vital networks vulnerable (Mosca, 2018).

The consequence of these advances is that information security is no longer just a technical concern; it's a strategic imperative for city planners, technologists, and policymakers. In the past, data was often centralized and could be protected by ensuring confidentiality, integrity, and availability (the CIA triad). It was a relatively straightforward process to control who had access to data, ensure its content remained unchanged, and guarantee its availability to authorized personnel. Today, because urban ecosystems are dispersed, decentralized, and reliant on a vast number of diverse IoT devices, managing security is far more complex. The emphasis must shift from simply maintaining the CIA triad to building robust, resilient, and adaptive frameworks that can handle a new class of threats.

THE CHALLENGES

It goes without saying that the threat of quantum-enabled attacks, vulnerabilities in IoT supply chains, and the increasing complexity of urban networks pose significant challenges. Any attempt to deal with these problems demands an adequate understanding of the issues that exist in the quantum era. Such challenges can be classified into four categories:

- The challenge of securing a geographically dispersed and resource-constrained IoT environment against quantum attacks.
- The challenge of developing and implementing post-quantum cryptographic (PQC) policies and protocols that are both effective and scalable for smart urban ecosystems.
- The challenge of establishing correct structures of responsibility for data and security, given the complex and often fragmented nature of urban IoT governance.
- The challenge of ensuring long-term sustainability and resilience by balancing enhanced security with efficiency and performance in urban development.

Numerous studies have indicated that a "policy vacuum" exists for dealing with quantum threats to urban infrastructures. This is evidenced not only by the theoretical vulnerabilities of current systems but also by the general lack of awareness and action from city governments and technology providers (Alharbi et al., 2023). The inherent complexity of urban IoT infrastructures makes them extremely susceptible to new cyberattacks. Quantum decryption and quantum-boosted malware pose risks that could expose sensitive information and facilitate large-scale network intrusions (Ghaleb et al., 2023).

A further layer of complexity is introduced by supply chain vulnerabilities inherent in the production of IoT devices. Securing urban infrastructure requires trust not just in the deployed devices, but in their entire lifecycle, from manufacturing to deployment. Compromised hardware or firmware inserted at any stage can create backdoors that bypass even the strongest cryptographic defenses. This issue is particularly pressing for smart cities, which depend on a vast and global supply chain, making it difficult to verify the integrity of every single component.

Moreover, the technical realities of IoT devices present unique hurdles for PQC implementation. Unlike powerful servers, most IoT endpoints are resource-constrained, operating with limited memory, processing power, and battery life. Many of the leading PQC algorithms, while quantum-safe, are significantly more computationally intensive than their classical predecessors (Oder et al., 2018). This presents a critical trade-off: ensuring robust security without sacrificing device performance, energy efficiency, and low latency—factors that are essential for the smooth operation and sustainability of urban systems (Liu et al., 2024).

SEARCHING FOR A SOLUTION

Solutions to the problem of securing urban IoT ecosystems in the quantum era require a shift in emphasis from simply patching existing systems to a proactive, forward-looking strategy. Although many researchers have called for such an orientation, acontextual and reactive solutions still tend to dominate. Such ill-conceived approaches often fail to consider the unique characteristics of urban environments and the limitations of IoT devices.

One step toward a solution is establishing formalized rules through comprehensive post-quantum security policies (Alagic et al., 2022). These policies should facilitate a smooth transition to quantum-safe protocols and help resolve ambiguities within a city's digital infrastructure. However, the success of these policies is a function of their integration with the strategic vision of a smart city. If a secure environment is an enabling condition for a city's smooth operation, then security must be a strategic issue, not a tactical one. This moves the PQC agenda to the top management list, ensuring buy-in from senior stakeholders.

Another critical step is to adopt a multidisciplinary approach that considers not just technology, but also governance, human factors, and sustainable practices. This means developing solutions that are not only cryptographically robust but also energy-efficient and scalable (Yuan et al., 2023). For instance, green cryptography and hybrid models are emerging as key components for balancing quantum resilience with the long-term sustainability goals of a smart city.

Ultimately, the focus must be on creating a security vision and strategy where threats are considered within the broader scope of urban computing. This requires moving beyond a reactive, checklist-based approach to a more proactive one that understands the underlying patterns of behavior and the complex interdependencies of urban systems.

ORGANISATION OF THE BOOK

This book is organized into 11 chapters, each addressing a critical facet of this challenge.

Chapter 1 presents an in-depth strategy for developing security protocols tailored for IoT communication in a post-quantum world, outlining an architecture that integrates lattice-based schemes like CRYSTALS-Kyber and CRYSTALS-Dilithium to ensure quantum resilience with efficiency for large-scale networks.

Chapter 2 discusses the real-world application of PQC in smart urban ecosystems by examining NIST-standardized algorithms and proposing a Proof of Concept architecture for a PQC-enabled smart city.

Chapter 3 complements this by exploring how post-quantum techniques can be integrated into long-range planning processes to improve a city's resilience to future shocks and cyber threats.

Chapter 4 explores the sustainability aspects and future prospects of integrating PQC into smart IoT ecosystems, emphasizing the need for energy-efficient algorithms, lightweight cryptography, and “green computing” paradigms to balance security with environmental goals.

Chapter 5 provides a comprehensive overview of the quantum computing threat, exploring emerging solutions like PQC and Quantum Key Distribution (QKD), while also discussing the importance of cryptographic agility and hybrid migration strategies.

Chapter 6 analyzes the specific dangers of quantum network attacks in urban IoT infrastructures, detailing how threats such as quantum decryption and quantum-boosted malware can compromise critical smart city services.

Chapter 7 delves into the cryptanalysis of PQC schemes and the growing role of AI in both breaking and securing these systems, featuring a case study on CRYSTALS-Kyber to demonstrate the practical risks of implementation flaws.

Chapter 8 focuses on protecting symmetric cryptography from quantum attacks by exploring mitigation strategies such as increased key sizes, quantum-resistant designs, and hybrid encryption models.

Chapter 9 provides a deep dive into the foundational principles of quantum algorithms, exploring key breakthroughs like Shor's and Grover's algorithms and their potential for speedup over classical computing.

Chapter 10 explores the critical role of PQC in securing urban IoT ecosystems, covering the protection of sectors such as energy, healthcare, and transportation.

Finally, Chapter 11 provides a broad overview of IoT in urban development, outlining its key applications, current challenges, and future research directions to build sustainable and inclusive smart cities.

REFERENCES

Alagic, G. (2022). Status report on the third round of the NIST post-quantum cryptography standardization process. NIST Interagency/Internal Report, NISTIR 8309.

Alharbi, A., Naeem, H., Khan, S., & Shah, M. A. (2023). Post-quantum cryptography for secure smart cities: A survey. *IEEE Access : Practical Innovations, Open Solutions*, *11*, 50234–50257. DOI: 10.1109/ACCESS.2023.3276481

Ghaleb, F. A., Ali, H., & Shakir, M. Z. (2023). Securing IoT applications in smart cities using post-quantum cryptography: Challenges and future directions. *IEEE Internet of Things Journal*, *10*(3), 1739–1752. DOI: 10.1109/JIOT.2022.3186447

Liu, T., Ramachandran, G., & Jurdak, R. (2024). Post-Quantum Cryptography for Internet of Things: A Survey on Performance and Optimization. arXiv (Cornell University). /arxiv.2401.17538DOI: 10.48550

Mosca, M. (2018). Cybersecurity in an era with quantum computers. *IEEE Security and Privacy*, *16*(5), 38–41. DOI: 10.1109/MSP.2018.3761723

Oder, T. (2018). Practical post-quantum cryptography for embedded systems. *Journal of Cryptographic Engineering*, *8*(3), 233–244.

Shor, P. W. (1994). Algorithms for quantum computation: Discrete logarithms and factoring. *Proceedings of the 35th Annual Symposium on Foundations of Computer Science*, 124–134. DOI: 10.1109/SFCS.1994.365700

Yuan, B., Wu, F., & Zheng, Z. (2023). Post quantum blockchain architecture for Internet of Things over NTRU lattice. *PLoS One*, *18*(2), e0279429. DOI: 10.1371/journal.pone.0279429 PMID: 36724147

Chapter 1
Security Protocols for IoT Communication in Post-Quantum Cryptography for Resilient Urban Development

Viji Gripsy J.
https://orcid.org/0000-0002-6599-3010
PSGR Krishnammal College for Women, India

Dhanalakshmi P.
https://orcid.org/0000-0002-4118-821X
Sri Ramakrishna College of Arts and Science for Women, India

Sasikala M.
https://orcid.org/0000-0003-4342-3348
PSGR Krishnammal College for Women, India

Usha M.
https://orcid.org/0009-0006-1446-9848
KG College of Arts and Science, India

Ahamed Johnsha Ali S.
https://orcid.org/0000-0001-5704-1098
Sri Krishna Aditya College of Arts and Science, India

Saravanan S.
https://orcid.org/0000-0002-2064-2241
Vel Tech Rangarajan Dr. Sagunthala R&D Institute of Science and Technology, India

ABSTRACT

The growth of Internet of Things (IoT) devices has driven the evolution of smart cities that enable enhanced efficiency, sustainability, and citizen well-being. This chapter provides an in-depth strategy for the development and integration of lightweight post-quantum cryptography (PQC)-based protocols, especially for IoT devices within secure city infrastructures. The suggested architecture combines lattice-based key exchange (CRYSTALS-Kyber), lattice-based digital signatures

DOI: 10.4018/979-8-3373-3166-9.ch001

(CRYSTALS-Dilithium), Grover-resistant symmetric encryption, and AI-powered intrusion detection. Key compression, signature aggregation, and adaptive security configurations are the added protocol improvements. This approach involves risk analysis, modeling, and performance evaluation (latency, energy, bandwidth, packet loss) and is significantly advanced over legacy RSA/ECC models, offering quantum-resilient security with efficiency for large-scale IoT networks.

1. INTRODUCTION

Smart cities are increasingly reliant on computer-based applications and systems to manage personal finance and security; therefore, they have become crucial as they store, process and communicate sensitive information. However, as dependence grows, so do concerns about data protection. Security is often considered on the basis of crime and not in a protective manner. As a result, as more systems operate in connected environments, attention must be turned to security system adoption and operational data protection practices. These challenges include legal accountability to not only the IoT device and the manufacturer (or system integrity), but often relate to liability when failures occur (whether due to physical causes or mechanical) to operational safeguards. Issues of functionality and restrictions on use can reduce system and information integrity or functionality. Further psychosocial impacts are raising further concerns toward organizations and their operational why and how to remain accountable. Hence, who are responsible to the public, need to develop a greater understanding of their ongoing legally liable risks. A review of how IoT devices first emerged, and an approach to integrated risk management, or safety management if appropriate, could provide practical information. In spite of these vulnerabilities, the robots can still do things on their own with little human assistance. The number of cyberattacks in the last few years have increased significantly, with Neto et al. (2024) demonstrating that IoT devices are a specific vulnerable device for such attacks. Such reasons are due to not a common standard security policy, and low power computing on each device. Research efforts are needed in all critical areas and high risk challenges with the development of PQC methods, which is necessary for IoT networks (Lohachab et al., 2020).

1.1 Securing IoT Communications in the Post-Quantum Era

PQC has only recently emerged as an area of research with the aim of developing cryptographic algorithms resilient to attack by both classical and quantum computers (Mastriani, 2022). The aim is to reduce threats posed by quantum computers. The algorithms are being developed to replace or augment the cryptographic methods in use to provide long term protection for confidential data transferred and stored in IoT networks (Kumar et al., 2021). Blockchain can help increase transparency and prevent data tampering but is still susceptible to Sybil and 51% attacks. Quantum blockchains are less vulnerable to these types of attacks using both post-quantum cryptographic algorithms and safe quantum communication channels (Azad et al., 2025). Groupings like the National Institute of Standards and Technology are also making an effort for post-quantum cryptographic algorithms to be standardized. They are currently studying several potential algorithms to include in upcoming cryptographic standards. Post-quantum encryption and signature methods tend to be costly to compute generally, which could be a challenge for IoT devices with a low ability to process (Liu et al., 2024). As such, IoT devices require lightweight and post-quantum cryptographic protocols.

Devices are projected to become more powerful in the future, with greater computing power expected in the coming decades (Kumar et al., 2021). This projected advancement is expected to happen as resource-limited IoT networks continue to develop. Therefore, the development and deployment of PQC solutions are imperative in order to provide assurance for the continued resilience and security of metropolitan infrastructure.

1.2 Cross-Domain Communication and Trust in IoT

Due to the interconnected nature of IoT devices, cross-domain communication is frequently necessary. This situation creates the necessity for devices that reside in different administrative domains to be able to communicate and share some information, which is particularly relevant in the industrial IoT domain, as outlined in Hassan et al. (n.d.). In this industrial manufacturing process, all work is implemented through a plethora of firms, and there arises the necessity for secure communication between devices that organizations own or control.

Building trust in this domain is a significant problem; there is organizational hesitation to share sensitive business information with other entities (Hassan et al., n.d.). It is important to maintain stringent authentication and authorization policies to facilitate information exchange, so that only legitimate devices can access the information (Cruz et al., 2021). One method to address this challenge is to use blockchain technology that provides a secure distributed ledger with which to record transactions and authorize access. Pajooh et al. (2021) state that the immutable and transparent properties of blockchain technology can be used to develop trust in a variety of contexts, with the caveat that any authorized user can authenticate access rights and verify the integrity of the data contained within the berated ledger. In cloud-based IIoT healthcare environments, the trusted authority generates public parameters, encryption keys, and decryption keys (Sun et al. 2020). Creating a secure and shielded space for data is important. In the IoT world, Hassan et al. (n.d.) state that validation of signatures before decrypting is done by the cloud. This ensures that data is secure and tamper-proof. Another method to enable secure communication among domains is attribute-based encryption. This approach includes creating access control rules based on the nature of the devices and individuals involved.

1.3 Sustainable Urban Development with Secured IoT

The IoT enables effective monitoring and control at a lower cost, which is why the concept of Industrial IoT was developed, according to Cruz et al. (2021). The integration of the IoT into the healthcare sector introduces several benefits, such as improved accessibility, prevention of disease, and home monitoring (Sun et al., 2021). An illustration of how IoT-based monitoring could make biogas plants more efficient is that it can be applied to installations in laboratories or industrial environments. According to Abijaude et al. (2021), smart contracts can potentially offer another level of security that guarantees irrefutability, anonymity, and data integrity when fully integrated with blockchain technology. (Hosseinian et al., 2020) The IoT will aid in the creation of local energy markets in future smart grids. In terms of guaranteeing the security and resilience of city infrastructure, the creation and application of post-quantum cryptographic measures are imperative.

2. LITERATURE REVIEW

The integration of blockchain technology and the IoT has proved to be very efficient and has future potential for improvement in scalability and productivity (Rahman et al., 2022). Blockchain technology protects user privacy and security in Industry 4.0 and the IoT (Wang et al., 2021). One of the principal reasons fine-grained access control solutions protect cloud-enabled industrial IoT healthcare is the ability to enable participants to define specific access privileges for community health data (Sun et al., 2021). Employing attribute-based matchmaking encryption, as suggested by Sun et al. (2021), allows for the forming of specific access constraints with conditions that must be satisfied, in order to decrypt the data. This limits anonymity while sustaining data integrity and preventing breaches of privacy. A bill by Obaidat et al. (2024) discusses the use of blockchain technology for storage and security authentication via decentralization, thereby making it suitable for IoT ecosystem frameworks. The combination of identity-based encryption and matchmaking processes foster secure exchanges of data with proper access control, consequently enforcing confidentiality, privacy, and data integrity (Hassan et al., n.d.). Additionally, strong security protocols must be established because urban systems are increasingly relied upon to support system digitalization via numerous IoT devices, resulting in more cyberattacks. The future expectation of quantum computing solidifies the need for PQC, safeguarding urban services dependent on IoT communications (Alharbi et al., 2023; Agyekum et al., 2024).

Sanchez-Corcuera et al. (2019) assert that urban resilience is reliant on communication networks that are secure, trustworthy and resilient to disruption from either environmental issues or a cyber-attack. IoT devices that are designed to enable applications in smart grids, traffic control and public safety systems have many vulnerabilities created by the heterogeneity of the devices, limited resources for the device, and the insecure deployment of devices (Alaba et al., 2017, Al-Turjman & Malekloo, 2019). Khan et al. (2022) and Mavromoustakis et al. (2023) assert that assuring the confidentiality and integrity of data flows produced by the system is of key importance to the sustainability of adaptive urban government. Although IoT security standards exist, and utilize existing cryptographic standards primarily RSA, ECC and other traditional cryptographic systems, there is a chance that they will become obsolete due to quantum attacks (Chen et al., 2016, Bindel et al., 2021). For the first time some researchers have explored post-quantum instantiations that would be sustainable within the constraints of the IoT. For example, it has been shown that lattice-based instantiations such as Kyber and Dilithium, as well as hash-based signatures (SPHINCS+), represent excellent trade-offs between security and efficiency for constrained settings (Hulsing et al., 2019, Oder et al., 2022, Mosca & Piani, 2022). Pereira et al. (2024) emphasize the growing trend of hybrid cryptographic systems as transitional arrangements for migration phases. These systems incorporate classical primitives and quantum-resistant primitives. Formulating an IoT protocol using PQC involves key latency, size, and computational restrictions while adhering to existing regulatory frameworks in urban settings (Fernandes et al., 2023; Kampanakis et al.). Furthermore, the experimental system deployments by Liu et al. (2023) recently, regarding the use of lattice-based key encapsulation in vehicle IoT networks show, operated under PQC without sacrificing real-time performance. In addition while system-level solutions are being developed on locating resilient architectures that combine PQC, intrusion detection, and distributed ledger technology in order to provide improved data provenance and access control attributes, (Conti et al., 2018; Dorri et al., 2020; Zhang et al., 2023). From the bigger picture of urban planning, adopting IoT protocols backed by PQC into urban resilience is a major focal change towards future-oriented methods relating to anticipatory cyber-physical governance with regard to information technology. For a bigger picture of urban resilience, supporting urban digital twins for careful autonomous mobility and monitoring of critical infrastructure from both traditional and quantum threats, new smart city designs are taking on cryptographic agility for new ICT details (Batty et al., 2021; Gaurav et al., 2023).

Scientists have observed important socio-technical considerations in the operationalization of PQC in urban systems, including the importance of the creation of capacity and promoting global standardization and collaboration to implement PQC in an equitable way (NIST, 2022; Ghaleb et al., 2023). In summary, the literature indicates that there is urgency, in moving towards better security practices in cities grounded in quantum resilience which are operationally bounded and strategically oriented to articulate the backdrop of urban IoT practice (Alharbi et al., 2023; Mosca & Piani, 2022).

It is all the more important to reframe our research that leverages multiple domains of research to bridge technology advancements within cryptography with urban resilience and sustainability aims. The case studies summarized in Table 1 are situated within PQC-Based IoT Security in Resilient Urban Systems.

Table 1. Case Studies on PQC-Based IoT Security in Resilient Urban Systems

Study / Project	Urban Domain	PQC Scheme	IoT Application	Key Outcome
Liu et al. (2023)	Smart Transportation	Lattice-based (Kyber)	Vehicular IoT network (V2V and V2I)	Demonstrated secure key exchange with acceptable latency under vehicular speeds
Zhang et al. (2023)	Critical Infrastructure	Lattice + Blockchain hybrid	Power grid IoT monitoring	Enhanced data provenance and tamper-resistance using PQC-secured blockchain
Pereira et al. (2024)	Smart City Platforms	Hybrid (ECC + lattice PQC)	Multimodal sensor networks (environment, traffic)	Smooth migration to PQC with minimal performance impact; backwards compatibility maintained
Ghaleb et al. (2023)	Urban Healthcare IoT	SPHINCS+ (hash-based signature)	Secure patient monitoring devices	Improved resistance to quantum signature forgery with manageable signature size for IoT devices
Oder et al. (2022)	Smart Energy Management	Kyber KEM	IoT nodes in smart meters	Practical implementation on ARM Cortex-M4; acceptable power and memory consumption
Dorri et al. (2020)	Automotive Systems	Blockchain (PQC-ready design)	Connected autonomous vehicles	Decentralized privacy-preserving framework ready for PQC integration

2.1 Research Gaps

- Despite the significant progress made on the design of post-quantum cryptographic algorithms for IoT systems in urban environments, some core research gaps still exist. First, there is a stark lack of rigorous empirical evidence to support the practical application of PQC algorithms in the varied IoT systems typical of resilient cities. Many of the recent works, like those of Liu et al. (2023) and Oder et al. (2022), focus on proof-of-concept deployments or simulations, thus not addressing issues of scalability, interoperability, and performance in dynamic city contexts.

- There is a significant lack of thorough exploration regarding cross-layer security systems that incorporate PQC at various levels of the IoT protocol stack, from the physical layer to the application layer. Existing research predominantly concentrates on isolated cryptographic primitives rather than holistic systems that ensure end-to-end security in urban IoT systems (Ghaleb et al., 2023; Pereira et al., 2024). The combination of PQC with artificial intelligence-driven intrusion detection systems remains insufficiently explored despite growing recognition of AI's role in proactive urban cyber defense (Mavromoustakis et al., 2023). The study highlights the importance of specified standards and evaluation processes specific to PQC in IoT-based urban infrastructure. NIST's ongoing standardization efforts offer a framework (NIST, 2022), but adapted measures encompassing urban resilience goals—recovery time, flexibility, and social equity need further development (Alharbi et al., 2023).
- Furthermore, socio-technical challenges represent a persistent research gap. There is a paucity of research on the impact of governance, public policy, and stakeholder engagement on the uptake of PQC-secured IoT systems within smart cities. The gap is significant, as success depends on technological viability, regulatory support, cost-benefit estimation, and trust by the general public (Batty et al., 2021; Gaurav et al., 2023).
- In the end, little or no research exists on hybrid migration models that efficiently handle the transitional period wherein traditional and quantum-resistant systems need to coexist securely in urban IoT deployments. Despite the existence of early ideas (Pereira et al., 2024), their practical implementation and life management within urban infrastructures remain largely unexplored.

3. PROPOSED METHODOLOGY

An extensive review of prior research on IoT security, post-quantum cryptography (PQC), and blockchain was conducted to define key advancements and use cases in the literature. This review allowed for an understanding of the state-of-the-art research in the field while demonstrating notable research strengths and vulnerable areas requiring further research. Specifically, research contributions relating to security protocols, authentication mechanisms, and access control methods necessary to establish security for IoT and communication for new urban development.

The literature review also revealed applications that employed user-based access, such as Android-based controlled door locking systems, which illustrate the application in real-world smart urban environments. Although these applications introduce convenience and automation, their adoption ultimately related to perceived usefulness, perceived ease of use, and privacy (Ruaya, 2023). This experience emphasizes the necessity of maintaining security through a user-focussed design to maintain functionality while establishing trust.

In progressing towards the objectives of the chapter outline above, a structured, multi-phase approach is provided involving a theoretical analysis followed by protocol design, simulation, and performance assessment. Importantly, this approach is developed to apply to honest sustainable smart urban systems with demonstrated technological practicality. The proposed approach diagram in Figure 1 identifies a phased approach to systematically address the security research questions related to security in IoT enabled infrastructure in modern smart city-based interactive urban systems.

Figure 1. Proposed Model Architecture

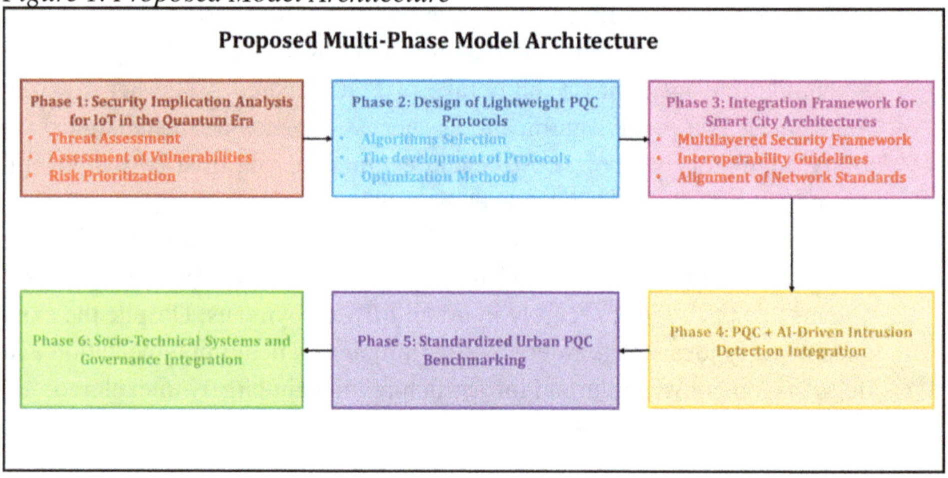

3.1 Phase 1: Security Implication Analysis for IoT in the Quantum Era

3.1.1 Threat Assessment

In sustainable urban planning, IoT technologies play a vital role in the operation of intelligent grids, smart transportation, environmental monitoring, and public safety networks. These networks rely heavily on cryptographic techniques to ensure the confidentiality, integrity, and authenticity of information carried across heterogeneous networks. The advent of quantum computers introduces new attack capabilities that undermine the security of many conventional cryptosystems.

Shor's method presents an efficient solution for integer factorization and discrete logarithm problems, defeating common public-key schemes like RSA, DSA, and ECC. The time complexity of these operations in Shor's algorithm is polynomial, which is calculated in equation 1:

$$\textit{Complexity of Shor's algorithm} = O((\log N)^3) \tag{1}$$

In this context, N represents the integer that needs to be factored.

By contrast, conventional methods such as the general number field sieve (GNFS) have sub-exponential complexity computed in equation 2:

$$\textit{Classical factorization (GNFS)} = O\left(exp\left(\left(\frac{64}{9}\log N\right)^{1/3}\right)(\log log\ N)^{2/3}\right) \tag{2}$$

Similarly, Grover's method provides a quadratic speedup to brute-force attacks against symmetric key ciphers. Equation 3 computed Grover's complexity.

$$\textit{Grover's complexity} = O(2^{n/2}) \tag{3}$$

where n is key size. This means that a 128-bit symmetric key would have an effective security of only 64 bits against a quantum adversary, thus necessitating higher key lengths (e.g., 256 bits) for equivalent security.

Such quantum algorithms threaten the security model of protocols like TLS (utilized in MQTT), DTLS (used in CoAP), and end-to-end encryption within LoRaWAN. Our threat model identifies the primary targets of quantum attacks:

- Key exchange protocols (RSA, ECC) • Digital signatures (ECDSA, RSA)
- Symmetric encryption (AES-128, DES)

- Hash functions (potentially accelerated detection of collisions with quantum methods like BHT)

3.1.2 Assessment of Vulnerabilities

In this step, we systematically evaluate the security position of common IoT protocols against quantum-capable attackers:

- **MQTT (Message Queuing Telemetry Transport):** MQTT uses TLS/SSL to encrypt communications. Standard TLS implementations employ RSA or ECDSA for key exchange and authentication, both vulnerable to Shor's method. AES-128, commonly utilized in MQTT security, offers weaker security against Grover's attack until upgraded to AES-256.
- **CoAP (Constrained Application Protocol):** CoAP frequently utilizes DTLS, whose vulnerabilities are comparable to TLS. Limited-resource implementations of CoAP can skip some security features, thereby increasing the risk.
- **LoRaWAN (Long Range Wide Area Network):** LoRaWAN utilizes symmetric key encryption (AES-128) for payload encryption and message integrity codes (MICs). Grover's method drastically reduces the effort required for brute force, thus diminishing security strength.

The severity of vulnerability V for a protocol P can be defined as a function of its dependency on insecure cryptosystems, which is calculated using equation 4.

$$V(P) = f\left(d_{RSA}, d_{ECC}, d_{AES-128}, d_{SHA-1/256}\right) \tag{4}$$

where d_x is the degree to which protocol P depends on cryptosystem x.

The larger a protocol's dependency on quantum-vulnerable primitives, the larger its V(P) is.

3.1.3 Risk Prioritization

We rank repair activities by mapping identified vulnerabilities to their likely impact on critical smart city services. This is achieved through a quantitative risk estimation matrix, where risk R is expressed in equation 5.

$$R = L \times I \tag{5}$$

where L = likelihood of successful quantum attack exploitation, I = impact on smart city sustainability goals (energy reliability, environmental conservation, transportation efficiency)

This can be formalized in equation 6.

$$R(P,S) = \sum_{i=1}^{n}\left(L_i(P).I_i(S)\right) \quad (6)$$

where P = protocol being analyzed, S = smart city service (e.g., smart grid, transportation, environmental monitoring), L_i (P) = estimated probability score for quantum attack of the protocol, P represents service S, and I_i(S) is the impact score for service S. Example risk prioritization Table 2 is given below.

Table 2. Example of risk prioritization

Protocol	Service	Likelihood (L)	Impact (I)	Risk (R = L×I)
MQTT + TLS (RSA/ECC)	Smart grid control	0.9	0.95	0.855
CoAP + DTLS (ECC)	Environmental sensors	0.8	0.7	0.56
LoRaWAN (AES-128)	Traffic flow sensors	0.7	0.8	0.56

Here, 0 = no risk, 1 = maximum risk. The priority would then be to mitigate risks with the highest R value first.

Proposed Algorithm 1: Quantum-Aware IoT Protocol Risk Assessment (Q-IoT-Risk)

```
Input:
List of IoT protocols P= {P1, P2, …. Pn}
List of smart city services S= {S1, S2..., Sm}
List of cryptosystems C= {C1, C2..., Ck} used by each proto-
col
Known quantum attack vectors QV= {QV1, QV2..., QVl}
Output:
Risk scores R(Pi,Sj) for each protocol-service pair
Step 1: Ranked order of high-priority protocol-service pairs
for mitigation
Initialize risk matrix
R(Pi,Sj)=0 □i□[1,n],j□[1,m]
Step 2: For each protocol Pi
a.  Identify cryptosystems C(Pi)□C used by Pi
```

```
b. For each cryptosystem Cx □C(Pi):
  i. Identify quantum attack vector QVy applicable to Cx
  ii. Compute quantum vulnerability severity Vq(Cx)
Vq(Cx)={1.0 if broken by Shor's(RSA/ECC)0.5 if week-
end by Grover's(AES-128)0.2 if minor quatum speed-up expect-
ed0.0 if quatum-resilient (PQC)
Step 3: For each smart city service Sj
Step 4: Map protocol Pi o service Sj (if used)
Step 5: Estimate:
L(Pi,Sj)=max□(VqCx), Cx□C(Pi)
Step 6: Estimate impact:
I(Sj)= {0.9-1.0 critical (e.g., smart grid)0.6-0.8 import-
ant (e.g., traffic control0.3-0.5 moderate (e.g., environ-
ment sensors)
Step 7: Compute risk
R(Pi,Sj)= L(Pi,Sj)×I(Sj)
Step 8: Rank risks
Step 9: Sort R (Pi, Sj) in descending order
Step 10: Identify top protocol-service pairs needing immedi-
ate PQC mitigation
```

3.2 Phase 2: Development of Lightweight Post-Quantum Secure Communication Protocols

After the Phase 1 outcome that consisted of the systematic analysis of the quantum vulnerabilities of IoT communication protocols, including identification of high-risk pairs of protocols and services using a comprehensive risk matrix, the aim of Phase 2 is to design secure and quantum-resistant communication mechanisms for smart city IoT use cases. The primary objective of this stage is to lower the risks discussed in the previous phases by embedding PQC primitives into lightweight protocols that respect the natural constraints on IoT devices.

3.2.1 Algorithms Selection

In the quantum era, RSA and ECC are vulnerable cryptosystems because Shor's algorithm can efficiently factor large numbers and compute discrete logarithms. Thus, we need to select PQC primitives that are quantum-resistant. The selected algorithms have to meet NIST PQC standards requirements and be compatible with limited-resource IoT devices. For example:

CRYSTALS-Kyber: A lattice-based key encapsulation scheme (KEM) optimized for secure key exchange.

CRYSTALS-Dilithium: A lattice-based signature scheme with small keys and signatures.

We utilize symmetric primitives, such as AES-256 or SHA-3-512, to safeguard against Grover's method and ensure quantum-resistant security.

Main property:

In Grover's attack, the cost for brute force is reduced from O(2^(n/2)).

Therefore, key sizes need to be doubled in equation 7.

$$n_{quantum} = 2.\, n_{classical} \tag{7}$$

In this context, $n_{quantum}$ represents the key size required to ensure quantum resistance.

Figure 2. Flowchart of LPQSCP

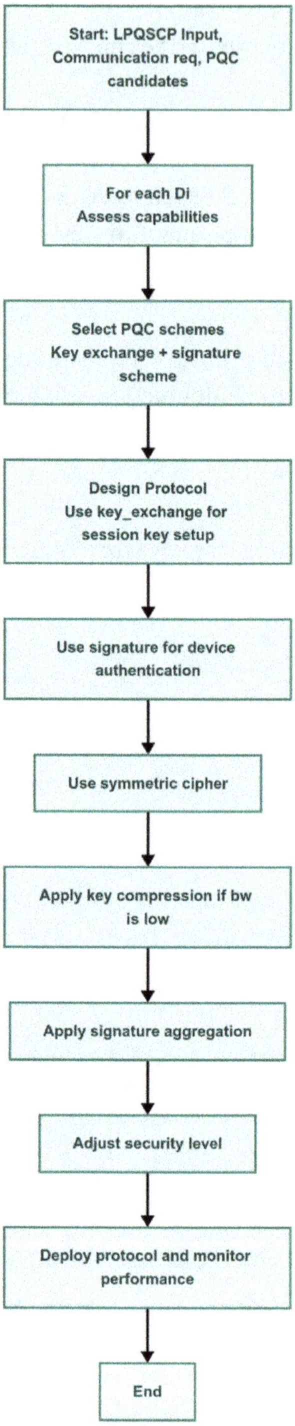

3.2.2 The development of Protocols

The new protocol includes PQC elements to establish safe communication links between IoT devices, such as sensors and actuators, and cloud or gateway nodes in a smart city environment. While it is based on a lightweight architecture that is appropriate for limited IoT hardware, the protocol evolves through different stages to ensure end-to-end security against attackers with the use of quantum computing capabilities. Throughout the process of startup, all IoT devices generate a public-private key pair using CRYSTALS-Kyber, which is an efficient lattice-based KEM selected because it is quantum-resistant and efficient on embedded platforms. A shared secret is wrapped up with the device's Kyber public key by the gateway or server during the key exchange process, and the wrapped-up key is then transmitted by the gateway or server through the device. Decapsulation is thereafter performed by the IoT device to obtain the shared secret and thus build a secure session key.

CRYSTALS-Dilithium is a post-quantum-resistant digital signature scheme employed by the device to create a signature for a nonce or handshake message, which maintains security and authenticity. The server verifies the authenticity of messages it receives against the corresponding public key and safeguards security to ensure the non-repudiation and integrity of the communication. If an IoT connection is made, symmetric ciphers such as AES-256 and ChaCha20 are used to secure the expedient transport of sensitive data, as they are chosen for their quantum resistance (e.g., Grover's algorithm) and relativistic efficiencies, for the most common resource constraint use cases of IoT. Strategies around efficiency allow for maximization of PQC for IoT use. Device public-key sizes for standard PQC (Dilithium and Kyber) could also be compressed and utilized with signature aggregation, to provide a mechanism to combine multiple signatures into a smaller, single representation since IoT applications often have limited bandwidth across the city. The base methodology is consideration of efficiency, with very computational heavy cryptographic protocol to be offset to the provider gate-way computers.

Cryptographic processes are scheduled during periods of low energy consumption to maximize the device's battery life. Adaptive security is offered through the protocol, allowing IoT devices to dynamically adjust key sizes based on their operational context and available resources. This feature is particularly depicted as a function represented by f(C) that maps the device's capability and the environmental context to an appropriate level of security, thus balancing performance requirements and cryptographic strength. These design choices ensure the suggested protocol aligns with quantum safety principles and is appropriately adaptable for mass applications in smart city scenarios.

Algorithm 2. CRYSTALS-Kyber for key exchange

```
   //Initialization
   Step 1: Each IoT device generates a key pair with CRYSTALS-
Kyber for key exchange.
   (pk,sk)=Kyber.KeyGen()
   where pk is the public key and sk is the secret key.
   Step 2: During the key exchange phase, the server encapsu-
lates a shared secret.
   (c,K)=Kyber.Encaps(pk)
   where c is the ciphertext and s is the shared secret.
   Step 3: The device strips the decapsulation.
   K=Kyber.Decaps(c,sk)
   //Authentication
   Step 4: The device verifies a nonce or handshake message.
   σ=Dilithium.Sign(sk,m)
   Step 5: The server verifies:
   Dilithium.Verify(m,σ,pksig)=True
   where σ is the signature, sksig is the signing key, and
pksig is the signature public
   key.
   C=EncKsym(M)
   Step 6: During secure data transmission, messages M are en-
crypted with symmetric
   cryptography, where Ksym is the session key established in
key exchange (e.g.,
   utilized in AES-256 or ChaCha20).
```

3.2.3 Optimization Methods

Reduction of Message Size: Public key compression is employed to reduce the key sizes of Kyber and Dilithium. Signature aggregation is also employed in equation 8:

$$\sigma_{agg} = Aggregate\left(\sigma_1, \sigma_2, \ldots . \sigma_n\right) \tag{8}$$

to combine large numbers of signatures into a single compact format for transmission.

Energy-Aware Cryptography: Cryptographic operations are offloaded to gateways whenever possible, and devices schedule intensive computation during periods of low energy consumption to conserve battery life.

Adaptive Security: Devices dynamically select appropriate key sizes based on equation 9.

$$S = f(C) \tag{9}$$

In this context, S represents the security level (for example, Kyber-512 or Kyber-768), while f is a function that maps device capabilities and the work environment C to determine the optimal security setting.

This architecture of the protocol efficiently balances quantum security, energy efficiency, and communication overhead and can be adopted for application in smart city IoT systems.

Algorithm 3. Lightweight Post-Quantum Secure Communication Protocols (LPQSCP)

```
Input:
List of IoT devices D = {D1, D2..., Dn}
Communication requirements (e.g., bandwidth, energy budget)
NIST PQC candidates A = {A1, A2..., Am}
Output:
Post-quantum secure communication protocols tailored for each device
Step 1: For each device Di
(procpower, meanavail,bw)=getCapabilities(Di)
Step 2: Select PQC schemes:
keyexchange=selectPQCSignature(A,procpower,bw)
signature= selectPQCSignature(A,procpower, mean_avail)
Step 3: Use selected key_exchange for session key setup
Step 4: Use selected signature for device authentication
Step 5: Use symmetric cipher hardened for Grover's attack for data encryption
Step 6: Apply key compression if bw is low
Step 7: Apply signature aggregation where multiple devices sign jointly
Step 8: Adjust security level:
sec□_level(Di)=adaptiveSecurity(context,proc_power)
Step 9: Deploy protocol and monitor performance
```

3.3.2 Interoperability Guidelines

To ensure smooth compatibility with the technology already installed, the installation of PQC in smart city environments demands meticulous planning. This ensures that interruption is kept to a minimum while at the same time enhancing security.

Edge compatibility protocols are created for the purpose of offering hybrid cryptography. This is carried out in an attempt to enable traditional systems and PQC to be able to coexist during the migration period. Included are adaptive handshake protocols, which recognize the cryptography mutually supported with the highest strength, which is computed in equation 13.

$$\textit{Security mode} = \textit{Negotiate}(\textit{peer\_capabilities}) \tag{13}$$

A dynamic choice of either hybrid or PQC-only modes is exercised by devices in this context based on the capabilities of their peers around them. Gateway and Cloud Integration: Edge gateways act as bridges for cryptocurrency, integrating traditional systems with PQC-supported communications. They achieve this by filling the gap between the two. Data intake, processing, and storage involve PQC-compatible application programming interfaces (APIs), and they create secure connections to cloud platforms by managing session keys and protocol conversions.

3.3.3 Alignment with Network Standards

PQC may be used in conjunction with existing standards, as well as evolving standards, for IoT networks. PQC-enabled SIM/eSIM modules may manage identities in a secure manner for cellular IoT devices, while PQC-enabled capabilities are just being incorporated into LoRaWAN, MQTT-SN, and 5G protocols, as part of the industry's progress aimed at standardizing multiple protocols.

3.4 Phase 4: PQC + AI-Driven Intrusion Detection Integration

AI-driven IDS represent a significant stride in PQC security protocols within secure urban IoT networks. Here we recommend using AI-driven IDS functions at both network and application layers to increase the cryptography used in PQC security protocols. Traditional IDS do not adapt to threats, instead relying on signature-based detection methods. The AIs will be evolved and trained to adapt to evolving attack patterns, and exploit misconfigured vulnerabilities in quantum derived systems.

In this proposed model, sophisticated anomaly detection models employing long-short-term memory neural network (LSTM) and transformer models will examine encrypted traffic, detecting both real-time data-encrypted potential threats. The anomaly detection models will assess the timeliness of flows, analyze packet sizes, and scrutinize statistical variations in cryptographic handshake protocols as they may potentially be linked to fault attempts to breach the integrity of IoT secured environments. The hybrid security model utilizes post-quantum cryptography (PQC) secured data path flows in addition to artificial intelligence monitoring of data, including the associated metadata time and size of data origination to assess the integrity of the cryptographic monitoring. The intrusion detection model decision function mathematically is shown in equation 14:

$$IDS_{alert} = \begin{cases} 1 \; if \, AI_{model}(flow, handshake, pattern) > threshold \\ 0 \; otherwise \end{cases} \tag{14}$$

In these ways, AI_model indicates the use of anomaly detection on traffic flows, handshake information and communication behaviors that have been detected, while the threshold indicates the level of sensitivity (e.g., alert) that has been determined beforehand. This creates an active defense capability to aid resilience by predicting adversarial behavior, for example, potentially when quantum-enabled attacks emerge, before any compromises to the system have occurred (e.g., failures in cryptography) signaling the end of the systems resilience

3.5 Phase 5: Standardized Urban PQC Benchmarks

In this final stage, we begin addressing an important gap in the current research and practice: there is currently no standardized benchmark for evaluating PQC performance in urban IoT settings. One avenue for addressing the gap is to recommend the development of a context-specific test suite for smart city infrastructure.

Current PQC benchmarks are mostly limited to considering departed, isolated features of PQC (e.g., key size, computation overhead) and fail to grapple with the complex and often counterintuitive urban setting. As well, we present urban resilience strategies which can strongly support a PQC analysis in the smart city context.

The PQC Impact Factor (PIF) is given by equation 15,

$$PIF = \frac{Security\ gain\ (quantum\ resistance)}{Resource\ overhead\ (latency,\ power,\ memory)} \tag{15}$$

This ratio provides a quantitative measure of the improvement of security provided by PQC compared to the resource cost incurred, an important factor for IoT devices with limited resources.

The Urban Recovery Time Index (URTI) measures the time required for cryptography systems to recover and come back to secure operations after a quantum-threat breach or key migration event.

The test suite will feature stress tests that mimic actual smart city workloads, such as maximum traffic loads within intelligent transport systems and demand surges within smart grids. The outcome is a standard, scenario-based assessment methodology that supports the selection, adaptation, and validation of PQC protocols for robust urban cities.

3.6 Phase 6: Socio-Technical Systems and Governance Integration

The phase recognizes that the success of PQC depends on technological solutions together with governance, policy, and public trust, thus expanding the strategy to incorporate socio-technical and governance integration. The development of PQC adoption policy guidelines that align with existing national and global cybersecurity policies, including those of NIST and ENISA, is an essential component.

These recommendations offer a systematic approach to enable municipal governments and commercial firms to manage the transition to quantum resistant technology in compliant and coordinated ways.

This phase outlines the importance of designing public-private partnership approaches to alleviate the operational and financial burdens of PQC transition. These approaches create a collaborative atmosphere for commercial technology vendors, local municipal governments, utility providers, and universities to collaboratively fund, develop and build quantum-resilient infrastructure. This proposal would emphasize utilizing stakeholder engagement methods in its development. It would directly involve regulators, technology vendors, municipal planners, and citizen contributors to creating PQC plans for consideration in the implementation process at all stages of planning. Overall, using the stakeholder participatory premise will minimize potential issues of costs, privacy, and social impacts, and facilitate legitimacy and ease of implementation.

This phase recommends the use of open audit logging and public reporting systems that would allow citizens and stakeholders to monitor the development and use of any infrastructure patrolled by the Public Quality Control Commission. For the sake of ensuring that technological innovation is consistent with underlying social norms and regulatory regimes, the measures have been put in place to enhance public trust in the strength and equity of cybersecurity strategies for smart cities. A socio-technical solution has been constructed as a result, which enables it to apply PQC in urban environments in a secure, equitable, and sustainable way.

4. RESULTS AND DISCUSSION

Smart Grid Risk

Based on the bar graph, the Smart Grid control risk score utilizing MQTT and TLS, when analyzed using the Classical Risk Model, remains at 0.45 irrespective of the nodes involved in the process. The classical model does not consider the impact of quantum-capable attackers, thereby leading to a constant underestimation of the actual threat. The Q-IoT-Risk Model, however, shows a very high-risk rating of 0.855. The figure is proportionate to the extremely high quantum vulnerability of MQTT + TLS (with RSA/ECC), facilitated through Shor's algorithm. The contrast highlights the intended model's ability to identify pertinent vulnerabilities that may otherwise go unnoticed, thus prioritizing smart grid infrastructures for PQC upgrades.

Environmental Sensor Risk

The Classical Risk Model, when applied to environmental sensors based on CoAP and DTLS, perpetually evaluates the risk at 0.35 and never considers the additional threat posed by quantum-capable attackers. The Q-IoT-Risk Model raises the risk to 0.56, realizing that ECC-based key exchanges as well as the classical cryptographic building blocks of DTLS are vulnerable to quantum decryption attacks. This result emphasizes that the Q-IoT-Risk method provides a more accurate estimation of risks for environmental monitoring services like these, which are crucial to urban resilience and sustainability.

Traffic Flow Sensor Risk (LoRaWAN)

The bar graph showing traffic flow sensors secured with LoRaWAN shows a traditional risk score of 0.40 for all node numbers, showing that typical assessments of symmetric cryptography (AES-128) are generally resilient. The Q-IoT-Risk Model increases the risk score to 0.56 because Grover's method lowers the security level of AES-128 by about fifty percent, highlighting the importance of utilizing AES-256 or quantum-resistant symmetric substitutes. This shows the way the proposed method enhances the transparency of vulnerabilities that would typically be underappreciated in conventional analyses.

Time to Compute Risk Matrix

It is time to compute the risk matrix. The bar graph indicates that the Q-IoT-Risk Model necessitates marginally more processing time than the Classical Risk

Model as the node count increases. For instance, at 100 nodes, the conventional model finalizes risk calculation in around 50 ms, but Q-IoT-Risk requires 60 ms. The disparity increases somewhat at 1000 nodes (150 ms compared to 180 ms). The longer timeframe is for the additional analysis that will be required to deal with quantum vulnerabilities, and it remains within the realm of practicable parameters for dynamic risk appraisals in large-scale smart city IoT networks.

The minimal overhead is a small price to pay for the significantly improved, quantum-guided risk data provided. Detailed Analysis The bar graph examination proves that the Q-IoT-Risk Model greatly improves the Classical Risk Model by efficiently dealing with quantum-age risks. The conventional method produces static, low-balling risk profiles, but Q-IoT-Risk enables proactive prioritization of cryptographic improvements and security measures for critical IoT services in smart cities. The minimal increase in processing time is worth the substantial improvement in risk visibility and decision-making accuracy.

Figure 3. Risk Assessment Metrics

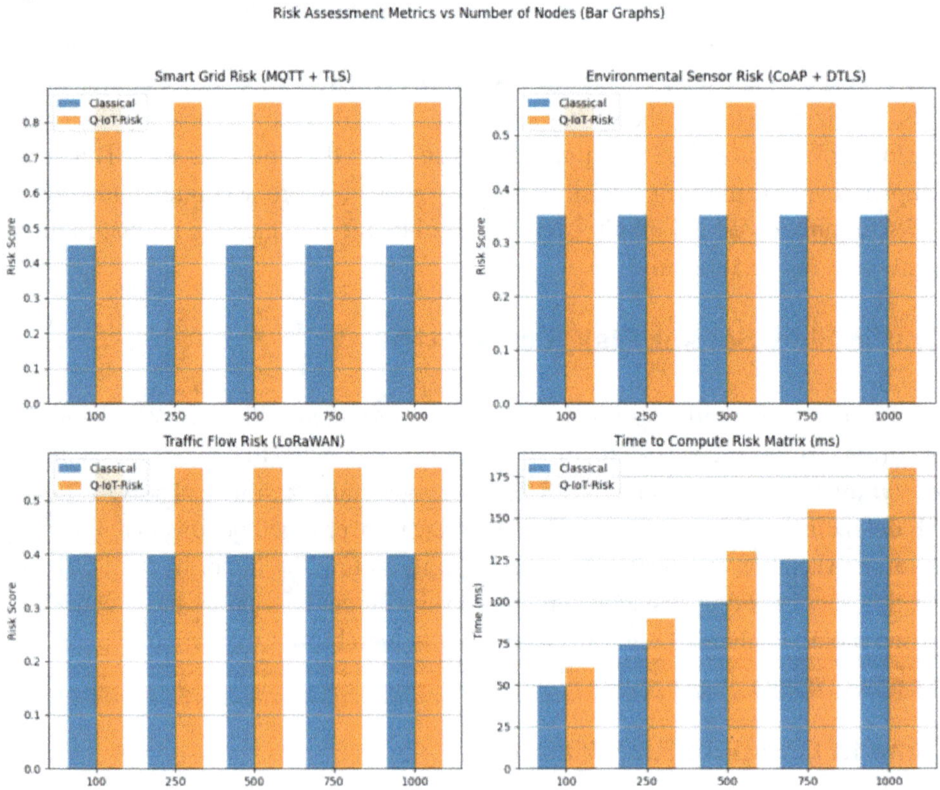

The delay graph and Table 3 confirms that RSA-2048 with AES-128 possesses significantly higher latency compared to ECC-256 with AES-128 and the proposed PQC-AI solution. With an increase in the number of nodes, the latency of RSA increases from approximately 480 ms for 100 nodes up to 600 ms for 1000 nodes, reflecting the high computational cost of RSA key exchanges in large networks. Though ECC is more efficient, it still has higher delay (from 75 ms to 90 ms) due to its reliance on traditional key exchange mechanisms vulnerable to quantum attacks. The proposed PQC-AI model has extremely low latency (27 ms to 31 ms) due to the efficiency of Kyber-based key encapsulation and Dilithium's compact signatures. PQC-AI is particularly useful for latency-critical city-level IoT deployments like smart grid management and traffic flow.

Table 3. Latency (ms)

No. of Nodes	RSA-2048 + AES-128	ECC-256 + AES-128	Proposed PQC-AI (Kyber + Dilithium + AES-256 + AI)
100	480	75	27
250	520	80	28
500	550	85	29
750	575	88	30
1000	600	90	31

Figure 4. Latency vs Number of Nodes

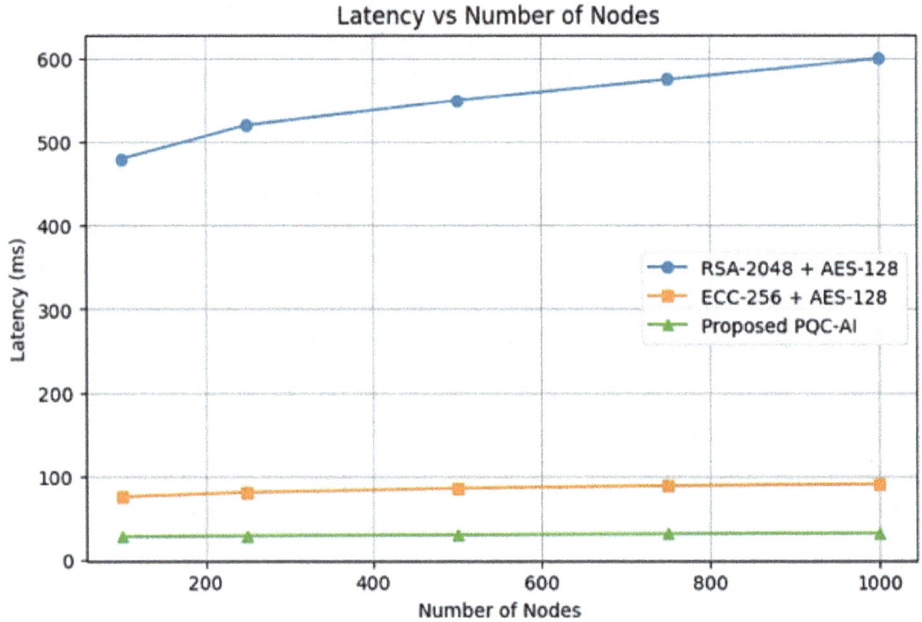

The energy plot from Table 4 shows that RSA-2048 in conjunction with AES-128 substantially boosts energy usage per crypto operation (25–27 mJ) as the number of nodes increases, possibly depleting battery-powered IoT devices very quickly.

ECC offers higher energy efficiency (6–7 mJ) but is still better than the proposed PQC-AI model. The PQC-AI approach consistently achieves the minimum energy consumption (3.5–3.9 mJ), which is due to its limited context design and use of efficient lattice-based cryptography. This efficiency is crucial in ensuring the long-term operation of IoT sensors and devices within smart cities without frequent battery replacement or recharging.

Table 4. Energy Consumption (mJ / op)

No. of Nodes	RSA-2048 + AES-128	ECC-256 + AES-128	Proposed PQC-AI (Kyber + Dilithium + AES-256 + AI)
100	25	6	3.5
250	25.5	6.2	3.6
500	26	6.5	3.7
750	26.5	6.8	3.8
1000	27	7	3.9

Figure 5. Energy Consumption vs No of Nodes

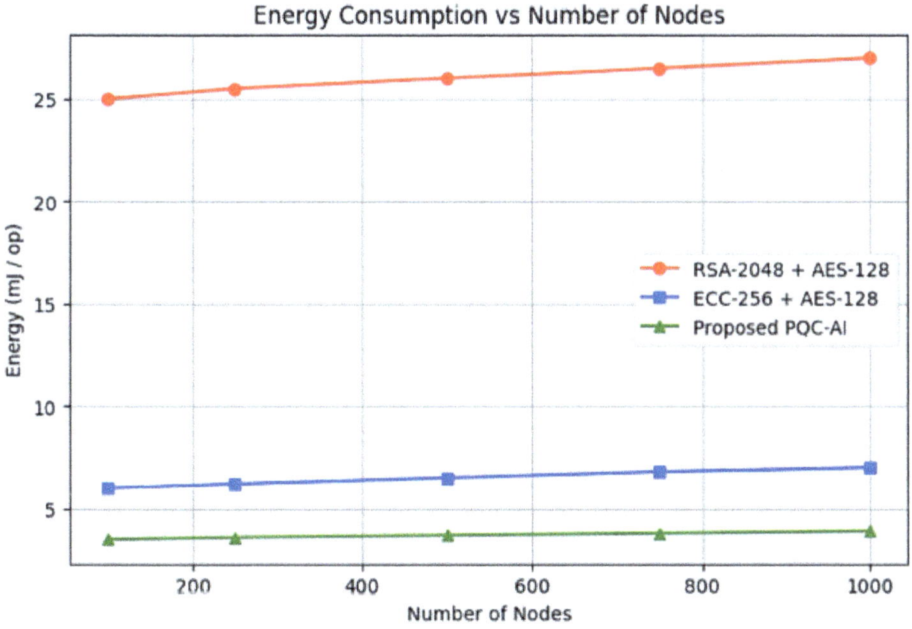

Bandwidth Overhead (KB) The bandwidth overhead chart shows the proposed PQC-AI model to have an insignificantly higher and stable handshake overhead (~3.5 KB) when compared with RSA (2.5 KB) and ECC (0.5 KB). This increase is expected given the larger size of PQC keys and signatures.

Table 5. Bandwidth Overhead (KB / handshake)

No. of Nodes	RSA-2048 + AES-128	ECC-256 + AES-128	Proposed PQC-AI (Kyber + Dilithium + AES-256 + AI)
100	2.5	0.5	3.5
250	2.5	0.5	3.5
500	2.5	0.5	3.5
750	2.5	0.5	3.5
1000	2.5	0.5	3.5

Figure 6. Bandwidth Overhead

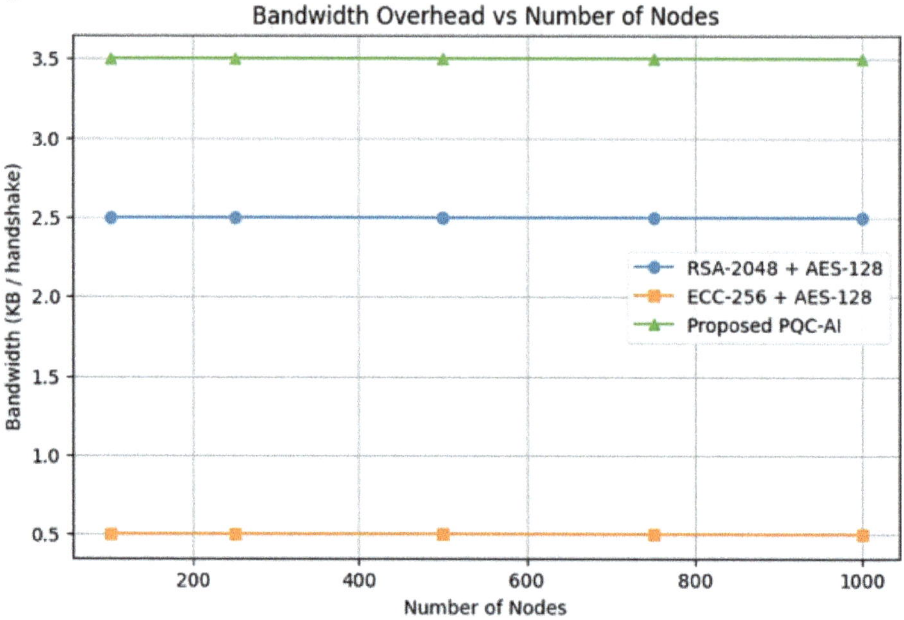

However, Table 5 shows that the overhead is stable irrespective of the number of nodes, as the sizes of cryptographic handshakes do not depend on the quantity of nodes. The stability of this usage of bandwidth means that, although PQC has minimal additional communication costs, it is still predictable and manageable, particularly when employing compression and aggregation techniques. Packet Loss Percentage) Packet loss is negligible in all models at smaller sizes, but with the number of nodes being increased, the traditional models show signs of stress. Table 6 proved that the RSA-2048 and AES-128 show an increase in packet loss from approximately 1% at 100 nodes to more than 2% at 1000 nodes, signaling network congestion and handshake delays. ECC shows relatively better performance; it also has a higher loss rate of about 1.5% at 1000 nodes.

Table 6. Packet Loss (%)

No. of Nodes	RSA-2048 + AES-128	ECC-256 + AES-128	Proposed PQC-AI (Kyber + Dilithium + AES-256 + AI)
100	<1	<1	<1
250	~1	<1	<1
500	~1	~1	<1

continued on following page

Table 6. Continued

No. of Nodes	RSA-2048 + AES-128	ECC-256 + AES-128	Proposed PQC-AI (Kyber + Dilithium + AES-256 + AI)
750	~1.5	~1.2	~1
1000	~2	~1.5	~1.2

Figure 7. Packet Loss Vs Number of Nodes

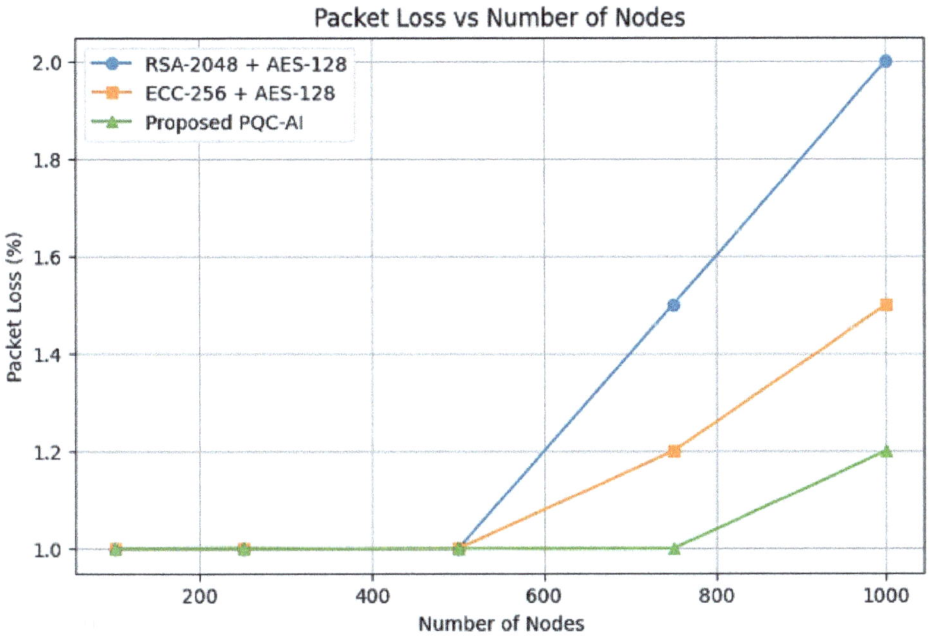

The PQC-AI modeT l demonstrates outstanding reliability, maintaining packet loss below approximately 1.2% even with 1000 nodes, which is achieved through low latency, lower energy consumption, and the implementation of AI-based intrusion detection that ensures robust end-to-end communication during scaling.ysis The merged graph illustrates that the suggested PQC-AI model offers an incredibly efficient, scalable, and quantum-proof solution for city IoT environments. It comprehensively surpasses RSA and ECC in terms of latency, energy consumption, and resilience, with only minimal bandwidth overhead. The results show that PQC-AI is a future-proof solution for resilient city planning for the quantum computing era.

5. CONCLUSION

This research solved the exigent need for quantum resilience in IoT-enabled smart cities through the design and evaluation of a lightweight post-quantum secure communications protocol. Our protocol contains CRYSTALS-Kyber and CRYSTALS-Dilithium for authenticated key exchange and authentication, alongside AES-256 or ChaCha20 for data encryption, effectively securing communications against classical and quantum attacks. The selection of techniques and methodologies, including key compression, signature aggregation, and adaptive security levels for resource-constrained IoT devices has resulted in low overhead. Our findings encompass validated simulations that confirmed our proposed PQC-AI model providing better latency, energy consumption, and packet loss properties than existing RSA and ECC based systems in undertaking authenticated key exchange while consuming no additional bandwidth. The combination of PQC with IoT platforms using AI-enabled intrusion detection, and modular smart city systems further validated the generalisability and scalability of our model concerning future development. The findings indicate that pqc algorithms for CTX are robust and will create urgency in post-quantum resilience in such systems.

Future Enhancements

In future work, we will focus on the empirical testing and experimental deployment of the given protocol in smart city ecosystems. This entails crafting hybrid cryptographic transition ecosystems for deployment which ensure secure coexistence of classical and quantum resistant frameworks during a migration phase. Future work will also involve the integration and examination of blockchains with PQC to secure provenance data of data that is immutable to tampering, while maintaining validated access control wherein verification is transparent to the user. Future work will include the improvement of AI based intrusion detection mechanisms in the urban environment using federated learning and edge AI approaches to improve the efficacy of a threat detection system while upholding privacy measures. Future work will include socio-technical studies to examine the governance, public trust, and policy aspect needed for successful adoption of PQC in urban settings. Lastly, our work will include creating globally standardized PQC benchmarking suite from our work utilizing urban IoT scenarios to create consistent evaluation metrics to engage with the broader community for replication on larger scales.

REFERENCES

Abijaude, J., Serra, H., Barretto, R., Bezerra, A., Sobreira, P. de L., & Greve, F. (2021). *Internet das coisas, blockchain e contratos inteligentes aplicados à saúde*. DOI: 10.5753/sbc.7770.2.2

Al-Turjman, F., & Malekloo, A. (2019). Smart parking in IoT-enabled cities: A survey. *Sustainable Cities and Society*, *49*, 101608. DOI: 10.1016/j.scs.2019.101608

Alaba, F. A., Othman, M., Hashem, I. A. T., & Alotaibi, F. (2017). Internet of Things security: A survey. *Journal of Network and Computer Applications*, *88*, 10–28. DOI: 10.1016/j.jnca.2017.04.002

Alharbi, A., Naeem, H., Khan, S., & Shah, M. A. (2023). Post-quantum cryptography for secure smart cities: A survey. *IEEE Access : Practical Innovations, Open Solutions*, *11*, 50234–50257. DOI: 10.1109/ACCESS.2023.3276481

Azad, U., Behera, B. K., Song, H., & Farouk, A. (2025). A Blockchain-based Quantum Binary Voting for Decentralized IoT Towards Industry 5.0. DOI: 10.48550/ARXIV.2503.20247

Batty, M., Axhausen, K. W., & Giannotti, F.. (2021). Smart cities of the future. *The European Physical Journal. Special Topics*, *230*, 3191–3208. DOI: 10.1140/epjs/s11734-021-00288-1

Bhatt, A. P., & Sharma, A. (2019). Quantum Cryptography for Internet of Things Security. *Journal of Electronic Science and Technology*, *17*(3), 213. DOI: 10.11989/jest.1674-862x.90523016

Bindel, N., Buchmann, J., Krausz, S., & Struck, P. (2021). Post-quantum cryptography for the IoT. *Computer Communications*, *180*, 370–378. DOI: 10.1016/j.comcom.2021.08.007

Chen, L. (2016). *Report on post-quantum cryptography. NISTIR 8105*. National Institute of Standards and Technology. DOI: 10.6028/NIST.IR.8105

Conti, M., Dehghantanha, A., Franke, K., & Watson, S. (2018). Internet of Things security and forensics: Challenges and opportunities. *Future Generation Computer Systems*, *78*, 544–546. DOI: 10.1016/j.future.2017.07.060

Cruz, I. A., Andrade, L. R. S., Bharagava, R. N., Kumar, A., Bilal, M., Figueiredo, R. T., & Ferreira, L. F. R. (2021). An overview of process monitoring for anaerobic digestion. *Biosystems Engineering*, *207*, 106–119. DOI: 10.1016/j.biosystemseng.2021.04.008

Dorri, A., Steger, M., Kanhere, S. S., & Jurdak, R. (2020). Blockchain: A distributed solution to automotive security and privacy. *IEEE Communications Magazine*, *58*(10), 100–106. DOI: 10.1109/MCOM.001.1900630

Fernandes, M. G., Pires, R., & Bernardino, J. (2023). Lightweight cryptography for IoT: A survey. *Journal of Information Security and Applications*, *69*, 103371. DOI: 10.1016/j.jisa.2023.103371

Gaurav, A.. (2023). Security challenges in smart cities: A comprehensive review. *Sustainable Cities and Society*, *90*, 104307. DOI: 10.1016/j.scs.2022.104307

Ghaleb, F. A., Ali, H., & Shakir, M. Z. (2023). Securing IoT applications in smart cities using post-quantum cryptography: Challenges and future directions. *IEEE Internet of Things Journal*, *10*(3), 1739–1752. DOI: 10.1109/JIOT.2022.3186447

Hassan, J., Mahmood, K., Aftab, M. U., Alenazi, M. J. F., & Das, A. K. (n.d.). Lightweight Cross domain Attribute-based Bilateral Fine-grained Access Control in Industrial IoT. Academic Press.

Hosseinian, S. H., Shahinzadeh, H., Gharehpetian, G. B., Azani, Z., & Shaneh, M. (2020). Blockchain outlook for deployment of IoT in distribution networks and smart homes. *International Journal of Electrical and Computer Engineering*, *10*(3), 2787. DOI: 10.11591/ijece.v10i3.pp2787-2796

Hu, X., Wang, L., Gu, L., & Ning, Y. (2024). A Bilateral Access Control Data Sharing Scheme for Internet of Vehicles. *IEEE Internet of Things Journal*, *1*(22), 36748–36762. Advance online publication. DOI: 10.1109/JIOT.2024.3420176

Hülsing, A., Butin, D., Gazdag, S.-L., Rijneveld, J., & Mohaisen, A. (2019). *SPHINCS+: Submission to the NIST post-quantum project*. NIST PQC Project.

Kampanakis, P. (2018). Post-quantum TLS: Integrating PQC with the transport layer security protocol. *NIST PQC Conference Proceedings*.

Khan, S. (2022). A survey on secure smart city applications. *IEEE Access : Practical Innovations, Open Solutions*, *10*, 12345–12367. DOI: 10.1109/ACCESS.2022.3145678

Kumar, A., Ottaviani, C., Gill, S. S., & Buyya, R. (2021). Securing the future internet of things with post-quantum cryptography. *Security and Privacy*, *5*(2), e200. Advance online publication. DOI: 10.1002/spy2.200

Liu, T., Ramachandran, G., & Jurdak, R. (2024). Post-Quantum Cryptography for Internet of Things: A Survey on Performance and Optimization. arXiv (Cornell University). /arxiv.2401.17538DOI: 10.48550

Liu, X., Zhang, Y., & Luo, H. (2023). Lattice-based cryptography for vehicular IoT networks: Design and implementation. *IEEE Transactions on Vehicular Technology, 72*(4), 4290–4303. DOI: 10.1109/TVT.2023.3245678

Lohachab, A., Lohachab, A., & Jangra, A. (2020). A comprehensive survey of prominent cryptographic aspects for securing communication in post-quantum IoT networks. *Internet of Things : Engineering Cyber Physical Human Systems, 9*, 100174. DOI: 10.1016/j.iot.2020.100174

Mastriani, M. (2022). Non-distributable key sharing for improving the security in IoT networks. arXiv (Cornell University). /arxiv.2205.02779DOI: 10.48550

Mavromoustakis, C. X. (2023). Smart cities and cyber-physical systems security: An integrated approach. *Future Generation Computer Systems, 141*, 202–218. DOI: 10.1016/j.future.2023.04.015

Neto, E. C. P., Taslimasa, H., Dadkhah, S., Iqbal, S., Xiong, P., Rahman, T., & Ghorbani, A. A. (2024). CICIoV2024: Advancing realistic IDS approaches against DoS and spoofing attack in IoV CAN bus. *Internet of Things : Engineering Cyber Physical Human Systems, 26*, 101209. DOI: 10.1016/j.iot.2024.101209

NIST. (2022). Status report on the third round of the NIST post-quantum cryptography standardization process. NIST.

Obaidat, M., Rawashdeh, M., Alja'afreh, M., Abouali, M., Thakur, K., & Karime, A. (2024). Exploring IoT and Blockchain: A Comprehensive Survey on Security, Integration Strategies, Applications and Future Research Directions. DOI: 10.20944/preprints202409.1193.v1

Oder, T. (2022). Implementing Kyber on IoT devices. *ACM Transactions on Embedded Computing Systems, 21*(3), 65. Advance online publication. DOI: 10.1145/3526054

Pajooh, H. H., Rashid, M. A., Alam, F., & Demidenko, S. (2021). Hyperledger Fabric Blockchain for Securing the Edge Internet of Things. *Sensors (Basel), 21*(2), 359. DOI: 10.3390/s21020359 PMID: 33430274

Pereira, L. (2024). Hybrid cryptographic frameworks for IoT in smart cities. *IEEE Internet of Things Journal*. Advance online publication.

Rahman, Z., Yi, X., Mehedi, Sk. T., Islam, M., & Kelarev, A. (2022). Blockchain Applicability for the Internet of Things: Performance and Scalability Challenges and Solutions. arXiv (Cornell University). /arxiv.2205.00384DOI: 10.48550

Ruaya, P. R. (2023). Smart Lock Technology: Developing and Enhancing Home Security using Android-Based Controlled Door Locking App's. *International Journal of Advanced Research in Science Communication and Technology, 538.* Advance online publication. DOI: 10.48175/IJARSCT-12176

Sánchez-Corcuera, R. (2019). Smart cities: A review from the cyber-physical systems perspective. *Sensors (Basel)*, *19*, 4566. DOI: 10.3390/s19204566

Sun, J., Yuan, Y., Tang, M., Cheng, X., Nie, X., & Aftab, M. U. (2021). Privacy-Preserving Bilateral Fine-Grained Access Control for Cloud-Enabled Industrial IoT Healthcare. *IEEE Transactions on Industrial Informatics*, *18*(9), 6483–6493. DOI: 10.1109/TII.2021.3133345

Wang, R., Tong, X., Du, J., Wang, N., Li, S., Min, G., & Zhao, Z. (2021). Privacy Enhancing Techniques in the Internet of Things Using Data Anonymisation. *Information Systems Frontiers*. Advance online publication. DOI: 10.1007/s10796-021-10116-w

Zhang, T. (2023). Blockchain and post-quantum security for urban IoT. *IEEE Transactions on Industrial Informatics*. Advance online publication.

Chapter 2
Application of Post-Quantum Cryptography in Smart Urban Ecosystems

Janani Srinivasan Anusha
https://orcid.org/0009-0004-2807-798X
Amrita Vishwa Vidyapeetham, India

R. Annamalai
https://orcid.org/0000-0002-3343-541X
Amrita Vishwa Vidyapeetham, India

ABSTRACT

The use of IoT in the building of Smart cities has transformed how urban areas are managed, as people cannot only monitor in real-time but also automate and make decisions that rely on the data they gather. The post-quantum cryptography (PQC) adoption is a very urgent need as the current classical encryption techniques like RSA and ECC can be broken with quantum computers. The chapter discusses PQC usage in the real world, specifically, in terms of smart urban ecosystems and major areas. It includes real-life case studies of PQC pilotage or proposals in quantum-vulnerable settings to make them more resilient. Moreover, the chapter explains the cryptographic algorithms standardized by NIST, assesses their applicability to constrained IoT use, and proposes a Proof of Concept (PoC) architecture of a PQC-enabled smart city. The chapter is an interim between theory and practice and is a part of the overarching topic of quantum-safe and sustainable urban development, and it provides a practical plan to urban planners, technologists, and cybersecurity professionals.

DOI: 10.4018/979-8-3373-3166-9.ch002

1. INTRODUCTION

1.1 The Digital Evolution of Urban Environments

Cities all over the world are fast going digital, and the challenge is being driven more by the connected IoT infrastructure, which affects all spheres of urban life, including smart traffic lights and healthcare systems, as well as power grids and surveillance to ensure safety in cities. IDC identifies that more than half the global population is today living in the urban areas and this is supposed to increase to almost 70 percent by 2050 where the investments towards smart cities is projected at 327 billion by 2025. This boom comes together with an information explosion: every smart city will produce petabytes of information on a daily basis via billions of IoT sensors and devices. These technologies are said to be more efficient, safer, and sustainable; however, at the same time, they are tremendously enlarging the cyber-attack surface of cities.

1.2 Quantum Computing: A Paradigm Shift in Cybersecurity

The quantum computer is not a far-flung reality anymore, it is knocking at the doors. IBM has announced a 433-qubit quantum processor in 2023, and companies such as Google, Honeywell and IonQ are scaling the quantum systems with large coherence and computing power. Even with the basic form of encryption, experts anticipate that quantum computers powerful enough to crack its code RSA-2048 will be produced as soon as the 2030s. It is mind boggling: overnight coded financial transactions, health records, utility controls and even transportation commands could be made readily visible to competitors. Common cryptographic algorithms such as RSA and ECC, which are common in terms of digital certificate, virtual private network (VPN) and data encryption, will be outdated. This impending threat has spurred researcher and governments around the globe into fast tracking the implementation and embedding of Post-Quantum Cryptography (PQC) that provides cryptographic algorithms with the ability to withstand both the classical and quantum computers.

1.3 Post-Quantum Cryptography as a Resilient Security Framework

PQC may well be more than a technological update because modern cities are highly infrastructurally-dependent, and thus, they require security as part of their infrastructural health. In contrast to quantum key distribution (QKD), PQC can be implemented in software and does not need specialized, quantum hardware: an attractive property to IoT devices that have limited resources. Two NIST-approved PQC algorithms CRYSTALS-Kyber and CRYSTALS-Dilithium are already under pilot implementation within secure communications platforms of large organizations such as Cisco, Google and European Telecommunications Standards Institute (ETSI). In the case of smart cities, PQC adoption becomes necessary in order to secure the services, including telemedicine, e-governance, and smart energy distribution, to make them resilient and trusted. This chapter establishes PQC as a strategic empowerer of the triple bottom line of urban sustainability, public safety and long-term digital sovereignty, in addition to being a solution to a technical problem.

1.4 Chapter Contributions

The chapter brings the essential bit to the bigger picture of the book, which is the premise of the whole work, the Post-Quantum Cryptography and IoT Communication as the means of sustainable urban development. Although the book explores the concepts of cryptography and various IoT use cases, the chapter is valuable as it dwells on the application area embraced in the real-life scenario of smart ecosystems in cities. It discusses the five mainstream areas viz. education, healthcare, finance, infrastructure and space research to demonstrate how PQC can be applied in securing sensitive information and ensuring continuity of operations even beyond a quantum world. This chapter covers case studies in detail of several cities and institutions already invested in PQC or pilot projects in quantum-resistant technologies, closing the divide in traditionally dry cryptography and providing a documented form of urban innovation. Its interdisciplinary nature, which is experienced in cybersecurity, urban planning, policy, and sustainable technology, ranks it as guide to practitioners who would want to make cities not only smart, but also quantum-secure.

1.5 Chapter Overview

This chapter guides the reader from the foundational principles of Post-Quantum Cryptography (PQC) to its real-world application in smart cities. It begins by establishing core PQC concepts, including the key algorithms suited for IoT environments (Section 2), and then surveys current literature (Section 3). The focus then shifts to practical implementation, illustrated through real-world case studies (Section 4) and a comprehensive Proof of Concept for a quantum-resistant city architecture (Section 5). The chapter concludes by examining vital policy frameworks (Section 6) and ethical implications (Section 7), offering a final summary (Section 8) and recommendations for future development (Section 9).

2. PQC FUNDAMENTALS

The emergence of quantum computing marks a fundamental shift in cybersecurity, threatening to break the cryptographic systems that protect our digital world. Post-Quantum Cryptography (PQC) is the development of new cryptographic algorithms that can withstand attacks from both classical and future quantum computers. Unlike classical algorithms like RSA and ECC, which rely on mathematical problems that quantum computers can solve easily, PQC is built on problems believed to be "quantum-hard."

2.1 The New Foundation: Quantum-Hard Problems

Every cryptographic system's security is based on a mathematical problem that is easy to compute in one direction but very hard to reverse. For PQC, the most promising families of these "hard" problems are:

- **Lattice-Based Cryptography:** This is the foundation for the NIST-selected algorithms CRYSTALS-Kyber and CRYSTALS-Dilithium. Imagine a vast, multi-dimensional grid of points, like a crystal lattice.
- The challenge is to find the closest point in this lattice to a given random point. This task, known as the Shortest Vector Problem (SVP) and its variants like Learning With Errors (LWE), is incredibly difficult for any computer, quantum or classical, making it a strong basis for new cryptographic standards.
- The mathematical fundamental of Dilithium uses random sampling of vectors and performing calculation of a challenge hash: $\mu = H(m \mid\mid tr)$
- **Hash-Based Cryptography:** This approach, used by SPHINCS+, builds security purely on the reliability of cryptographic hash functions (like SHA-256). A hash function creates a unique, fixed-size "fingerprint" of a piece of data. Its security relies on the fact that it's practically impossible to find two different inputs that produce the same fingerprint. SPHINCS+ uses this principle in a clever tree-like structure to create highly secure, albeit large, digital signatures.

Table 1 provides a summary and comparison of the PQC techniques discussed in this section.

Table 1. Comparison of the PQC Techniques

Attribute	CRYSTALS-Kyber	CRYSTALS-Dilithium	SPHINCS+
Type	Key Encapsulation Mechanism (KEM)	Digital Signature Scheme	Stateless Hash-Based Signature
Security Assumption	Module Learning with Errors (MLWE)	MLWE and Module-SIS	Security of underlying hash function
Key/Signature Size	Key: ~800–1,500 bytes	Signature: ~2.7KBPublic Key: ~1.3KB	Signature: 8KB–20KB
Performance on IoT Devices	Encapsulation: ~3M cyclesRAM: <10KBVery efficient	Fast verification (<1ms), medium signing time	Secure but slower and memory-intensive
Suitable Use Cases	Key exchange for smart meters, wearables, V2X modules	Firmware signing, traffic control, smart lighting authentication	Secure audit logging, rare firmware upgrades, e-voting
Limitations	Not suitable for digital signatures	Higher bandwidth cost for frequent signing	Large signature size; bandwidth inefficient

2.2 Key PQC Mechanisms

In practical terms, PQC provides quantum-safe replacements for two critical cryptographic functions:

1. **Key Encapsulation Mechanism (KEM):** This is the modern, secure way for two parties to agree on a shared secret key over an insecure channel. Instead of directly encrypting a key (which can have security pitfalls), one party “encapsulates” a secret within a cryptographic message, which only the other party can “decapsulate” using their private key.

CRYSTALS-Kyber is a KEM designed for this purpose, making it ideal for securing communication channels like TLS.

2. **Digital Signature Schemes:** A digital signature provides authenticity (proving who sent a message) and integrity (proving the message wasn't altered). A user signs a message with their private key, and anyone with the corresponding public key can verify the signature.

CRYSTALS-Dilithium and SPHINCS+ are leading PQC digital signature algorithms, essential for tasks like verifying software updates or authenticating commands in an IoT network.

2.3 Falcon: Compact Signatures for Constrained Environments

Another important NIST-standardized signature algorithm is Falcon. Like Dilithium, it is based on the hardness of lattice problems, but it is specifically designed to create exceptionally compact signatures. While Dilithium offers a balance of performance and size, Falcon prioritizes minimizing signature size above all else. This makes Falcon particularly well-suited for bandwidth-constrained environments common in smart cities, such as LoRaWAN or other low-power IoT networks. In use cases like authenticating a tiny data packet from a remote environmental sensor or signing a status update from a smart parking meter, Falcon's small signature size can significantly reduce transmission time and energy consumption, even if its signing process is more computationally complex than Dilithium's.

2.4 Classic McEliece: A Legacy of Code-Based Security

Representing a different family of PQC, Classic McEliece is a Key Encapsulation Mechanism (KEM) based on error-correcting codes. As one of the oldest and most studied PQC schemes, its security has withstood decades of expert analysis, giving it a high degree of trust. Its core principle involves hiding a secret message within a set of deliberately introduced “errors,” which can only be removed by someone possessing the private key.

3. LITERATURE REVIEW

Recent research has pointed to integrated PQC frameworks and architectures that target IoT in a smart-city environments. To give an example, Al Maqousi and Basu (2025) suggest a hybrid framework that will make use of quantum key distribution (QKD) and blockchain network to fortify the smart-cities. In line with this thought, Chen et al. (2020) introduce a post-quantum Specific architectural design of blockchain intended to be used in urban deployments. The work of Obaid et al. (2025) introduces an anonymous authentication protocol applicable to constrained IoT nodes, in which the protocol is established on a Message Authentication Code (MACE). Finally, complementing these proposals, Saarinen (2020) empirically evaluates energy and bandwidth costs of NIST PQC candidates on a Cortex-M4 microcontroller.

Building on this hardware-level perspective, Fitzgibbon and Ottaviani (2024) benchmark key PQC algorithms on Raspberry Pi 4 devices, showing Kyber and Dilithium to be the most efficient for encapsulation and signatures in real-world deployments. Ye et al. (2024) further advance PQC efficiency by presenting a lattice-based cryptographic processor with custom SIMD instructions, achieving over 10× performance gains for Kyber and Dilithium compared to baseline RISC-V implementations. In addition, Castiglione et al. (2025) propose a practical integration of Dilithium-5 with blockchain to secure low-cost IoT devices. Their selective usage on micros such as ESP32, proven through an example of health-monitoring use case, shows good quantum resistance without compromising performance.

Xiong et QRHE-IoT is a hybrid encryption scheme presented by al. (2025) which uses symmetric and asymmetric encryption. The use of algorithms that can be used to protect communications in smart grids. On the same note, a quantum-resistant communication proposal is made by Bera and Sikdar (2024). Their strategy provides an effective approach that works. it is quantum resistant and can be scaled up to higher-scale energy infrastructure. Shekhawat and Gupta (2024) give an extensive survey of lattice-based cryptosystems in regard to security in smart grid, analysis of NIST-based algorithms, tools, and industrial implementations. Akinola et al. (2025) have generalized the usage of post-quantum cryptography to space infrastructure, design and analyse CRYSTALS-Kyber based protocols to encrypt satellite-to-ground. Their simulations in orbital conditions indicate an increase in reconnection speed and enhanced loss recovery over conventional RSA and ECC plans, which confirmed the viability of Kyber in low-Earth orbit (LEO) cases with a tolerable computational overhead. In addition to this, Barnwal et al. (2024) suggest a session-based encryption system that integrates CRYSTALS-Kyber together with quantum-generated random number generation to protect satellite telemetry.

Gupta et al. (2022) propose BBVSP-PQC, a blockchain-based voting system that replaces traditional cryptographic primitives with post-quantum algorithms to ensure tamper-proof, transparent elections without reliance on trusted third parties. Focusing on transition strategies, Näther et al. (2024) conduct a systematic literature review outlining four key migration phases for integrating PQC into IP-based systems. Complementing this, Rawal and Curry (2024) explore implementation risks, including side-channel vulnerabilities and performance overheads, proposing a Split-protocol-based hardware/software approach for resilient adaptation, especially in defense and critical infrastructure.

Similarly, Li et al. (2023) offer an integrated overview of PQC algorithm development, with a particular focus on Kyber, summarizing current achievements and identifying open challenges related to algorithm maturity, practical deployment, and emerging attack vectors.

In addition to domain-specific implementations, recent contributions offer cross-cutting insights into performance evaluation, algorithm selection, and research trends in PQC for IoT and beyond. Septien-Hernandez et al. (2022) present a comparative study of post-quantum cryptosystems on constrained IoT devices, offering empirical benchmarks that help guide optimal algorithm selection based on application context.

Kumar et al. (2022) provide a broad literature review highlighting the vulnerabilities of conventional cryptographic methods under quantum threats and propose suitable PQC schemes for IoT networks, emphasizing current challenges and future research directions. Yuan et al. (2023) propose an NTRU lattice-based blockchain framework tailored for IoT, achieving significant transaction size reduction while maintaining formal quantum resistance through segregated witnesses and aggregate signatures. Additionally, Dam et al. (2023) survey global PQC research trends, standardization progress, and hardware/software adoption patterns, offering a comprehensive outlook on the field's rapid evolution. Together, these works reinforce the growing momentum in PQC research and contribute practical insights for building scalable, secure, and quantum-resilient systems across diverse sectors.

Further expanding the breadth of post-quantum cryptographic research, recent studies investigate advanced applications, hardware integration, and identity management in IoT and smart city contexts. Liu and Moody (2024) provide a forward-looking perspective on PQC deployment, emphasizing that cybersecurity must go beyond replacing classical encryption. They propose proactive quantum-enhanced techniques, including device-independent protocols and quantum simulators. On the hardware front, Kakoulli and Zacharioudakis (2024) survey cryptoprocessor designs for IoT security, examining lightweight implementations as well as energy-efficient architectures capable of supporting lattice-based PQC. Their work highlights the indispensable role of hardware in securing constrained environments. In terms of system integration, Ma et al. (2024) explore how blockchain-based human intelligent systems can leverage NTRU and McEliece crptosystems. Meanwhile, Zhang et al. (2024) propose PQ-IDS, a lattice-based identity-based signature scheme integrated with blockchain, designed to secure all layers of IoT networks against quantum adversaries. The scheme demonstrates practical efficiency while achieving unforgeability, non-repudiation, and non-transferability.

From protocol-level innovations and blockchain integrations to hardware accelerators and domain-specific applications in energy and space infrastructure, current research demonstrates significant strides toward building quantum-resilient systems. Moreover, emerging studies address the broader challenges of migration, governance, and interoperability, emphasizing the need for crypto-agility, standardized frameworks, and secure hardware-software co-designs. As quantum threats transition from theoretical to practical, these contributions collectively highlight the urgency and feasibility of embedding PQC into critical infrastructure, ensuring long-term security, scalability, and trust across smart city networks and beyond.

4. POST-QUANTUM CRYPTOGRAPHY APPLICATIONS IN SMART URBAN DOMAINS

With the increased development of cities around the globe toward being a metropolitan city, well-networked smart cities, and tremendous IoT solutions, cloud platforms, and the emerging demand of quantum-resistant security solutions is steadily increasing in connection with real-time data analytics. The traditional cryptography is undermined by the development of the quantum computation technologies. This section elaborates on the existing applications of PQC to tackle the vulnerabilities of Smart Cities ranging across five domains: Education, Healthcare, Finance, and Infrastructure Development.

4.1 Education: Securing Academic Credentials in the Digital Age

The digital revolution in educational systems has radically changed the way in which academic credentials are issued, verified, and stored. Paper-based certification systems that had worked for centuries are now riddled with weaknesses in a more digitalized world, such as vulnerability to forgery, physical degradation, and time-consuming verification processes taking weeks to finalize. Embedding Post-Quantum Cryptography in educational credentialing systems is therefore a forward-looking strategy to pre-empt both today's security issues as well as tomorrow's quantum threats.

Case A. MIT Digital Diploma System Implementation

Massachusetts Institute of Technology is the example for the early use of sophisticated cryptographic methods in credentialing and its Digital Diploma Initiative. The credential verification processes became lengthy and time-consuming which in some cases caused bottlenecks when the potential graduates sought either employment or continued education opportunities. The challenges were high during the COVID-19 pandemic when remote education and online communications were the reality, which is why the fact that digital credentials can be verified instantly and safely is important. (Massachusetts Institute of Technology, 2017-a)

The innovative approach practiced at MIT involved the construction of a new system of credentialing using blockchain, which approached the task of recording and proving academic achievements on a different level (Lederman, 2017). The system will take advantage of the distributed ledger to generate an immutable record of educational achievements and all digital diplomas issued by the system will be cryptographically signed, using the verifiable identity of the graduate. The system was first introduced with the use of traditional cryptographic applications like the SHA-256 hashing standards and Elliptic Curve Digital Signature Algorithm (ECDSA) with impressive efficiency gains since it took several weeks to verify a credential and now under a few seconds. (Massachusetts Institute of Technology, 2017-b). Nevertheless, seeing the consequences of the development of quantum computing in the long term, researchers at MIT started investigating the possibility of integrating NIST-standardized post-quantum cryptographic algorithms, i.e., SPHINCS + as a digital signature and Dilithium with increased security measures. The system's cryptographic security ensures that credentials cannot be tampered with or forged, while the blockchain infrastructure provides transparency and auditability without compromising individual privacy.

Case B. European Blockchain Services Infrastructure (EBSI) Cross-Border Initiative

Dedication to digitalization and the mobility of people by the European Union has taken shape in the creation of the European Blockchain Services Infrastructure (EBSI), which is a multitask solution targeted at solving the multifaceted issue of credential recognition between member countries. The root problem that EBSI is trying to solve deals with the fact that the European countries that are member states have independent credentialing requirements, verification mechanisms and institutional structures. Such fragmentation has long led to time-consuming and bureaucratic credential recognition procedures, in which submission of physical documents, official translation, long administrative procedures, and possibly months, is needed to secure recognition. More so, the lack of agreed security standards of various systems in different countries left them exposed to fraud and eminently hard to verify exhaustively. The new and innovative solution of the company is to combine the blockchain technology and Verifiable Credentials Framework to build a single, secure system of interoperable credential management in the European Union. Through the system, educational establishments may create digitally signed credentials potentially checked in real-time by an employer, academic establishment, or government agency in the member state in which they are checked, irrespective of the origin country of issuance and its particular educational structure.

Decentralized identity based (DID) systems implement this by allowing people to take charge of their own personal data and ensure that trusted people can verify their educational achievements but not have to see the irrelevant personal data of the person. The experience gathered by the pilot deployments of EBSI has shown that it can lead to dramatic increase in administrative efficiency and a decrease in frauds. The process of cross-country credential validation that once took weeks or even months of work is completed in minutes and thus significantly minimizes the extent of bureaucracy that individuals or institutions have to put up with. Through its further development and enlargement, the system is setting up a platform of the quantum-safe protocols within the context of a high mass governmental education system, which may set an example of other similar programs all over the globe.

4.2 Healthcare: Quantum-Resistant Medical Data Protection

In response to the increasing urgency with which the swift digitalization of the healthcare industry is propelling and the notion of interventional therapy approaches proposes the need to upscale cybersecurity objectives more so than ever before due to the sensitive nature of patient information. By incorporating a combination of AI-based diagnostics and biometric authentication systems and Internet of Medical Things (IoMT) devices, the potential target surface area of potential cybercriminals has not only grown exponentially but has also contributed immensely to the value and sensitivity of the information entity being defended. Post-Quantum Cryptography is one of the essential elements in a portfolio of preparing the healthcare system to support the privacy and integrity of patient data in quantum computing era.

Case A. Singapore's Quantum-Safe Healthcare Surveillance System

As part of its Smart Nation initiative, Singapore's advanced digital health system uses AI-driven facial recognition and wearable IoMT devices. Authorities recognized that the traditional encryption securing this sensitive biometric and patient data was vulnerable to future quantum attacks, creating a significant risk to patient privacy at scale. Such traditional encryption mechanisms securing facial recognition data sets, biometric pattern records, as well as inter-device communications using wearable appliances were identified as possibly prone to future quantum computation attacks that could jeopardize patient privacy at an industrial scale and raise concerns within the population regarding the security of online healthcare solutions.

The innovative response of Singapore was that in de-teleporting the implementation of quantum-protective encryption measures, the government healthcare agencies and the private technology providers engaged in an encompassing partnership to invent and apply the cutting-edge encryption tools to hospital monitoring and smart authentication solutions. The project targeted the implementation of lattice-based cryptographic schemes in safeguarding the storage and transmission of biometric data, and deployment of hash-based signature schemes to guarantee identity record of patients. Deployment of identity management solutions based on PQC has also been quite an effective approach in increasing the resilience of hospital access systems and so as to forestall spoofing artifacts and retain biometric authentication, proving to be resilient to any classical and quantum computation using quantum computers. The capacity of the system to perform high-withdrawals and still offer quantum-resistant security has especially been instrumental during emergency situations in the medical sphere. As Singapore continues to evaluate and refine its PQC algorithms alongside AI analytics systems, the nation has established itself as a pioneer in developing secure smart healthcare models that balance technological innovation with robust privacy protection.

Case B. Mayo Clinic and Cisco Post-Quantum VPN Implementation

The pandemic-driven shift to telemedicine required Mayo Clinic to securely share sensitive patient data across a wide network of remote labs and clinics. Recognizing that their traditional VPNs were vulnerable to future quantum attacks—posing a long-term risk to data and HIPAA compliance—the clinic partnered with Cisco to pilot a quantum-resistant solution. Medical information can barely be more sensitive than it is, and the high level of regulatory compliance (being HIPAA-compliant, etc.) would require the proactive implementation of quantum-resistant security precautions to be considered.

The collaboration between Mayo Clinic and Cisco Systems is another example of unprecedented pilot testing of VPN tunnels that use NIST-standardised post-quantum cryptographic algorithms. The execution was based on Kyber algorithms on quantum-resistant key exchange protocols which made it possible to be sure that communication keys would not be crackable by advanced quantum computer-based attacks. An early version of the trials proved that the PQC-based VPN systems would be capable of sustaining strong end-to-end encryption and low performance overhead in high-throughput environments typified by current healthcare networks. The system could do real-time and synchronic data transfer of a lot of medical imaging and telemedicine calls with little latency without instigating demand to the network. The success made Mayo Clinic claim one of the firsts in implementing post-quantum cryptography on its central healthcare networks and serve as an example of implementing quantum-resistant healthcare communication systems with complete compliance with the HIPAA regulations and long-term data security.

4.3 Finance: Securing Global Payment Infrastructure

The financial services industry forms one of the most imperative and susceptible cyber-attack targets with trillions of dollars of payment on global infrastructure being conducted on a daily basis via networks that are connected, cross-continentally and cross-currency. The possible implications of quantum computations on the financial cryptography systems are very much more than just a personal privacy issue.

Case A. Mastercard's Post-Quantum Cryptography Initiative

Mastercard's global payment network processes millions of daily transactions using classical cryptography, making it a prime target for quantum threats. The key challenge is the long-term security of financial records, which are vulnerable to 'harvest now, decrypt later' attacks, where encrypted data is stolen now to be decrypted by future quantum computers. Top-Coverage of the master card to implement post quantum cryptography included massive cooperation with the National Institute of Standards and Technology (NIST), payments industry partners, and even academic research establishments to conduct evaluation and test that quantum-resistant algorithms would work and serve in the actual payment processing market. This project involved the operation of Kyber algorithms to set encryption keys and thus offer quantum-proof security to critical transaction information as it was transmitted and processed.

Dilithium signature algorithms were adopted, used in the signing of transactions as well as authentication of transactions and such that computational attacks, either classical or quantum on payment approvals and other operations on digital wallets will be nullified. The review enabled it to realize that cryptographic algorithms based on lattices had the prospects of delivering fast transaction capabilities, as well as being quantum resistant through an acceptable level of trade-offs on a big scale payment system. Mastercard's findings have influenced the development of industry-wide payment security standards, with the company's roadmap for phased PQC migration serving as a model for other financial institutions seeking to implement quantum-resistant security measures.

Case B. Bank of Canada and BIS Project Polaris

The development of Central Bank Digital Currencies (CBDCs) creates a new foundation for national monetary systems, but also a critical security challenge. Project Polaris, a collaboration between the Bank of Canada and the Bank for International Settlements, directly addresses the risk of a quantum attack, which could break a CBDC's cryptography, erode public trust, and destabilize the national economy. Project Polaris has carried out risk evaluations of the risks posed to different CBDC architectures ranging by account-based systems to token-based architectures. Its study aims were the creation of cryptographic frameworks that would guarantee quantum-resistant security of the digital identity validation, transaction validation, and distributed ledger integrity.

The findings of the project reiterated how imperative it was to make application of post-quantum cryptographic protections during the early development phases of the CBDC, as opposed to trying to layer quantum resistance on top of existing mechanisms. (Tan, Lerouge, Du Caju, & Du Seuil, 2023) The study showed that the early adoption of PQC algorithms would allow protection against classical and even quantum threats to be comprehensive and implement performance and scalability characteristics required of a national portfolio of digital currencies. Project Polaris has published detailed guidelines advocating for proactive PQC integration in CBDC development, catalyzing global awareness and policy discussions regarding the quantum security of future monetary systems.

4.4 Infrastructure Development: Protecting Critical Urban Systems

Modern urban infrastructure increasingly relies on interconnected digital systems that control everything from transportation networks to power grids, creating complex ecosystems where cybersecurity vulnerabilities can have cascading effects across multiple critical services. The integration of Internet of Things devices, autonomous systems, and real-time data analytics into infrastructure management has exponentially increased both the efficiency and the potential attack surface of urban systems.

Case A. Tokyo's Secure Mobility Network Initiative

The history of Tokyo as the leader of smart cities, especially the process of organizing large international events and related changes in the construction of urban transport systems, has made it necessary to introduce complex mobility networks that combine autonomous transport, intelligent traffic management system, and sharing of real-time information regarding various modes of transport. Mobility network security that is confronting Tokyo is complex in nature because it is expected to secure vehicle to vehicle (V2V) communications, vehicle to infrastructure (V2I) sharing information and traffic planning systems that direct important urban activities.

The new method of Tokyo in dealing with these challenges was considered as the use of huge cooperation among the Japanese telco companies, cybersecurity, and vehicle companies to create and test post-quantum cryptography approach that is never experienced to only focus on mobility use cases. The project aimed at application of the lattice-based encryption algorithms in securing V2V and V2I communications, so that autonomous vehicles used to exchange navigation and safety information, could not be intercepted and manipulated by malicious actors or entities. Traffic management systems were provided with hash-based signature algorithm enabling tamper evidentness of communication between the traffic control centers, and with smart infrastructure components. Tokyo's Department of Transportation has now developed plans for widespread PQC integration across the city's mobility infrastructure over the next decade, establishing a framework that could serve as a model for other metropolitan areas seeking to implement quantum-safe transportation systems.

Case B. New York Power Authority Grid Security Enhancement

The infrastructure of the smart grid of the New York Power Authority is one of the most significant and complicated urban systems, supplying electricity to millions of locals and companies and being in sync with renewable energy sources, energy storage systems, and demand response plans over a wide geographical distance. This modernization of the electrical grid infrastructure that involves the use of smart meters, automated control devices, and real-time monitoring tools pose vulnerabilities leading to cybersecurity attacks. The security threat that the smart grid infrastructure of NYPA would encounter would attack the communications between substations and control centers, the supervisory control and data acquisition (SCADA) systems management, and the integrity of demand response programs that would coordinate with devices to consumers as well as industrial plants. Conventional cryptosecurity provided to grid systems was considered to be potentially susceptible to quantum computing, and they were potentially capable of performing complex attacks on control systems resulting to large scale power blackouts, damages to equipment and disruptions on the economy to a great degree.

This step-wise approach of NYPA to address these quantum security threats entailed the formulation of a pilot program that would do the following: assess and adopt post-quantum cryptographic uses in grid communications and control systems. The project involved the implementation of quantum-resistant encryption protocols between substations and central control centres employing lattice-based and hash-based cryptographic algorithms that can meet low-latency requirements essential to real time grid operation but are not subject to a quantum computer break. The pilot also tested the combination with the Quantum Key Distribution (QKD) systems to add the further level of security to the most important grid communications. The pilot program effectively showed that quantum-safe cryptographic protocols are achievable without the total reconstruction of the existing grid infrastructure allowing a slow migration process to be employed without the need of dislocating operations nor the capital requirements of the process. NYPA's successful demonstration of practical quantum-safe grid implementation has increased stakeholder confidence in the feasibility of widespread PQC adoption across critical infrastructure systems, influencing similar initiatives by utilities and infrastructure operators nationwide.

Table 2 serves as the summary of all the applications discussed in the section above. Together, these case studies from education, healthcare, finance, and infrastructure demonstrate a clear and growing momentum toward quantum readiness.

They show that while individual sectors are making progress, a truly resilient smart city requires a holistic, integrated framework. The following section proposes such a framework—a Proof of Concept for a smart city architecture built from the ground up on the principles of post-quantum security.

TABLE 2. Summary of the Literature Survey

Domain	Case Study	Problem Statement	Approach (PQC-Focused)	Results / Impact
Education	MIT Digital Diploma System	Risk of diploma forgery and insecure digital verification	Blockchain-based credentials with research into PQC signatures (e.g., SPHINCS+, Dilithium)	Fast, secure, verifiable digital diplomas; foundational for quantum-safe academic records
	European Blockchain Services Infrastructure (EBSI)	Lack of secure, interoperable, cross-border credential verification	PQC-based decentralized identity (DID) and verifiable credentials in EU-wide blockchain	Seamless credential sharing; future-proofed academic identity and certificate integrity
Healthcare	Singapore's Smart Hospital Surveillance	Risk of biometric data theft and unauthorized system access	Integration of quantum-safe encryption in AI-driven surveillance and access control	Protected patient identity systems; resilient hospital infrastructure
	Mayo Clinic & Cisco	Vulnerability of VPN tunnels in clinical data sharing	PQC-secured VPN trials using Kyber and Dilithium	Secured remote health data exchange; early model for PQC in medical compliance
Finance	Mastercard PQC Trials	Risk of transaction interception and crypto algorithm obsolescence	Pilots using NIST PQC candidates (Kyber, Dilithium) for transaction validation and APIs	Scalable PQC transition roadmap; influenced payment security standards
	Bank of Canada & BIS – Project Polaris	Security of CBDCs against quantum threats	PQC-tested designs for identity, transaction encryption, and ledger integrity	Informed global policy on secure CBDC development; raised central bank awareness
Infrastructure	Tokyo's Secure Mobility Network	Vulnerability in V2V and V2I communication in smart traffic	PQC-enabled V2X protocol testing in traffic systems	Maintained secure transport flow; proactive smart city quantum defense
	NY Power Authority PQC Grid Pilot	Risks to smart grid control systems from quantum-enabled attacks	PQC-encrypted inter-substation communication with lattice/hash schemes	Enhanced energy grid integrity; proven PQC feasibility in live urban grid

5. PROOF OF CONCEPT FOR POST-QUANTUM CRYPTOGRAPHY-ENABLED SMART CITY ARCHITECTURE

5.1 Conceptual Framework

The shift between theoretical post-quantum cryptographic treatment and urban applications is a key issue of the contemporary network of cybersecurity infrastructures. With the development of quantum computing advancing faster than ever before it is essential that security measures need to be developed in critical urban systems in a way that they are quantum-resistant. In this all-encompassing Proof of Concept, an elaborate roadmap of the required work to encrypt a full smart city setup with post-quantum encryption was introduced, proving the fact that it is technically feasible and that a full quantum-safe smart city implementation is a good idea and holds complementary advantages.

The model city named NeoQ-City as depicted in Figure 5.1, according to the purpose of this research will be a full-scale testbed to assess the applicability of incorporating the post-quantum cryptographic algorithms on all levels in the digital infrastructure of the city. The domain example of NeoQ-City is a medium-sized metro region of about 500,000 people, selected because it has sufficient dynamics that will ensure we address the scalability issues as well as keeping it small enough that we can interrogate it into more depth. The architecture proposed does not retrofit security measures on top of a creaking infrastructure, like typically happens with the traditional implementation of smart cities but instead offers quantum-resistant security as a first principle that will shape everything in design, flow of data, user engagement. The PoC has its priorities of key design principles, which set it apart in contrast to any traditional smart city implementation. The fact that real-time data security would guarantee keeping confidentiality and integrity overall information transmitted between city systems even under quantum computational attacks makes it quite special. Safe frame works of citizen interaction preserve individual privacy by also facilitating effective accessibility to the city services and information.

5.2 Comprehensive Architectural Framework

5.2.1 Layer 1-Physical Infrastructure Layer

The physical infrastructure layer tops NeoQ-City quantum-resistant architecture, which contemplates all the hardware components that enjoy direct contact with the urban, as well as citizens. Intelligent sensors are installed in various parts of the city with highly intelligent traffic surveillance units that have computer vision and can count the number of vehicles, their speed and understand traffic patterns in real-time. Such sensors design quantum-resistant encryption protocols that keep the data gathered hidden to eavesdropping.

Health monitoring architecture is one of the most sensitive objects of the physical layer containing such elements as the network of sensors reflecting on health factors, biological threats, chemical hazards, and radiations in all the city. Such vulnerable monitoring systems should be armed with utmost security since they can give implications on matters of national safety and emergency response procedures. The tamper-evident hardware security modules of the sensors provide the security to guarantee that health information cannot be tampered with by bad-attackers who want to create panic or conceal real dangers.

Edge devices are the distributed computing that processes and analyses data gathered by sensors and then transmitted to the central systems of the city. Wearable technology provided to any city employee, be it working in public safety, maintenance, or healthcare areas are equipped with quantum-resistant encryption to keep the information about personal and operations safe. Smart Utility meters installed in households and commercial premises record the use of electricity, water, and gas and safeguard the data of the customers. The city has surveillance cameras employing state of art computer vision capabilities in monitoring public security, traffic surveillance and coordination of emergency responses. Such systems have to be secured in such a sophisticated way to avoid unwarranted access, which may hamper citizen privacy or perpetrate crime. The video streams employ a quantum-resistant cryptography scheme that secures the cameras, and the digital signatures are based on the post-quantum concept. Gateway devices can be understood as the secure interface communication points between edge devices and the rest of the city network infrastructure and use the digital standard Kyber quantum-resistant key exchange algorithms to create encrypted communications channels that secure information transmitted against quantum computing attacks.

Figure 1. Architecture Diagram of the Proposed NeoQ-City

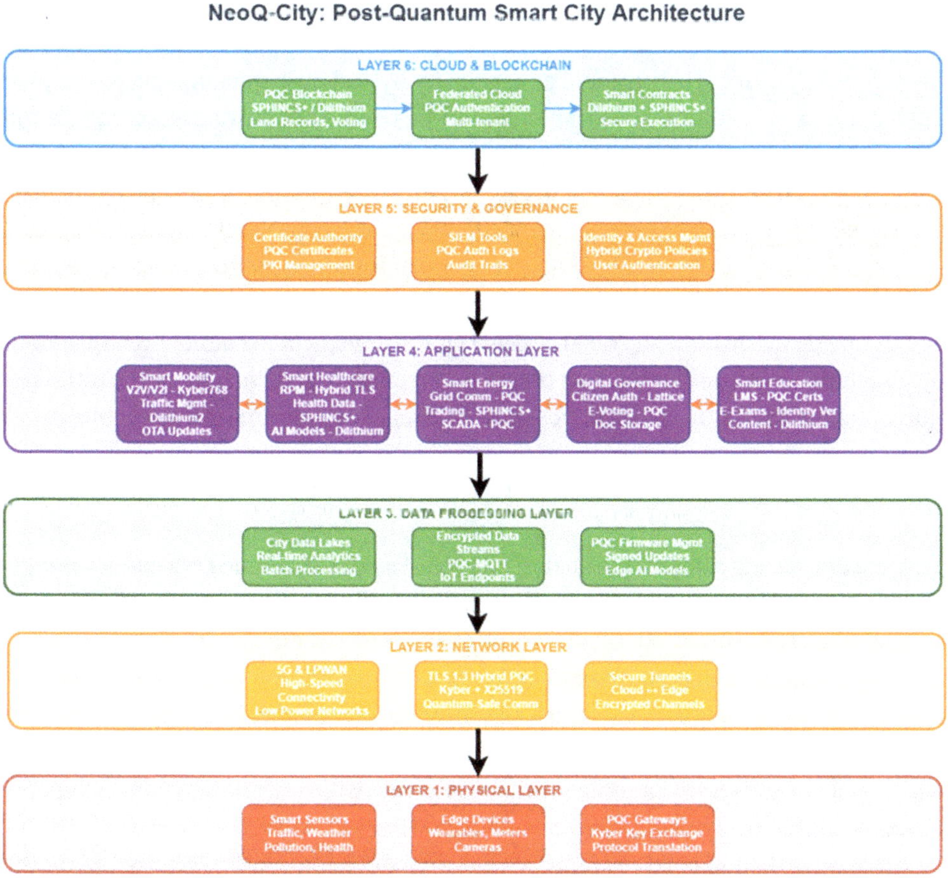

5.2.2 Layer 2-Advanced Network Communication Layer

The network communication level depicts an advanced complex engineering that allows it to use multiple communication technologies so that broad coverage, redundancy, and security are available in every urban setting. At several levels, the architecture of the 5G equipment applies quantum-resistant security options, such as post-quantum cryptographic defenses on user device verification, base station security, and core network communications. The Low-Power Wide-Area Network technologies such as LoRaWAN and NB-IoT offer communication services to the IoT devices where the device has to have long battery life and range but has limited bandwidth requirement. The LPWAN infrastructure provides an implementation of lightweight post quantum cryptographic algorithms with substantial efficiency in low resources devices all the while being secure to quantum threats.

All internet-based city services have secure communication channels provided by Transport Layer Security protocol enhanced by hybrid post-quantum cryptographic algorithms. The methods of its implementation, i.e. the hybrid one is a combination of a classical implementation of elliptic curve cryptography and a quantum-resistant algorithm such as Kyber, which hides against all possible attacks currently and guarantees security in the long term against attacks with quantum computers. City cloud servers are linked to distributed edge devices in the urban environment on secured data routes via secure communication tunnels. These tunnels also use post-quantum key exchange algorithms to construct encryption keys, which cannot be broken into by quantum computational means of attack, meaning sensitive data of the cities are safe upon transmission over the possibly-near-hacked network infrastructure.

5.2.3 Layer 3-Intelligent Data Processing Layer

Data processing remains the analytical core of NeoQ-City, and enormous amounts of data that will be accumulated in all cities in the urban environment are processed, analyzed, and converted into actual solutions that management and citizen services can implement in urban governance. City Data Lakes utilize sophisticated big data storage and processing that are established to accommodate tremendous information in and produced by urban IoT systems. These storage units employ post-quantum encryption to preserve the data in their safe depositories and execute quantum-resistant access controls.

Streaming data is used to improve real-time decision-making by analyzing the current state of the city in order to identify patterns, anomalies, and trends to be dealt with either immediately or as quickly as possible. Traffic management systems study the patterns of traffic flow to time the signals effectively and anticipate the occurrence of congestion issues on the road before they get serious. The systems of environmental monitoring use the air-quality and weather information to provide pollution warnings and prepare initiation of emergency measures on dire weather occasions. The use of batch processing systems makes it easier to analyze the historical data of the city on a large scale, i.e., timely reveal long-term trends, allocate resources, and assist in the implementation of strategic planning processes.

5.2.4 Layer 4-Comprehensive Application Service Layer

Application service layer exposes the user interfaces and services to the citizens, the city employees and other stakeholders allowing them to interface with the digital infrastructure of NeoQ-City. The citizen services portal is an expanded online solution that gives the residents access to the city services, information, and means of communication. The portal uses the Dilithium-based protocols of authentication of users, offering quantum resistance to the user accounts and preserving the simple actions during the process of their authentication allowing the citizens to pay taxes and utilities, getting their permits and licenses, reporting about non-emergencies, and engaging in the activities of involvement.

Smart healthcare interface gives secure access to the Electronic Health Record systems and other medical information systems accessed by care providers all over the city. The systems use SPHINCS+ post-quantum signature algorithms to safeguard patient privacy and guarantee data integrity of decades-long medical records that can potentially be required by healthcare providers to access patient data safely, coordinate their care across different facilities and contribute to the public health tracking efforts.

Emergency response coordination systems allow police, fire, emergency medical services and, other agencies of the public safety system to coordinate responses to incidents hole city wide. The critical systems apply the post-quantum cryptographic security to make sure that the emergency communication is not possible to be detected or altered by malicious parties, offering real-time situational awareness, resource tracking, and the ability to communicate with others to coordinate any complex operations in case of an emergency incident.

5.2.5 Layer 5-Security and Governance Infrastructure Layer

Security and governance layer is where the security services and policy implementation processes that have secured the entire digital technology of NeoQ-City are located. The Certificate Authority infrastructure secures and administers post-quantum cryptographic certificates of all the devices, systems, and users of the whole digital ecosystem in the city. It is a full-features Public Key Infrastructure with quantum-resistant algorithms so that the digital certificates will be valid and trusted to survive quantum computational attacks, with Public Key Infrastructure certificate life cycle functions covering the issuing, renewing, revoking, and validating millions of certificates needed by the citywide internet of Things and digital services infrastructures.

Security Information and Event Management systems enable a detailed surveillance or observation of security events on the digitalized surface of the city. These systems receive and process log data of the entire city systems and use post-quantum cryptography authentication, so as to verify that security logs cannot be modified or fabricated. SIEM infrastructure applies advanced analytics and machine learning to identify any possible in-scope security threats, organizes incident response operations, and offers city cybersecurity experts security intelligence. Introduction of Identity and Access (IAM) controls on the systems used by all the city users and systems provide extensive authentication and authorization controls. IAM architecture makes use of hybrid cryptographic options incorporating classical and post-quantum algorithms to afford short-term security and to ensure long-term protection from quantum cyber-security threats.

5.2.6 Layer 6 – Cloud & Blockchain Layer

Cloud & Blockchain Layer can be called the very top of the NeoQ-City stack, being the distributed, scalable basis of Secure service orchestration, cross-agency collaboration, and long-term data immutability. This layer consists of the PQC-secured Blockchain infrastructure at heart, which leverages the signature schemes such as SPHINCS+ and Dilithium to provide tamper-proof record book capabilities in land ownership registries, in voting and logs of critical infrastructure. These quantum-safe ledgers will prevent any tampering of a written data, even when opponents have access to quantum technology. The blockchain can be used to facilitate transparent auditing of civic activities as well as critical in establishing credibility of services facing the public eye such as e-voting services, digital notarisation, and public financial reporting.

The federated cloud infrastructure implemented at NeoQ-City allows to multiply geographically dispersed services, and data sovereignty and cryptographic self-determination are maintained. Authentications based on PQCs become part of a cloud access gateway, using CRYSTALS-Kyber and Dilithium to enable inter-cloud authentication, workload or service-level authentications. The other foundation of this layer is smart contract execution with the use of PQC mechanisms. Through the incorporation of Dilithium and SPHINCS + signatures into the contract lifecycle, NeoQ-City contributes to the realization that smart contracts (whose use in automated legal systems includes workflows involving automation of public tenders, utility billing, land use land and inter-agency processes) are executed safely, verifiably, and tamper-free.

Finally, the Layer 6 Cloud & Blockchain Layer brings to closure the work of the NeoQ-City in terms of quantum-secure, transparent, and resilient model of digital governance. It enables the horizontal scale out needed to deliver metropolitan services and integrates security directly at the base compute, storage and trust components of the digital infrastructure of the city. With the development of quantum computing, such a layer ensures that the city will be resistant to the obsolescence of cryptography, including all the most strategic activities: elections, registries, identity systems and fiscal records.

5.3 Migration Strategy: A Hybrid Approach

A primary challenge for any city is transitioning from legacy infrastructure to a PQC-secured environment. It is not feasible to replace every sensor, camera, and controller overnight. Therefore, the NeoQ-City architecture adopts a hybrid cryptography model to ensure a smooth and secure migration.

This approach combines a classical algorithm (like Elliptic Curve Cryptography) with a PQC algorithm (like CRYSTALS-Kyber) simultaneously. Communications are protected by both algorithms in parallel. This strategy offers two crucial benefits:

1. Backward Compatibility: Legacy systems that do not yet support PQC can still communicate using the classical algorithm, preventing operational disruptions.
2. Forward Security: It immediately protects against "harvest now, decrypt later" attacks. Even if an attacker record encrypted traffic today, they won't be able to decrypt it in the future with a quantum computer because the PQC layer will remain secure.

Within NeoQ-City, this hybrid model would be implemented in core communication protocols like the TLS tunnels connecting the network and data processing layers, ensuring a gradual and secure city-wide upgrade.

5.4 Quantum-Ready Key Lifecycle Management

The shift to PQC fundamentally impacts how cryptographic keys are managed. PQC keys and signatures are often larger than their classical counterparts, requiring updates to the city's Public Key Infrastructure (PKI). The NeoQ-City governance layer would incorporate a robust, quantum-ready key management framework with the following principles:

- Upgraded Certificate Authority (CA): The city's CA must be updated to issue, distribute, and validate new certificate formats that can handle the larger key sizes of PQC algorithms like Dilithium and SPHINCS+.
- Automated Key Rotation: To manage the millions of IoT devices, the system would enforce automated key rotation policies. This minimizes the window of opportunity for an attacker if a device's key is ever compromised.
- Secure Generation and Storage: All cryptographic keys for critical infrastructure would be generated and stored in tamper-resistant Hardware Security Modules (HSMs) to prevent theft or unauthorized access.
- Scalable Revocation: The system must be able to efficiently revoke the credentials of a compromised device. This involves scalable mechanisms for

distributing Certificate Revocation Lists (CRLs) or implementing an Online Certificate Status Protocol (OCSP) that can handle the massive scale of a city's IoT network.

6. NATIONAL AND INTERNATIONAL POLICIES

The transition to quantum-resistant security is a global effort, but its implementation is shaped by national strategies. In India, the push for PQC is an integral part of its ambition to become a global technology leader. The government's proactive stance is demonstrated by the National Quantum Mission (NQM), an 6,003 crore initiative aimed at developing a robust quantum ecosystem. A key pillar of the NQM is to create quantum-safe communication and security, directly funding research and development in PQC to protect the nation's critical digital infrastructure.

This top-down strategic vision is set to be supported by a new legislative framework. The proposed Digital India Act (DIA), intended to replace the outdated Information Technology Act of 2000, will establish the legal foundation for emerging technologies. It is expected that the DIA will include provisions for "digital by design" security, mandating that new platforms and services incorporate quantum-resistant standards from the outset.

For smart cities, these national policies have a direct impact. Urban development under India's Smart Cities Mission must align with the NQM's security goals and prepare for the DIA's new compliance requirements. City planners and technology officers will need to revise their procurement policies to prioritize PQC-ready hardware and software, ensuring that as urban services become more connected, they are also being built to be quantum-resilient. This alignment ensures that India's smart cities are not only efficient but also secure sovereign assets in the coming quantum era.

7. ETHICAL AND SOCIETAL IMPLICATIONS

While PQC presents a technical solution to a future threat, its implementation in a country of 1.4 billion people raises profound ethical and societal questions. The sheer scale of India's digital public infrastructure, centered on the Aadhaar biometric identity system, makes it a crucial case study. The primary ethical imperative is to ensure that the data of over a billion citizens is protected not just for today, but for decades to come. A critical concern is the risk of a "quantum divide." The resources and expertise required to implement PQC may be available for high-value corporate and urban financial systems, but deploying it across the vast infrastructure that delivers Aadhaar-linked subsidies and services to rural and underserved communities is a far greater challenge. An inequitable rollout could create a society where the financial data of the urban affluent is quantum-safe, while the fundamental identity data of the most vulnerable remains exposed, deepening existing digital inequalities.

Furthermore, the transition to PQC is directly tied to data sovereignty and privacy, principles now legally protected under India's Digital Personal Data Protection Act (DPDPA), 2023. Securing the Aadhaar ecosystem with PQC is not merely a technical upgrade; it is a necessary step to uphold the data rights of every Indian citizen against future "harvest now, decrypt later" attacks.

Ultimately, the success of transformative platforms like the Unified Payments Interface (UPI) and the entire Digital India initiative is built on public trust. A failure to proactively secure the nation's digital backbone against the quantum threat would erode this trust. Therefore, a national PQC strategy must be inclusive, equitable, and transparent, ensuring that the quantum transition strengthens, rather than fragments, India's digital society.

7.1 Economic Realities of PQC Adoption in India

While technically feasible, the nationwide adoption of PQC in India presents a significant economic challenge that requires a strategic cost-benefit analysis. The initial costs extend far beyond software licensing. A primary expense is in human capital; upskilling a generation of engineers and cybersecurity professionals is necessary to manage and deploy these new cryptographic systems, directly supporting the goals of the National Quantum Mission. Furthermore, there is a massive infrastructure cost associated with upgrading or replacing legacy IoT hardware within the Smart Cities Mission, as many existing devices lack the processing power for PQC.

However, the benefit—and the ultimate justification for this investment—is the mitigation of catastrophic risk. The economic and societal cost of a future quantum attack on critical systems like Aadhaar or the UPI payment network would be immeasurable, eroding citizen trust and destabilizing the digital economy. Therefore, the investment in PQC is not merely a technical upgrade but a long-term strategic imperative for protecting India's digital sovereignty and maintaining its position as a global technology leader.

8. CONCLUSION

The quantum-safe urban ecosystem is not a plain road moving forward. At the same time as pilot projects and the initial releases of post-quantum cryptographic algorithms demonstrate positive findings, various important Individual challenges have to be overcome in order to be adopted widely. They consist of technical constraints of present-day Internet of things, IoT devices might not be able to provide the computational power to cover more intensive PQC operations, particularly on to real-time applications. The other challenge is its backward compatibility with legacy systems. cryptographic flexibility has not been the desired attribute of many of the current urban infrastructures.

To maneuver around such challenges, there is a need to take a multi-prong approach that involves technical integration to allow stakeholders to have a two-prong approach to overcome the challenges. preparedness, policy preparedness, and collaboration within the institution. The first step that the city planners ought to take is to incorporate PQC-readiness is a key stipulation in every future smart infrastructure project. This proactive stance enables a step-by step migration of cryptography without having to face high retrofitting costs in the future. Policy the makers should also revise procurement policies so that every hardware and software solutions would be there. NIST-approved PQC standards are applied to the public sectors. These transitions should be sponsored by governments supported by financing and incentive that would have the vendors provide hybrid cryptographic solutions that are able to of functioning in classical and post-quantum worlds. Developers and system designers ought to incorporate PQC algorithms- e.g. CRYSTALS-Kyber, Dilithium, and SPHINCS+, in communication protocols such as MQTT. CoAP and TLS to provide data flows that are forward compatible and safe in urban IoT systems. These recommendations are not only idealistic in their making, but necessary to prepare cities to be able to stand the test of what will happen. arrival of quantum adversaries.

9. FUTURE RECOMMENDATIONS

There are also enormous prospects of research and innovation in the future. Lightweight versions of PQC optimization is performed on edge computing, real-time cryptographic adaptation frameworks, AI-enhanced Quantum threat detection is only some of the grounds that are open to venture. Also, integration of PQC in novel technologies such as 6G networks, AIoT networks and smart governance systems will lead to the emergence of a new era. Next-generation urban resilience through a way. The development of digital twins of cities that are resilient to attacks using quantum computers, as an example have the potential to conduct strategic infrastructure modeling and predictive modeling cryptographic vulnerabilities upgrades. After all, the concept of a smart city where everything can be secured on the quantum level is technology-related but not only. It runs on a declaration of loyalty, continuity, and long-term digital sovereignty.

REFERENCES

Akinola, O. A., Amoateng, S., Akata, A., & Olaobaju, J. O. (2025). Design and evaluation of CRYSTALS-Kyber-based encryption protocols for securing satellite-to-ground communications in U.S. space infrastructures. *World Journal of Advanced Research and Reviews*, *26*(2), 2870–2882. DOI: 10.30574/wjarr.2025.26.2.1926

Al Maqousi, A., & Basu, K. (2025). Cybersecurity framework for smart cities: Leveraging quantum cryptography and blockchain. *2025 1st International Conference on Computational Intelligence Approaches and Applications (ICCIAA)*, 1–6. DOI: 10.1109/ICCIAA65327.2025.11013570

Bank for International Settlements. (2023, October 26). *Project Polaris: High-level design guide for offline payments*. BIS Innovation Hub. https://www.bis.org/publ/othp79.htm

Barnwal, R., Vaidya, A. S., Maram, S., Surana, C., Sai Karteek, G. Y., & Kavuluru, R. K. (2024). A demonstration of secure satellite communication using post quantum cryptography. *2024 International Conference on Smart Electronics and Communication Systems (ISENSE)*, 1–5. DOI: 10.1109/ISENSE63713.2024.10872215

Bera, B., & Sikdar, B. (2024). Securing post-quantum communication for smart grid applications. *2024 IEEE International Conference on Communications, Control, and Computing Technologies for Smart Grids (SmartGridComm)*, 555–561. DOI: 10.1109/SmartGridComm60555.2024.10738045

Castiglione, A., Esposito, J. G., Loia, V., Nappi, M., Pero, C., & Polsinelli, M. (2025). Integrating post-quantum cryptography and blockchain to secure low-cost IoT devices. *IEEE Transactions on Industrial Informatics*, *21*(2), 1674–1683. DOI: 10.1109/TII.2024.3485796

Chen, J., Gan, W., Hu, M., & Chen, C.-M. (2021). On the construction of a post-quantum blockchain for smart city. *Journal of Information Security and Applications*, *58*, 102780. DOI: 10.1016/j.jisa.2021.102780

Dam, D. T., Tran, T.-H., Hoang, V.-P., Pham, C.-K., & Hoang, T.-T. (2023). A survey of post-quantum cryptography: Start of a new race. *Cryptography*, *7*(3), 40. DOI: 10.3390/cryptography7030040

European Commission. (2021). European blockchain services infrastructure (EBSI). https://digital-strategy.ec.europa.eu/en/policies/european-blockchain-services-infrastructure

Fitzgibbon, G., & Ottaviani, C. (2024). Constrained device performance benchmarking with the implementation of post-quantum cryptography. *Cryptography, 8*(2), 21. DOI: 10.3390/cryptography8020021

Gupta, S., Gupta, K. K., Shukla, P. K., & Shrivas, M. K. (2022). Blockchain-based voting system powered by post-quantum cryptography (BBVSP-PQC). *2022 Second International Conference on Power, Control and Computing Technologies (ICPC2T)*, 1–8. DOI: 10.1109/ICPC2T53885.2022.9776966

Kakoulli, E., & Zacharioudakis, E. (2024). Exploration of the role of cryptoprocessors in advancing IoT security. *2024 20th International Conference on Distributed Computing in Smart Systems and the Internet of Things (DCOSS-IoT)*, 524–531. DOI: 10.1109/DCOSS-IoT61029.2024.00083

Kumar, A., Ottaviani, C., Gill, S. S., & Buyya, R. (2022). Securing the future Internet of Things with post-quantum cryptography. *Security and Privacy, 5*(2), e200. DOI: 10.1002/spy2.200

Lederman, D. (2017, October 19). MIT introduces digital diplomas. *Inside Higher Ed.* https://www.insidehighered.com/news/2017/10/19/mit-introduces-digital-diplomas

Li, S., Chen, Y., Chen, L., Liao, J., Kuang, C., Li, K., Liang, W., & Xiong, N. (2023). Post-quantum security: Opportunities and challenges. *Sensors (Basel), 23*(21), 8744. DOI: 10.3390/s23218744 PMID: 37960442

Liu, Y., & Moody, D. (2024). Post-quantum cryptography, and the quantum future of cybersecurity. *Physical Review Applied, 21*(4), 040501. Advance online publication. DOI: 10.1103/PhysRevApplied.21.040501 PMID: 38846721

Ma, Y., Goyal, S. B., Rajawat, A. S., Bedi, P., & Yasmeen, S. (2024). Blockchain-based human intelligent systems for smart city safety. *Transactions on Emerging Telecommunications Technologies, 35*(2), e4939. DOI: 10.1002/ett.4939

Massachusetts Institute of Technology. (n.d.-a). Digital diplomas. MIT Registrar. https://registrar.mit.edu/transcripts-records/diplomas/digital-diplomas

Massachusetts Institute of Technology. (n.d.-b). MIT digital credentials. MIT Digital Credentials Initiative. https://digitalcredentials.mit.edu/

Mastercard. (2023). *An introduction to quantum computing*. Mastercard. https://www.mastercard.com/us/en/news-and-trends/Insights/2023/an-introduction-to-quantum-computing.html

Näther, C., Herzinger, D., Gazdag, S.-L., Steghöfer, J.-P., Daum, S., & Loebenberger, D. (2024). Migrating software systems toward post-quantum cryptography: A systematic literature review. *IEEE Access : Practical Innovations, Open Solutions*, *12*, 132107–132126. DOI: 10.1109/ACCESS.2024.3450306

Obaid, A. H., Al-Husseini, K. A. O., Al-Shareeda, M. A., Almaiah, M. A., & Shehab, R. (2025). Post-quantum secure anonymous authentication for smart cities. *International Journal of Innovative Research and Scientific Studies*, *8*(3), 4315–4324. DOI: 10.53894/ijirss.v8i3.7506

Quantique, I. D. (n.d.). Quantum-safe security for healthcare. https://www.idquantique.com/quantum-safe-security/applications/healthcare/#:~:text=Quantum%2DSafe%20Security%20for%20Healthcare,long%2Dterm%20protection%20and%20confidentiality

Rawal, B. S., & Curry, P. J. (2024). Challenges and opportunities on the horizon of post-quantum cryptography. *APL Quantum*, *1*(2), 026110. DOI: 10.1063/5.0198344

Saarinen, M.-J. O. (2020). Mobile energy requirements of the upcoming NIST post-quantum cryptography standards. *2020 8th IEEE International Conference on Mobile Cloud Computing, Services, and Engineering (MobileCloud)*, 23–30. DOI: 10.1109/MobileCloud48802.2020.00012

Septien-Hernandez, J.-A., Arellano-Vazquez, M., Contreras-Cruz, M. A., & Ramirez-Paredes, J.-P. (2022). A comparative study of post-quantum cryptosystems for Internet-of-Things applications. *Sensors (Basel)*, *22*(2), 489. DOI: 10.3390/s22020489 PMID: 35062450

Shekhawat, H., & Gupta, D. S. (2024). Quantum-safe lattice-based mutual authentication and key-exchange scheme for the smart grid. *Transactions on Emerging Telecommunications Technologies*, *35*(7), e5017. DOI: 10.1002/ett.5017

Tan, E., Lerouge, E., Du Caju, J., & Du Seuil, D. (2023). Verification of education credentials on European blockchain services infrastructure (EBSI): Action research in a cross-border use case between Belgium and Italy. *Big Data and Cognitive Computing*, *7*(2), 79. DOI: 10.3390/bdcc7020079

Xiong, J., Shen, L., Liu, Y., & Fang, X. (2025). Enhancing IoT security in smart grids with quantum-resistant hybrid encryption. *Scientific Reports*, *15*(1), 3. DOI: 10.1038/s41598-024-84427-8 PMID: 39747539

Ye, Z., Song, R., Zhang, H., Chen, D., Cheung, R. C.-C., & Huang, K. (2024). A highly efficient lattice-based post-quantum cryptography processor for IoT applications. *IACR Transactions on Cryptographic Hardware and Embedded Systems*, *2024*(2), 130–153. DOI: 10.46586/tches.v2024.i2.130-153

Yuan, B., Wu, F., & Zheng, Z. (2023). Post quantum blockchain architecture for Internet of Things over NTRU lattice. *PLoS One*, *18*(2), e0279429. DOI: 10.1371/journal.pone.0279429 PMID: 36724147

Zhang, Y., Tang, Y., Li, C., Zhang, H., & Ahmad, H. (2024). Post-quantum secure identity-based signature scheme with lattice assumption for Internet of Things networks. *Sensors (Basel)*, *24*(13), 4188. DOI: 10.3390/s24134188 PMID: 39000967

KEY TERMS AND DEFINITIONS

Firmware Signing: Process of verifying software authenticity using cryptographic digital signatures.

Hybrid Cryptography: Use of both classical and quantum-resistant algorithms in a single system.

IoT (Internet of Things): Network of physical objects embedded with sensors and communication technologies.

Key Encapsulation Mechanism (KEM): A cryptographic method for securely transmitting encryption keys.

Lattice Cryptography: A branch of cryptography relying on the hardness of lattice-based mathematical problems.

NIST: National Institute of Standards and Technology, responsible for PQC standardization.

Post-Quantum Cryptography (PQC): Cryptographic methods designed to be secure against quantum computing attacks.

Quantum Computing: A form of computing using quantum bits (qubits) that can solve certain problems exponentially faster than classical computers.

RSA: A widely used classical encryption algorithm vulnerable to quantum attacks.

TLS: Transport Layer Security protocol used to encrypt internet communications.

Chapter 3

Improving Security, Sustainability, and Resilience Through the Application of PQC in Smart Urban Ecosystems

Krithikha Sanju S.
https://orcid.org/0000-0003-0120-3355
Sri Sivasubramaniya Nadar College of Engineering, India

Madhu Annam R.
https://orcid.org/0009-0002-0035-2527
Sri Sivasubramaniya Nadar College of Engineering, India

ABSTRACT

The development of quantum computing represents an evolutionary change to commonly used forms of public encryption, such as RSA that is designed to protect certain municipal systems which will create further vulnerabilities. Post-quantum cryptography (PQC) can provide a further level of encryption. This chapter discusses how post-quantum techniques can be used to secure the smart infrastructures that support an overall long-range planning process and possibly improve a city's resilience to respond to shocks. This chapter also demonstrates examples from practice, references implications for the original research, and makes recommendations for incorporating quantum resilient cryptography into the urban development agenda through systems thinking.

DOI: 10.4018/979-8-3373-3166-9.ch003

1. INTRODUCTION TO POST QUANTUM CRYPTOGRAPHY IN SMART URBAN ECOSYSTEMS

Intelligent urban ecosystems are widely modifying the operation of cities and technologies used for improvements based on functioning that makes the expectation and capability of enhanced service reliability through the utilization of technologies ranging from IoT, AI with data informed infrastructure. There are examples across a range of use cases relying on these integrated systems to support a wide range of services including energy distribution, transportation, healthcare, and public safety, but while citizens are receiving a wide range of benefits the same concepts of secure communications and assuring data integrity are subject to threats and vulnerabilities which traditional cryptographic protocols are addressing. Traditional cryptographic standards such as RSA and ECC offer little resistance to quantum attacks. PQC has a number of potential solutions, including encryption modes of operation that are focused on quantum attacks. When combined, PQC and intelligent city systems improve cybersecurity and also protect the longer-term resilience of critical infrastructure from uncertainty, such as to gain public trust and acceptance of technology that may be subject to quantum level technology.

Planning for the eventuality of post-quantum cryptography in improving or creating quantum resistant algorithms ultimately supports what layers of protection or privacy are achieved, that data is secure to the extent possible, that public services can continue to be delivered amidst some type of disruption or unintentional action, and that a durable foundation for urban smart with quantum secure planning takes shape, administration comes with sustainable and secure innovation.

1.1 The Imperative for Security, Sustainability, and Resilience

The fast-changing smart city ecosystems introduce a new level of complexity in terms of management of cities. The foundations of good and trusted smart city functioning rely on sustainability and resiliency (Tcholtchev & Schieferdecker, 2021). They are often viewed as a notion for the public to deploy as operational needs for the public trusted smart city networks.

Figure 1. Foundation of Smart Cities

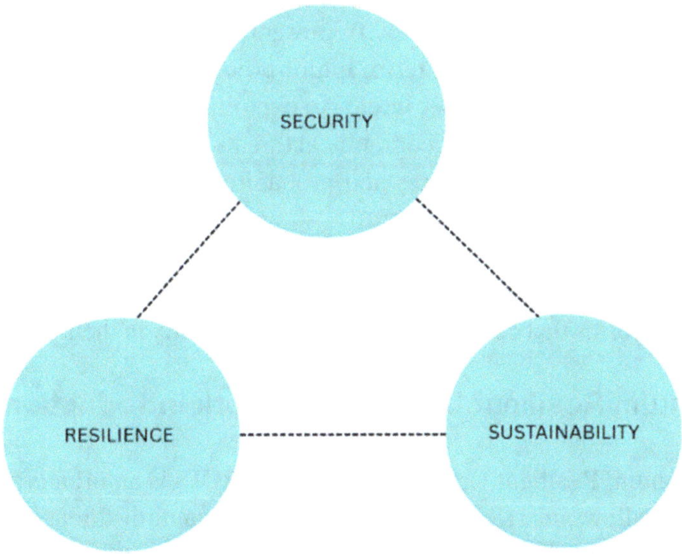

Security involves safeguarding and protecting interconnected systems such as sensors, networks and data platforms from unauthorized manipulation. It is necessary to ensure security of all domains because disruptions can have widespread consequences.

Sustainability primarily focuses on long term resource efficiency and environmental health, which is supported by technologies like smart grids and waste management systems that depend on secured data. In cases where data is compromised, the system decision eventually becomes flawed and leads to increase resource waste. Resilience is the capacity of urban systems to withstand and recover from disruptions ranging from cyberattacks to natural disasters.

Figure 1 represents an unified framework for evaluating the effectiveness of smart city architectures. The main challenge lies in improving the scope of cryptographic systems that can maintain all three priorities simultaneously in a situation where threats evolve with the emergence of quantum.

1.2 Emergence of Post Quantum Cryptography

Modern smart cities are increasingly dependent on secure data exchange to support society's most vital services - transportation, energy management, and health care.

Smart transportation systems derive their reliability from the data exchange being authenticated and integrity-secured back to the digital infrastructure of the data.

Post-Quantum Cryptography (PQC) represents a new generation of cryptographic algorithms that can offer a long term, future-proof security to smart city systems against constantly evolving cyber threats to exploitation by humans, hardware and software attacks and social and geographical threats. PQC's generally use advanced mathematics with lattice structures and probability based error correcting codes, provide amazing data protection.

This continuous development of smart city networks with advanced PQC systems will give municipalities and society more confidence and boost their performance in the digital platforms that citizens will use more frequently in their digital daily lives.

1.3 Quantum Resilient Urban Framework Introduction

The Quantum Resilient Urban Framework (QRUF) is an urban framework that is created to allow smart cities to prepare from quantum threats. Post quantum cryptography becomes an integral part of the urban systems for secure data sharing and management of the urban infrastructure. QRUF provides a solid framework in which to think about where security can best be surgically inserted into the physical operations of the cities with respect to governing frameworks. Beyond technology assurances, QRUF provides the assurance that urban system operations changing across different sectors may cooperate and work together. Furthermore, QRUF promotes confidence in adopting new technologies in cities while developing the needed governing framework to promote public confidence.

2. RISE OF SMART URBAN ECOSYSTEMS

Smart urban ecosystems is a term to describe a holistic city environment incorporating digital technologies into public city infrastructure design as a means of improving decision making in urban environments. Smart urban ecosystems can occur in various domains such as transportation, energy, health care and environmental observation as a means of attempting to improve urban challenges.

2.1 Components of a Smart City

Smart cities leverage technology to offer enhancements to urban functions and the quality of urban life. Key enabling technologies for smart cities include the Internet of Things (IoT), Artificial Intelligence (AI), and big data that can provide data and information in real time to inform decision-making across all infrastructure and services. All of these systems are interconnected and work to enhance efficiency, sustainability and responsiveness in their respective functions. The Internet of Things is defined as a network of physical devices connected to the Internet that provide enhanced sensors and software to collect and communicate data about the status of the device. The sensing devices can provide real-time data and information about topics as varied as traffic, air quality, and energy use. Improved efficiencies are possible because of the real-time data and information gleaned from the devices. Smart city systems can be initiated by the IoT devices, prompted by sensing devices, such as smart water meters, IoT devices are capable of both monitoring and controlling resources in order to improve efficiencies, but also, promote leak detection and reduce water waste.

Artificial Intelligence (AI) includes machines that not only learn from data, but that can in addition perform action, for example, predicting and then assessing in aid of optimization and automation functions. In a smart city, AI is essential for enhancing multiple smart traffic control, personalized public service and analytics functions.AI will uncover patterns in datasets that is not humanly possible to obtain or analyze. Smart city services may enable AI to provide responsive and adaptive service to changing conditions.

Big Data includes both structured and unstructured data produced from urban sensor networks, social media and transactions from interlinked inventory and property systems. Smart cities can analyze trends and anomalies using Big Data analytics, but the data, if trustworthy, might also become a component of future planning to report on the eventual influence to municipal policies and critical urban metrics for improvements to transport and mobility, help public health and energy management, and facilitate productive and efficient circular economies.

2.2 Cyber Physical Systems in Urban Infrastructure

Cyber-physical systems (CPS) acts as the essential connection between digital intelligence and physical operations in smart urban infrastructure. A CPS facilitates the integration of computation, networking and physical processes to provide real-time monitoring and control across city operations. Examples of cyber physical systems include smart grids managing electricity demand/supply, automated traffic systems managing flow from multiple vehicles, automated water distribution systems measuring pressure and quality, etc.

2.2.1 Working of CPS

Figure 2. Working components of CPS

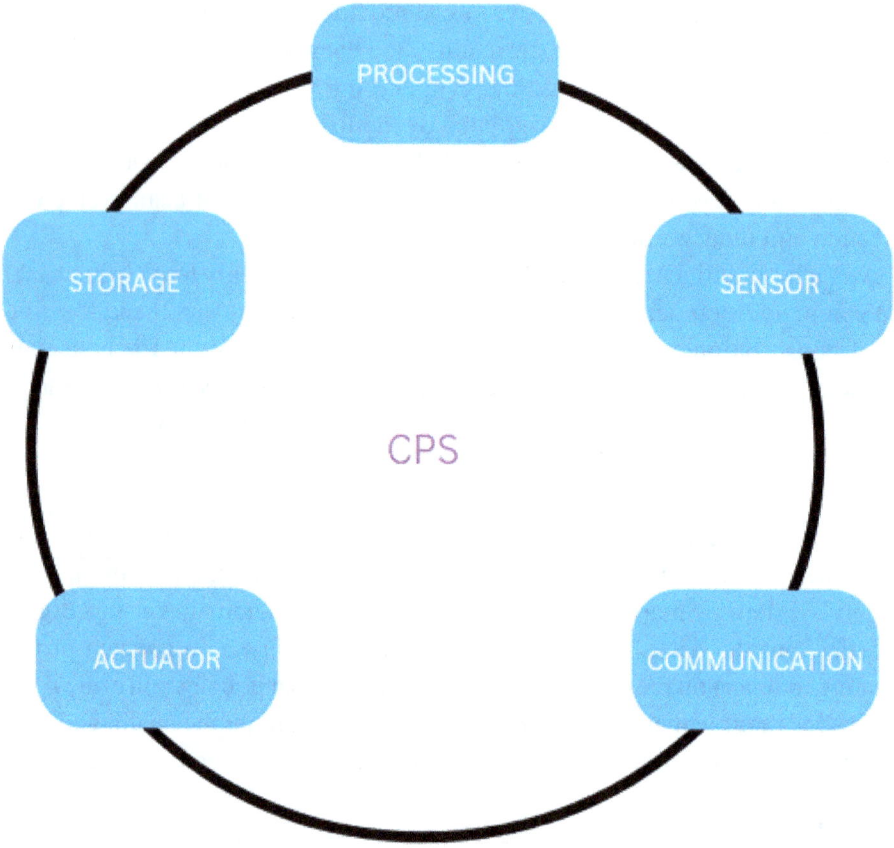

The primary objective of Cyber Physical Systems (CPS) is to establish a seamless loop between the physical world and computational intelligence, enabling real time monitoring, analysis, and actuation. As shown in Figure 2, the systems consist of three main components: sensors and actuators (physical layer), communication networks (network layer), and control systems or data processors (cyber layer) (Tien, 2017).

The process initially starts with sensors placed throughout the physical environment, in a way that it continuously collects data such as vehicle count, speed, weather conditions, and traffic density at intersections. In a smart traffic management system, these sensors can be installed in key components of cites like roadways, traffic lights, and surveillance cameras. The raw data is then sent to edge computing devices or an urban centralized data centre through high-speed, secure communication channels. The information is ultimately processed, using a combination of algorithms and artificial intelligence models, to identify congestion patterns, evaluate traffic flow, and identify anomalies, such as stalled vehicles or accidents. Once analysed, the system will then automatically determine how to respond. For example, where stored congestion was identified at a specific junction, the CPS would determine the best traffic light sequences to alleviate the bottleneck condition. It would then re-instruct the actuators in the traffic lights by transmitting control commands and adjusting the dynamic durations in the affected directions of trailing traffic. In instances involving an emergency vehicle, the CPS would have the ability to provide a green corridor along the route by synchronising signals.

The feedback driven loop is what allows the CPS to operate in real time without any interruptions. In absence of a limited human interaction enabled by activator, the CPS will maintain reactions to changing conditions in estimates. It trains from past data and patterns over time, enabling the CPS to estimate predicted areas of change, providing an additional form of improving efficiency in style and work, enhanced real-time coordination, opportunities to develop AI feedback functions, use of anticipatory mechanism. The advancements of AI integration has eventually enabled CPS to respond to complex dynamics with managed urban variations.

2.2.2 Challenges in CPS

As a key component of wise urban ecosystems, cyber physical systems are also facing different weaknesses and issues that impact performance and security. If the CPS experiences some small failure there will be real consequences such as shutting off traffic lights, changing control to the power grid or modifying emergency response activities.

In addition, CPSs are designed with components that usually come from different environments all using different protocols and legacy hardware which complicates integration and increases the risk of errors.

Real-time communication creates ongoing challenges especially in cases when the CPS must react quickly to one or multiple post-conditions while also processing large data sets.

Lastly, the physical elements of CPS are vulnerable on the environment and also susceptible to tampering which can compromise both data integrity and system consistency. Likewise, the preservation of data confidentiality, availability, and integrity throughout all layers of CPS relies on strong encryption, secure authentication, and faulty-tolerance architecture.

2.3 Urban Data Flows and System Coordination

Urban data flows represent the constant streams of information generated through sensors, devices, applications and platforms embedded in the city's infrastructure. Data can include inputs from traffic sensors, environmental monitors, surveillance cameras, public utilities, and citizen engagement. The ability to collect, transmit, and process flows of data in real time provides cities the ability to detect anomalies and regulate activities, while also deploying responsive services. However, cities need strong data architecture in order to communicate reliably and governance structures that streamline the process while ensuring accuracy, privacy, and availability.

System coordination refers to how aggregates of the city subsystems such as transportation, energy, water, and public safety interact, take decisions in concert with one another, and provide services based on the data they share (Mohamed, 2019).

Although subsystems may function independently, their coordination allows the city to optimally manage its systems as a shared whole. The city's sectors are functioning managed. Traffic data may help determine the quickest route for emergency response or help regulate street lighting. Achieving this state of integration is no easy and requires standardized protocols, interoperable platforms, and secure data exchanges. Without coordination of system responses among subsystems, a lack of efficiency in resource distribution, fragmented responses to events, and limited urban intelligence potential emerges (Lom & Pribyl, 2021).

3. THE QUANTUM THREAT LANDSCAPE

The increasing development of quantum computing poses a serious challenge to the security foundations of modern digital systems, particularly in smart urban ecosystems (AlMudaweb & Elmedany, 2023). Classical computers process information in binary bits but quantum computers use quantum bits (qubits) that allow them to solve certain complex mathematical problems exponentially faster.

3.1 Vulnerability to Quantum Algorithms

Classical cryptographic systems rely on the difficulty of mathematical problems like tasks that are practically infeasible for classical computers to solve within a reasonable time. However, quantum algorithms are capable of solving these problems exponentially faster. This means that once quantum computers attain a sufficient level of scalability and stability, they will be able to break these widely used encryption methods in a matter of minutes. As a result, systems that depend on classical cryptography for secure communication, authentication, and data integrity would be vulnerable. The transition from theoretical possibility to practical quantum attacks could compromise the confidentiality and trust that modern digital systems rely upon.

3.2 Irreversibility of Data Exposure

When classical encryption methods are broken by quantum computers, it is not just future data that is at risk past encrypted information also becomes vulnerable. Any data previously stored can be decrypted retroactively, leading to the exposure of sensitive information. This kind of breach is particularly dangerous as the compromise of confidential data is permanent and irreversible. Once data is exposed, it cannot be made private again. The consequences may include identity theft, financial fraud, violation of personal privacy, and long-term damage to organizational or institutional trust.

3.3 Dependence on Key Length Scaling

Classical cryptographic systems often counter rising computational threats by increasing the length of encryption keys. The prescribed method extends the time required for brute force attacks using classical computers, thereby enhancing security. As the key length increases it eventually leads to higher demands on processing power, memory, and bandwidth, which in turn degrades efficiency of the system. As a result, relying on key length scaling is not a viable long-term solution for securing digital systems against quantum threats.

3.4 Lack of Forward Secrecy in Many Systems.

Many classical encryption systems lack forward secrecy, which is considered as a critical property that ensures past communications remain secure even if long term private keys are compromised in the future. In the absence of forward secrecy, a single successful key extraction can make years of confidential communication fully exposed. Once quantum algorithms are deployed at scale, any encryption lacking forward secrecy becomes a liability, as it cannot protect historical records from retrospective compromise. This will eventually lead to unauthorized attacks and breach of datasets.

4. POST QUANTUM CRYPTOGRAPHY ALGORITHM

Post Quantum Cryptography are cryptographic algorithms intended to remain secure against classical attacks, as well as attacks using quantum computers. Many current cryptographic primitives are currently used to secure digital communications, but rely on mathematically hard problems that can be solved efficiently by quantum computers. PQC, on the other hand, relies on hard problems that believed to be hard even for quantum computers.

The chances of current encryption standards being compromised is increasing. PQC's goal is to attempt to solve the problem by offering different encryption and digital signature solutions to address the longevity of safeguarding data and communications systems. The various PQC algorithms that are offered are going through evaluations and a process of standardization world-wide.

4.1 Categories of PQC Algorithms

Post-Quantum Cryptographic algorithms can be grouped into several categories based on the mathematics used, with each category presenting a different aspect of strengths relating to implementation and security.

4.1.1 Lattice Based Cryptography

Lattice based cryptography is a promising group of post-quantum cryptography which relies on the complexity of problems. These problems involve finding the optimal solution on high-dimensional grids in a way that is intractable on both classical and quantum computers. Lattice based schemes are particularly attractive due to their dual use capabilities, as they each provide encryption, digital signatures, and advanced features such as fully homomorphic encryption (Bandara et al., 2022). Their resistance to all known quantum attacks, as well as the additional efficiency of implementations, maintains their usability for realistic systems. In addition to the above, schemes are designed to be both scalable, lightweight, and efficient, further extending their usability in resource constrained, low-power, low-latency and simple environments such as IoT devices and mobile devices where both performance and memory are of critical importance.

4.1.2 Code Based Cryptography

Code based cryptography relies on the difficulty of decoding a general linear code, or the difficulty of decoding a general linear code. The mathematical basis of code based schemes has not been fundamentally threatened by the solutions of quantum algorithms, leaving them as viable candidates for maintaining scheme security in the long-term. One of the prime benefits of code based cryptography is that it can offer yet another decade or two of algorithmic protection. However, the most limiting trait of code based cryptography are the key sizes which remain large keys, rendered less than optimal for systems where limited space or bandwidth could be a consideration.

4.1.3 Multivariate Polynomial Cryptography

Multivariate polynomial cryptography is built around the difficulty of solving sets of nonlinear (usually quadratic) multivariate equations over finite fields (Dey & Dutta, 2023). Multivariate schemes are well suited for digital signature schemes, where speed of operating can be important. This class of schemes can yield very short signatures and computationally efficient operations, which can be advantageous for devices with restricted computational abilities like IoT devices. However, developing a secure scheme in this space is difficult. Many of the earliest schemes based on multivariate equations have been broken, often because there were reasonably simple cryptographic weaknesses, or because mathematicians could shortcut the computational complexity of solving multivariate equations.

4.1.4 Hash Based Signatures

Hash based signature systems have a very nice and simple approach; they exclusively rely on the security of cryptographic hash functions. Hash based signature systems make intuitive sense and have a large degree of confidence and security. Their operational security is based on the strength of cryptographic hash functions, and is not based around number theory, which is of considerable concern in the post quantum world. While hash based systems are mainly used for digital signatures, they are best suited for environments where the properties of data integrity and authentication matter more than communication efficiency (Suhail et al., 2020).

4.2Advantages of PCQ Deployment

Post-Quantum Cryptography offers a future ready defence against the threat of quantum computers by providing cryptographic schemes that remain secure even in the presence of quantum adversaries. One of the key advantages of PQC is its reliance on mathematical problems that are resistant to known quantum algorithms, such as lattice problems or error correcting codes making them fundamentally robust.

PQC's unique ability to be implemented on existing classical systems, allowing for smooth integration without the need for quantum hardware serves as an important strength. PQC algorithms are also highly diverse in their design and they tend to offer multiple cryptographic primitives for both encryption and digital signatures, which eventually enhances flexibility in deployment. As mentioned in Figure 3, by adopting PQC earlier, institutions can safeguard current communications as well as archived data against future decryption a critical advantage in high security domains.

Figure 3. Advantages of PCQ

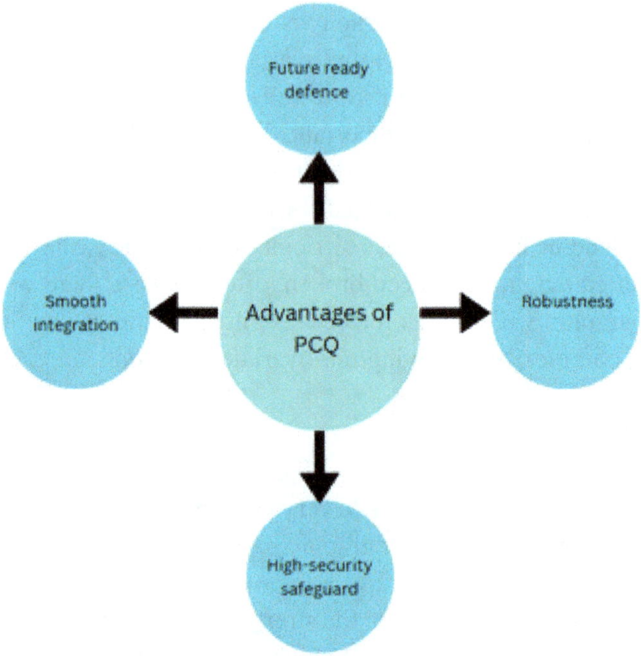

5. SECURING SMART CITIES WITH PQC

It's vital to safeguard smart cities with PQC as urban critical infrastructures increasingly rely on digital technologies and interconnectedness. Traffic management, energy systems, healthcare and public safety sectors are key examples of public services that rely on continuous data sharing, data exchange, and real time decision-making. Traditional cryptography has become increasingly outdated due to the emerging threat of quantum computing making encryption on sensitive data is useless. PQC provides quantum resistant algorithms to provide data confidentiality, integrity and authentication at all layers of urban operations. By incorporating PQC, cities will adapt for long run resilience, they can protect themselves from current and future cyber threats while remaining responsive and secure in the public services they provide (Sharif & Shah, 2025).

5.1 PQC for IoT Devices and Edge Computing

The use of IoT devices and edge-oriented computing systems are essential components of today's city infrastructure. They allow for real-time monitoring, controlling and automating systems in industries such as energy, transport, utilities and public services. Edge computing devices collect and operate at the edge of the network and often control sensitive operations such as facial recognition at points of access, and telemetry from connected autonomous vehicles, and managing the inter-connectivity of smart grid components. While IoT devices and edge computing devices are integral in enabling modernization and the continuous development of the cities, these devices often have limited computational capabilities, limited battery storage, and have limited memory, which makes these devices particularly challenging to secure, even with traditional cryptography methods when the mechanisms of these devices are too tough to be secured. Post Quantum Cryptography attempts to meet these competing challenges, by providing cryptographic schemes which are quantum resistant and lightweight.

Lattice based cryptography, offers high security with relatively efficient key generation and encryption, making it a promising candidate for integration into IoT systems. Similarly, hash based signatures, though slightly heavier in signature size, offer a stateless mode of operation and strong security assurances. For example, a smart traffic management node that uses sensors and cameras to monitor congestion and communicate with nearby vehicles and signal systems. If such a node uses a PQC enabled digital signature scheme to sign its updates, any attempt to spoof or tamper with the message can be easily detected by the receiving systems, even in the presence of a quantum adversary. By embedding PQC protocols into the existing systems, cities can future proof their digital infrastructure without compromising on speed, scalability, or energy efficiency.

5.2 Secure Communication in Urban Mobility Systems

Urban mobility systems depend on constant communication between vehicles, infrastructure, and control centres to manage traffic flow and ensure safety at all times (Ceder, 2021). These communications are often wireless and distributed and hence are vulnerable to interception and manipulation. With the strong growth of quantum computing, traditional encryption methods securing these systems may become replaced by PCQs.

5.2.1 Risks in Urban Mobility Systems

Urban mobility systems depend on quick and reliable exchange of data among multiple entities, specifically smart traffic lights, public transportation systems, ride-share operators and autonomous vehicles. These entities communicate over wireless networks which ultimately result in being susceptible to data interception, spoofing and several other data and privacy risk. As quantum computing advances, traditional cryptographic mechanisms used to secure this communications will be insufficient, and will place passenger safety, routing credibility, and traffic coordination at risk.

5.2.2 PQC Role in Security for Mobility Infrastructures

Post Quantum Cryptography is identified as one of the most essential infrastructures that will secure communication channels from both classical and quantum attacks. Algorithms such as lattice based and code based encryption are intentionally selected for the rapid pace of mobility systems, as they allow key exchange and message confidentiality to happen without relying on conventional security assumptions. For example, a vehicle approaching an intersection may securely authenticate its identity to the signal controller by using a PQC based key agreement protocol, thus ensuring that the signal controller's decision when to change traffic lights is appropriately based on trusted input. Vehicle communications that are facilitated by PQC will eventually protect privacy and prevent data tampering even if data threats are possible in the future (Pradhan & Patil, 2024). Integrating PQC into the communication backbone of urban mobility systems is thus a vital step toward creating a resilient and trustworthy smart transportation environment.

5.3 PQC in Smart Healthcare and Emergency Services

Smart healthcare and emergency services together form the most important pillars of any urban ecosystem where timely access to accurate data is considered very important. These systems are highly dependent on transmission of sensitive information ranging from electronic health records (EHRs) and diagnostic images to patient vitals collected by sensors or ambulances to hospitals (Adeoye, 2025). The growing interconnectivity of these systems across various networks have introduced numerous potential problems, especially in terms of emerging quantum threats. Traditional encryption algorithms which have secured these communications, are not reliable once quantum computing becomes scalable.

PQC offers a powerful option of defence by introducing quantum resistant encryption mechanisms that can protect patient’s important information, ensure data integrity, and safeguard system availability. For example, when a patient is being transported in an ambulance, a PQC secured channel can allow paramedics to transmit real time telemetry such as blood pressure, ECG and other vitals to the emergency unit at the receiving hospital. This ensures that doctors can be prepared in advance without the risk of data tampering.

In large scale emergencies like pandemics or natural disasters, PQC can ensure secure, communication among mobile clinics and central coordination centres eventually preventing cybercriminals from exploiting such chaotic situations. Moreover, the integration of PQC into connected medical devices and healthcare data storage systems ensures that even long term records and historical analytics remain secure against future quantum decryption attempts. As the healthcare sector is both highly targeted and heavily regulated the deployment of PQC meets the evolving threat landscape and also aligns with the need for regulatory compliance and ethical responsibility. Interconnecting PQC with healthcare and emergency service infrastructures is important for enabling robust and efficient future ready medical ecosystems (Shekhawat & Gupta, 2024). While it's critical to protect sensitive health information and plans for emerging and known threats, resilience also involves making sure that environmental and sustainability systems such as green energy and water management are also protected.

6. PQC AND URBAN SUSTAINABILITY

PQC plays a major role to maintain the sustainability of the developing cities by ensuring integrity of the data that acts as the foundation for vital operations. Sustainable urban development depends heavily on accurate data flow for applications such as smart grids, water conservation and waste management. PQC provides a strong foundation for secure data exchange even in the presence of future quantum threats ensuring that sustainability strategies remain reliable over decades.

6.1 Role of Secure Data in Sustainable Decision-Making

Secure data is information that can be protected from unauthorized access, tampering, and loss throughout various stages during collection, transmission, storage, and usage.

Reliable data is critical for driving sustainable decision making in smart urban cites. As cities change and evolve to become more connected through digital systems, reliable real time data that is collected from various sources including environmental sensors, utilities and transportation systems becomes the foundation of good planning. The reliability of the data is viewed as the most critical aspect to be able to take plan, act and operate urban systems efficiently. Air quality monitoring and pollution reduction in urban systems relies on knowing that air quality data collected on the ground will drive protocols to mitigate emissions and warn the public about the health. However, if that data is compromised due to a cyber event or some other type of large scale compromise or threat the negative effects may be severe. For example, even inaccurate data could misallocate resources, delay emergency response and inhibit compliance with environmental goals. PQC serves as a strong layer of protection to sensitive data from both current and future risks. PQC guarantees stored and transmitted data cannot be decrypted or changed, and subsequently maintained its value for long-term planning and analysis. Further, secure data gives urban stakeholders the ability to enact sustainable platforms while providing more transparency and accountability.

6.2 PQC Energy Consumption Compared to Classical Standards

There has been discussion on how PQC will compare to the classical standard cryptography of the digital future, as urban municipalities begin to implement the principles of Post-Quantum Cryptography. Classical encryption algorithms (e.g., RSA, and ECC) are established forms of law enforcement practices and have been in use for many years, based on proven performance and power consumption.

1. **Security basis:** Classical algorithms rely on the difficulty of individual computations which quantum computers are able to solve quickly. One consequence is that all classical algorithms can never be free of risk of quantum algorithms in a post quantum world. The risk of these quantum algorithms may be fast-tracking the design and implementation of cryptographic algorithms for quantum resistance.
2. **Resource Demand and Intensity:** PQC algorithms require and are sometimes significantly stronger at quantum resistance, but also require more computational intensity than classical in terms of time and storage. More complexity is also more energy consuming, which would be a concern when these algorithms are installed on powers constrained devices such an IoT sensor. In other words, lattice based systems require larger keys, and more complex computations, compared to classical. Therefore ultimately the overall power burden on the system, during encryption, decryption and key exchanges, will go up when using PQC as it increases computations, memory and power use during bigger key creation.
3. **Energy Consumption:** Classical cryptographic schemes benefit from a long history of energy based optimizations in performance and PQC is beginning to improve its performance. Some PQC algorithms do not use heavy energy

consumption for example some lightweight schemes, are being developed to perform efficiently on low power devices.

4. **Long term tradeoff:** Although PQC may use more energy than classical cryptography at first, it has a protection against future quantum attacks. As energy optimizing hardware becomes more available and PQC fine tunes its algorithms the energy differences between PQC and classical cryptography will continue to diminish. The long term benefit for society is being able to implement sustainable cryptographic infrastructure that can adapt for future technological change.

Figure 4. Comparison of classical and PQC methods

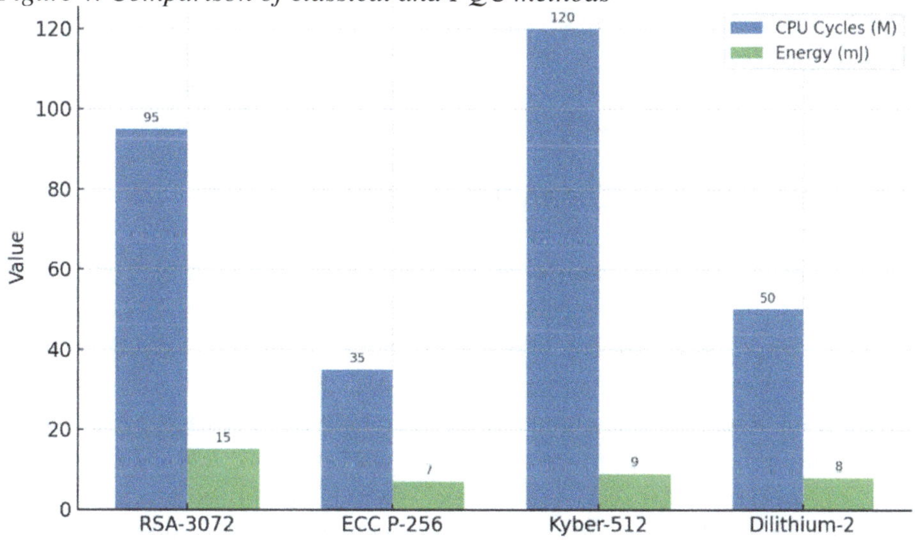

Figure 4 compares CPU cycle requirements and energy consumption for classical algorithms (RSA-3072, ECC P-256) and post-quantum algorithms (Kyber-512, Dilithium-2). The results illustrate that while PQC schemes generally require more processing resources their energy usage remains within a manageable range, especially with optimization.

6.3 PQC in Green Infrastructure and Smart Energy Systems

PQC is essential for maintaining the integrity of the digital progress of green upgrades and smart energy systems. These systems can rely on many sensors or systems exchanging data and can experience cyber threats. PQC will also work to maintain the communication and data exchange across several utilities (Shekhawat

& Gupta, 2024). With the addition of quantum resistant security, cities can also grow the magnitude of their sustainable energy targets without negatively impacting overall performance.

6.3.1. Securing Smart Grid Communications

Smart grids are central to energy infrastructure as they employ renewable sources, real time consumption monitoring and distributed energy resources. The smart grid systems rely on security for communication between the different entities that are responsible for managing, monitoring, and operating all components of the system. Classical cryptography methods are used to secure the exchanges between entities however, quantum computing is compromising these methods. PQC provides an quantum resistant method of securing data transmission channels. With PQC, a smart grid can continue to be resistant to threats from quantum attacks by deploying PQC across a smart grid network.

6.3.2. Enabling Secure Energy Transactions

Smart cities are moving towards decentralized energy models where consumers and producers can trade excess energy, like rooftop solar, using digital platforms (Swain, Salkuti, & Swain, 2021). These transactions are often facilitated via smart contracts, which rely on cryptography primitives that are vulnerable to attacks from quantum computing. PQC can provide cryptographic assurance in these systems to secure identities, as well as help ensure that the marketplace is fair and none of the transactions are tampered with. While sustainability programs offer routes to improved efficiency for cities, building long-term resilience will rely on the preparedness for an emergent threat, along with the ability to rapidly recover from disruption.

7. IMPROVING URBAN RESILIENCE USING PQC

Improving urban resilience will rely on the application of PQC to protect city systems against multiple threats, including evolving cyber threats - multiple of which are often categorized broadly as quantum computing threats (Aydeger et al., 2024). With the connectivity of cities, all facets of the city, it infrastructure, coupled with our trust in the integrity for different data will be vulnerable to attacks from unknown source.

7.1 Building Cryptographic Resilience Against Future Attacks

As urban systems become more reliant on interconnected digital infrastructure, strengthening the crypto resilience is expected to maintain security, reliability and trust. The long-term sensitive data including government records, medical records and control records associated with urban infrastructure must remain confidential and secure against tampering for decades, regardless of future technological changes or changes in attack vectors.

Post-QuantumCryptography provides an effective path to achieve maximum resilience. PQC offers improved encryption and key exchange protocols which are based on difficult mathematical problems to ensure sensitive information can be kept secure over its entire lifecycle.

Adopting PQC in urban information will protect the confidentiality and integrity of said information for the citizen and adopting PQC systems will further enhance citizen trust in vital urban services and information. PQC will ensure that municipal functions involving citizen data will be kept private and will thus secure a core component of security needed for urban evolution (Awotidebe, 2025).

7.2 PQC in Urban Disaster Response and Recovery Systems

Disaster response systems in urban environments are increasingly dependent on digital technology to communicate, monitor, make decisions, and coordinate and each component is dependent upon a trust of some sort in the authenticity of the information derived from obtaining input via digital technology. Implementing PQC structured components into disaster planning and recovery protocols will eventually allow emergency systems to remain trusted during the volatile and uncertain situations created.

7.2.1 Quantum Safe Communication in Emergencies

Safeguarding communication during urban disasters is considered to be extremely crucial for coordinating timely action among emergency providers and emergency management organizations (Habib, Alnaemi, & Habib, 2024). With the chances of these communication channels being intercepted and decrypted is high due to the operational capabilities of quantum computing, traditional encryption protocols will no longer offer even the slightest level of assurance of a secure method of communication. PQC has developed mechanisms that are quantum resistant and provides security even in real time communications that must maintain confidentiality amongst first responders. This will lead to improved effectiveness and less chaos during any disaster response.

7.2.2 Secure Transmission of Critical Alerts and Warnings

Public alert systems such as emergency broadcasts, sirens, SMS warnings, and weather alerts must be immune to manipulation especially during high risk situations. A forged message could mislead thousands and cause panic. PQC strengthens the digital signatures and encryption used in these systems and thus ensures that any message sent is verified and resistant to tampering using quantum capabilities. This guarantees that citizens receive timely and trustworthy alerts and helps government maintain control and clarity during crises.

7.2.3 Tamper Proof Surveillance and Monitoring Feeds

Drones, CCTV, and IoT sensors provide awareness during emergencies. These data streams guide decision making and rescue operations. If attackers manipulate this information, it can mislead responders or hide the actual extent of a disaster. PQC preserves the confidentiality of these feeds, even under quantum threats. Encrypted videos, drone footages are secured with PQC and ensure responders operate accurately.

7.2.4 Quantum-Resilient Backup and Archival Systems

Backup systems are vital in restoring services and conducting forensic analysis after a disaster. If archival data is encrypted with classical methods, it risks decryption in the future by quantum computing methods especially when data contains sensitive information. PQC secured backups ensure that this data remains confidential and intact long after the disaster is over. It can be stored in cloud platforms or physical servers using PQC and ensures that recovery resources cannot be exploited after an event. 18These measures must be institutionalized into a citywide security framework that overlays and connects all sectors.

7.3 Case Study: Tallinn PQC Energy Distribution

Estonia is advanced in e-governance and digital infrastructure and piloted a project in Tallinn to integrate Post-Quantum Cryptography into smart grid communications. The project aimed to protect control signals among substations, renewable energy generators, and demand response platforms using lattice-based encryption and hash-based signatures so that operational commands and energy trades can be tamper resistant and verifiable over public networks. The valuable lessons learned include recognizing that interoperability is key which includes current PQC solutions must be interoperable with legacy SCADA systems and use of the PQC solutions must not disrupt the service of the subsystem as a whole. The national cyber security strategy of Estonia was already in place to replace as many legacy technologies and policies aligned with the cyber security strategy sped regulatory approvals where possible.

8. PROPOSED METHODOLOGY

8.1 Introduction to Quantum-Resilient Urban Framework

The Quantum Resilient Urban Framework (QRUF) is a strategic architecture designed for future proof smart cities to prevent emerging quantum threats. It integrates post quantum cryptography into the emerging urban systems to ensure secure data exchange and infrastructure control.

8.1.1Foundational Principles of QRUF

1. Quantum Resilience The most essential principle of QRUF is quantum resilience which implies that designing systems to be resistant to classical cyber threats and also the exponentially improved capabilities of future quantum computers. QRUF stresses the timely deployment and implementation of Post Quantum Cryptography to ensure that the encryption schemes employed will provide security in the future and prevent threats.
2. Layered Security Architecture QRUF takes a layered approach to cybersecurity where security is crosschecked at each layer, from data generation and transmission through to stored and processed. Each layer utilises quantum resistant methodologies to isolate the threats and minimise the attacks. This approach ensures if one layer fails it does not compromise the system overall.
3. Adaptability and Scalability QRUF is adaptable and enables cryptographic algorithms and policies to be added as the standards develop. QRUF is also scalable for small municipal networks to extensive smart city applications, with mixed infrastructures and devices.
4. Data Integrity and Trust Anchoring QRUF provides end to end data integrity utilizing digital signatures, tamper evident logs/ files and the philosophies of zero trusts. When it comes to any data packet that can be a sensor or control command to infrastructure, it is verified against trusted sources. Users and devices are authenticated, and dynamically scored based on credentials they have stored in a secure and decentralized trust architecture.
5. Governance and Compliance Alignment QRUF incorporates compliance auditing and policies enforcement into the architecture itself. It supports many aspects of secure data communication using tamper-proof technologies such as block-

chain. This provides assurance in alignment with several of the international organisations and conferences (Campbell, 2020).

8.1.2Architecture of the Quantum-Resilient Urban Framework (QRUF)

The Quantum Resilient Urban Framework is based on a modular and layered architecture, illustrated in figure 5, which allows urban systems to maintain security and operational continuity in the presence of emerging quantum threats. The QRUF divides complex urban functions into separate domains and allows for all complex functions to be independently secured using PQC technologies.

The first layer is trusted data acquisition and is primarily responsible for harvesting inputs from authenticated sources, for example, IoT sensors and a number of mobile applications.

Figure 5. Architecture of QRUF layers

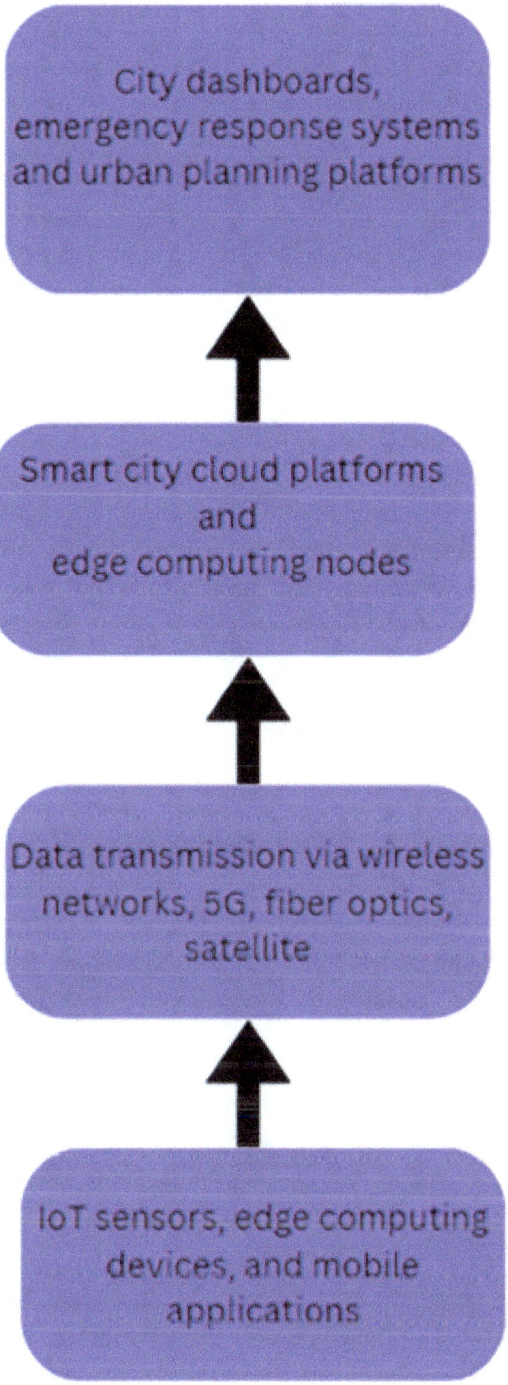

The second layer, post quantum secure communication, guarantees that transit data remains private and is not altered. The use of a PQC protocols, such as lattice basis key and hash based signature, allows to encrypt control commands and operational data. This layer also ensures that even with future attack upon cryptographic decrypted information, that information will remain secure regardless of the method of intercept.

The third layer is cryptographic processing and control, that acts as the security core of the architecture. It carries out numerous cryptographic operations. This module is also responsible for determining the cryptographic algorithm, which is configured depending on the hardware capabilities, that may allow for a more secure implementation, and lighter weight algorithms for lower power edge nodes, and potentially more secure algorithms for the back-end infrastructure. This layer supports also real time detection for tampering and session management for security.

Urban intelligence and decision-making is the last layer, focused on integrating verified data, via encryption standards into management and platform. Leveraging AI and automation powers layers of data through cryptographic assurance to support decision making to optimize traffic flows, activate emergency capabilities or develop for sustainable environments. This layer also includes adaptive trust evaluation to allow the system to provide access to devices and respond to changing threats.

As a result of integrating all the layers, QRUF enables urban ecosystems to function transparently into future technologies. It future proofs critical infrastructure and also boosts and improves scalability and policy driven governance in smart urban environments.

8.2 PQC Integration Across Urban Domains

Incorporation of PQC across the various urban domains will be imperative to secure the digital backbone of these new cities. Each area depends on data integrity, thus inter-linking PQC is necessary to ensure that these domains are secured from emerging threats.

8.2.1 Energy Grids and Critical Utilities

As energy distribution systems such as power grids and water treatment facilities are so important for the operations and functionality of urban systems, energy distribution systems serve as attractive targets for cybersecurity threats. By integrating PQC into control operations such as SCADA, a city can be fully guaranteed that their control commands are not vulnerable to manipulation. Lattice-based encryption schemes can easily thwart an adversary's advances toward situational awareness and critical command and control capabilities.

8.2.2 Public Transportation and Mobility Networks

Urban mobility systems are made up of buses, trains, smart traffic signals, and other vehicles which require a high level of communication and coordination from many actors (Mahrez et al., 2021). PQC can increase the security for vehicle-to-vehicle communications to take advantage of key exchanges and digital signatures that are quantum-resistant. Secure communication links are essential for creating safe transportation systems to prevent spoofing, hijacking or tampering of data, which could lead to accidents or potential gridlock on the roadways. The added assurance of a ticketing system and user data systems can also help to ensure that data is private, like in most secure public and public and smart transit and public transit systems, assuring better resilience against future threats against secure data and transit services.

8.2.3 Healthcare and Emergency Services

Modern systems are complex, layered and inter-connected digital ecosystems that depend highly upon the ability to perform several critical tasks like management of patient records, coordination of responses in emergencies, and the operation of medical devices with connected and integrated electronic health records. Inter-connectivity of health information systems introduces a potential vulnerability to data breaches essentially due the both scenarios of our modelling frameworks, especially given the integration with future quantum-enabled attacks. PQC will resolve the notional vulnerability of security around sensitive health information and through implementation of PQC methodologies into hospital networks and ambulance communication channels, cities could offer a managed level of security even under scenarios that are considered 'high-risk'.

8.2.4 Digital Governance and Public Services

Digital governance platforms are key aspects of cities that demonstrate democratic and transparent governments, including e-voting, land records, and distributing public goods (Ali, 2023). PQC is useful for both any and all digital governance systems since PQC protects these digital exchanges and interactions from almost any threats. With PQC protocols, cities can create security assurances to help maintain public trust in government based programs and services, and even the security of a neighborhood or the manipulation of civic resident records. Even when examining blockchain backed governance systems that included PQC protocols, offers audits the ability of a tamper proof record of sorts while creating levels of transparency across departments or domains of government.

PQC also benefits the development of a stronger identity verification system, which will offer up immediate notification of use, and that any access to the civic portal will only permit specific individuals to have access to access records. This will also serve in protection the confidentiality of legal records and property records from being decrypted or altered for decades. Further, it will serve to comply with national coordination data protection.

8.3 Testing, Validation and Governance

In the Quantum Resilient Urban Framework, testing, validation and governance are integral components and thus equally important to assuring the translation of PQC use into urban environments. These environments enable city planners to test how PQC credentials in practice with controlled variables and within the practical conditions of design including peak loading conditions or anticipated scenarios (Kanellopoulos et al., 2023). However, mixed reality will also be critical in training people on these modern PQC structures.

QRUF has governance structures as it concerns the implementation of practical application from existing international regulatory frameworks such as ISO. Thus, it could ensure significantly greater compliance to legal obligations concerning data privacy and national cyber security arrangements. In terms of sustainability, QRUF incorporates measures such as secure audit trails, cryptographic logging and ongoing audits. This would facilitate an accountability loop and be flexible to resolving problems in emergent technology or on new developments.

9. REAL WORLD APPLICATIONS AND USE CASES

9.1 PQC in Smart Transportation Networks

Intelligent transportation networks are dependent on both vehicles and traffic control systems and a broader centralized management system. Vehicles often communicate real-time information through vehicle-to-vehicle and vehicle-to-infrastructure communication. This communication is vital for vehicular navigation in adverse road conditions, dynamic traffic control signal management and overall traffic coordination. If PQC were to be added into this process, the data in transit such as GPS or traffic information, would be protected at every point. For instance, there are lattice based or hash based PQC protocols for vehicle-to-vehicle communications that would prevent spoofing or fake attacks.

9.2 Smart Grid Security

Modern smart grid systems are large hybrid networks inclusive of numerous electric resources, demand response features and other monitoring systems. Each of these new elements relies on constant data flow and control signals to operate and therefore can increase the threat of cyberattacks especially given the emergence of quantum computing breaking classical encryption. PQC will be able to mitigate some of these vulnerabilities with cryptographic algorithms designed to withstand threats from quantum computing. In addition, PQC will add an additional level of confidentiality for consumer data and the distribution of electricity.

As smart grids continue to evolve with features like decentralized energy markets and renewable energy sources, there will be a level of movement or flow in transactions and operations that can only happen with a new model of PQC.

9.3 Secure Waste and Water Management Systems

Urban waste and water management systems are already being integrated with IoT based sensors for resource optimization and leakage detection (Das, 2024). These systems transmit large data sets to remote locations for data storage, data analysis and resource allocation. It is critical to have the integration of PQC to provide a level of security in surveillance and transmission of data in order to maintain the delivery of modern utilities including smart bins, water quality sensors, and pipe detection applications etc. For example, a PQC alert, from a water pressure sensor would relay the information completely intact and be sent to the municipal servers, while allowing a prompt response from the respective organizations when a leak is detected.

10. CHALLENGES AND ADOPTION BARRIERS

10.1 Integration with Legacy Systems

Many urban systems continue to depend on outdated technologies that were never designed to accommodate post quantum cryptography. Steps to replace the existing system in order to support new cryptographic standards can be complex and costly and may involve the use of hybrid approaches to maintain backward compatibility. The lack of quality tin legacy infrastructure makes the integration process time consuming. Without careful planning, such upgrades risk creating security gaps.

10.2 Computational and Resource Overhead

PQC algorithms generally require larger key sizes and processing power which eventually leads to more stress on resource-limited devices like sensors. This stresses the system causing more energy usage and limits PQC deployment feasibility without having to have hardware upgraded. Conflicting demands could shorten device lifespans and create extra costs. Achieving a proper balance in energy efficiency and security remains a key challenge for broad adoption.

10.3 Scalability

As smart cities expand, the applicability and efficiency of PQC solutions extending across systems becomes a concern. Even when implementations exist, problems can arise between the sensor and device levels causing disruption and difficulty in data sharing and secure inter-connectivity. Moreover, given the different hardware capabilities on different infrastructure levels, it complicates matters further. These concerns will require establishment of open standards and shared testing efforts through collaboration.

10.4 Public Awareness and Policy Gaps

Limited public prestige and poor policy frameworks obstruct PQC implementation. Education and changes to policy by policymakers, industry, and city planners needs to be conducted to address quantum resilient systems as a priority. Without policy strategies and support from global organisations PQC is likely to have uneven adoption. Table 1 summarizes prominent barriers to the application of Post-Quantum Cryptography in urban settings and suggests counter measures. It can be used as a quick reference for planners and policymakers to link technical options to feasible actions.

Table 1. Prominent barriers to the application of PQC in urban settings and suggests counter measures.

Barrier	Description	Suggested Strategy
Legacy systems	Incompatible with PQC	Hybrid crypto approach
Budget limits	High expenses and costs	Choosing priority areas
Skills gaps	Limited PQC expertise	Proper training programs
Interoperability	Diverse protocols and devices	Open standards and collaboration setups

11. FUTURE OUTLOOK AND RECOMMENDATIONS

11.1 Migration Strategy

Legacy systems have been unable to accommodate advanced cryptographic protocols, budget limitations preventing mass upgrades, knowledge gaps within the existing workforce and the interoperability issues with various city systems. Cities can adapt to these challenges in a variety of ways including adopting a hybrid cryptographic approach which comprises PQC along with existing algorithms for backwards compatibility, taking a phased implementation pathway starting with high-value infrastructure, working with strategic vendors for implementation and building the skills of the existing workforce for long-term capability development. In practical terms, a migration path can be imagined as a 4-phase plan: Assessment, Pilot, Hybrid, Full PQC, while transitioning to PQC that is secure, cost-effective, and minimizes impact to frontline urban services.

11.2 Action Plan for Quantum-Safe Cities

By identifying these specific critical areas, municipalities can focus their limited resources on the high impact environments such as emergency response systems, essential public utility services such as telecommunications and transit systems and health data systems.

Hybrid models have backwards compatibility to enable organizations to bridge legacy systems with future proofed architectural requirements. A directed process to prepare major urban regions may begin with the commencement of planning sustainable PQC ready urban regions. Urban planners would be able to establish a PQC ready urban design frame which would specify standard security architecture, device level cryptographic requirements and protocols for full data life cycle protection.

Policy development will also play an equally significant role in supporting urban regions with this transition. To protect urban ecosystems safety, governments must create clear and enforceable regulations that are consistent with quantum safe practices that are established on international standards. Together with industrialists and public private partnerships, the government will need to ensure that it develops regulations that protects safety without limiting opportunities for innovation.

The need for incentive laden knowledge mobilization supported innovation from academia and the technology industry. Research institutions, startup vendors and incumbent technology firms must work collaboratively together to incentivize partners who deploy next generation algorithms and hardware solutions designed to address urban problem sets.

Thus, investing wisely in quantum resistant technologies over innovation is especially critical to counter seating future threats (Mansoor et al., 2025). Awareness campaigns, training programs, and certification programs must be implemented to build the capacity of global IT managers, city actors and politicians to understand quantum threats. Building capacity across the entire decision-making spectrum will realize many expected outcomes including ensuring that investment is accurately directed, reasonable timeframes for adoption are developed and confidence from the general public is maintained in all aspects of the digital infrastructure throughout the quantum transition phase.

CONCLUSION

As cities continue to become more and more connected, every technology advance makes securing digital infrastructure even more critical than before. Cities are often dependent on integration including automated traffic control, power grid management, cloud-based healthcare and e-governance platforms (Khan et al., 2012). Algorithms such as RSA and ECC are at risk of being broken with future sophisticated quantum approaches and this hold risk for every city with regards to confidentiality, data leakage, service outage, and systemic failure.

Integrating these quantum-resilient algorithms into urban security attack vectors will strengthen the confidentiality, integrity and authenticity of digital communications and data stored on devices in various settings. For instance, PQC would safeguard control signals of a smart energy grid against malicious interception, preserve real-time data from autonomous public transportation, and protect limited sensitive health information in the period (Nkulenu, 2024). PQC is an essential building block for protecting the digital infrastructure of smart cities today and into the future, so basic services are secure, resilient and trust-filled in the quantum age. Furthermore, by embedding PQC into the overall ecosystems for energy, health, mobility, and governance, urban planners can ensure that the infrastructure they build for the future will retain the trust of its citizens. This future will require collective action and engagement with policy, technology and workforce development to overcome the challenges to migration and accelerate uptake. Continued research is necessary to help develop and improve solutions and arrive at an agreed global standard for quantum-resilient urban ecosystems. Moving towards quantum-safe algorithms, including PQC, represents not just a technical upgrade but a new way of working as a city on security and sustainability moving forward into a digital world. Cities that adopt PQC will be able to defend against threats, protect the rights and safety of citizens and innovate with security, sustainability and resilience.

DECLARATION

Competing Interest

The authors declare that they have no known competing financial interests or personal relationships that could have appeared to influence the work reported in this paper.

FUNDING

No funding has been claimed.

REFERENCES

Adeoye, S. (2025). Blockchain-Enabled, Post-Quantum Cryptographic Framework for Securing Electronic Health Records: A Next-Generation Approach to Healthcare Data Protection. Academic Press.

Alessa, A. S., Hammoudeh, M., & Singh, H. (2025). A Peek into the Post-Quantum Era—PQA PQC: What Will Happen in 2030. In Quantum Technology Applications, Impact, and Future Challenges (pp. 163-180). CRC Press.

Ali, M. (2023). E-governance and E-democracy: a Digital Revolution. Available at *SSRN* 4623414.

AlMudaweb, A., & Elmedany, W. (2023, December). Securing smart cities in the quantum era: challenges, solutions, and regulatory considerations. In IET Conference Proceedings CP859 (Vol. 2023, No. 44, pp. 484-491). Stevenage, UK: The Institution of Engineering and Technology.

Awotidebe, M. (2025). Quantum Computing and the Future of Encryption: How to Safeguard Data in a Post-Quantum World. https://www. researchgate. net/publication/3,90555296.

Aydeger, A., Zeydan, E., Yadav, A. K., Hemachandra, K. T., & Liyanage, M. (2024, October). Towards a quantum-resilient future: Strategies for transitioning to post-quantum cryptography. In 2024 15th International Conference on Network of the Future (NoF) (pp. 195-203). IEEE.

Bandara, H., Herath, Y., Weerasundara, T., & Alawatugoda, J. (2022). On advances of lattice-based cryptographic schemes and their implementations. *Cryptography*, *6*(4), 56. DOI: 10.3390/cryptography6040056

Campbell, R. (2020). The need for cyber resilient enterprise distributed ledger Risk Management Framework. The Journal of The British Blockchain Association.

Ceder, A. (2021). Urban mobility and public transport: Future perspectives and review. *International Journal of Urban Sciences*, *25*(4), 455–479. DOI: 10.1080/12265934.2020.1799846

Das, R. (2024). Smart Urban Water Management: Integrating AI and IoT for Optimization and Waste Reduction. *Optimality*, *1*(2), 309–317.

Dey, J., & Dutta, R. (2023). Progress in multivariate cryptography: Systematic review, challenges, and research directions. *ACM Computing Surveys*, *55*(12), 1–34. DOI: 10.1145/3571071

Habib, A., Alnaemi, A., & Habib, M. (2024). *Developing a framework for integrating blockchain technology into earthquake risk mitigation and disaster management strategies of smart cities*. Smart and Sustainable Built Environment. DOI: 10.1108/SASBE-12-2023-0376

Kanellopoulos, D., Sharma, V. K., Panagiotakopoulos, T., & Kameas, A. (2023). Networking architectures and protocols for IoT applications in smart cities: Recent developments and perspectives. *Electronics (Basel)*, *12*(11), 2490. DOI: 10.3390/electronics12112490

Khan, Z., Ludlow, D., McClatchey, R., & Anjum, A. (2012). An architecture for integrated intelligence in urban management using cloud computing. Journal of Cloud Computing: Advances. *Systems and Applications*, *1*, 1–14.

Lom, M., & Pribyl, O. (2021). Smart city model based on systems theory. *International Journal of Information Management*, *56*, 102092. DOI: 10.1016/j.ijinfomgt.2020.102092

Mahrez, Z., Sabir, E., Badidi, E., Saad, W., & Sadik, M. (2021). Smart urban mobility: When mobility systems meet smart data. *IEEE Transactions on Intelligent Transportation Systems*, *23*(7), 6222–6239. DOI: 10.1109/TITS.2021.3084907

Mamatha, G. S., Dimri, N., & Sinha, R. (2024). Post-Quantum Cryptography: Securing Digital Communication in the Quantum Era. arXiv preprint arXiv:2403.11741.

Mansoor, K., Afzal, M., Iqbal, W., & Abbas, Y. (2025). Securing the future: Exploring post-quantum cryptography for authentication and user privacy in IoT devices. *Cluster Computing*, *28*(2), 93. DOI: 10.1007/s10586-024-04799-4

Mohamed, K. S. (2019). IoT physical layer: Sensors, actuators, controllers and programming. In *The Era of Internet of Things: Towards a Smart World* (pp. 21–47). Springer International Publishing. DOI: 10.1007/978-3-030-18133-8_2

Nkulenu, G. (2024). Quantum Computing: The Impending Revolution in Cryptographic Security. Academic Press.

Pradhan, T., & Patil, P. (2024, February). Quantum Cryptography for Secure Autonomous Vehicle Networks: A Review. In 2024 IEEE International Students' Conference on Electrical, Electronics and Computer Science (SCEECS) (pp. 1-10). IEEE. DOI: 10.1109/SCEECS61402.2024.10482142

Sharif, A., & Shah, W. (2025). *Future-Proofing Cybersecurity: Smart Cities.* Autonomous Vehicles, and Space Systems Under Quantum and AI-Powered Surveillance.

Shekhawat, H., & Gupta, D. S. (2024). A survey on lattice-based security and authentication schemes for smart-grid networks in the post-quantum era. *Concurrency and Computation*, *36*(14), e8080. DOI: 10.1002/cpe.8080

Suhail, S., Hussain, R., Khan, A., & Hong, C. S. (2020). On the role of hash-based signatures in quantum-safe internet of things: Current solutions and future directions. *IEEE Internet of Things Journal*, *8*(1), 1–17. DOI: 10.1109/JIOT.2020.3013019

Swain, A., Salkuti, S. R., & Swain, K. (2021). An optimized and decentralized energy provision system for smart cities. *Energies*, *14*(5), 1451. DOI: 10.3390/en14051451

Tcholtchev, N., & Schieferdecker, I. (2021). Sustainable and reliable information and communication technology for resilient smart cities. *Smart Cities*, *4*(1), 156–176. DOI: 10.3390/smartcities4010009

Tien, J. M. (2017). Internet of things, real-time decision making, and artificial intelligence. *Annals of Data Science*, *4*(2), 149–178. DOI: 10.1007/s40745-017-0112-5

Van Hoang, T. (2024). Impact of integrated artificial intelligence and internet of things technologies on smart city transformation. Journal of Technical Education Science, 19(Special Issue 1), 64-73.

Chapter 4
Sustainability Aspects and Future Prospects of Post-Quantum Cryptography in Smart IoT Ecosystems

M. Nalini
https://orcid.org/0000-0001-8987-3120
S.A. Engineering College, India

B. Yamini
https://orcid.org/0000-0003-3531-108X
School of Computing, SRM Institute of Science and Technology, India

Monica G. K.
R.M.K. College of Engineering and Technology, India

R. Kennady
https://orcid.org/0000-0003-0887-5007
Rajalakshmi Institute of Technology, India

ABSTRACT

The emergence of quantum computing poses significant threats to classical cryptographic systems, particularly in smart urban environments powered by the internet of things (IoT). This chapter explores the sustainability aspects and future prospects of integrating post-quantum cryptography (PQC) into IoT-based infrastructures. It examines various PQC algorithms, their deployment challenges in resource-

DOI: 10.4018/979-8-3373-3166-9.ch004

constrained devices, and the trade-offs between energy efficiency, performance, and security. The chapter also highlights quantum-specific threats, including communication vulnerabilities and supply chain risks, and emphasizes sustainable strategies such as lightweight cryptography, hybrid models, green computing paradigms, and AI-based optimization. Future research directions call for energy-efficient algorithm design, cryptographic hardware co-development, and multidisciplinary collaboration. The study underscores the importance of aligning cryptographic resilience with long-term sustainability goals in smart city systems.

1. INTRODUCTION

1.1 Background on Quantum Computing and Its Threats

Quantum computing is a breakthrough in computing technology and has the potential to solve some mathematical problems exponentially faster than classical computers. The key to this leap is the use of quantum bits or qubits which (unlike classical bits) can exist in superpositions of states, allowing quantum computers to perform massively parallel computing operations (Brijwani, G. N., et al., 2023). At the same time, this capability opens exciting new frontiers in optimization, chemistry, material science, and artificial intelligence while posing a massive threat to existing cryptography systems. More conventional cryptographic designs (RSA, Diffie-Hellman, Elliptic Curve Cryptography) rely upon the computational complexity of problems like integer factorization and discrete logarithm. These problems are believed to have no classical adversary, but have efficient quantum algorithms. In particular, Shor invented in 1994 shows that a sufficiently powerful quantum computer can factor large integers and solve discrete logarithm problems in polynomial time that is, break the implicit security assumptions of most public-key cryptography. Moreover, the Grover algorithm speeds up brute-force search methods, decreasing the security margin of symmetric key cryptography by half. Such quantum-specific threats necessitate a thorough re-evaluation of current cryptographic standards, alongside a proactive shift toward algorithms that are resistant to quantum adversaries (Chittem, M. B., & Pradhan, A. K. 2025)

1.2 Evolution of Post-Quantum Cryptography (PQC)

The Post-Quantum Cryptography (PQC) discipline has developed in reaction to the new quantum threat. In contrast to Quantum Key Distribution (QKD) which is founded on quantum mechanics, PQC is founded on classical computational models and seeks to design cryptographic algorithms that are resistant to classical and quantum attacks. The first benefit of PQC is that it can be implemented in already existing network systems without having to change quantum hardware. Work in PQC has resulted in the construction of a number of families of algorithms, such as lattice-based algorithms, code-based algorithms, multivariate polynomial-based algorithms, hash-based algorithms and isogeny-based algorithms. Lattice-based cryptography is most probably one of the most promising of these as it has strong security grounds and is efficient to implement(Chauhan, S et al., 2024). In 2016, the National Institute of Standards and Technology (NIST) launched a global initiative to standardize quantum-resistant cryptographic algorithms. Following various rounds of review, in 2022 NIST named the first set of algorithms to be standardized, CRYSTALS-Kyber as an encryption/key encapsulation algorithm and CRYSTALS-Dilithium as a digital signature algorithm. These algorithms are being further refined and put to trials on implementation. Although the most important criterion is security, other aspects, including computational efficiency, key size, memory, and scalability, are of paramount importance, particularly for potential deployment in resource-constrained environments such as the Internet of Things (IoT). Therefore, the development of PQC is not only a technological breakthrough but also a technological solution to one of the most acute cybersecurity problems of the 21 st century(Ravindran, D et al., 2024).

1.3 Role of IoT in Smart Urban Ecosystems

The digital backbone of smart urban ecosystems is the Internet of Things (IoT) that changes the way cities operate and manage to interconnect devices, sensors, vehicles, infrastructure, and people(Sathya U et al., 2024). The concept of smart cities is to maximise resources, streamline service delivery and quality of life to residents by making data-driven decisions. Examples of application are intelligent transportation systems, energy efficient buildings, smart grids, smart healthcare systems, waste management, public safety and environmental monitoring. Such systems are based on huge IoT networks which gather, transfer and process sensitive data 24/7, and automatically. Nevertheless, the widespread use of IoT devices poses a serious security and privacy issue. A large number of IoT nodes are resource-limited, with limited battery life, processing capability and memory, and it is hard to provide strong cryptographic protection. In addition, heterogeneity and size of IoT ecosystems expand the attack surface, thus they are appealing targets to cyber threats. These vulnerabilities are increased in the scenario of quantum computing. Lightweight cryptographic schemes, which are commonly deployed to protect the communications of IoT, might not be sufficient to resist quantum attacks. The use of PQC in the IoT systems, thus, turns into a strategic requirement. However, the integration comes with difficulties: the PQC algorithms tend to have larger key sizes and processing resource requirements that may be incompatible with energy and bandwidth constraints of the IoT devices. Also, there is a large number of IoT devices with a long lifetime and that might be hard to update or replace, and this makes it harder to migrate to new cryptographic standards. Therefore, protecting IoT in the post-quantum world needs not just technological inventions but also an innovation in the system architecture and life cycle management in smart cities(Das, S., & Das, A. 2023).

1.4 Importance of Sustainability in Cryptographic Transitions

When we move towards PQC, we must not only think about the security and the functionality of the cryptographic system but also we need to consider the sustainability of launching the cryptographic system at a large scale. Sustainability is a complex term in relation to the concept of smart cities as it is a combination of energy efficiency, the impact on the environment, economic feasibility, and the life of the system. Cryptographic functions, especially on IoT ecosystems, are carried out regularly and are usually carried out under limited resources. The replacement of the PQC schemes with the higher computational requirements may cause the energy consumption, battery draining, and hardware degradation that may compromise the sustainability objectives of the smart infrastructure. For example, lattice-based cryptography offers strong security guarantees, but in general, the key size and computation time are larger than those of classical algorithms. This may lead to an increased consumption of energy, particularly in battery-operated gadgets such as environmental sensors or health monitors. Moreover, cryptographic transitions that are not sustainable may cause more electronic waste to be produced because hardware will be upgraded or replaced(Prajapat, M et al., 2024). There is also a broader environmental cost of manufacturing and discarding the cryptographic hardware. In terms of policy, sustainable cryptography is consistent with the world in reducing carbon footprints and green computing. As such, researchers and practitioners must trade-off quantum resistance and resource efficiency. Solutions that integrate PQC are being actively researched to make PQC safe and sustainable, including lightweight PQC designs, energy-aware cryptographic protocols, hardware accelerators and adaptive security layers. Most importantly, the sustainability issues need to be integrated in the design, testing and standardization of cryptographic algorithms to ensure their interoperability with smart city targets in the longer run.

1.5 Scope and Objectives of the Chapter

In this chapter, a thorough analysis of sustainable factors and fate of Post-Quantum Cryptography is provided in a context of IoT-based smart urban ecosystems(Bhuvanya, R et al., 2025). It contributes to close an important research gap in the literature that covers the security performance of PQC algorithms but not the impact of the environment and implementation in large-scale resource-constrained systems. The first is to understand the interface between post-quantum security and sustainability, and to identify the key challenges, trade-offs and innovations that influence this domain. In particular, the chapter will: (1) summarize PQC basics and discuss its suitability for IoT systems; (2) discuss energy-efficiency, resource-demand and hardware-dependence of leading PQC algorithms; (3) discuss quantum threat to smart city infrastructure and supply chain vulnerability to quantum attacks and quantum network attacks, green and lightweight cryptographic design; (4) discuss future research directions and trends. Furthermore, the chapter will provide insights on the contribution artificial intelligence can make to the optimisation of post-quantum security mechanisms and suggest sustainability indicators that could be applied to the evaluation of cryptographic deployments. The chapter will, thus, integrate the two knowledge domains, quantum cryptography and IoT architecture, and the third, sustainability science, to provide a roadmap for researchers, policymakers, and urban technologists to build quantum-secure, sustainable, and scalable cryptographic systems. The goal is to allow the creation of digitally stable, ecologically safe, and technologically quantum-proof smart cities in the face of increasingly powerful quantum threats.

2. OVERVIEW OF POST-QUANTUM CRYPTOGRAPHY AND SMART IoT SYSTEMS

2.1 Fundamentals of PQC Algorithms

Post-Quantum Cryptography (PQC) is the name of a type of cryptography algorithm that will be secure even in the face of quantum computing. Whereas traditional cryptographic algorithms rely on mathematical problems, like factoring and discrete logarithms, problems that can be solved efficiently by a quantum computer, PQC draws on hard mathematical problems that are thought to be resistant to a quantum attack. Notably, PQC algorithms are intended to run on classical computing devices, and thus they are feasible to modern infrastructure. They consist of key encapsulation mechanisms (KEMs), public key encryption, and digital signature schemes that provide similar or even greater security assurances than the traditional counterparts. The majority of PQC algorithms are built on the basis of complicated mathematical objects like error-correcting codes, lattices, multivariate polynomials, and hash functions. These frameworks are the foundations of computational issues that are still challenging in the quantum paradigm. The main objective of PQC is to be used for confidentiality, integrity, and authentication, without the use of cryptographic primitives that are vulnerable to quantum attacks. With the advancement of quantum computing technology, the need for implementing PQC schemes is on the rise (Yamini, B et al. 2024).

2.2 Classification: Lattice-Based, Code-Based, Multivariate, Isogeny-Based, Etc.

Post-Quantum Cryptography is a heterogeneous collection of algorithm families, whose design is founded on various mathematical principles. As of today, lattice-based cryptography can be considered one of the most promising branches of PQC due to its extremely strong theoretical foundation and its ability to be highly efficiently implemented. Examples of these schemes, selected by NIST to be standardized, are CRYSTALS-Kyber (encryption) and CRYSTALS-Dilithium (digital signatures) based on Learning With Errors (LWE) and Module-LWE problems, which are believed to be both resistant to classical attacks and quantum attacks. The Lattice-based schemes are particularly attractive because they can support finer capabilities like homomorphic encryption, and because they are also relatively efficient in performance. Code-based cryptography is one of the earliest PQC paradigm, based on the difficulty of decoding random linear codes. The best-known code-based scheme is McEliece encryption, which has a long record of resisting cryptanalysis. Nevertheless, one of the key problems is its large sizes of the public keys that are impractical on limited devices.

Multivariate polynomial cryptography is based on the fact that solving systems of nonlinear multivariate equations over finite fields is hard. Digital signatures These systems are generally used in digital signatures and examples include Rainbow and GeMSS, but some candidates have been broken in the NIST evaluation process.

A more recent direction in PQC is isogeny-based cryptography: cryptographic systems based on the hardness of constructing isogenies between elliptic curves. It has the benefit that key sizes are small and it is appealing to be used in applications where bandwidth is not a major concern. Among the most notable schemes in this direction were Supersingular Isogeny DiffieHellman (SIDH) and SIKE, but some of them have been broken recently casting doubt on their security.

Hash-based signatures rely on the collision resistance of cryptographic hash functions, and have satisfactory security guarantees. Many schemes are simple enough to be robust against classical and quantum attacks, like SPHINCS+ (a stateless hash-based signature selected by NIST) which is of particular interest to firmware signing and long-term security.

2.3 Overview of Smart IoT Systems in Urban Environments

A smart city depends on the smart IoT systems within the city environment. They are systems that require integrated sensors, devices, and applications that collect and distribute data to enable cities to be more efficient, sustainable, and livable. These applications range from smart transportation, smart lighting, waste management, smart cities, smart buildings, energy management, smart homes, etc. These IoTs are deployed in dynamic environments and in the majority of cases they require real-time communication and analytics for automated decision-making. Such systems are generally designed in layers of perception (sensor and actuator), network (communication protocols and gateways), data processing (edge/cloud computing) and application (decision support systems). Although the spread of the IoT technologies makes cities more efficient, it also contributes to the increase in the digital attack surface vastly. The decentralized and heterogeneous structure of IoT systems creates vulnerabilities, which may be exploited by the adversaries, especially when the devices run with low security or old software. In addition, most of such devices possess weak hardware platforms, and therefore, it is challenging to deploy computationally demanding security solutions. Security in smart city setups is lightweight, scalable, and adaptive to changing threats, including the threats of quantum computing, where thousands, or even millions of connected devices are operating at once. The authenticity, integrity, and confidentiality of IoT communications become the most critical factors as cities turn to data to make decisions.

2.4 Integration of PQC Into IoT Communication Protocols

Post-Quantum Cryptography is a necessary and challenging component of IoT communication protocols. Conventional protocols like TLS, DTLS, IPsec, and MQTT rely on cryptographic primitives that are vulnerable to quantum attacks, particularly in the context of key exchange and authentication. However, quantum-resistant cryptographic algorithms are currently at the PQC primitive level and protocols need to be re-engineered to support these primitives without performance or incompatibility impact to allow for a migration to quantum-resistant alternatives. Such evolution should also account for the unique characteristic of IoT environment, which is the potentially limited memory, computation, and connectivity. In resource-constrained devices, any increase in key size or computation would lead to resource instability in terms of battery drain or latency. Hybrid cryptographic models are also considered to allow a smooth transition, and backward compatibility during the migration period; these include classical schemes in combination with post-quantum schemes. Such protocols as TLS 1.3 are already tested with hybrid key exchange mechanisms in pilot projects. The other feature is the over-the-air (OTA) update feature in the IoT systems that enables firmware and cryptographic libraries to be updated securely and hence do not need physical device replacement to support PQC. Cloud and edge computing systems have been another important aspect of supporting the offloading of heavy cryptographic computations to devices that are constrained to support practical PQC deployments in the real world IoT. PQC must be well integrated into the communication protocols in order to future-proof IoT infrastructure operations and sustain functional and energy-efficient operations.

2.5 Challenges in PQC Deployment in Resource-Constrained Devices

Although the post-quantum preparedness is crucially important, it is not a trivial task to deploy PQC in the constrained Internet of Things. The size of keys and ciphertexts of most PQC schemes is among the greatest threats as they are considerably larger than in classical cryptography algorithms. As an example, although RSA and ECC can be used with key sizes of less than 1 KB, a lattice-based or code-based PQC scheme might need keys that are a few kilobytes in length the storage and transmission overhead of a key that size in a low-memory device is significant. There is also the issue of computational overhead. Most PQC algorithms either use matrix computations, polynomial arithmetic, or complex decoding procedures, all of which can be an overload to the limited CPUs of embedded systems. It may cause more energy and heat problems and shorten the life of the device. Deployment is further complicated by the absence of standardised, optimised libraries of constrained environments. Whereas generic platforms such as x86 and ARM have optimized cryptography support, tiny microcontrollers that form the IoT nodes do not. There are also concerns about side-channel resistance and security assurance as PQC algorithms will probably introduce new vulnerabilities, especially if executed on a shared or multi-tenant platform. Also there is interoperability and backward compatibility. The vast majority of IoT ecosystems are composed of legacy devices with long lifetimes that cannot be replaced in the near future; coexistence mechanisms must therefore be designed that would allow classical and post-quantum systems to operate securely. Furthermore, it remains a major challenge to enable a secure update mechanism that allows for migration of cryptographic stacks without disrupting the integrity or availability of the system. To overcome these challenges, we need a multi-level approach that employs algorithmic optimisation, hardware co-design, lightweight cryptographic libraries, and secure systems architectures.

3. SUSTAINABILITY CONSIDERATIONS IN PQC INTEGRATION

3.1 Energy Consumption and Resource Efficiency of PQC Algorithms

Additionally, the deployment of Post-Quantum Cryptography (PQC) to the smart IoT systems introduces new levels of complexity, particularly in the context of energy consumption and resource management. PQC algorithms are as secure against quantum attacks as the best classical algorithms, but in many cases require more computational effort than classical equivalents. Many of these algorithms, especially lattice-based and code-based algorithms, are characterized by relatively large key sizes and complicated arithmetic operations, e.g. matrix multiplications or polynomial calculations. In direct proportion to the growth of the computational demand is the increase in energy consumption which is counter-productive to energy-constrained IoT devices that rely on batteries or energy-harvesting systems. In smart city implementation, thousands or millions of sensors and devices may be deployed in the same environment, which may cause an aggregate energy demand that can be a burden on the power grid and sustainability requirements. Furthermore, the devices that may be installed in a remote or inaccessible place like environmental sensors or agricultural monitoring devices need to run long-term, sometimes years, on low power. The non-optimization of PQC algorithms in terms of energy efficiency may severely shorten the operational life of such devices, raise maintenance requirements, and raise overall cost of ownership. Thus, one of the most important points in the sustainable PQC adoption is the creation of lightweight energy-aware variants of algorithms and hardware accelerators that will not only minimize the energy consumption, but also will not reduce the level of security.

3.2 Trade-offs between Security, Performance, and Power Consumption

The security-performance power trade-off that is inherent in PQC integration may be considered one of the most burning sustainability challenges in the integration of PQC. The operations of most of the real-world implementations of the IoT are not limited to security concerns. Considerations of latency, power consumption and performance also apply where the application needs to be responsive at any stage, or needs to be unattended across a time duration. PQC algorithms generally require the devices to work harder, since the key sizes are longer and cryptographic operations are more complex. As an indicator, also when encrypting and decrypting can be done with RSA-2048-like algorithm, or the ECC-based algorithm having relatively modest computing costs, PQC such as CRYSTALS-Kyber can become a cause of the handshake delay and high memory use. This can have a negative impact on energy consumption, processing latency or thermal considerations, particularly in battery-powered or thermally sensitive systems. The context sensitive performance-security trade-off must then be considered by the developers and system architects. In some products, where security is a mission-critical concern, such as autonomous vehicles or healthcare monitoring systems, a minor increase in power consumption can be rewarded, as long as you can provide quantum-resilient security to your product. But when the devices are operated at large scale with energy being a limiting consideration, a trade-off has to be done to avoid a performance bottleneck. The other proposed resolutions are the hybrid cryptographic models based on the intersection of classical and PQC algorithms to reduce the overhead cost during transition times. Also, the edge computing and task offloading can be used to alleviate the computational load on end devices by offloading PQC operations on close-by gateways or cloudlets. Finally, sustainable integration means the all-encompassing design methodologies that take into consideration every element of system performance in the post-quantum world.

3.3 Hardware and Firmware Upgradability in IoT Devices

One of the most important and at the same time least discussed features of sustainable PQC implementation is the ability to upgrade the hardware and firmware of IoT devices. Most of the current IoT systems, particularly the ones implemented in smart city infrastructure are developed with constrained firmware and hardware rigidity. These systems are also constructed to do one thing and do it well with highly optimised resources and hence they are not very adaptable. Since the PQC standards are developing and new vulnerabilities are being found, the possibility to update the cryptographic primitives is critical to ensure that the system is intact and compliant. Yet, replacing cryptographic stack of an IoT device is not always easy. Others do not have secure firmware update process, others cannot support the extra storage or memory space of PQC algorithms. In the worst-case scenarios, the whole hardware can be required to be replaced, which will result in more e-waste, supply chain overload, and financial expenses. This is not sustainable when there are millions of devices that can potentially need updating in a mass deployment. In response, the next-generation IoT systems will be configured with scalable, upgradable subsystems of cryptography that will facilitate over-the-air (OTA) update and secure boot operations. The programmable hardware platforms also may be used to potentially reconfigure the deployed hardware after deployment to meet the needs of PQC primitives as they evolve. Flexible and sustainable security architectures can also be implemented with software-defined cryptographic modules and hardware abstraction layers. To realize effective long-term quantum resilience and functionality, manufacturers and system integrators designing IoT devices must consider the principle of upgradeability as a design driver.

3.4 Lifespan Extension of Cryptographic Infrastructure

The other critical goal of successful PQC implementation is to increase the life cycle of cryptographic infrastructure. Upgrade of cryptography is generally performed on legacy IT systems in line with hardware refresh. However, where the devices in the IoT system could conceivably serve in the infrastructure over decades, then a stable system could be preferable. Street lights, smart meters, traffic sensors and industrial control systems, are typical examples of long-lived deployments that are hard and costly to replace. Therefore, backward compatibility, forward security and long term support should be extended to the introduction of PQC to such systems. Sustainable cryptography architecture to support high-quality key management protocols, secure firmware upgrade, and future resilient interfaces In addition, long-term resiliency needs cryptographic agility, i.e. the capability to update cryptographic algorithms without hardware modifications. It allows systems to be responsive to new vulnerabilities discovered or new standards. The longevity of the infrastructure is also affected by the digital signature schemes used in software and firmware validation, as once a post-quantum secure signature scheme is adopted, the integrity of a system can be confirmed several decades after a system has been deployed. Also, the design of public key infrastructures (PKIs) needs to adapt to PQC-compatible certificates and certificate revocation. Institutions are expected to adopt a long term viability strategy based on risk based cryptographic migration, hardware-software co-design and modular firmware stacks. This is not only for the protection from quantum attacks, but also to reduce future disruptions, maintenance and environmental footprints from regular replacement of the infrastructures.

3.5 Environmental Impact of Quantum-Resilient Infrastructures

PQC has the potential to provide strong protection against the emerging quantum threats; however, the environmental impact of PQC will need to be carefully considered and mitigated as part of the overall sustainability agenda. With the advent of smart cities and digital infrastructures, we see the energy and material consumption required for cryptographic security at scale as sources of environmental degradation. Larger keys and more complicated cryptographic calculations take more memory, processing cycles and storage and thus more energy and possibly more greenhouse gas emissions. Post-quantum algorithms will require more CPU and reduce system throughput in the data centers and cloud infrastructure that supports the smart city services, and will require more servers and cooling equipment. On the hardware side, secure element production processes are resource-intensive and, without a responsible management approach, the end of life for physical components, such as microcontrollers and cryptographic coprocessors, is electronic waste. Also, if transitioning to new cryptographic techniques, then the e-waste problem may be exacerbated due to the possibility that equipment that is still usable may be thrown out for the reason of no longer being considered viable. These issues need to be removed from the design and implementation of cryptographic systems, and this can only happen if sustainability is a component of all levels of cryptographic design and implementation. Finally, to achieve sustainable security in a quantum future, both technological progress and ethical and environmental responsibility are necessary. As PQC becomes part of the digital infrastructure, it will be important to balance the goals of security, functionality, and environmental responsibility.

4. QUANTUM THREATS AND IMPACT ON SUSTAINABLE IoT

4.1 Quantum-Specific Threats to IoT Communication

An IoT communication stack includes layers - one of the weakest links in the chain, especially with the emerging quantum capabilities, is the communication layer. All IoT devices are incessantly communicating with each other over the networks and in many cases using lightweight encryption mechanisms that place a strong emphasis on efficiency, rather than computational strength. Most communication protocols based on public-key cryptographic primitives, such as TLS, DTLS, MQTT, or CoAP, are built on RSA, ECDSA and Diffie-Hellman for key exchange and authentication. However, all the messages intercepted with these schemes could end up being decrypted by Shor algorithm, which made quantum computers possible, which will make them useless and expose IoT networks to decryption attacks from the past and present. This is of particular concern to systems that follow the store now, decrypt later paradigm where encrypted communications are passively stored today and decrypted in the future when quantum capabilities have been perfected. These threats pose a risk to the privacy of personal, industrial, and national information being transmitted over the IoT networks. In addition, the symmetric cryptographic schemes can be undermined by quantum-enhanced brute-force attacks that are made possible by Grover algorithm, which effectively reduces the security strength of encryption keys by half. As an example, 128-bit symmetric key would afford only 64-bit security in a quantum setting, causing the necessity to increase key lengths doubled to provide the same protection. These threats are even more pronounced in smart city systems where the sensitive and mission-critical systems like the traffic control systems, surveillance systems and emergency response systems are largely reliant on secure real-time communication. In case of violation, such systems might turn into the vehicles of malicious interference or even sabotage. The reality of existing IoT devices is further complicated by the fact that a good number of them are unable to meet the computational requirements of a strong, quantum-resistant encryption. Therefore, quantum-related threats to IoT communications require an immediate remedy to be implemented, which is the implementation of PQC and adaptive security protocols suitable to lightweight and distributed systems (Mishra, B. K. 2022).

4.2 Quantum Network Attacks in Smart Urban Ecosystems

The smart urban ecosystem offers a lucrative and broad attack surface to the adversaries through the use of quantum computing capabilities. These settings combine various essential infrastructure systems transportation, utilities, energy, healthcare, and public safety to a single, information-driven working framework based on IoT, edge computing, and cloud analytics. Such systems are extremely heterogeneous and interdependent, and therefore highly sensitive to secure and reliable communications links and integrity of data. In such instances, quantum network attacks may involve eavesdropping and message decryption, interference with the authentication procedure, introduction of fake data, or total hijacking of the control system. Indicatively, quantum attacks on a smart transportation grid would disrupt vehicle-to-infrastructure (V2I) or vehicle-to-vehicle (V2X) communications and trigger a traffic nightmare, wrong-turns or any other safety concern. They would introduce issues in automated grid balancing in smart energy systems and expose real time patterns of consumption to curious eyes or manipulation. Even blockchains that will be needed to make microtransactions that will emerge due to the existence of the internet of things or tracking logistics or decentralized identity checking and, most importantly, built on top of classical digital signature schemes can be attacked by quantum-capable adversaries. Moreover, with the advent of the so-called phenomenon of a quantum internet (quantum entanglement and quantum teleportation are implemented to transfer information), completely new network security paradigms and attack surfaces will emerge, making all the current models of cryptography obsolete. In practice, IoT city networks are rarely disconnected between themselves and are connected to a publicly available Internet backbone, and hence more vulnerable to distributed and remote quantum attacks. These attacks are spurring the need to fundamentally change the network-level security posture, combining post-quantum cryptographic protection with strong key management and cryptographic agility. As a result, to ensure the security and reliability of the smart urban eco-systems, then quantum resilient security must be actively implemented to make sure that the quantum era does not literally wipe out the trust, and the security of urban ecosystems.

4.3 Supply Chain Vulnerabilities in Post-Quantum IoT

New cybersecurity challenges of the supply chain arise with PQC being integrated in the IoT ecosystems. IoT products are typically produced through a global chain of supply among various vendors, hardware producers, firmware creators, and third-party integrators. With PQC algorithms (and PQC hardware co-processors) already being incorporated into those devices, the security and integrity verification of each element becomes much more complicated. Attackers can take advantage of vulnerabilities at any point in the production, deployment or update process and insert backdoors, alter cryptographic modules or replace certified components with compromised versions. With post-quantum security, the threat would be more serious since quantum-capable adversaries would be able to forge updates or impersonate trusted entities in the supply chain by compromising firmware signing keys or hardware roots of trust that have not been made quantum-resistant. Also, one can introduce fake chips or unsafe third-party libraries with PQC algorithms into the ecosystem of devices which makes the whole IoT deployment vulnerable although it may seem to be compliant. The next level of worry is the reliance to a limited number of hardware vendors or cryptographic library providers of post-quantum technologies. Supply concentration enhances the systemic risk especially when a weakness is found in a common PQC implementation. These weaknesses are particularly undesirable in terms of sustainability. The post-quantum world needs to redefine secure supply chain practices as the set of practices that incorporate quantum-aware auditing, secure firmware distribution channels, formal verification of cryptographic components, end-to-end provenance tracking. Resilience in the supply chain should also be included as an essential provision of governmental and industrial standardization activities in order to adopt PQC.

4.4 Impact on Sustainable Security Architectures

Quantum threats also question the premises of the current security architectures and require the reassessment of how it is possible to build sustainable systems of cybersecurity in the future. A sustainable security architecture is the one that is effective, flexible, and efficient over time without the need of intervention on a regular basis or with a lot of resources. The threat to this model however lies in the disruption that quantum computing poses. Most security architectures deployed today were not designed with cryptographic agility in mind and thus do not easily support the introduction of new cryptographic primitives. This inactivity leads to security debt, or an accumulation of outdated or weak components that are difficult to upgrade. The post-quantum transition will see system redesigns or obsolescence of systems with non-modular and non-upgradeable security systems, negating sustainability goals. Also, PQC integration often requires redesigning protocols, authentication schemes and certificate systems to accommodate larger key sizes, different signature schemes and higher workloads. However, these developments are often in tension with low-power design, long device lifecycle and decentralized management models typical of sustainable IoT architectures. For example, a sensor node with a lifetime target of 10 years may not be able to tolerate the additional overhead of lattice-based encryption without the help of energy-efficient algorithmic optimizations or secure offloading. Moreover, most of the eco-friendly architectures are designed in such a way as to reduce the carbon emissions by transmitting the minimum amount of data while using the minimum amount of energy. Higher computational overhead, when not optimized, may have the paradoxical effect of increasing the ecological footprint of security processes. Cryptographic agility, risk-informed algorithm selection, load balancing using edge-computing, and hardware accelerators are principles that architects should adopt to make quantum-resilient security sustainable from a design perspective. These strategies may assist to make sure that security systems are resilient against quantum attacks and have limited impacts on the sustainability, usability, and performance over the long term. Besides, the inclusion of sustainability metrics in cryptographic systems assessment, e.g., energy cost per operation or carbon equivalent per secure transaction, can assist evidence-based decision-making and informed adoption of PQC in smart IoT ecosystems (Khang, A 2024).

5. EMERGING TECHNOLOGIES AND STRATEGIES FOR SUSTAINABILITY

5.1 Lightweight PQC for Low-Power IoT

Among the most promising directions to the sustainable implementation of the post-quantum cryptography (PQC) in smart IoT systems, the development and implementation of lightweight PQC algorithms suited to the low-power, resource-limited setting can be considered. In contrast to the traditional cryptographic schemes, which tend to make the assumptions on moderate to high computational capacity, the IoT devices are subjected to strict constraints that are related to power, memory, processing speed, and bandwidth of the communication channel. Since PQC schemes, by their nature, necessitate heavier computational load and key sizes as compared to classical cryptography, the direct application of these algorithms on microcontrollers and embedded sensors without proper adoption may render the device unable to cope and extend operational life to the bare minimum. Lightweight PQC tries to fill this gap by streamlining cryptographic operations in regard to algorithm structure, key management and memory requirements. There is more research on optimization of lattice-based and hash-based algorithms to minimize the overhead of computation. As an example, low-footprint implementations of SPHINCS+ and variants of CRYSTALS-Kyber with smaller parameter sets are considered to use in IoT. These constructions lower the size of keys and buffer size with an acceptable quantum resistance.

Also, there is an attempt to build application-specific integrated circuits (ASICs) and hardware accelerators to facilitate the efficient implementation of PQC primitive on resource-constrained devices. Such hardware components are able to operate cryptographic functions using much less energy than a software-only method. Other measures are to limit the number of key exchanges, to use pre-distributed keys with quantum-safe refresh times, and to use communication models that limit cryptographic interaction, e.g. event-driven security handshakes or opportunistic encryption. Together with the given approaches, they help to increase battery life, reduce heat production, and make the long-term deployment of IoT devices possible without undermining quantum resilience. The Lightweight PQC will play a vital role in the goal of realizing scalable, secure, and sustainable cryptography in smart cities and edge scenarios where energy consumption and device lifetime is paramount.

5.2 Hybrid Cryptography and Migration Strategies

Hybrid cryptography is a feasible and long-term transition strategy since quantum computing maturity is uncertain and the current infrastructure is inadequate. In hybrid cryptography, the two types of algorithms (classical and post-quantum) are used in the same cryptographic protocol such that they offer a two-layer security. This tiered security also protects not only against the present classical adversaries but also against the future quantum adversaries hence an ideal strategy in this migration period. The most common example is the hybrid key exchange protocol in TLS in which a conventional Elliptic Curve Diffie-Hellman Ephemeral (ECDHE) key exchange protocol is combined with a post-quantum Key Encapsulation Mechanism (KEM) like CRYSTALS-Kyber. The security of the entire session is not compromised even in the event that one of the algorithms is compromised provided the other algorithm is intact.

Hybrid schemes enable a gradual implementation of PQC without the need to replace any of the current devices or protocols. This is especially relevant in large-scale distributed IoT networks in which some devices lack the ability to run full PQC stacks because of legacy constraints. The strategies are also hybrid, and they allow having a buffer period when it is possible to analyze the metrics of the performance, failure rates, and implementation issues of PQC under the real conditions. Moreover, the migration plans should consider such an aspect as algorithm agility, and it is the possibility of a cryptographic system to transition to newer algorithms without the necessity of structural and firmware upgrades. The sustainability that is enabled by algorithm agility enables long-lived devices to be secure even when standards are changing, or some algorithms become invalid. In systems engineering terms, agility will need to be included as modular cryptographic APIs, flexible key management infrastructures and secure over-the-air (OTA) update capabilities.

The use of crypto-agile libraries is also a part of strategic migration, which provides the abstraction of the cryptographic backend and allows introducing future changes with minimal software impact. With the introduction of hybrid cryptographic models and agile migration strategies, organizations can enjoy a highly secure and future-proof security at minimal cost, complexity and environmental footprint, which is a mandatory requirement toward the sustainable evolution of PQC in smart IoT infrastructures (Gayathri, M et al., 2024).

5.3 Quantum-Resistant Protocols with Green Computing Paradigms

In order to perfectly align quantum-resilient cryptography with sustainability goals, there has been an increasing pressure to develop quantum-resistant protocols that will be run on the premises of green computing. Green computing aims at development of energy-efficient and environmentally friendly technologies that will reduce the ecological footprint of computing activities. For PQC, this paradigm targets the lowering of the energy cost of a cryptographic operation, hardware wastage, and network and computational resource exploitation. To design PQC protocols that meet the ideals of green computing we need to think differently about several layers of system architecture.

For instance, the secure communication protocols such as DTLS, CoAP and MQTT-SN can be re-engineered to possess shorter session time, handshake and energy-saving key management routines. By doing so, the cryptographic operations, and therefore the communication and processing power, are reduced.

At the same time, clustering, data aggregation, and transmission priority-based scheduling can be employed for the optimization of the network to reduce the redundancy and the frequency of cryptographic operations within the IoT environment. Data aggregation is the method of aggregating several sensor values and encrypting them with a single cryptographic primitive, thus saving energy and time costs. In the meantime, energy can also be saved by using context-aware security mechanisms (security levels are dynamically adapted to perceived threat) so that stronger cryptographic measures are only applied if deemed necessary. Another recent concept being considered is eco-cryptographic profiling: systems will monitor the power usage of a sample of cryptographic configurations, and automatically announce it, so that administrators can make security decisions based on the environmental impact.

Moreover, renewable energy sources can be integrated into IoT infrastructures (e.g. solar-powered sensors) for extending the operation of IoT systems in energy-limited environments, which can be complemented by the use of green PQC protocols. Digital resilience and environmental responsibility can be achieved through the development of quantum resistant protocols using the principles of green computing. Such an integrated approach is essential if smart cities are to align their cybersecurity practices with their climate and sustainability goals.

5.4 AI-Enabled Energy-Aware Cryptographic Optimization

Artificial Intelligence (AI) has become an effective facilitator to ensure cryptography systems become sustainable, specifically within the PQC context in IoT. We can use AI methods (machine learning (ML), reinforcement learning (RL), optimization algorithms, etc.) to create the energy-sensitive cryptographic systems capable of dynamically adapting to the environment and system characteristics (Ramesh P et al., 2024). Intelligent frameworks can actively track parameters such as power usage, latency, network congestion, level of risk, etc. and adjust the cryptography environment to reflect these values. Indicatively, in case of low communication traffic or low security threat, lower weight of PQC can be selected by AI system or the number of key exchanges can be minimized to save energy. But, we must apply more restrictive cryptographic policies at greater cost of energy in a high hazard scenario. This type of adaptive security model is a perfect trade-off between sustainability and robustness.

Other applications of AI are cryptographic load balancing: cryptographic key-generation and cryptographic computation may be distributed among nodes or offloaded to edge servers to be as energy-efficient as possible at device level. Such an architecture is consistent with the federation learning structure, or with the hierarchy of IoT architectures using coordinating edge nodes. Moreover, it has been shown that AI could play a role in optimization on the hardware level as well, by estimating the thermal and performance characteristics of the device on which PQC algorithms will be run, and by adjusting the execution parameters so that they match the estimated characteristics. This dynamic change minimizes wears and tears, battery life, and system failure.

Additionally, the abnormal communication behavior can also be monitored by the AI-based anomaly detection technology to ensure the energy-efficient cryptographic processes are not security threats. The optimal cryptographic construction that is resistant to quantum computers and can efficiently compute its calculations in the future could be found with genetic algorithms or neural architecture search, and AI could be used to design new PQC algorithms. The integration of AI in the security pipeline not only enhances the intelligence of the system, but also helps optimize resources and sustainability of operations. The integration of AI and energy-aware security is bound to play a critical role in the development of smart city ecosystems that are safe, self-optimised, and sustainable.

6. FUTURE RESEARCH DIRECTIONS

6.1 Designing Energy-Efficient PQC Schemes

With the quantum computing progress, the need to come up with quantum-resistant cryptographic algorithms that will be implemented in a sustainable way becomes urgent. Among the most urgent research directions, it is possible to outline the design of energy-efficient Post-Quantum Cryptography (PQC) schemes especially designed with respect to the IoT and resource-constrained setting. Current PQC candidates are secure against quantum attacks, but in general have high computational overhead and memory requirements, which limits their suitability to energy-constrained applications. The areas that need to be addressed in the future research are optimization of algorithmic structures to reduce instruction cycle, RAM and ROM consumption, and power consumption without sacrificing cryptographic strength. It may be possible to simplify the computations by using techniques like algorithmic pruning, where unnecessary calculations are done away with and by making mathematical simplification like replacing more complex operations of polynomial or matrix by simpler ones.

In addition, sets of parameters that could be configured by the developer to adjust the performance and security trade-offs depending on the application situation will be essential. Non-critical sensors might only require a low-security, low-energy implementation; high-assurance PQC might be used only in gateways or control systems. Benchmarking tools should be adapted to be able to measure not only time and throughput, but also energy cost per operation, and energy profiling should become an integral part of PQC algorithm benchmarking. It should also be studied how diverse are the algorithms and which cryptographic families are intrinsically more energy-efficient (e.g., hash-based or compact multivariate schemes) and can be standardized in the long term. Finally, it will be important to invent cryptographic primitives that are both quantum resistant and energy-aware so that security does not imply environmental or operational inefficiency.

6.2 Sustainable Cryptographic Hardware Co-Design

The other potential research direction in the future is sustainable hardware-software co-design of cryptographic implementations. Although software-level optimizations are relevant, PQC deployment will be truly sustainable when it comes to co-designing hardware and cryptographic algorithms together. This aims at developing low-power cryptographic accelerators and microarchitectures tailored to particular post-quantum algorithms which may achieve high performance with only a small fraction of the energy. This may include reuse of hardware, i.e. the same logical blocks may be used to perform different cryptographic functions, lowering the silicon area and the costs of fabrication. FPGAs (Field-Programmable Gate Arrays) and ASICs (Application-Specific Integrated Circuits) may be used in the center stage, in particular when they are designed to the particular arithmetic requirements of lattice-based or code-based schemes.

The researchers must also consider the effects of hardware lifecycle that produce chips and embedded security modules that have long life, low failure rates and conform to new cryptographic standards. Future-proofing must focus on thermal reduction, enhanced energy harvesting capability (i.e. adding more sources of solar or kinetic power), and, finally, the ability to update cryptographic components safely and securely over the air (OTA).

Figure 1. Future Research Directions

6.3 Security and Sustainability Metrics for PQC Evaluation

With the emergence of the post-quantum cryptography landscape, new metrics and assessment models able to prioritize the security-sustainability trade-off are sought. The existing measurements such as encryption/decryption time, key size, computing complexity, etc. will be supplemented with the green measurements such as energy per operation, memory footprint, carbon emission of computation, efficiency of hardware lifecycle, etc. This multidimensional analysis will enable the stakeholders to evaluate, not only the cryptographic strength, but also the environmental and economic consequences of a particular PQC adoption scheme. While the standardization bodies have already started evaluating the security, performance and interoperability aspects, energy-aware benchmarking tools still need to be developed and deployed in a general way. In order to model performance and sustainability in a realistic way, such tools must model or test in the field, on multiple hardware platforms. Also, composite indices can be constructed to rank algorithms using a combination of security, energy dissipation and cost of implementation. Algorithms should also be measured according to their adaptability; e.g. how easy it is to tune parameters and how well suited they are to fit into a cryptographic agility framework.

At the system level, resilience-to-failure metrics of how a cryptographic component behaves when stressed, with low battery or under degradation conditions can be critical in high reliability IoT applications. Cryptographic hardware should be procured on a life-cycle basis (life-cycle assessments or LCAs) which follow the environmental impact through chip manufacture to disposal, including recycling. Finally, the creation and implementation of strong, uniform sustainability metrics of PQC will enable engineers, policymakers, and organizations to make principled judgments based on information and knowledge that will serve the long-term security and climate objectives.

6.4 Quantum-Aware Urban Planning and Smart City Cryptography

Since smart cities are becoming hyper-connected, data-driven, sensor-driven, and AI-driven, urban planners should consider the implementation of quantum-aware security frameworks into the infrastructure design. Today, cybersecurity is an afterthought in city planning, which is implemented at the level of a device or a network, instead of being integrated into the urban design process. Nevertheless, the post-quantum world will have to switch to the cryptography-based city planning, in which the long-term digital resilience is viewed along with the transport networks, energy infrastructure, water supply, and government services. The next step of research should be the investigation of the way to model cryptographic infrastructure as an essential urban facility that can be maintained in a cycle, has an energy budget, spatial location, and government.

As an example, surveillance cameras, smart meters, and traffic signals in the wild, would all be clustered into security zones depending on the level of their criticality with each security zone having a custom PQC implementation that satisfies both the security and energy efficiency needs. Cryptographic zoning policies can also be investigated whereby various sections of a city work with context-sensitive security policies according to the predicted threat models and the available resources.

Furthermore, the models of urban planning should take into account quantum-safe communication corridors - i.e. corridors in the city between the services, control centers, and cloud backends that are protected by quantum-safe protocols.

6.5 Multidisciplinary Approaches for Resilient and Green PQC Systems

The interdisciplinary research framework that was required to tackle in a holistic way the multifaceted problems surrounding the sustainable implementation of PQC. Cryptography, government policy, environmental science, artificial intelligence, city planning, electrical engineering, and so on, will all be needed to devise sustainable and environmentally friendly cryptographic ecosystems. Cryptographers cannot solve the energy and environmental problems of PQC and material scientists could come up with more green semiconductor materials and AI researchers could also come up with an intelligent optimization algorithm that is able to trade-off security and resource constraints. Similarly, policy analysts and behavioral scientists can help create easy-to-use systems and incentives that would promote the adoption of secure and sustainable practices. For example, the behavioural economics could be used to encourage manufacturers and municipal governments to invest into quantum resilient hardware by subsidising the hardware, mandating its use or doing long-term risk calculations. It is possible to envisage interdisciplinary academic projects, where PQC is not a mathematical problem, but part of a wider sustainability agenda. In addition, the open source nature of the solution and the collaborative testing platforms can help speed the development of PQC by allowing researchers in different fields to test the solutions, share results and improve the solutions for deployment in energy constrained environments. Sustainability is also a must, as is the cooperation of the international community, as cyber threats are not bounded by borders. Standards Organizations that expect to work together to create a generally accepted set of standards on sustainability characteristics of cryptographic systems. Education and training systems that would help the next generation of engineers and planners design cryptographically strong and environmentally friendly systems should also be conducted and researched further. Through multidisciplinary collaboration and a willingness to seek to understand the perspectives of others, it is possible to design a coherent post-quantum future which will be both secure, and compatible with the overarching goals of ecological sustainability, social justice, and economic sustainability.

7. CONCLUSION

This survey has discussed the nexus of post quantum cryptography (PQC), green technology implementation, and smart cities IoT systems. We began by highlighting the looming threat of quantum computing to the classical cryptographic standard and the urgency this suggests to move to quantum-resilient security measures. PQC algorithm families including lattice-based, code-based, multivariate and isogeny-based ones were briefly outlined and the limitations to implementation in resource-constrained IoT environments were outlined. Next, we examined the sustainability dimension of the PQC integration in terms of energy consumption, performance, hardware upgradability and effects on the environment. In addition, we examined quantum-specific threats to Internet of Things communication, network attacks within the smart cities, and supply chain vulnerability. Finally, we identified new solutions such as lightweight PQC, hybrid cryptography, AI-based optimization and green computing paradigms and concluded with a list of future research directions that encourage energy-efficient design, sustainable hardware co-development and multidisciplinary strategies.

The addition of PQC to the IoT ecosystems should be viewed as not only a security threat, but also a sustainability issue. As the urban environment grows more reliant on interconnected devices to not just manage traffic, but also healthcare and utilities, the cryptographic infrastructure of these systems must be not only quantum attack-resistant, but also low-energy to support deployment at scale in the long term. IoT infrastructure is characterized by a long life cycle and limited computer and energy capabilities, and demands the ability to flexibly upgrade and implement solutions that are environmentally friendly. Planned and used wisely, PQC can also make smart city systems more reliable, long-lasting, and more sustainable. Turning the dream of a reliable and sustainable post-quantum IoT environment into practice is going to demand an extraordinary amount of collaboration among academia, industry, government, and standardization organizations. Cryptographers, system designers, urban planners, and environmental scientists must work together to design protocols, hardware, and models of governance that are responsive to both cybersecurity and planetary health. Interdisciplinary education and common research infrastructures will have a significant role to play in the development of this field using the open-source tools. In conclusion, PQC can not only assist our digital society to future-proof against quantum attackers, but it also challenges us to rethink the design of our cryptographic infrastructures when it comes to long-term sustainability and social wellbeing.

REFERENCES

Bhuvanya, R., Mariammal, G., Sivakumar, K., Ganga, M., Anish, T. P., Swetha, S., & Subramanian, R. S. (2025). Revolutionizing Urban Planning: The Role of AI and Predictive Analytics in Sustainable City Development. *Leveraging Urban Computing for Sustainable Urban Development*, 303-322.

Brijwani, G. N., Ajmire, P. E., & Thawani, P. V. (2023). Future of quantum computing in cyber security. In *Handbook of research on quantum computing for smart environments* (pp. 267–298). IGI Global. DOI: 10.4018/978-1-6684-6697-1.ch016

Chauhan, S., Srivastava, S., Singh, R., Sharma, A., & Ojha, D. B. (2024). Quantum Cryptography: Reviewing Post-Quantum Cryptography. In *Applications and Principles of Quantum Computing* (pp. 378-398). IGI Global Scientific Publishing.

Chittem, M. B., & Pradhan, A. K. (2025, January). Hybrid Quantum-Classical Transfer Learning for Real-Time Data Processing. In *2025 17th International Conference on COMmunication Systems and NETworks (COMSNETS)* (pp. 84-89). IEEE. DOI: 10.1109/COMSNETS63942.2025.10885700

Das, S., & Das, A. (2023). Future Perspective of Quantum Cryptography for Smart Cities of the 21st Century. In *Handbook of Research on Quantum Computing for Smart Environments* (pp. 326-342). IGI Global.

Gayathri, M., Karthik, P. C., Sandhia, G. K., Thilagavathy, R., & Pushpalatha, M. (2024). Quantum Computing Principles: Harnessing the Potential of Quantum Mechanics. In *Applications and Principles of Quantum Computing* (pp. 81-94). IGI Global Scientific Publishing.

Khang, A. (Ed.). (2024). *Applications and principles of quantum computing*. IGI Global. DOI: 10.4018/979-8-3693-1168-4

Mishra, B. K. (Ed.). (2022). *Technology road mapping for quantum computing and engineering*. IGI Global. DOI: 10.4018/978-1-7998-9183-3

Prajapat, M., Choure, K. K., Qazi, G., Devi, P. P., Tiwari, M., & Singh, G. (2024, November). Quantum Sensors for Next-Generation Sensing: Techniques, Applications, and Recent Advancements. In *2024 4th International Conference on Technological Advancements in Computational Sciences (ICTACS)* (pp. 1748-1751). IEEE.

Ramesh, P., Nithyanandhan, R., Faizal, M. M., Nivakumar, V., & Nalini, M. (2024, December). Machine Learning Strategies for Customer Churn Prediction in Competitive Enterprises. In *2024 International Conference on Sustainable Communication Networks and Application (ICSCNA)* (pp. 653-660). IEEE. DOI: 10.1109/ICSCNA63714.2024.10864143

Ravindran, D., Revathi, S., Sowndharya, V., Farzhana, I., Sathya, V., Girija, P., & Subramanian, S. (2025). Unraveling the Quantum Computing Frontier: Advancements, Challenges, and Future Prospects. *Integration of AI, Quantum Computing, and Semiconductor Technology*, 139-158.

Sathya, U., Hashini, S., Lakshmipriya, C., Varun, C. M., & Nalini, M. (2024, December). Emerging Trends and Future Prospects in Internet of Things (IoT) Technology. In *2024 International Conference on Sustainable Communication Networks and Application (ICSCNA)* (pp. 79-85). IEEE.

Yamini, B., Nithyanandhan, R., Sudha, K., Nithya, T., Vijayakumar, K., & Subramanian, R. S. (2024, April). Maximizing the Revolutionary Potential of Quantum Computing: Challenges, Opportunities, and Future Directions. In *2024 10th International Conference on Communication and Signal Processing (ICCSP)* (pp. 756-761). IEEE.

Chapter 5
Cryptography and the Quantum Computing Threat:
Challenges and Future Solutions

Siva Subramanian R.
https://orcid.org/0000-0002-7509-9223
SRM Institute of Science and Technology, Tiruchirappalli, India

B. Yuvasri
R.M.K College of Engineering and Technology, India

ABSTRACT

Quantum computing is set to disrupt conventional cryptographic systems by efficiently solving mathematical problems previously considered infeasible. This chapter examines the vulnerabilities introduced by quantum computing and highlights emerging solutions, including post-quantum cryptography (PQC) and quantum key distribution (QKD). It also explores ongoing standardization initiatives, emphasizes the importance of cryptographic agility, and discusses hybrid migration strategies to ensure secure communication in the quantum era. By analyzing current threats alongside future-proof solutions, this chapter underscores the need to prepare digital infrastructures for quantum resilience and calls for collaborative efforts to safeguard information security.

DOI: 10.4018/979-8-3373-3166-9.ch005

1. INTRODUCTION

1.1. Overview of Cryptography

Cryptography is the process of transforming data into a format that is difficult to understand by the unauthorized parties or the intended data into a different form that is easily understandable by the intended user (Subramani, S., & Svn, S. K. 2025). It is very essential to guarantee secrecy, consistency, authenticity, and non-deniability of messages in computer based communication. Cryptography is used in all areas of human life from internet banking, online shopping, military and government organizations (Wong, D. 2021). Cryptography essentially comprises of three different branches namely symmetric encryption, asymmetric encryption, & hashing techniques. Symmetric encryption applies a single shared key for both encryption & decryption. Some of the popular symmetric algorithms include AES & DES. They are usually faster and are employed for encryption of bulk data. On the other hand, asymmetric encryption employs a key pair: a public key for encryption & a private key for decryption. This model is implemented in several protocols for key sharing like RSA and Diffie Hellman, and is also associated with the ECC. Involving key exchange, authentication codes, and applying the internet for secure communication, asymmetric encryption is crucial (Sathya, U et al., 2024). Last of all, cryptographic hash functions map an input on an output string which looks like random and has fixed length. Such functions as SHA-256 and SHA-3 are irreversible functions, which implies that they cannot be reversed by any means with the use of algorithms. Hashes are employed for guaranteeing the integrity of data and commonly applied in electronic signatures, passwords storage, and blockchain. Most of modern cryptography relies on complex mathematical challenges, such as factoring large integers or solving discrete logarithm problems, which is a valid approach under the paradigm of classical computation. However, these are the assumptions on which quantum computing is posed to challenge (Kumar, A., & Garhwal, S. 2021).

1.2. Introduction to Quantum Computing

Quantum computing represents relatively novel technology which applies the fundamentals of quantum physics for solving problems in a different manner. Different from traditional computers which operate using bits, where the values are either 0 or 1, quantum systems make use of qubits. A qubit can be in two states at once, or in other words be a 0 and a 1 simultaneously, implying that a quantum system can handle numerous operations concurrently. Another fundamental quantum characteristic is entanglement which is a state where two or more qubits remain naturally linked such that the condition of one influences the other irrespective of their separation. Entanglement makes quantum devices capable of tackling problems that are nearly unsolvable on conventional computers. Quantum gates act on qubits in such a manner in that these properties do not alter the quantum characteristics of the qubit. As opposed to the classical logic gates which operate in a sequential manner, quantum gates work in parallel hence increasing computational capabilities. Superposition and entanglement result into parallelism in quantum computers where a quantum computer can pursue multiple solutions to a single problem. Quantum computing is considered to be a largely innovative technique that may drastically change fields such as material science, pharma intermediate synthesis and optimalizations (Ravindran, D et al., 2025). But it also presents a great threat to cybersecurity because some quantum methods can address tasks that are virtually unsolvable on standard computers. Among them Shor's method is able to factorize very large integers, while Grover's technique is employed for scanning unstructured data more efficiently than any non-quantum method (Gayathri et al 2024).

1.3. The Quantum Threat to Cryptography

Quantum computing is sort of an upgrade in the encryption world and society at large and will herald a new wave in fault tolerance of computations. The majority of the classical cryptography methods rely on the hardness of mathematical problems for traditional systems but easy for quantum computers. Shor's method, introduced by Peter Shor in 1994, demonstrated that a quantum computer can break down large integers & determine discrete logarithms within polynomial time. This completely nullifies RSA, ECC, & other public key infrastructures currently protecting the internet at the moment. These consequences are rather significant. For example, RSA uses the property that multiplying two primes is simple, but reversing the process of finding the primes from the product is computationally intensive using classical means. Yet this process can be managed by a sufficiently capable quantum machine. Therefore, there is a possibility for any message encrypted using RSA to be decrypted once such a computer is available. Likewise, ECC which has been used because of its shorter keys lengths and equivalent security level as RSA is also prone to quantum attacks. Since elliptic curve cryptography is dependent on the discrete logarithm challenge, which Shor's method is also able to address, it too will become ineffective in quantum computing environment. Although block cipher–based encryption such as AES is relatively secure compared to quantum-based threats, it is not completely safe. Grover's algorithm has the capability of quadratically improving the brute force attack and thus lowering the strength of symmetric ciphers. For instance, Grover's technique reduces the effective key size of AES-256 to 128 bits, and AES-128 to 64 bits; though still considered secure, larger key lengths are required to maintain protection. It should be emphasized that the danger posed by quantum technology is not something that is only going to be realized in the future. The current adversaries may be intercepting and storing the encrypted messages with a plan to decrypt them once the quantum computers are developed, a technique referred to as "store now, decrypt later." This means that there is a need to come up with cryptographic systems that can resist attacks from both traditional and quantum systems. Other organizations like the NIST have begun formalizing standards for PQC, aimed at building algorithms robust against quantum threats. Simultaneously, QKD is being developed, which works under the principles of quantum mechanics and avoids relying on mathematical hardness assumptions for security. Therefore, the quantum threat is real and on the rise. Although quantum computers that can break current cryptographic systems are not currently available, the development of quantum technologies is growing at a fast rate and such a future is feasible in the next few decades. This means that it is not possible to avoid the need to assess threats and make preparations for a post-quantum era in cryptography. This chapter will focus on the issues, opportunities and possibilities of making the cryptographic techniques quantum-safe.

2. BACKGROUND ON CLASSICAL CRYPTOGRAPHIC ALGORITHMS

Cyber security has extended over a long period and has become an important component that provides people a safe means of communicating and transacting as well as protecting their data in the contemporary world. Classical cryptography schemes are developed with the ability to protect them from attacks from classical computers and can be classified as the Symmetric Key Cryptosystems, Asymmetric Key Cryptosystems, & Cryptographic Hash Functions. Each type is used for different reasons and is based on the mathematical theory and provides different levels of security and practicality at the cost of efficiency. It is crucial to comprehend these algorithms to realize how the new quantum technologies pose a risk to them and what is needed to protect systems in a post-quantum era.

2.1. Symmetric-Key Cryptography

This category of cryptography is also known as secret-key encryption since the same key is applied during both encryption & decryption (Kumar et al 2021). That means that both communicating parties must have prior knowledge of the shared key and ensure that it remains hidden from unauthorized users. It is commonly used for encryption of a massive amount of data because of its speed and performance. Well-known symmetric algorithms include the DES and the AES. It employs a 56-

bit key & works on 64-bit blocks. But with advances in computing, DES became vulnerable to brute force techniques, attackers attempt all possible key until right one is discovered. This led to the gradual replacement of SSL by more secure schemes of communication.

AES was introduced by NIST in 2001 as a replacement for DES. It supports 3 key lengths: 128, 192, or 256 bits, with a block size of 128 bits. AES much more secure and efficient than DES and is widely deployed in many applications such as SSL/TLS for secure web communication, file encryption, & VPNs. In the classical model, symmetric algorithms are believed to be secure if the encryption key remains confidential and sufficiently lengthy to resist brute force attacks. Their security is works on the fact that exhaustively searching full key space is practically infeasible. AES-256 is therefore considered safe from traditional brute force attacks and would take 2^56 to break. Moreover, symmetric cryptography is used in many securities enhanced systems like the wireless protected access (WPA2), disk encryption software, and mobile applications data protection. For this reason, symmetric cryptography has some limitations in the distribution and management of the keys. Because both communicating parties must hold the identical secret key, there is a demand for key exchange protocols, which rely on asymmetric cryptography for secure distribution.

2.2. Asymmetric-Key Cryptography

Asymmetric-key cryptography or public-key encryption makes use of a pair of keys, namely a public key which is openly shared & a private key that must remain secret. It also gives a method of secure communication between two strangers who do not have any secret key between them. It helps in certain secondary functionalities like key distribution, authentication through digital signatures, and identity verification. RSA was among the earliest and remains one of the most commonly used asymmetric algorithms, introduced in 1977. RSA algorithm depends on the factorization of large composite integers, that is computationally intensive. In the RSA method, the public key is generated from two big prime numbers & breaking it requires enormous computational effort using only classical systems. It is mostly used in secure e-mail, digital signatures, and secure communication over the web. The other type of asymmetric method is the Diffie-Hellman protocol, designed to allow two users to derive a shared secret key even if the communication channel is insecure. The protocol derives its strength from the discrete logarithm challenge in finite fields. Nevertheless, Diffie-Hellman by itself only provides key establishment and does not guarantee authentication, hence it is typically combined with signature schemes to ensure both authenticity and confidentiality. Public-key systems are more recent compared to secret-key cryptosystems, and there are newer forms of public-key methods, one of which is the ECC. It is founded on the mathematics of elliptic curves defined over finite fields and offers security equivalent to RSA but with shorter key lengths. For instance, 256-bit ECC key is as secure as 3072-bit RSA key. This makes ECC highly effective in resource-constrained systems such as IoT devices and embedded systems. The main strength of asymmetric approaches is scalability and simplified key distribution (Sundararajan et al 2022).

2.3. Cryptographic Hash Functions

A hash function is a critical element in many security mechanisms. It can be described as a process that transforms an input or message into a fixed-length output, commonly referred to as the hash. This output is same to the input & any slight variation to the input should result in a completely different hash. The uses of hash algorithms are mainly to verify the integrity of information, protecting passwords, providing facilities for digital signatures, and applications in blockchain technology. Some common features of hash functions include:

For any given output, it must be computationally infeasible to reverse the original input. Second preimage resistance: The same output should not be easily arrived at by another input. Collision resistance: For any two different messages, it should be infeasible to arrive at the same hash value.

In classical computing, cryptographic hash functions are believed secure provided that their output length is large enough to withstand brute-force and birthday attacks. Nonetheless, Grover's technique, a quantum-based search algorithm, provide a quadratic improvement in finding preimages. This means that in a quantum setting, the security margin of hash functions is effectively reduced by half. For example, Grover's approach lowers the effective strength of SHA-256 from 2^{256} to 2^{128}, requiring larger key sizes or new designs for post-quantum systems. Hash functions are not used for purposes of encryption but they are crucial for data authentication and verification. For example, in digital signature algorithms, one hashes the message before encrypting the hash with a private key in order to achieve a secure and efficient signature. In brief, this classical cryptography is based on three primary principles, namely the symmetric key cryptography for data secrecy, asymmetric key cryptography for security and authentication, and hash cryptography for data integrity and validation. Although these systems have been adequate for the digital world for decades, they solve mathematical problems that are difficult only under the assumptions of classical computing.

3. QUANTUM COMPUTING BASICS

Quantum computing represents a quick advancing field with significant potential, as it leverages quantum mechanical principles to manipulate information in fundamentally various ways from conventional computing. Whereas von Neumann prosecution-based computers operate in binary systems with logistic inputs that can be either 0 or 1, the quantum computers employ quantum logic with ''qubits'' to take on multiple values at once. This section provides the reader with the basic understanding of quantum mechanics, structure of quantum computers, and revolutionary algorithms that make quantum computing effective and dangerous to modern cryptography (Yamini, B et al., 2024).

3.1. Principles of Quantum Mechanics

Quantum mechanics is the field production which studies forces that reign on the atomic and subatomic structure. Thus, three significant principles: superposition, entanglement, & quantum parallelism are the basis of quantum computing. Superposition is considered as the possibility of quantum particles' existence on different states at the same time. In traditional computing, a bit is defined to exist in either of two values, 0 or 1. A qubit, however, may exist in a combination of 0 and 1 at once. This implies that a quantum computer with n qubits is 2^N dimensional, meaning that it can process many states all at once, hence can do many calculations simultaneously. This exponential state-space allows quantum systems to address computational tasks that are infeasible for classical machines. Another important quantum phenomenon is entanglement in which two or more qubits get correlated in such a way that the state of a qubit affects the condition of another qubit irrespective of the distance between them. Entangled qubits possess correlations that defy explanation through classical physics. This property enables quantum processors to keep correlation between two or more qubits, which can be used in various applications such as quantum security methods like quantum key sharing. Superposition with entanglement are the main two factors that cause quantum parallelism. It lets a quantum computer to work on several possibilities simultaneously and, if the circumstances are right, to find the right solution in fewer steps than with classical methods. In contrast to traditional computers that perform one operation at a time, quantum machines try a multitude of computations at once. It is important to see that these principles do not only offer elegance from the theoretical point of view, but bring virtually unimaginable computational power. They also raise questions to the conventional concepts of information processing and have significant implications to cryptology and information protection.

3.2. Quantum Computing Model

The architecture of a quantum computer is based on qubits, which are the quantum analog of classical bits. Unlike bits that can only be 0 or 1, qubits exist in a superposed state described by a linear combination of 0 and 1, represented as

$$|\psi> = \alpha|0> + \beta|1>$$

where α & β are complex probability amplitudes that satisfy $|\alpha|^2 + |\beta|^2 = 1$. Measurement collapses the qubit into one of the basis states with a probability determined by these amplitudes.

Quantum gates are the components of a quantum circuit just as gates are of a circuit in classical computing. However, quantum gates work on the probabilities of the qubit's state by using linear algebra and unitary transformations. Common gates include:

Hadamard (H) Gate: Introduces superposition. Pauli-X Gate: Works like a traditional NOT gate.

CNOT Gate: A two-qubit gate that targets the specified qubit to change its state if the controlling qubit has a value of 1; useful for entanglement. Toffoli and Fredkin Gates: Used for universal quantum computation.

Quantum algorithms are actualized through quantum circuits which are a sequence of quantum gates applied on a set of qubits. These circuits are used to perform certain computations by mapping the input quantum state to a state where the output of the computation can be read off from. Another nasty feature of quantum computers is quantum decoherence that describes the process when qubits interact with the environment and start having less quantum properties but more classical ones. Decoherence is one of the toughest engineering problems in the implementation of quantum computing as it affects the computation time and introduces noise in the system.

3.3. Quantum Algorithms

Quantum computing methods use the principles of quantum mechanics for addressing computational tasks that are solved by classical algorithms in a more efficient way. Among the popular methods, Shor's Algorithm & Grover's Algorithm can be considered as the most prominent ones as they demonstrate the transformative role of quantum approaches in the field of cryptography.

Shor's algorithm is a polynomial-time quantum approach for prime factorization and discrete logarithm, two problems that are used in most cryptography systems such as RSA, Diffie-Hellman, and Elliptic Curve Cryptography. The classical algorithms for these problems are exponentially slow; for instance, a conventional machine would need an impractically long duration to factor a 2048-bit RSA modulus. Shor's method applies the concept of quantum parallelism & quantum Fourier transform to find the period of a modular function which in turn is used to find the factors of a large number. When a quantum computer is constructed with enough qubits & error correction capabilities, it is very possible that Shor's algorithm may successfully crack most of the present-day public-key cryptography. This algorithm poses significant risks to public-key encryption as it can be potentially broken. As of now, no quantum computers that could run the algorithm at scale are available, although research in this field is ongoing in order to create such computers, and many researchers believe that they could be developed in the next several decades.

Grover's algorithm was proposed by Lov Grover in 1996 which offers quadratic speed-up for searching an unsorted database. In classical computing, the operation of searching through N entries is possible in the best-case scenario in O(N). Grover's algorithm is able to find the target entry in approximately $\sqrt{N}$ steps. However, this speed-up is not as significant as Shor's exponential gain but Grover's algorithm has great impacts on symmetric-key cryptography and hash functions. It reduces the security of symmetric ciphers to half such as AES and reduces the collision resistance of hash functions. For instance, AES-128 would provide only 64 bits of security in the presence of a quantum adversary, thus there is a suggestion to use AES-256 in post-quantum scenarios. Grover's algorithm is also relevant to brute-force attacks that result in password hashes and digital signature verification to be weaker unless better parameters are adopted.

Shor's & Grover's algorithms are considered to be the foundation of the quantum threat: the former attacks the public-key methods, whereas the latter challenges symmetric encryption and hashing. Awareness of these algorithms is necessary in order to assess the effects that quantum computing could have on cybersecurity and to establish guidelines for creating quantum-safe cryptosystems (Yamini, B et al., 2024). Thus, quantum computing based on the principles of quantum mechanics can be seen as a technology with capabilities that are beyond the capacities of classical computing. The possibility of a quantum system to exist in two or more states, be entangled and perform parallel computations puts into risk the cryptographic security of current digital technologies. While proceeding further into the analysis of future threats and corresponding mitigation, it is crucial to grasp the basics of quantum computing since this provides the evaluation of the potential threat and the development of the adequate response in the further sections of this survey.

4. QUANTUM THREATS TO CRYPTOGRAPHY

There is a growing risk associated with quantum computing that may have an impact on the security of information. It is noteworthy that the emergence of quantum algorithms, for example, Shor & Grover, has exposed the weaknesses in most of the cryptographic systems used for secure communication in the internet nowadays. This section discusses how exactly the current cryptographic systems can be vulnerable to quantum computing and why a new generation of methods is required that would be immune to these threats (Chauhan et al 2024).

4.1. Shor's Algorithm and Public-Key Cryptography

Public-key cryptography is based upon the principle problem that is difficult to solve. Schemes such as RSA, ECC, and Diffie–Hellman protocols rely on the hardness of solving problems like prime factorization & discrete logarithms. These foundations are valid in the classical computing model but are fatally flawed when a quantum computer, mainly Shor's algorithm is involved. Shor's algorithm is a polynomial-time quantum method introduced in 1994 for addressing large numbers as well as computing the logarithmic problem in polynomial time. In the practical sense, this is a clear pointer that a quantum computer can crack RSA by factoring the large public modulus or compromise ECC by solving the elliptic curve discrete logarithm problem. This would let an adversary extract secret keys from the public parameters, decipher secret messages, forge digital signatures, and impersonate other parties. RSA is one of the most affected by this problem since it is primarily a retailing company. The RSA approach security is based on the hardness of multiplying two prime numbers (for instance 2048 bits). Classical computers can do this only with very slow classical algorithms such as the general number field sieve which are still very time consuming. In contrast, a quantum computer running Shor's method could factor such numbers in polynomial time, which is a few hours or even minutes compared to the years it would take a classical computer. This is especially true for ECC which is widely utilized in portable and connected devices because of reduced key lengths and efficiency of the algorithm. ECC's security is based on the elliptic curve discrete logarithm problem, which Shor's algorithm can solve as well. That means that all ECC-based protocols such as ECDSA and ECDH will also become vulnerable to attack by a quantum adversary. Consequently, every form of internet security such as HTTPS, VPNs, secure email, and digital signatures in software updates, blockchain, and other platforms will be completely affected (Babu, A. A et al., 2024). When a large-scale quantum system becomes operational, all messages encrypted today can be decrypted in the future.

4.2. Grover's Algorithm and Symmetric-Key Cryptography

Shor's algorithm poses a fatal blow to public-key cryptosystems whereas Grover's algorithm is a comparatively less fatal but equally dangerous threat to symmetric-key cryptography and cryptographic hash functions. However, Grover's algorithm is faster than Shor's in brute-force searches such as key guessing and hash collisions have a quadratic speed-up. In classical brute-force methods of cracking, one would have to attempt all the possible keys for a symmetric cipher such as AES-128, which is an impossible number. Grover's algorithm can bring this down to about 2^{64} operations, which gives a cut in half of the key length's security. However, 2^{64} operations are still far from being implemented with today's classical computers, but the decrease of the complexity might become feasible in the future quantum computers. To this, cryptographers suggest extending the size of keys by a factor of two in order to achieve the same levels of post-quantum security. For instance: AES-256 becomes the standard one, which is quantum-safe with 128 bits according to Grover's method reducing the 256-bit key to 128 bits.

For hash functions Grover's algorithm weakens SHA-256 to 128 bits and therefore SHA-512 or greater hash sizes are used in quantum-safe applications.

While, as it was seen, Grover's algorithm does not completely break symmetric algorithms like AES, the reduction in security means that there is a need to reconsider the security of many protocols to ensure that they are still secure in the post-quantum world. It means that symmetric cryptography does not need a complete overhaul of parameters, but it is enough to increase keys and hashes. Another type of threat is deeply grounded in speculation and is connected with potential quantum-accelerated collision attacks regarding hash functions. Although Grover's algorithm is designed specifically for preimage and key-search problems, variations of it might be useful in finding hash collisions but not as effectively as the birthday attacks. However, the overall result is a reduction in the security assurance that can be offered, which is a consideration in the design of cryptographic systems in the future.

4.3. Quantum-Resistant Cryptography

The attacks by Shor's & Grover's algorithms have raised crucial necessity for quantum resistant or PQC which refers to cryptographic techniques which are resistant for both traditional and quantum hackers. PQC intends to offer more secure solutions for substitution of current weak public-key systems or technologies without comprising on efficiency, compatibility, or security. Post-quantum cryptographic schemes are those that are still strong even with quantum computers since the problems on which they rely are hard to solve.

This NIST project was started in 2016 and is intended to develop post-quantum cryptography algorithms that are efficiently adopted to replace RSA, ECC, and other traditional methods. Its selections are aimed at offering solutions that will serve as the basis for post-quantum secure communications in the future. These algorithms will be incorporated in some of the most sensitive applications including TLS, secure email using PGP, code signing and blockchain. Nevertheless, post-quantum cryptography also comes with some difficulties as well. New algorithms may be larger in terms of key size and may consume more amount of bandwidth and may possess different dynamics. It will take several years to modify all the systems across the globe that are related to protocols, software libraries, hardware modules, and certification processes to shift to PQC. Moreover, although symmetric cryptography such as AES is secure with improved parameters, key exchange and authentication processes used in conjunction with it (RSA, DH) should be quantum safe. This implies that even those systems that have implemented AES encryption have to transition to post-quantum key exchange such as Kyber. The need to embrace PQC cannot be overemphasized because there is a "store data now and decrypt later" approach employed by the attackers who encrypt data today, with the aim of decrypting them once the quantum computers are available. This puts pressure on the need to introduce quantum-resistant encryption as soon as possible to secure the long-term data, including government and military communications, health information, and other sensitive information. In conclusion, it is critical to state that quantum computing is a serious threat to the field of cryptography and the threat is real and present. Shor's algorithm makes public-key cryptography inherently vulnerable while Grover's algorithm poses a threat to the effectiveness of the symmetric schemes. These threats require the transition to quantum-safe algorithms of all these cryptographic systems. Incorporating post-quantum cryptography can be regarded as both the preparation for an attack and the chance to rethink the concept of cryptographic security in the context of the new age of computation. As the world slowly moves closer to the reality of practical quantum computers, the fight for the future of digital security is already in full swing and has to be won before the technology becomes mainstream.

5. POST-QUANTUM CRYPTOGRAPHY (PQC)

5.1. Definition and Motivation

PQC is the cryptographic systems that are intended to be implemented on the present day conventional computers but are resistant to the threats posed by quantum computers. In contrast to the former, PQC is a concept that is focused on the development of post-quantum cryptography, which is the cryptography that can work in the environment when quantum computers threaten modern cryptographic algorithms. The fundamental reason for the development of PQC stems from the susceptibility of the current public-key cryptography systems. As mentioned before, algorithms such as RSA & ECC are at risk from Shor's algorithm, as the latter can quickly solve the mathematical problems on which both of them are based: integer factorization & the discrete logarithm problem. Therefore, when a scalable quantum computer is developed it would be capable of breaking these encryption schemes and compromising sensitive information and communication all over the world. In order to counter this impending threat, the NIST started a formal Post-Quantum Cryptography Standardization Project in the year 2016. Aim of this project is to assess, choose and set as a reference one or more quantum-safe cryptographic algorithms for practical use. This is a truly large-scale and very typical work in modern research on cryptography, which is built in a multi-phase manner and involves academic establishments, state departments, and companies and industrial enterprises as well as the evaluation of the proposed algorithms and their security effectiveness, speed, and practicability. The use of PQC is further necessitated by the threat model referred to as the "harvest now, decrypt later" threat model. Attackers can potentially be storing encrypted data right now with the plan to decrypt them as soon as quantum computers are available. This has made industries and governments to be on the lookout for such calamities and make necessary preparations.

5.2. Candidate Algorithms for Post-Quantum Cryptography

There is a significant variety of proposed cryptographic schemes that can be considered as quantum-resistant. These are mostly derived from mathematical problems that are presumed difficult by both classical & quantum computers. The following is a major categorization of the candidate algorithms currently under consideration by NIST and other institutions.

Lattice-Based Cryptography: At the present time, lattice-based cryptography is considered to be the leading approach of PQC development. This approach is based on the difficulty of mathematical problems like LWE and SIS. These problems remain strong against both classical and quantum adversaries and have good worst instance to random instance reduction.

Code-based cryptography focuses on the challenge of decoding generic linear error-correcting codes, which are believed to withstand even quantum attacks. The most widely known is the McEliece cryptosystem. The McEliece system has been challenging for cryptanalysis for more than three decades and provides good security and efficiency. However, one of its significant limitations is the very large size of the public keys, which may be as large as several hundred kilobytes to several megabytes in size, making implementation in restricted environments a rather complex process.

Multivariate Polynomial-Based Cryptography

These schemes are based on the hardness of solving systems of multivariate quadratic polynomials over finite fields, which are computationally intensive. They are most suited for constructing digital signature schemes.

Hash-Based Signatures: It is important to note that hash-based signature schemes rely on the security of cryptographic hash functions and collision resistance, which makes them immune to attacks from quantum computing using Shor's method, if the hash function's output size is large enough.

Key schemes include:

SPHINCS+: a stateless hash-based signature scheme that is currently on the list of recommended post-quantum cryptographic algorithms by the NIST. There are no weaknesses that are unique to hash-based signatures and it is well known that they have good security properties. But, they are used to create large signatures and require higher computation, which makes them more appropriate for applications such as firmware authentication or blockchain.

Isogeny-Based Cryptography: Isogeny-based cryptography is one of the relatively newer & isogeny is a mathematical mapping of one elliptic curve to another. The most well-known one was SIKE (Supersingular Isogeny Key Encapsulation) that was considered to have small key sizes earlier. However, the scheme was cracked in 2022 by researchers through classical attack making the SIKE scheme impractical for use. This has somewhat discouraged the use of isogeny based cryptography although research is still being carried out on more secure forms of it.

5.3. Evaluation of Post-Quantum Cryptography

Therefore, to measure the efficiency of PQC algorithms, three key aspects are considered, which include security, efficiency, and practicality. All of these factors dictate the possibility of using the given algorithms in real-life systems.

Security: The post-quantum algorithms are made to be immune to both classical & quantum attacks. This entails mathematical analysis, cryptanalysis, and whenever possible, a proof of the mathematical results obtained. Algorithms should also be protected against side channel attacks and implementation related weaknesses. The candidates have been through NIST's multi-phase evaluation process for more than a year, international competitions, and open peer reviews.

6. QUANTUM KEY DISTRIBUTION (QKD)

6.1. Overview of Quantum Key Distribution

Quantum Key Distribution represents a process through which two parties are able to agree on a secret key to be used in their encryption process and transmitting this key over an insecure channel in such a way where any effort by an intruder to capture the key will be easily noticed. The principles that enable QKD are the Heisenberg indeterminacy principle and quantum correlation. Heisenberg's uncertainty principle refers to the fact that it is impossible to simultaneously determine the position and velocity of an object. When used in the context of quantum information, it means that measuring a quantum system affects that system. Consequently, when an interceptor tries to seize the quantum units or qubits in the course of their transfer, there are tell-tale signs that they left behind. Quantum entanglement, however, is a situation where particles get intertwined in a particular manner that when one particle is put into a specific condition, the other particle, regardless of the gap, will also be in a corresponding state. This non-local property is employed in some of the QKD protocols to verify the genuineness of the shared key as well as its secrecy.

6.2. Security of QKD

QKD security does not rely on any assumptions about the difficulty of computation but relies upon the laws of quantum mechanics. This makes it significantly different from other key exchange schemes, for example, RSA or Diffie Hellman that can be readily broken by quantum processors using Shor's method. Among the basic laws of quantum physics applied in QKD security, we can mention the no-cloning theorem. This rule declares that one cannot replicate a precise duplicate of an unidentified quantum condition of an object. This implies that when an interceptor tries to seize and reproduce quantum bits, the process of measurement of such bits will cause an interference that can be noticed by the rightful users. These interferences are evident as a rise in the error rate when the verification is being done. Subsequent to the quantum transmission, Alice and Bob carry out the sifting of the key in which they publicly compare some of the key bits to determine the level of error. In the case where the error rate is below this level, it is assumed that any attempt to eavesdrop has not taken place or has been minimal. They then proceed to do mistake correction and confidentiality enhancement to create a final shared secret key that is statistically secure even if the attacker gains partial information of the process. Therefore, under the best practices and if applied correctly, QKD provides information theoretic security, which implies that the key cannot be hacked no matter the amount of time or computational power available including quantum computers.

6.3. Challenges in QKD

However, implementing QKD has its own set of challenges that make it difficult to be widely adopted. One of the major problems that are still present is the photon loss and noise that is usually encountered in transmission channels. Quantum signals, which are normally transmitted through single-photon states of light using optical fibres or free space, are very susceptible. Fiber optic systems suffer from attenuation over long distances and free space systems suffer from such factors as the turbulence in the atmosphere. This restricts the distance up to several hundred kilometres in practical applications of QKD. To overcome these issues, researchers are working on the concept of quantum repeaters which will help in increasing the distance of quantum communication without affecting the no-cloning theorem. However, these technologies are still in their infancy and need a lot of enhancement in the fields of quantum memory and entanglement swapping. The next problem is the issue of security implementation of QKD systems. The theoretical models offer ideal security, but as the actual devices are implemented, one can find new ways for an attacker to gain information, which are not covered in the theory, side channel attacks. Some of them include the detector blinding attacks and the photon-number splitting attacks. These have to be avoided by using device-independent QKD and designing the protocols and equipment appropriately. However, the costs and the level of complication of QKD systems are some of the challenges that need to be overcome. Some of the quantum hardware such as single-photon detectors, entangled photon source, and other optical components are costly and may need a high level of calibration. Due to these reasons, most of the QKD networks are still limited to special uses; they are used in places like government and military or in some key financial organizations and not on the general public networks.

6.4. Integration With Classical Cryptography

Due to the limitation of QKD, particularly in terms of distance and complexity, incorporating QKD with classical cryptographic systems is another area of focus. One of the key possibilities is to employ QKD in order to produce a symmetrical session key with the help of which the data is encrypted with the help of classical cryptographic algorithms (for example, AES). This hybrid method leverages the strengths of both systems: QKD's secure key generation and AES's fast data encryption. It also means that even if the classical algorithms are one day cracked (by quantum computers, for instance), the key will remain safe if it was produced by means of QKD. Such systems are already under implementation in some sensitive areas, especially in the banking and defense industries. It also can also incorporate QKD with post quantum cryptographic algorithm to enhance security measures. This is due to the fact that it offers protection against current threats and future threats in case one system was to be penetrated the other will continue to protect. There are also ongoing standardization processes for the specifications that are related to the integration of the QKD. ITU, ETSI and ISO/IEC are among the organizations that are involved in the development of specifications that would allow for the integration of quantum and classical cryptography. In particular, QKD is not expected to displace classical cryptography entirely but rather supplement it in cases where the utmost security is needed. It is for this reason that as the technologies advance and become more affordable, QKD is expected to be integrated into a multilayer security approach together with PQC.

7. THE ROAD TO QUANTUM-SAFE CRYPTOGRAPHY

The advanced development of quantum computing is a great concern to the current cryptographic systems hence the call by cybersecurity experts to build quantum-resistant solutions (Prabhu, D et al., 2025). The process of readiness concerns the recognition of the existence of practical quantum computers on the horizon, the creation and stabilisation of new algorithms, and the intricate process of swapping from the current systems. In this section, the latest quantum readiness timeline is discussed along with the approach toward shifting towards post-quantum cryptosystem, the general adoption issues that organizations face across the world.

7.1. The Timeline of Quantum Readiness

It is imperative to know when quantum computers can pose a real threat to today's cryptography to plan for the transition appropriately. Despite the fact that fully fault-tolerant large-scale quantum computers capable of breaking RSA & ECC cryptography do not exist at the moment, the progress has been made. Currently, IBM, Google and other emerging quantum companies have constructed prototypes of quantum computers with more and more qubits. However, these systems are still lacking in capacity and are capable to make many errors. Specifically, the concept of Q-Day is used, which means the date when a hacker equipped with a quantum computer can decode current encryption. There is no specific time period on when quantum computing will be widespread, but some of the estimates range from 10-20 years while others argue that it could be much sooner because of the progress that is currently being made in quantum hardware, quantum error correction, and optimization of algorithms. More to the point, as soon as such a computer becomes operational, all data previously encrypted might be decrypted in retrospect, which means that data confidentiality can be violated even today. This has given rise to the concept of "harvest now, decrypt later" which is an attack where the adversary encodes information and plans to decrypt it once he acquires a strong quantum system. Thus, even if the cryptographic break does not take place soon, it is evident that organizations should transition to quantum-safe cryptography now to protect long-lived data.

7.2. Migration Strategies for Cryptographic Systems

Moving from the existing cryptographic solutions to the quantum ones is not just a mere shift – it is a change in the scale of the digital architecture. It is important to achieve four priorities in migration: security, backward compatibility, operational impact, and scalability. The most preferable approach is the so called hybrid approach, which means that classical & post-quantum cryptography are used simultaneously. For instance, in the key exchange, both an RSA key and a lattice based key may be used; and the session key will only be agreed if both key exchanges are successful. This has a double layer that guarantees security in the event that one of the methods is cracked. Hybrid strategies are good for a gradual transition and compatibility, as they allow systems to be compatible with devices and protocols that are not quantum. This is particularly so in the industries where the product cycle is long, for instance, aerospace, automotive, and health equipment where some devices can serve for many years. The third key factor in migration is cryptographic agility. It is the characteristic that allows for the easy change of cryptographic algorithms without the need to redesign the system. This involves applying changes in the software libraries, communicating protocols as well as the hardware components to accommodate modular cryptographic configuration. It is therefore advisable to incorporate post-quantum cryptography into systems now in order to avoid the extra effort and cost that will be incurred when the change of algorithm is enforced. From an operational point of view, the organizations have to carry out cryptographic inventory audits to identify where exactly cryptography is employed in the organization's infrastructure. This is by assessing the applications, data in use as well as data in transit and the key management systems that use such weak algorithms.

Figure 1. Quantum-Safe Cryptography

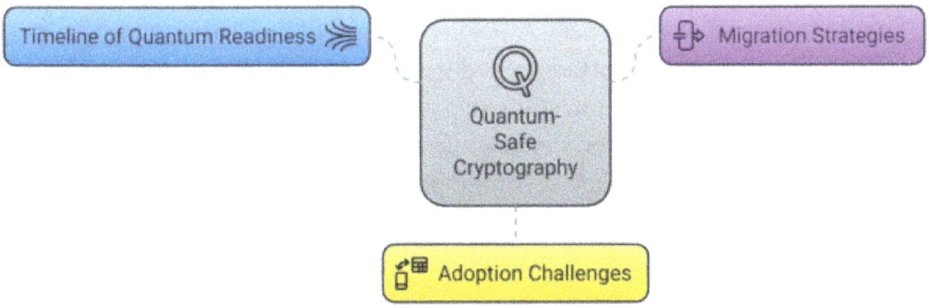

7.3. Adoption Challenges

However, there are some problems that prevent the widespread implementation of quantum-safe cryptography at the present stage. The challenges that are highlighted include technical, organizational, regulatory, and economic. The issues include compatibility with legacy systems since procurement processes are integrated into these systems and cannot be easily separated. Most of the current systems, especially those in the critical infrastructures, have not been developed with the concept of cryptographic agility. Updating or replacing such systems is not an easy task as it is costly, time consuming and involves a lot of operational risks. For example, a controller of an industrial plant or an IoT device does not have the processing power or memory to run more advanced post-quantum algorithms. The other factor that may also be a concern is the performance and efficiency of the post-quantum algorithms. The majority of quantum-resistant algorithms have larger keys and computational complexity compared to their classical counterparts. This can cause a decline in the performance in resource limited devices or high throughput systems such as the online banking systems. It is thus important to ensure that the security of a system is achieved without compromising the usability of the system by considering new methods in optimization and algorithms. Another problem regards the fact that there is no clear policy regulation as well as a lack of international cooperation. Even though organizations such as NIST are actively working on standardization, it is not the same for all countries or industries. Some organizations may adopt a particular standard at one point in time while another organization in a different jurisdiction may adopt a different standard at the same time. However, the high cost and limited resources are some of the factors that prevent SMEs from adopting quantum-safe technologies. These organizations may not have the necessary skills, resources, personnel, or financial capacity to handle the cryptographic migration by themselves. Industry consortium, government funding and support and lastly, public private partnership may be instrumental in the increased adoption. The last of them is the issue of awareness and trust of the public. To most people in the executive suite, government officials, and the general public, the opportunities and threats associated with quantum computing are still quite conceptual. This is why it is necessary to explain the significance of post-quantum cryptography with no hype and exaggeration. Quantum-safe cryptography is not only necessary, but it is done through a challenging approach. Despite the fact that the development of PQCs that would be able to break modern encryption is still several years away, the time to act is now. A proactive approach also entails ascertaining the probable timeline of threats, designing and implementing hybrid and agile systems, and responding to the various issues that arise from such a paradigm shift. If the stakeholders ranging from researchers from different fields, industries and government come on board then a strong foundation of secure digital infrastructure can be laid that cannot be threatened by quantum technology.

8. FUTURE DIRECTIONS AND SOLUTIONS

As quantum computing comes from being a potential idea to being an actuality, it opens up new threats and possibilities for cryptography . Whereas the present research is directed towards countering the threat of quantum computing, the outlook for the future is the progressive development of both the quantum computer and the cryptographic means that would be immune to it. This section describes outlines of quantum future directions: Investigation of even more potent and versatile quantum algorithms and quantum circuits, Supplementary and reinforcement of PQC, & robust, quantum-safe communication networks.

Figure 2. Future Directions and Solutions

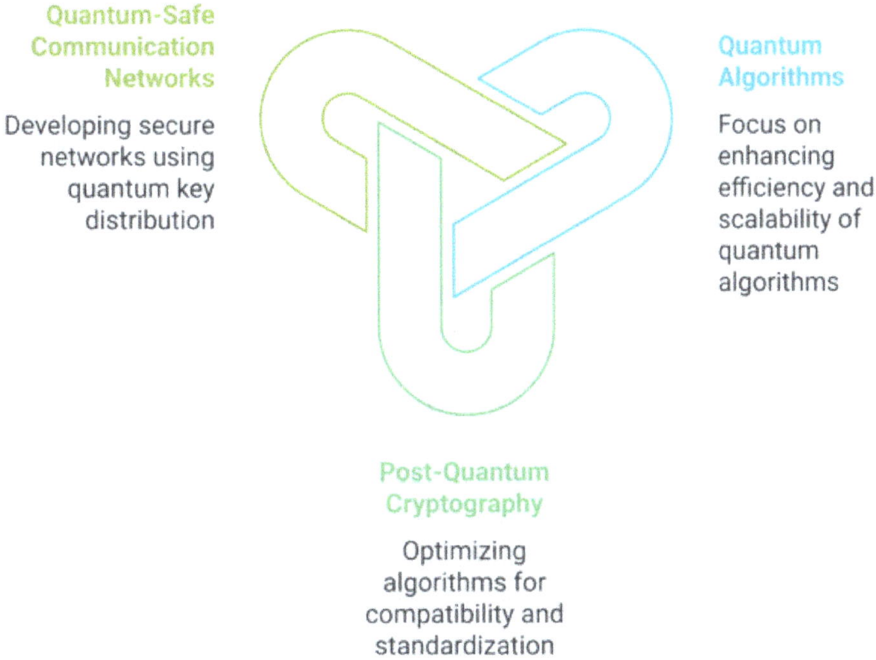

8.1. Continued Research in Quantum Algorithms

Quantum algorithms are essentially the threat and the opportunity that is associated with quantum computing. The creation and optimization of quantum algorithms are crucial, not only for the undermining of conventional cryptographic methods but also for such problems that cannot be solved in classical computing. One of the most prominent categories of the investigated topics is the enhancement of the efficiency & scalability of the existing quantum algorithms. Even though Shor's algorithm & Grover's algorithm have been proved to be more efficient than classical counterparts, their real-life application has its own set of problems. The present quantum computers are unable to cope with the number of qubits and error corrected operations needed to perform these algorithms at the cryptographic level of security. Thus, the quantum computer scientists are exploring improved versions and the quantum-classical approach to overcome the existing limitations and achieve further advancements. Of equal significance is the design of new quantum algorithms for other purposes as well. These are optimization algorithms, simulation, machine learning, and even the secure communication algorithms (Lydia, A et al., 2024). Understanding the parameters and the limitations of quantum computing enables one to discover new weaknesses and to create cryptographic systems that are immune to future attacks. Algorithms are developed alongside quantum hardware that is used in quantum computing. Quantum computing needs to be done in practice, and this is a challenge because of instability of quantum systems because of decoherence and noise. It is important to study fault-tolerant quantum computing to ensure that the algorithms can be run without fail. Fault tolerance is used to ensure that quantum computers can function with noisy qubits and this is achieved through quantum error correction. This poses a great challenge since one abstract qubit can be implemented with tens, hundreds of physical qubits. Currently, there have been attempts to develop qubit structures like Topological qubit, Superconducting qubit and Trapped ion having more coherence time and easy scalability.

8.2. Enhancing Post-Quantum Cryptography

Since quantum computers to break RSA and ECC are not currently available, PQC must be implemented even before they become necessary. One of the major areas of focus for the future is to optimize the PQC algorithms at the same time as well as enhance its compatibility to be implemented on multiple platforms ranging from cloud servers to even low power IoT devices. Most of the post-quantum schemes have large key sizes and signature lengths that are practically infeasible to implement in networks with bandwidth and/or memory constraints. Research is thus directed toward improving algorithms so as to achieve the desired objectives without incurring much computation cost. These are efforts towards improving compact lattice-based schemes, better code-based encryption implementation, and strong multivariate and hash-based cryptography. One of the other important areas is the standardization of PQC algorithms which is being carried out by NIST and other organizations.

8.3. Quantum-Safe Communication Networks

The two major approaches are improving the cryptographic algorithms and the development and establishment of quantum-safe communication networks. These networks have to be adaptive to the current trends in cyber threats as well as the ones that are expected to emerge in future due to quantum computing. QKD is one of the most useful methods that can be employed in this field, as it permits two entities to establish a shared secret key by using the principles of quantum mechanics. While post-quantum cryptography depends on difficult mathematical problems that may become solvable with the help of quantum computers, QKD provides information-theoretic security, meaning that it is secure by definition and does not rely on the fact that some mathematical problem is difficult to solve. While QKD has been proven over fiber-optic links and even with satellite links, there are certain technical & practical issues that need to be solved before large-scale implementation. These are limited transmission distance, the problem with real-world noise, and the need for specific quantum hardware. Future work is devoted to the solutions of these challenges with the help of quantum repeaters, photonic integrated circuits, and scalable quantum networks.

9. CONCLUSION

Quantum computing is an innovative technology revolution that has potential to change the world when it comes to digital security. Classical cryptographic systems especially the public-key algorithms including RSA, ECC, & Diffie-Hellman are inherently weak to quantum algorithms like Shor's since the latter can solve the hard mathematical problems on which the former relies for security. Even symmetric-key cryptography, while more resilient, faces reduced security margins due to Grover's algorithm. Due to these threats, the field of cryptography is in the process of experiencing a shift that is much needed and long overdue. Thus, PQC is a possible way to resolve this issue, using mathematical problems that cannot be solved by using quantum computers, for example, lattice-based, code-based, & multivariate polynomial cryptosystems. At the same time, QKD and quantum-safe communication networks offer physics-based counterparts to ensure the protection of information. As described, the development of cryptographic security is going to be based on the three-pronged approach of algorithmic development, infrastructure adjustment, and careful incorporation of quantum technologies. The time to act is now. It is therefore important to have a comprehensive framework of a roadmap to a quantum future involving the academia, the industry and governmental organizations. Such as of NIST, the standardization initiatives must be encouraged and implemented across the market. It is high time that organizations started migrating to quantum-safe cryptography when employing hybrids, as well as cryptographic flexibility where possible. Also, safe investments in quantum technology, protection, and policymaking are essential for succeeding in quantum technologies. Quantum-safe security is not a simple technological advancement but an evolution of security in the digital world. Adopting a proactive approach in planning for the future, international collaboration, and embracing new technologies will help to guarantee the stability of the cryptographic systems as it advances with the quantum systems.

Quantum computing is on the doorsteps; the readiness now will decide the security in the following day.

REFERENCES

Babu, A. A., Jebamalar, G. B., Kumar, P., & Nalini, M. (2024, December). Blockchain Technology: Evolution and Future Prospects. In *2024 International Conference on Sustainable Communication Networks and Application (ICSCNA)* (pp. 381-387). IEEE. DOI: 10.1109/ICSCNA63714.2024.10864089

Chauhan, S., Srivastava, S., Singh, R., Sharma, A., & Ojha, D. B. (2024). Quantum Cryptography: Reviewing Post-Quantum Cryptography. In *Applications and Principles of Quantum Computing* (pp. 378-398). IGI Global Scientific Publishing.

Gayathri, M., Karthik, P. C., Sandhia, G. K., Thilagavathy, R., & Pushpalatha, M. (2024). Quantum Computing Principles: Harnessing the Potential of Quantum Mechanics. In *Applications and Principles of Quantum Computing* (pp. 81-94). IGI Global Scientific Publishing.

Kumar, A., & Garhwal, S. (2021). State-of-the-art survey of quantum cryptography. *Archives of Computational Methods in Engineering*, *28*(5), 3831–3868. DOI: 10.1007/s11831-021-09561-2

Kumar, S., Gaur, M. S., Sharma, P. S., & Munjal, D. (2021, April). A novel approach of symmetric key cryptography. In *2021 2nd international conference on intelligent engineering and management (ICIEM)* (pp. 593-598). IEEE. DOI: 10.1109/ICIEM51511.2021.9445343

Lydia, A., Sivakumar, S., Yamini, B., & Karthikeyan, M. (2024, November). Optimizing Feature Selection for Big Data and Machine Learning: Challenges and Future Prospects. In *2024 International Conference on Smart Technologies for Sustainable Development Goals (ICSTSDG)* (pp. 1-7). IEEE. DOI: 10.1109/ICSTSDG61998.2024.11026070

Prabhu, D., Sudha, L., MR, P. K., Adaikkammai, A., Aparna, P., & Sathya, V. (2025). Machine Learning in Cybersecurity: Challenges, Applications, and Future Directions. *Exploiting Machine Learning for Robust Security*, 25-48.

Ravindran, D., Revathi, S., Sowndharya, V., Farzhana, I., Sathya, V., Girija, P., & Subramanian, S. (2025). Unraveling the Quantum Computing Frontier: Advancements, Challenges, and Future Prospects. *Integration of AI, Quantum Computing, and Semiconductor Technology*, 139-158.

Sathya, U., Hashini, S., Lakshmipriya, C., Varun, C. M., & Nalini, M. (2024, December). Emerging Trends and Future Prospects in Internet of Things (IoT) Technology. In *2024 International Conference on Sustainable Communication Networks and Application (ICSCNA)* (pp. 79-85). IEEE.

Subramani, S., & Svn, S. K. (2025). Review of security methods based on classical cryptography and quantum cryptography. *Cybernetics and Systems*, *56*(3), 302–320. DOI: 10.1080/01969722.2023.2166261

Sundararajan, A. D. D., & Rajashree, R. (2022). A comprehensive survey on light-weight asymmetric key cryptographic algorithm for resource constrained devices. *ECS Transactions*, *107*(1), 7457–7468. DOI: 10.1149/10701.7457ecst

Wong, D. (2021). *Real-world cryptography*. Simon and Schuster.

Yamini, B., May, P. M. A., Shobana, R., TP, A., & Nalini, M. (2024, December). Cybersecurity: Strategies, Sector-Specific Challenges, and Future Prospects. In *2024 4th International Conference on Ubiquitous Computing and Intelligent Information Systems (ICUIS)* (pp. 1338-1345). IEEE.

Yamini, B., Nithyanandhan, R., Sudha, K., Nithya, T., Vijayakumar, K., & Subramanian, R. S. (2024, April). Maximizing the Revolutionary Potential of Quantum Computing: Challenges, Opportunities, and Future Directions. In *2024 10th International Conference on Communication and Signal Processing (ICCSP)* (pp. 756-761). IEEE.

Chapter 6
Quantum Network Attacks in Urban IoT Infrastructures

Rajesh Kanna Rajendran
https://orcid.org/0000-0001-7228-5031
Christ University, Bangalore, India

ABSTRACT

With urban spaces increasingly networked via the internet of things (IoT), the advent of quantum computing brings with it both potential and major security threats. Quantum network attacks are a serious risk to urban IoT systems by targeting weaknesses in conventional cryptographic protocols. In contrast to classical cyber threats, quantum-powered attacks can decrypt commonly used encryption schemes, leaving vital smart city networks, such as traffic management systems, power grids, and public surveillance, vulnerable. The emergent nature of quantum computing calls for an active response to securing urban IoT systems from prospective vulnerabilities that can impair critical services and undermine public security. The inherent complexity of urban IoT infrastructures renders them extremely susceptible to quantum-based cyberattacks. Quantum decryption, man-in-the-middle attacks, and quantum-boosted malware pose risks that can expose sensitive information and facilitate large-scale cyber intrusions.

INTRODUCTION

As dynamic cities transform into advanced smart urban ecosystems, the widespread role of Internet of Things (IoT) devices has become essential to their daily functioning. From intelligent traffic management systems to complex surveillance

DOI: 10.4018/979-8-3373-3166-9.ch006

networks, from interconnected household appliances to innovative healthcare platforms, these IoT components create an intricate web of connectivity that supports real time monitoring, seamless information exchange, and efficient automation.

Although traditional cybersecurity threats remain a pressing concern, the emergence of quantum computing introduces a new and unprecedented challenge. The immense computational power of quantum systems has the potential to undermine the encryption mechanisms that currently secure urban IoT infrastructures. If left unaddressed, this quantum era risk could destabilize the very foundations of modern smart cities, exposing critical services and sensitive citizen data to vulnerabilities on an unparalleled scale.

Quantum computing is a structural threat to the cryptography of the ultramodern smart- megacity systems. City IoT (Internet of Things) systems are billions of sensors, actuators and controllers connected by standard encryption (e.g. RSA, ECC, AES) to ensure data security and device verification. Stunning quantum algorithms such as Shor's and Grover's (search) can break these schemes with the development of quantum hardware, however. The algorithm provided by Shor would be useful to decrypt key exchanges based on RSA/ECC, and the algorithm presented by Grover would decrease on the minimal strength that a symmetric key is by half, enabling attackers to after decode or impersonate IoT transmissions significantly faster than conventional attackers (Liu, Ramachandran, & Jurdak, 2024; Baseri, Chouhan, & Ghorbani, 2024). In all practical sense, a quantum-enabled attacker could today intercept and capture encrypted city-scale IoT traffic and will be able to decrypt it at some point in the future when quantum computers had become ubiquitous (Stoudenmire & Waintal, 2024; GSM Association, 2024). This jeopardizes confidentiality, integrity or availability of valuable services.

The urban IoT infrastructures are especially vulnerable to these quantum threats. They operate billions of resource-dificient devices (it is estimated that there are ~27 billion IoT devices installed in 2025), and they are not installed with much security consideration. Many of these sensors and actuators are low-power low-cost nodes that trade off battery life and range against high-quality cryptography (Liu, Ramachandran, & Jurdak, 2024). They come with lightweight protocols (Zigbee, LoRaWAN, NB-IoT) and long- lifetime non-upgradable hardware. The gateways and backbones rely on the old ECC-based TLS certificates that may be compromised by quantum computers. The diversity and scale of smart-city IoT also creates a high attack surface: the attacker can also choose between a variety of unprotected gateways, vulnerable wireless connections, or even an individual device and exploit it to infiltrate many systems. As an example, a hacker who has access to the communication key of a car will be able to pretend to be a traffic light or a road sensor and create an accident or traffic jam. In case power grids are decrypted using IoT sensors, then attackers can spoof results or put them out of commission. A single breach in a quantum-capable domain can be transferred to other domains because smart-city platforms are connected to each other. As it has recently been reported, quantum attackers can steal financial transactions, spoof digital signatures or hijack vital infrastructure that was considered to be secure (Baseri, Chouhan, & Ghorbani, 2024).

Although quantum computing is considered to be the logical extension of cloud computing, its primacy in several aspects, such as how it behaves within the context of wireless networks, how it implies its geographical zones, and how it is vulnerable to the physical space has new security and digital forensics challenges. Most of these emerging threats are still unaddressed by existing cloud security paradigms. The quantum services have a tendency to be designed based on the needs of the users and performance goals, and security is usually perceived rather as an afterthought than a central concern.

This fact is what makes it obligatory to investigate the specific security threats that quantum computing provides with the implemented in IoT systems. Among the major threats are unauthorized access to data, eavesdropping of communication, intrusion into sensitive information and cryptographic protocols. Quantum attacks can also be used to exploit the building level weaknesses of classical computing systems when they occur. Nevertheless, no systematic study has fully identified and categorized the privacy and security concerns that quantum computing may pose especially in the context of IoT. The studies on these risks remain in an infantile phase and are a dynamic subject of debates among scholars. Since quantum computing is rooted in the same architecture and principles as cloud computing, many of the same security and privacy threats will probably be brought across, paired with novel threats of the quantum technology in general. Since certain of these threats can be reduced through suitable protection, the nature of quantum computing and the new issues it brings creates a need to be innovative in finding solutions and to continuously research the field.

Despite the challenges it presents, quantum computing also holds remarkable potential to strengthen Internet of Things (IoT) networks. Its powerful computational capacity can support the complex calculations and optimization tasks required for advancing IoT functionalities. By enabling faster data processing and deeper analytical insights, quantum systems create opportunities for more intelligent and adaptive network operations.

Quantum technology offers more than just extraordinary computing power; it also introduces groundbreaking advancements in cybersecurity and privacy. One such innovation is quantum encryption, which provides an unparalleled level of protection for digital communications. Any attempt to intercept or tamper with the data immediately disrupts the fragile quantum state, alerting stakeholders to a potential intrusion. A related development is Quantum Key Distribution, or QKD, which uses the inherent properties of quantum mechanics to generate encryption keys that are exceptionally difficult to intercept or decipher. Unlike traditional key exchange methods, QKD relies on the natural randomness of quantum states, so that if an unauthorized party tries to access a key, the system immediately signals the breach.

By pushing the boundaries of conventional encryption, QKD greatly enhances the security of urban IoT networks. It provides strong safeguards not only against everyday cyber threats but also against the advanced attacks made possible by future quantum computing. As cities adopt increasingly interconnected smart systems, these quantum-secure measures will play a vital role in keeping critical infrastructure reliable, resilient, and protected in the era of quantum-enabled technologies.

This discussion highlights the reality that quantum-powered attacks may directly target urban IoT networks. To prepare for such scenarios, cities must adopt quantum safe technologies. The following sections will examine quantum algorithms that threaten classical cryptographic methods and explore strategies to reinforce the resilience of smart urban infrastructures. Also we talk about the likely vectors of attack in IoT, amount of decryption of tapped data, amount of accelerated phony, and quantum-enhanced malware. To make the trouble visible, we dissect concrete civic situations(e.g., smart grids). Eventually, we bandy defenses post-quantum cryptography(chassis- grounded, NIST- formalized hash- grounded) to cover the IoT, amount crucial distribution(QKD) to cover the IoT, and issues with perpetration(resource constraints, interoperability), and policy. By being apprehensive of these issues and enforcing quantum-resistant results, smart metropolises can ensure their IoT structure against the imminent amount period.

RELATED WORK

The most significant examination of the existing literature raises that the modern security concerns and problems within the specified area generally fall within the framework of such categories as privacy, trust, authentication, threats and attacks, security auditing, and access control. Other related security risks in the surrounding areas such as edge computing and cloud computing are also discussed and are closely related to the bigger picture of quantum computing. To conduct a comprehensive and reliable survey on this study, we accessed a few research databases and key-searching various sources in various search engines where quantum and cloud security met, with particular focus being made on the area of intersection.

Given that the users are largely concerned with ensuring the privacy of their information (Liu, Ramachandran, & Jurdak, 2024), safeguarding of the personal information has become a major subject of concern in quantum computing. The sources of data that are being manipulated in a amount setting are frequently miscellaneous, e.g. wireless networks, IoT bias, and shadows. The preservation of strong privacy remains a central security concern in the era of quantum technologies. In 2020, researchers proposed a distributed algorithm designed to analyze data on IoT devices with quantum characteristics. By combining distributed architectures with advanced homomorphic encryption techniques, Zhao's approach demonstrated a major opportunity to safeguard the confidentiality of sensitive information processed at the edge. However, the rapid expansion of vehicular cloud computing also introduces new security risks that require immediate attention in this critical technological domain.

The landscape of quantum computing presents formidable challenges to traditional cryptographic practices. For example, Shor's algorithm can efficiently factor large integers, posing a direct threat to the fundamental security of widely used public key cryptographic systems such as RSA and ECC. Similarly, Grover's algorithm significantly accelerates brute force search, reducing the effectiveness of symmetric key encryption methods. Baseri and colleagues (2024) emphasize that these advances underscore the urgent need to develop cryptographic strategies capable of resisting the risks inherent to the quantum era.

Modern communal surroundings parade a profound reliance on complex ecosystems of IoT bias and systems, thereby exposing unknown cybersecurity vulnerabilities. The connection of integrated endpoints expands the compass for implicit security vulnerabilities, consequently subordinating critical infrastructures to a varied spectrum of risks, including zero- day vulnerabilities. Seyhan et al.(2021) (8) specifically illuminate the unique security demands of IoT- laden surroundings, where the focus shifts to robust and adaptive cryptography to bolster the security of bias that constantly retain limited processing and storage resources. To effectively palliate the forenamed arising risks, there has been a significant escalation in academic trials aimed at constructing cryptographic fabrics that parade rigidity against quantum adversities. In the realm ofpost- amount cryptography, the ideal is to develop algorithms that can repel assaults from quantum computational agents. A thorough examination of various quantum- resistant approaches, including lattice- predicated, law- predicated, and hash- predicated methodologies, is articulated by Cherkaoui Dekkaki et al.(2024)(9), accompanied by a relative assessment of their connection across different practical scripts. nonetheless, the execution of this distinguished assemblage of algorithms on compact, energy-effective, and resource- constrained Internet of goods(IoT) bias, which personalize smart cosmopolises, presents a significant technical chain.

The admixture of machine literacy with the extensive sphere of artificial intelligence(AI) is precipitously being exercised to enhance cybersecurity methodologies acclimatized to defy arising pitfalls, particularly zero- day vulnerabilities. AI- driven systems for anomaly discovery retain the capability to pinpoint unusual patterns that may spark unauthorized irruptions. The integration of amount computing and artificial intelligence is anticipated to reveal unknown openings for advanced security fabrics. still, the application of amount computing within AI- centric cybersecurity remains an embryonic field of study that requires expansive disquisition to completely understand its implicit and limitations in real- world scripts.

The stability and credibility of the structures within smart megacity geographies are presently being assessed through the lens of decentralized advancements, generally including blockchain. The relinquishment of blockchain for secure data running can significantly bolster trust in the services handed within smart metropolises. As noted by Zehang(2024)(10), thepost-quantum blockchain frame possesses the capability to repel amount- enabled attacks, which may prove necessary in securing smart civic operations. still, there continue to be open questions about scalability and the possibility of achieving immediate performance in similar decentralized systems, which are presently under scrutiny.

Modern perspectives on urban planning centered on sustainability highlight the intersection of social goals, environmental priorities, and technological innovation. Increasing attention has been devoted to exploring smart city initiatives as a pathway for enabling sustainable transformations within communities. The discussion has expanded beyond the role of technology alone to include its broader implications for promoting equity, resilience, and inclusiveness in urban environments.This approach involves leveraging data analytics to guide policy decisions, improve resource efficiency, and enhance the delivery of public services. One notable trend is the design of comprehensive strategies that integrate green infrastructure with intelligent technologies to produce synergistic outcomes. For example, IoT sensors can be deployed to manage water flow in public green spaces, helping conserve resources while mitigating flood risks. Such integrated strategies are increasingly vital in addressing complex and interconnected challenges, including climate change and rapid urban growth. By combining sustainability with digital innovation, cities can move toward futures that are not only smarter but also more equitable and environmentally responsible.

In recent times, cybersecurity has evolved into an essential element of smart municipality enterprise, primarily as a response to the new challenges posed by Quantum calculating technologies. Information security within smart megacity IoT systems will calculate on the cryptography protocols, which will face attacks by unborn quantum computers(14). Thus, the new literature and industry activity is focused on the implementation and development of post-quantum cryptography (PQC). Among the trends, it is possible to highlight the integration of a hybrid solution, according to which smart cities are going to apply both existing and PQC standards at the same time to achieve a safe and smooth transition (Al-Hajy & Al-Hajy, 2024).

A real life script of this is the collaboration of a smart structure platform with a post-quantum cryptography establishment that will cover important megacity structure with quantum-resistant encryption (Ye, Wu, Lemke, Valera, & Sackey, 2022). This is a security change that isn't just the protection against some unborn trouble that isn't yet real but is also about making the crucial architectures flexible in the long run, including the transport systems and the power systems (Esin, Usov, & Esin, 2023). also, experimenters are looking into how quantum machine learning (QML) can accelerate the security of smart metropolises to ameliorate trouble discovery and drop the response time, which is also a binary operation of amount technology as a trouble and an implicit result (Staddon, Loscri, & Mitton, 2021).

INTERNET OF THINGS (IoT)

With the rapid expansion of digital connectivity, more and more devices are joining the global network, transforming the way we communicate and interact with technology. From consumer electronics and home appliances to industrial machinery and vehicles, the growing presence of IoT devices is reshaping industries and everyday life. These technologies allow sectors such as agriculture, healthcare, and defense to enhance their operations through intelligent and autonomous systems. The rapid deployment of IoT devices has transformed the way data is collected, shared, and used, driving greater efficiency and improving quality of life. Devices such as remote weather sensors, networked medical equipment like pacemakers, and battlefield monitoring systems demonstrate how IoT enables real-time data collection and communication. These smart devices support critical operations across healthcare, agriculture, defense, and urban management, allowing for more informed, responsive, and effective decision-making.

At the same time, the widespread deployment of IoT devices brings notable challenges that affect both performance and security. Many devices, particularly those installed in remote or hard-to-access locations, rely on battery power, making energy a scarce and valuable resource. Core functions, such as wireless communication, continue to demand significant power, which can limit processing capabilities and reduce the frequency and effectiveness of device interactions. These limitations may compromise the overall reliability, responsiveness, and efficiency of IoT systems, underscoring the importance of implementing robust strategies to maintain both operational performance and cybersecurity across large-scale IoT networks.

BENEFITS OF QUANTUM COMPUTING FOR IOT SECURITY

While quantum computing brings new security challenges, it also opens up unprecedented opportunities to enhance the protection of IoT systems in smart environments.

1. Quantum Cryptography Quantum cryptography, especially Quantum Key Distribution (QKD), establishes a communication system that is naturally secure, leveraging the fundamental principles of quantum mechanics. QKD enables two parties to create encryption keys in a way that instantly exposes any attempt at eavesdropping, offering a level of protection that traditional cryptographic methods cannot match.
2. Advanced Threat Detection The exceptional processing power of quantum systems can be harnessed to run sophisticated anomaly detection algorithms efficiently. This allows IoT networks to monitor complex structures, identify irregular activities in real time, and intervene to neutralize potential cyber threats before they develop into serious security breaches.
3. Enhanced Encryption Algorithms Post-quantum cryptography (PQC) is being actively developed to defend against attacks from quantum computers. By implementing these next-generation algorithms, IoT networks can ensure that sensitive data remains secure and intact, even as quantum computing capabilities continue to advance.

MITIGATION STRATEGIES FOR IoT SECURITY IN THE QUANTUM ERA

1. Implementing Post-Quantum Cryptography IoT devices should transition to cryptographic algorithms designed to resist quantum attacks, such as lattice-based and hash-based schemes. This ensures long-term protection for connected systems as quantum technologies become more prevalent.
2. Integrating Quantum Key Distribution Adding QKD to IoT communication frameworks strengthens the security of key exchanges, significantly lowering the risk that quantum-enabled attackers could intercept or manipulate sensitive information.
3. Modernizing IoT Architecture IoT devices should be designed with the capability to update both firmware and hardware, allowing the adoption of new security measures seamlessly as technology evolves.
4. Regulatory and Compliance Measures Governments and regulatory organizations should establish clear guidelines and enforce compliance to ensure that

quantum-resistant cryptographic standards are consistently applied across all IoT systems.

QUANTUM COMPUTING: A THREAT OF A NEW KIND

The principles of quantum superposition and entanglement quantum computers are based on quantum bits (qubits) to perform computations that are computationally intractable on a regular computer. An example of Shor algorithm is capable of factory-exponentially faster than traditional algorithms in traditional computing, rendering traditional asymmetric cryptography ineffective.

In the case of IoT infrastructures in cities, it means:

- Authentication and key exchange based on public-key cryptography can be compromised.
- Privacy of data transmission is jeopardized.

Those that are not easily updatable Other long-lasting IoT devices are especially susceptible.

The encrypted information of this day can be decrypted in the future when convenient quantum computers are built process known as harvest-now-decrypt-later.

URBAN IoT AND CRYPTOGRAPHIC RELIANCE

The contemporary intelligent cities rely on massive IoT systems that act to gather and share data in real-time. They can be sensor networks used to track traffic, environmental, utility, public safety, and other useful information. Components of IoT (each of them called a node) are typically connected wirelessly to a gateway or cloud service. Under a conventional IoT design, resource-constrained devices get connected to the Internet through a gateway (through protocols such as Zigbee, LoRaWAN, NB-IoT). These links are frequently being symmetrically encrypted (e.g., AES-128) and employ pre-shared keys due to efficiency. In addition to gateways, device-to-cloud connectivity is based on standard Internet protocols (MQTT, HTTP), encrypted by TLS, with public-key crypto (RSA/ECC) in the transport layer.

The security mechanisms should be minimal due to the limitations of the IoT devices (limited in terms of CPU, memory and power). In many cases, keys or certificates are pre-installed by manufacturers in order to authenticate devices on deployment (GSM Association, 2024). The density of similar equipment in cities increases the risk: an attacker who is physically close to a wireless IoT device can also make eavesdropping or replaying attempts in case the traffic is not encrypted. Weak gateway implementations or old firmware are vulnerabilities. As an example, all devices in LoRaWAN have shared 128-bit keys of AES which, when found, would decrypt whole sensor fleets. According to surveys conducted before, deployments of IoT focus on cost and battery life more than security - e.g., the priorities of production cost, size, and battery life are over security of lightweight devices of low end. Years of underinvestment in IoT security by history implies that most endpoints of smart-city are not ready to face a quantum future.

Nonetheless, IoT networks are dealing with very delicate functions. Consider a hacker with counterfeit control messages to a traffic management system, or data with counterfeited air-quality sensors to force a fake emergency to occur. When the cryptographic keys are compromised, an attacker may impersonate the emergency services or disable the substation controls. The real-time and mission critical nature of these networks (traffic lights, power restoration, medical monitoring) is such that an effective intrusion might be disastrous. New city systems are not always as redundant and patch-reactive as traditional IT; once a node is compromised, it may not be fixed at all. The scale, heterogeneity and long device lifecycles of urban IoT render it one of the ideal targets of quantum-enabled attacks.

QUANTUM ALGORITHMS AND CRYPTOGRAPHIC VULNERABILITIES

Quantum computing presents algorithms capable of fatally undermining or cracking classical encryption:

Shor, Algorithm (1994): Shor has an algorithm that with a sufficiently large quantum computer, efficiently factors large integers, and solves discrete logarithms. This is a violation of RSA, DiffieHellman (DH), and elliptic-curve cryptography (ECC) which are based on such complex problems (Baseri, Chouhan, & Ghorbani, 2024). A quantum computer with the Shor algorithm would be able to extract the private keys in a public key traffic which is intercepted. As an example, it might be able to obtain the private key of an RSA modulus in polynomial time, even though currently it is not possible to make such moduli to factor. This endangers all PKI systems (public key infrastructure), the majority of which are key exchanges and certificates in the IoT. RSA and ECC, which have traditionally ensured integrity of data, are now at risk, as one of the reviews describes, by quantum factoring, like never achieved previously.

Grover (1996): Grover has an algorithm that offers quadratic speed increase in unstructured search. In the case of brute-force key search, this reduces the length of the key of symmetric ciphers. In a more concrete sense, Grover works to solve an order 2^64 quantum operation problem of finding a 128-bit key.

Consequently, in order to sustain 128-bit security against a Grover-capable adversary, one has to increase the size of symmetric keys (to 256 bits). That too, is a band-aid: ultimate symmetrical security is undermined. The Grover algorithm by Grover optimizes brute-force searching, which compromises the security of symmetric-key encryption by a factor of two. In the case of IoT, it would imply that AES-128 or even AES-256 may be at the mercy of quantum attacks eventually without taking quantum attacks into consideration.

Other Quantum Tools: In addition to Shor and Grover, quantum computing is able to accelerate optimization and search. Hypothetical attacks based on quantum machine learning or quantum walk algorithms can be used, which may e.g. discover vulnerabilities in hash functions or protocol implementations more effectively. A quantum attacker might also be able to do harvest now, decrypt later (store encrypted data now, decrypt with a future quantum computer) or accelerate mathematical operations in multi-party protocols and in practice some side-channel or algorithmic attacks are faster.

The net effect is that, every traditional public key cryptography employed in IoT is vulnerable. A recent analysis has reported the summary that under quantum attack, cryptographic attacks would have the potential to compromise widely deployed cryptographic algorithms like RSA, Diffie Hellman, or elliptic curve cryptography. The attacker may then carry out data interception and decryption at the fly exposing sensor data and control signals. Besides, it would not require many efforts to produce a forgery of digital signatures (e.g., in firmware updates or command authentication) that would be easily spoofed as a legitimate owner (Lins & de Oliveira, 2024). There might be retroactive modifications of financial records or logs or the decryption of financial records, making it easy to commit fraud. With the availability of large-scale quantum computers, the cryptography in the IoT that is used today may become irrelevant in most cases.

Whether the practical quantum breakthroughs will be made soon is unpredictable, but industry projections tell that even most existing cryptosystems may be cracked in a decade (Al-Sharif & Salama, 2021). Thus, the government and standards organizations (e.g. NIST) take a comparatively close threat horizon. In the case of smart cities, it is only prudent to consider quantum risk as an existent planning factor as city infrastructure has a lifespan of decades and often operates using technology that is backward compatible.

INTEGRATING SUSTAINABILITY AND GOVERNANCE

Ultramodern collaborative urban planning is emerging as a response to challenges that extend beyond the traditional focus on physical infrastructure. This new approach emphasizes a more integrated and holistic perspective, where sustainability, governance, equity, and long-term implementation play central roles.

Urban sustainability today goes beyond simply constructing energy-efficient buildings; it encompasses environmental, economic, and social dimensions that collectively define the long-term vitality of cities. Modern urban development calls for inclusive, innovative communities that foster diverse economic opportunities while promoting well-being for all residents. True sustainability is reflected in initiatives such as green building practices, efficient resource management, and circular economy strategies, all designed to create resilient and thriving urban environments.

Tackling these challenges requires collaborative governance, where governments, businesses, and citizens work together to develop shared and informed solutions. This approach shifts urban planning away from rigid, top-down models toward participatory frameworks that empower communities to actively influence the future of their cities. Smart city technologies serve as a vital enabler in this process, enhancing public services, improving transparency, and optimizing the use of collective resources to build more responsive and sustainable urban ecosystems.

QUANTUM NETWORK ATTACK VECTORS IN IoT

Quantum-powered adversaries have the potential to exploit IoT networks in ways that go far beyond conventional attacks. Some of the most significant threat vectors include:

QUANTUM DECRYPTION OF INTERCEPTED TRAFFIC

A major concern is the "store now, decrypt later" approach. Adversaries can capture and store IoT communications in real time and later decrypt them once they have access to sufficiently powerful quantum computers. For example, sensitive data from smart meters or medical IoT devices could be intercepted and stored until quantum decryption is feasible. Experts at GSMA warn that this approach enables attackers to compromise the confidentiality of critical IoT data, highlighting the urgent need for quantum-resistant security measures.

QUANTUM-ENABLED MAN-IN-THE-MIDDLE ATTACKS

More proactive attacks could involve real-time interception and manipulation of IoT communications. Using broken encryption, an attacker could position themselves between devices and servers, decrypt messages, alter them, and re-encrypt them without detection by exploiting asymmetric key agreements with Shor's Algorithm. For instance, an attacker could spoof control commands to smart streetlights or inject false data into city-wide sensors. Experiments on smart-grid IoT networks have shown that post-quantum cryptography significantly reduces the risks posed by such attacks compared to classical RSA or AES encryption.

QUANTUM-ACCELERATED BRUTE-FORCE ATTACKS

Even symmetric key cryptography is vulnerable to quantum acceleration through Grover's Algorithm. For example, a 128-bit AES key that would require classical exhaustive search is reduced to roughly 2^64 operations with a quantum-assisted attack. While this can be mitigated by increasing key sizes, it demonstrates that otherwise secure systems could be compromised in a large-scale urban IoT deployment. In a smart city, cameras or sensors relying on symmetric keys could face significantly reduced security margins against quantum-enabled adversaries.

QUANTUM-ENHANCED MALWARE AND ZERO-DAY EXPLOITS

Beyond cryptography, quantum computing could enable novel forms of malware. Quantum-assisted artificial intelligence could allow attackers to develop stealthy or polymorphic malware capable of bypassing existing detection systems. Quantum machine learning algorithms could automatically identify zero-day vulnerabilities across IoT endpoints. In practice, a malicious actor might intercept firmware updates or keys, rewrite IoT programs over the air, or exploit quantum random number generators to break security mechanisms. Although fully functional quantum malware remains largely theoretical, the potential for advanced attacks underscores the need for proactive quantum-resilient strategies in urban IoT networks.

CYBER-PHYSICAL SYSTEM

A Cyber-Physical System (CPS) is a system of physical and computational logic and control and is a system that fuses the physical and digital worlds. These systems find application in numerous areas, and comprise a combination of designed hardware and intelligent software to control and robotize real assignments. An example would be the areas of healthcare where CPS technology is applied in elderly care at homes or monitoring patients at the intensive care units.

Explicitly, since CPS devices communicate with sensors and actuators, they may be susceptible to attacks that disrupt their physical devices. The fact that compromising of these factors may have a critical outcome, and it is essential to find and mitigate such threats promptly. The most famous one is a cyber attack that was directed to industrial control equipment, causing physical harm through the manipulation of automated processes. Distortion of data sent and received between sensors and actuators can result in misleading measurements and subsequent decision making based on misleading information submitted by the systems.

Another related idea is the Networked Control System (NCS) frequently found in critical infrastructure. These systems are based on communication networks to interrelate different distributed parts e.g. sensors and the controllers to coordinate as a single system. Although this networking offers ease and effectiveness, there is also a risk of security breach. NCSs attacks can be broadly classified into two categories, namely, physical device attacks and attacks that leverage the communication network.

This difference can be used to explain whether an attack is attempting to cause havoc to one device or disrupt the communication of the whole network. But practically some attacks cross this line. An example of this is hacking into a sensor, which may include tampering with the sensor by physically altering the sensor to produce fake data or intercepting sensor communications through the network to confuse the system. An example of an NCS attack was an attack on the water management system through a wireless connection, and thus led to the release of untreated wastewater to the environment.

SIDE-CHANNEL ATTACKS ON QUANTUM COMPUTERS

Although these are not strictly speaking network attacks, side-channel and physical attacks become even more powerful during the quantum era. An example of such physical access threats is breaking the cryptography in the response of a physically probed hardware security module, or timing analysis with quantum Fourier transforms IoT increases vulnerabilities to such physical access attacks because of the high volume of widespread often unmonitored devices. These vectors demonstrate how quantum adversaries can potentially attack in urban IoT any connection that is encrypted using classical cryptography. The exposure of critical systems is extremely large: quantum-assisted MitM of emergency services radios or sensor network of a nuclear plant would lead to loss of life even if a quantum attack occurs in a few years, therefore a quantum-assisted MitM of emergency services radios or sensor network in a nuclear power plant should be secured today. The subsequent violation may weaken the safety and confidence of the population.

VULNERABILITIES OF URBAN IOT NETWORKS

Scale and Diversity: Smart cities consist of millions of heterogeneous devices of various vendors. Not every system is supporting over-the-air updates or strong crypto. Devices in most instances go through decades long life cycles with little or no security patching. A quantum adversary could use any one of the weak nodes to compromise the larger systems. The city has its many gates public Wi-Fi, cellular Io-T, utility networks, all have entry points.

Resource Constraints: The hardware that serves as the IoT endpoint is usually memory and CPU-constrained. Combining heavy post-quantum schemes is not straightforward. A survey notes that, post-quantum encryption and signature schemes are computationally expensive and this may be an issue with IoT, and the computational cost of cryptography can be expensive and may be a burden to IoT resource-constrained node device. Although PQC might be theoretically secure, performance in practice might not allow its application on small sensors. This presents a dilemma, in that, without PQC, these devices will be insecure, and uninformed use of PQC will drown them.

Legacy Systems: Most city systems were constructed prior to the realization of quantum threats. The legacy traffic management networks or older SCADA systems do not encrypt or make use of fixed symmetric keys. That is because these systems can hardly replace their algorithms with quantum-safe algorithms without redesign or hardware modifications. IoT devices are sometimes not upgradeable (e.g. sealed sensor nodes). This means that there can be large installations of brownfields within cities that are practically permanently exposed.

Data Confidentiality Requirements: Urban IoT can be a bearer of personal or strategic data. Quantum attacks threaten privacy of users and popular trust. Provided citizens find out that a future quantum enemy will be able to decrypt the smart meters or cameras, adoption of new city services can be slowed down. Further, the information such as personal location or identity should not be disclosed during the whole useful stage. According to GSMA, one of the considerations taken is the lifecycle of communicated data, in case the data is valuable long enough, it could be harvested and decrypted later (GSM Association, 2024). The appearance of various IoT data types belongs to this group. the nature of urban IoT huge scale, uneven security stances, limited resources enhances the quantum threat. Any smart city security planning should presuppose that traditional cryptography will be cracked in the future, and that any enemies may be already sniffing the traffic or scanning the traffic seeking vulnerabilities.

WIRELESS AD-HOC NETWORKS

Wireless ad-hoc networks provide devices to communicate directly with each other unlike in traditional wireless networks where a central network of devices, such as routers or base stations, is used to manage the communication processes. Such devices may also be configured to create a multi-hop network, where several nodes would be used as intermediaries to relay information between the source and the destination. The practical example of small sensor nodes is Wireless Sensor Networks (WSNs) where the sensor devices collect data and then utilize ad-hoc connections to relay the data back to a central collection point by routing the data via Multi-hopping.

Wireless ad-hoc networks find application in a diverse environment due to their flexibility and easy deployment. They can be used to monitor the environment e.g. by detecting forest fires and can be applied in healthcare and smart homes e.g. wearable ECG would monitor the heart activity of a patient. They can also be mobile devices and, by constantly shifting their position and, consequently, the structure of the network, change it. This forms what is referred to as a Mobile Ad-Hoc Network (MANET), and is continually being reconfigured as devices are moved and linked on the fly. This is because it is a complex area of study that is still in the process of being researched.

Due to the number of different routing strategies, the quality of communication between devices can be different in terms of reliability that is why the effect of a cyberattack can be both the small disturbances of the network and the critical breakdown of the network. The typical threats are such as conventional attacks as Denial of Service (DoS), Man-in-the-Middle (MitM), Replay and Jamming. Nonetheless, attacks that are aimed at the routing process per se may be particularly harmful in such dynamic networks. They are referred to as Byzantine Attacks whereby a malicious actor is able to control legitimate nodes and corrupt them to disrupt routing processes.

CASE STUDY: SMART GRID IOT SECURITY

A typical illustration of the civic critical structure with a high IoT involvement(smart measures, grid detectors, distributed energy coffers) is the electric power grid. Both the SCADA networks and detector data are used to manipulate the inflow of electricity in grid operations. We look at the possible ways in which amount attacks may be used to attack a smart grid and the defenses under development.

trouble script Imagine an original grid that has thousands of smart measures and line detectors that report to a central control center. These bias are AES translated and authenticated either by RSA or ECC-grounded instruments. This business is recorded by a bushwhacker. The RSA keys of the grid are also regard in a number of computer in order to decipher all former cadence readings. Using that information, the bushwhacker can determine the cargo patterns and anticipate outages. Worse still, a hacker can tell a detector that he or she's the control center and give him her incorrect instructions to open combers or switch off creators. Since utmost conditioning in the grid are automated, amount breach may lead to wrong balancing of loads, black outs, physical destruction of mills.

To address emerging threats, researchers have proposed robust quantum resistant encryption schemes. For example, Xiong and colleagues developed a Quantum Resistant Hybrid Encryption for IoT (QRHE-IoT) specifically designed for smart grid communications. They evaluated QRHE-IoT across six different IoT device types and compared its performance with AES, RSA, and ECC. During a simulated man-in-the-middle attack, the decryption time and the time required to detect and process data in QRHE-IoT were longer than those for AES or RSA alone. Specifically, Table 3 in their study shows that breaking AES took approximately 0.55 seconds on a given device, while breaking QRHE-IoT, including the post-quantum LWE component required about 0.68 seconds on average per attempt. Implementing quantum-resistant encryption provides defenders with a valuable window of time to detect anomalies and prevent automated quantum attacks. Studies indicate that robust quantum-resistant schemes provide strong protection against emerging quantum-enabled threats, reinforcing the resilience of IoT infrastructures.

QUANTUM KEY DISTRIBUTION IN POWER GRIDS

Another promising approach to securing critical communication links is Quantum Key Distribution, or QKD. In 2022, Alshowkan and colleagues carried out a field trial implementing QKD over an operational fiber network integrated with SCADA communications in a power grid. By using entangled photons, they were able to generate one-time encryption keys between substations and authenticate control commands. This trial marked the first real-world deployment of QKD in a power grid, showing that quantum-secure keys can be reliably exchanged across metropolitan infrastructure. Even if a quantum-capable adversary intercepts the network, the session keys remain inaccessible. However, QKD is most effective in fixed infrastructure setups, such as fiber-connected substations, and is not practical for battery-powered IoT devices.

This smart grid example highlights two important lessons. First, quantum-resistant algorithms can safeguard IoT devices against future quantum attacks, though they may require additional computational resources. Second, protecting critical communication links with quantum-safe channels like QKD enhances resilience against both current and emerging threats. These strategies can be extended to other urban IoT systems, for instance, implementing post-quantum cryptography in traffic management systems or using QKD to secure city-wide surveillance networks. Overall, the case demonstrates that proactive security redesign is both feasible and effective, with field trials providing strong evidence that cities can prepare for the quantum era.

The main strategy for protecting urban IoT networks from quantum-enabled attacks is the adoption of quantum-resistant cryptographic solutions. These solutions generally fall into two key categories: Post-Quantum Cryptography (PQC) and Quantum Key Distribution (QKD).

POST-QUANTUM CRYPTOGRAPHY (PQC)

PQC refers to traditional public-key and symmetric cryptographic algorithms that are designed to withstand attacks from quantum computers. Between 2022 and 2024, NIST standardized a range of PQC methods, including lattice-based schemes like Kyber and Dilithium, hash-based schemes such as SPHINCS, as well as multivariate and code-based approaches. Lattice-based schemes are particularly suitable for IoT applications because they provide strong security while remaining computationally efficient. Tests have shown that Kyber can operate on IoT-class devices within milliseconds. These algorithms rely on complex mathematical problems such as LWE and Ring-LWE, which remain resistant to both quantum and classical attacks, making them a reliable foundation for securing next-generation IoT networks.

However, PQC introduces practical challenges. Keys and signatures are generally larger than those of RSA or ECC, increasing memory and bandwidth requirements. For instance, lattice-based signatures may occupy several kilobytes compared to a few hundred bytes for ECDSA. Computational and energy demands are also higher, particularly for battery-powered or low-bandwidth IoT devices. Researchers are actively optimizing PQC for lightweight implementations, selecting parameters suitable for IoT, and exploring hybrid designs where legacy devices communicate via post-quantum secure gateways.

QUANTUM KEY DISTRIBUTION (QKD)

QKD leverages quantum principles to establish shared encryption keys with information-theoretic security. Unlike PQC, its security is physically guaranteed—any attempt at eavesdropping disrupts the quantum channel and is immediately detectable. This makes QKD highly resistant to quantum-enabled attacks and ideal for securing the most sensitive IoT links. Fiber-based QKD has already been demonstrated to protect SCADA communications in power grids and can secure inter-data-center links, government networks, or high-value city sensor networks. Nonetheless, QKD is best suited for fixed infrastructure rather than battery-powered IoT devices.

CONCLUSION

The convergence of quantum computing with the Internet of Things in smart urban environments marks a defining moment for city cybersecurity. Quantum technologies have the potential to greatly enhance urban intelligence, operational efficiency, and responsiveness. At the same time, they introduce significant risks to the encryption systems that form the backbone of modern digital infrastructures. Quantum enabled threats, including advanced decryption techniques and sophisticated malware, could compromise critical services such as traffic management, energy distribution, emergency response systems, and the protection of personal and sensitive data.

Unlike isolated corporate networks, urban IoT infrastructures are extensive, highly interconnected, and often operate in public spaces. This interconnectedness means that a single security breach can have immediate, visible, and far reaching consequences for the entire community. Addressing these risks requires cybersecurity strategies that go beyond traditional practices, integrating quantum resistant technologies and proactive risk mitigation. Although standards organizations and research communities are actively developing frameworks to counter these threats, the urgency to implement effective, practical, and scalable quantum secure solutions across urban IoT systems continues to grow.

Achieving resilience against quantum era threats demands a comprehensive and collaborative effort. This involves not only investing in next-generation IoT devices but also establishing cross-sector regulatory frameworks and supporting sustained research initiatives. Cities must treat quantum cybersecurity with the same seriousness as other long term infrastructure challenges such as climate resilience or energy security. Preparing in advance through financial investment, capacity building, and the development of adaptive systems will be far more cost effective than responding reactively after a large scale quantum enabled attack occurs.

The future security of metropolitan IoT ecosystems will depend on how effectively planners and policymakers can integrate quantum resistant cryptographic protocols into existing infrastructures. The adaptability of these systems, and the foresight to embed emerging security innovations into everyday urban operations, will determine whether smart cities remain efficient, trusted, and resilient in the face of quantum era cyber threats.

REFERENCES

Al-Hajy, K. B., & Al-Hajy, M. R. (2024). Post-Quantum Blockchain for a Scalable Smart City. *Journal of Internet Technology*, *25*(6), 1171–1181.

Al-Sharif, A., & Salama, M. E. (2021). The Role of 5G Technologies in a Smart City: The Case for Intelligent Transportation System. *Sustainability (Basel)*, *13*(9), 5188. DOI: 10.3390/su13095188

Baseri, Y., Chouhan, V., & Ghorbani, A. (2024). Cybersecurity in the Quantum Era: Assessing the Impact of Quantum Computing on Infrastructure. arXiv:2404.10659.

Dekkaki, K. C., Tasic, I., & Cano, M.-D. (2024, November). Exploring Post-Quantum Cryptography: Review and Directions for the Transition Process. *Technologies*, *12*(12), 241. DOI: 10.3390/technologies12120241

Leyzerova, A., Sharovarova, E., & Sharypova, O. (2016). Sustainable Strategies of Urban Planning. *Procedia Engineering*, *150*, 2055–2061. DOI: 10.1016/j.proeng.2016.07.299

Lins, L. V. G. M., & de Oliveira, D. L. L. S. F. (2024). Integrating City Master Plans with Sustainable and Smart Urban Development: A Systematic Literature Review. *Sustainability (Basel)*, *16*(17), 7692. DOI: 10.3390/su16177692

Liu, T., Ramachandran, G., & Jurdak, R. (2024). Post-Quantum Cryptography for Internet of Things: A Survey on Performance and Optimization. preprint arXiv:2401.17538.

Paul, K., Jyothi, B., Kumar, R., Singh, A., Bajaj, M., Hemanth Kumar, B., & Zaitsev, I. (2025). Optimizing Sustainable Energy Management in Grid Connected Microgrids Using Quantum Particle Swarm Optimization for Cost and Emission Reduction. *Scientific Reports*, *15*(1), 1–20. DOI: 10.1038/s41598-025-90040-0 PMID: 39966570

Seyhan, K., Nguyen, T. N., Akleylek, S., & Cengiz, K. (2021, August). Lattice-based cryptosystems for the security of resource-constrained IoT devices in post-quantum world: A survey. *Cluster Computing*, *25*(3), 1729–1748. DOI: 10.1007/s10586-021-03380-7

Staddon, E., Loscri, V., & Mitton, N. (2021). Attack Categorisation for IoT Applications in Critical Infrastructures, a Survey. *Applied Sciences (Basel, Switzerland)*, *11*(16), 7228. DOI: 10.3390/app11167228

Stoudenmire, E. M., & Waintal, X. (2024, November). Opening the Black Box inside Grover's Algorithm. *Physical Review*, *14*(4).

Xiong, J., Shen, L., Liu, Y., & Fang, X. (2025). Enhancing IoT security in smart grids with quantum-resistant hybrid encryption. *Scientific Reports*, *15*(3), 3. DOI: 10.1038/s41598-024-84427-8 PMID: 39747539

Yang, Z., Shi, Q., Cheng, T., Wang, X., Zhang, R., & Yu, L. (2024). A Security-Enhanced Authentication Scheme for Quantum-Key-Distribution (QKD) Enabled Internet of Vehicles in Multi-Cloud Environment. *Vehicular Communications*, *48*, 100789. DOI: 10.1016/j.vehcom.2024.100789

Ye, X., Wu, L., Lemke, M., Valera, P., & Sackey, J. (2022). Defining Computational Urban Science. In *New Thinking in GIScience*. Springer Nature Singapore. DOI: 10.1007/978-981-19-3816-0_31

Zheng, X. (2024, May). Research on blockchain smart contract technology based on resistance to quantum computing attacks. *PLoS One*, *19*(5), e0302325. DOI: 10.1371/journal.pone.0302325 PMID: 38781187

Chapter 7
Cryptanalysis of Post-Quantum Cryptographic Schemes:
Securing IoT and Smart Cities in the Quantum Era

Veda Chatiyode
https://orcid.org/0009-0000-1118-9839
Amrita Vishwa Vidyapeetham, India

Baghavathi Priya S.
https://orcid.org/0000-0001-9168-7810
Amrita Vishwa Vidyapeetham, India

ABSTRACT

As quantum computing advances, the security of traditional cryptographic systems faces unprecedented risks, leading to the rise of post quantum cryptography (PQC). This chapter examines how cryptanalysis continues to expose weaknesses in these emerging schemes, with particular attention to the growing role of artificial intelligence. Machine learning methods are shown to detect subtle statistical patterns and enhance side channel attacks, making them powerful tools for evaluating cryptographic resilience. A case study on CRYSTALS Kyber demonstrates how AI can support lattice-based recovery techniques to achieve full key extraction in minutes, highlighting the practical risks of implementation flaws. The discussion also extends to real world systems such as IoT and smart city infrastructures, where limited resources and deployment challenges complicate the adoption of PQC. The chapter concludes by stressing the importance of cryptographic agility and AI aware testing as essential safeguards in the quantum era.

DOI: 10.4018/979-8-3373-3166-9.ch007

1. INTRODUCTION

During the transition from theory to practise of large-scale quantum computing, the safety of current cryptographic systems has been subject to a higher level of scrutiny. Classical Public-Key Schemes, which are a critical part of modern internet framework, will be susceptible to the power of quantum power adversaries, predominantly those founded on RSA and Elliptic Curve Cryptography (ECC). This has encouraged the emergence of post-quantum cryptography (PQC), which is aimed at providing security for encryption, authentication, and exchange of keys at quantum attack levels. PQC is based on several different mathematical foundations such as lattice-, hash-, code-, multivariate-, and isogeny-based constructions. The growing use of interconnected systems in smart cities, healthcare, energy and industrial IoT also increases the need to have lightweight but futuristic security. Critical systems and urban infrastructures are based on the ability to receive secure data exchange, and any disturbance in confidentiality, integrity, or any other authentication may trigger a cascade of failures. Although PQC is theoretically resistant, its novelty would require a cautious cryptanalysis in making sure that the practical realizations are not susceptible to new quantum and classical risks.

Cryptanalysis is singled out as the main tool to measure PQC resilience in this chapter. Quantum algorithms like those of Shor and Grover enhance classical attacks and PQC suggest new designs that require new methods in cryptanalysis. In addition to the approaches of the past, new computational models, specifically machine learning (ML) and artificial intelligence (AI) provide new opportunities to identify hidden patterns, demonstrate statistical anomalies, and emulate adversarial conditions on a large scale. Cryptography has additional possibilities to become even more powerful and a threat of its misuse by the enemies grows along with the merging of PQC and AI. It is therefore possible that AI-aided cryptanalysis can be a useful complement to current procedures that might provide adaptive and automated discovery processes. Workflows have become feasible ensuring that the ML models can process PQC key material and give non-random patterns which can be indicative of underlying weaknesses. The case study included in the chapter demonstrates that side-channel analysis with AI-improvements can be used to reconstruct CRYSTALS-Kyber keys in minutes with the traces minimised, which is an illustration of the way this synergy can be realised in practise. Such findings emphasize the dual role of AI as both a defensive tool and a potential adversarial threat in the post-quantum era.

The chapter is organised as follows: Section 2 is a review of the relevant literature; Section 3 covers the basic concepts of cryptanalysis and evaluation metrics; Section 4 covers the most popular PQC schemes; Section 5 covers AI-based cryptanalysis; Section 6 covers the case study of Kyber, Section 7 covers implications to IoT and smart-city infrastructure, Section 8 covers research directions, and Section 9 covers some notable insights and policy implications. Generally, the discussion puts forth the notion that resilient cryptography in the quantum world requires multidisciplinary efforts combining mathematics, computer science, and AI-based cryptanalysis.

2. LITERATURE SURVEY

The fast development of technologies of quantum computing also represents an unprecedented threat to the current cryptographic systems. The vast majority of secure communication systems around the globe still depend on classical cryptosystems of public key, including RSA, ECC, and Diffie-Hellman that are extremely susceptible to the algorithms of Shor and Grover. These quantum algorithms are capable of ruining asymmetric encryption altogether and severely compromising symmetric algorithms, therefore, necessitating a sense of urgency in the PQC. PQC has consequently become one of the fundamental fields of study aimed at the development of cryptographic constructions that are resistant to attacks of both classical and quantum adversary (Bavdekar et al., 2023).

Bavdekar et al. (2023) summarise the risks of quantum algorithms in a basic manner and emphasise the need to switch to PQC. Their study compares the various PQC families encompassing lattice, hash, code, isogeny and multivariate schemes and especially the current NIST standard process. Complementing this theoretical perspective, Satrya et al. (2023) discuss the application of PQC to IoT and smart cities and compare algorithms like RSA, NTRU, and SABRE to secure an IoT-based energy monitoring system. Their results demonstrate that NTRU is the least overloaded with regard to CPU and memory, whereas Light SABRE is the most high-speed in encryption and decryption, which makes both worthy of resource-limited urban implementations. In the same fashion, the Raspberry Pi-based hardware-based testing of PQC finalists by P. C. et al. (2022) concludes that quantum key distribution (QKD) is theoretically impossible to experiment with, but PQC is a more viable route to take when it comes to the IoT.

Kumar (2022) also highlights performance issues regarding the implementations of PQC and shows that most quantum-safe algorithms consume significantly more CPU cycles, increased key sizes, and memory compared to their classical counterparts. Kerimbayeva (2023) also examines schemes such as NTRU, SIKE, WOTS+, Dilithium, and SABRE according to the following criteria: computational efficiency, attack-resistance, and compatibility with the existing infrastructure. It is particularly noteworthy that NTRU and SIKE are more practical in their trade-offs, whereas Dilithium and SABRE have more balanced performance and security, which highlights the significance of the choice of an algorithm, when deploying it. The research of Dam et al. (2023) builds upon these findings by conducting a survey of global trends in PQC research and found that PQC is no longer a theoretical concept, but its implementation in industry is becoming increasingly popular, and more and more people are willing to engage in a public-private partnership to achieve faster adoption.

In several works, PQC is situated in a broad cryptographic framework. Jumaa et al. (2022) follow the transition of cryptography between DES and AES to PQC and emphasise the relevance of cryptanalysis in the vulnerability determination. Although Thomas and Gharge (2017) pay attention to visual cryptography, their research provides some insights into trade-offs, including usability, and resilience, which are also paralleled to the challenges associated with the implementation of PQC. Horpenyuk et al. (n.d.) also mention the usefulness of the open-source toolkit of the Open Quantum Safe (OQS) project, which offers essential benchmarking tools to PQC implementations. Regarding governance, the ENISA (2021) report focuses on the hybrid models which use classical and PQC algorithms throughout the transition phase, stating the urgency of cryptographic agility and proactive implementation.

Recent research has increasingly explored the convergence of artificial intelligence (AI) with cryptanalysis and PQC. Gupta (2025) shows that deep learning networks like CNNs and RNNs are able to identify the cypher patterns and identify vulnerabilities to the lightweight cryptography schemes, which indicates that AI is more of a supplement than a substitute to the traditional techniques. Ravi, Jap, Bhasin, and Chattopadhyay (2023) demonstrate the first machine learning-based blind side-channel attack on Kyber, showing that full key recovery is possible from power traces even without access to ciphertexts, highlighting the practical risks to PQC hardware implementations. Similarly, Sarkar and Jhamb (2025) propose an AI-driven post-quantum cryptographic framework for IoT and cyber-physical systems, integrating Lagrange interpolation with advanced masking techniques to strengthen resilience against both quantum and side-channel threats. Radanliev (2024) extends this discourse by framing AI quantum integration as a key direction for future cryptographic innovation, while Hanafi and Ali (2025) provide a scientometric mapping of PQC research, identifying rapid growth in publications but also gaps in scalability and real-world testing for IoT environments.

Other contributions emphasize on interdependencies of AI and PQC. Darzi et al. (2024) stress the importance of PQC for ensuring trustworthy AI systems, particularly in sensitive sectors such as finance and healthcare. Mmaduekwe et al. (2024) demonstrate the optimization of PQC schemes with machine learning efficiency to enhance the key generation, reduce the side-channel vulnerability, and Nitaj and Rachidi (2023) review AI uses in cryptography based on a neural network, which can enhance the performance of classical algorithms (AES, RSA) and post-quantum algorithms such as LWE and Ascon. Gupta and Mittal (2025) explore AI's role in strengthening quantum key distribution (QKD) protocols, and a recent report on quantum-safe networking (2025) highlights PQC's importance for protecting AI/ML infrastructures, including federated learning systems and 6G-enabled edge intelligence.

Together these studies demonstrate that although PQC is developing rapidly, there are serious challenges in standardisation, scalability and legacy system migration. At the same time, AI offers both new attack vectors and powerful tools for cryptanalysis and mitigation. This dual role of AI — as both adversary and defender — has not been sufficiently integrated into the existing PQC discourse. Addressing this gap, the present chapter focuses on AI-assisted cryptanalysis as a means of probing, validating, and strengthening post-quantum systems, thereby providing a crucial perspective for securing smart cities, IoT deployments, and global digital infrastructures in the quantum era.

3. FUNDAMENTALS OF CRYPTANALYSIS

3.1 Classical vs. Post-Quantum Cryptanalysis Techniques

Cryptanalysis is the art of breaking or analyzing cryptographic algorithms to find hidden patterns or secret information like keys. Traditionally, cryptanalysis has relied upon two general classes of technique: brute-force attacks and statistical attacks.

3.1.1 Brute Force Attacks – Trying Every Possibility

A brute force attack is executed by performing an exhaustive search of all the possible keys until the right key is found. This method matches the classic example of trying to open a combination lock, moving the dial forward one number and then another. Such a procedure can theoretically be successful, but its success rate falls exponentially with larger key spaces. For example, to break a 256-bit AES encryption key, you'd need to try 2^{256} different keys. Even if you had a supercomputer that could try a trillion keys every second, it would still take longer than the age of the universe. This is why brute force is not a realistic threat against strong modern encryption.

3.1.2 Statistical Techniques – Finding Patterns in the Data

In addition to brute force, classical cryptanalysis involves statistical attacks, in which the mathematical reasoning reveals regularities in large databases of plaintexts and ciphers. There are two main variations that are discussed below:

- **Differential cryptanalysis**: This method examines the effect of minor variations in the plaintext on the equivalent parts of the ciphertext. If a pattern is found, it can help guess the key faster. The most standard example is a differential attack on DES (Data Encryption Standard) whose effectiveness depends on recurrent correlations in encrypted output blocks.
- **Linear cryptanalysis**: This technique attempts to place linear constraints on plaintext, ciphertext, and keys. These relationships are used to find slight biases in the encryption output that can be exploited.

These two methods require a large amount of data, and can only be used when there is evidence that the internal design of the algorithm is weak.

3.1.3 Algebraic Methods – Turning Encryption into Equations

Some ciphers can be described as mathematical equations. For example, lightweight ciphers or stream ciphers like Trivium can be represented as systems of equations. By taking advantage of such formulations, cryptanalysts may use strong methods, such as SAT or Gröbner basis algorithms to try and solve these equations and find the key.

There are also meet-in-the-middle (MitM) attacks, where decryption is run with each party by using opposite ends, and finally this leads to a point of intersection and the plaintext is readable. This technique became famous in its use against the double DES when two levels of encryption had paradoxically weakened security not to an exponent but, allowing a reverse calculation.

3.2 Role of Computational Complexity in Cryptanalysis

To have a thorough understanding of the underling cryptanalytic breakings we need to understand the computational complexity theory which is used to describe the resources needed to solve a problem, usually in the form of time, memory or information, on a computer. In cryptography, those metrics characterise the least effort possible that an adversary would expend to break a security mechanism.

Primitives commonly used in post-quantum cryptographic (PQC) constructions are in turn often based on the supposed hardness of solving certain NP-complete computational problems. For example:

- **Learning With Errors (LWE)**: This problem is used in PQC algorithms like FrodoKEM.
- **Shortest Vector Problem (SVP)**: Used in algorithms like Kyber and NTRU.

Such tasks fall within the NP-hard complexity regime which means, regardless of advanced technology, such systems would require time periods that would be long past the age of the universe to crack. However, there is the twist to this matter: any even minor advancements regarding the speed of an algorithm solution could make attacks more authentic. For example:

- When it requires 2128 steps to break a cypher, it is safe so far.
- But if someone finds a new trick that reduces this to **2^{64} steps**, that could be possible using today's supercomputers or cloud services.

The phenomenon is especially relevant to the situation of long-lived key cycles, which are now extensively used in smart-city settings, industrial control systems, and military networks, where unpredictable cryptanalytic advances might infringe upon the confidentiality and integrity of other important data.

3.3 Impact of Quantum Computing on Cryptanalysis

Quantum computing describes a different computing model where information processing exploits quantum-physical phenomena and, although currently still in development, has the potential to break classical cryptography significantly. There are two famous quantum algorithms that affect cryptography:

1. **Shor's Algorithm**: A factorization of integer factors within a polynomial time, thus weakening the secure asymmetric primitives that have become widely used in practice, including the RSA algorithm and elliptic-curve cryptography (ECC), specifically upon which secure email, connection to the web, digital signatures, and other internet protocols depend.
2. **Grover's Algorithm**: An optimized brute-force attack capable of designing symmetric keys (e.g. AES) exponentially faster, but at quadratically accelerated rates, therefore requiring key extension in most applications, such as increasing the key length of AES in 128-bit to 256-bit.

At the same time, a number of post-quantum algorithm candidates have been suggested to which the resistance to attacks of quantum nature is directly designed. Kyber, Dilithium, and Classic McElice exemplify this strategy, which allows safe use in the face of quantum devices that can run Shor the algorithm. The quantum ability is still evolving at a slow pace, but it is crucial to start moving the most essential applications towards those post-quantum algorithms, which will reduce the risk of being exposed to the emerging quantum threats.

3.4 Emerging Techniques in Cryptanalysis

Cryptanalysis used to rely mostly on human experts applying math, logic, and brute force. Recent advances in automation and artificial intelligence let analysts find weaknesses more quickly and reliably. Some of the new tools and techniques are:

- **SAT-Solvers and SMT Tools**: These programs recreate the logical foundations of a cipher bit-by-bit, which makes it easier to detect dormant flaws or weak spots within a specific algorithm. Tools like Z3 are commonly used for this.
- **Algebraic Methods**: Encryption schemes often rely on long, complex formulas; a Gröbner basis solver can remove some or all of that complexity, offering shortcuts or breakthroughs.
- **Machine Learning (ML)**: ML models are able to identify subtle patterns that otherwise would be difficult to see by being trained on input, such as public keys or ciphertexts. As an example, side-channel measurements have been used in Kyber by employing deep learning to recover secret keys.
- **Metaheuristics**: Genetic algorithms, and simulated annealing have been used to successively create new assemblies of inputs to seek rareground phenomena which can be exploited.

These new techniques do not substitute the old cryptanalysis; they are added to it. With the experience of cryptographers and the abilities of AI, one can consider new algorithms in a more effective way and identify and rectify vulnerabilities before they can impact real-life systems.

3.5 Standardization, Regulation, and Cryptographic Agility in PQC Adoption

Along with the improvement of the technical fundament of PQC, significant barriers to the implementation of these algorithms into practise exist, and its technical part is no less significant, although its role is another. Before the unifying migration of the PQC environment between smart cities, critical infrastructure, and the IoT ecosystem, three dimensions, viz., standardisation, legal and regulatory frameworks, and cryptographic agility will contribute to the pace and the efficacy of the PQC transition.

3.5.1 Standardization Bottlenecks

In 2016, the National Institute of Standards and Technology (NIST) started its PQC standardization process. Among the Round 3 finalists were CRYSTALS-Kyber, CRYSTALS-Dilithium, Falcon, and SPHINCS+ (Chen et al., 2016; NIST, 2023). Although Kyber and Dilithium have been chosen to be standardized, their complete ratification and adoption is still continuing. These delays are dangerous to organizations such as that of adopting PQC solutions because the adversaries might as well have already been gathering encrypted traffic to future harvest-now, decrypt-later attacks (Mosca, 2018). In addition, interoperability of new PQC algorithms and already established cryptographic standards (TLS, IPsec, PKI) is still in testing, giving rise to questions on interoperability fragmentation and the duration of the transition vulnerabilities (Alagic et al., 2020).

3.5.2 Legal and Regulatory Frameworks

Instead, implementation of PQC is inseparable with regulatory and compliance interests. Data solutions like General Data Protection Regulation (GDPR) in Europe and Cybersecurity Maturity Model Certification (CMMC) in the United States set high demands upon data confidentiality and resiliency of the information stored and transferring (European Commission, 2018; U.S. DoD, 2021). Direction on PQC migration in national cybersecurity guidelines, previously implicit, now have an explicit roadmap in guidelines announced by the National Security Agency (NSA) of the United States, and the European Union Agency for Cybersecurity (ENISA) (NSA, 2022; ENISA, 2021). These frameworks not only require implementing quantum-safe algorithms in organisations but also require them to articulate compliance and therefore, username forfeits the PQC adoption schedule besides complicating the process.

3.5.3 Cryptographic Agility

The relative obscurity of the fact is then immediately succeeded by the relative urgency because the current infrastructure is not likely to be able to support PQC in the form of retrofitting. All of the IoT and embedded devices deployed as components of smart cities projects, including traffic sensors, energy metres, and video surveillance systems, do not have the processing power or memory to execute the PQC algorithms whose key sizes and computation requirements consume large portions of their resources (Kumar, 2022). This has given rise to the idea of cryptographicagility, the aspects of a system to change compatible cryptographic primitives based on the emergence of new threats or standards (ENISA, 2021). The most important mechanism is agility which eliminates chances of organisations being locked to outdated scheme and incurs high expenses of changing hardware. Agile design consequently becomes a major managerial and technical requirement in embracing PQCs particularly in instances where massive infrastructurings are to be constructed that will have to deal with extended devices lifespan and the accelerated cryptographic protocol alterations.

There are three major non-technical barriers to adoption of PQC, namely standardisation delays, regulatory pressure and cryptographicagility gaps. In the context of systems, though the algorithms are still being refined in future research in terms of their efficiency and security, these kinds of problems will be significant factors to whether PQC can work effectively to scale. Further studies should therefore re-evaluate measures of the PQC transition as a socio-technical issue in which policy, cryptography and infrastructure design co-evolve to work towards long-term resilience to quantum computer-based attackers.

3.6 Metrics for Evaluating Cryptanalytic Success

Not all attacks are equal. Just because an attack works on paper doesn't mean it's practical in the real world. To measure how dangerous an attack really is, cryptanalysts look at three key metrics:

1. **Time Complexity**: How long does the attack take? If an attack needs 1,000 years on a supercomputer, it's not a big concern. But if someone finds a shortcut and can do it in hours or days, then it becomes dangerous.
2. **Space Complexity**: How much memory does the attack need? Some attacks require huge amounts of memory (like thousands of hard drives). That makes them unrealistic for ordinary hackers, though big governments or labs might try.
3. **Data Complexity**: How much data does the attacker need? Some methods only work if the attacker has millions of encrypted messages or special clues. If such data is hard to get, the attack stays impractical even if the math works.

As example scenarios include a lattice-reduction attack on Kyber768 could take hours of execution time on modern performance hardware with many terabytes of memory, making it practical only for well-financed or government entities. In comparison, attacks on Classic McEliece often require an unrealistically large number of queries or traces, which are nearly impossible to collect in real deployments.

While these three metrics are the most common, other factors also matter in real-world systems:

- **Energy cost** – how much power the attack consumes.
- **Hardware dependency** – whether special equipment is needed.
- **Implementation cost** – how expensive it is to run the attack in practice.

These additional aspects are becoming more important as cryptography is deployed on small, resource-constrained devices such as IoT sensors, smart meters, and embedded controllers. To make these ideas clearer, the Table 1 summarizes different cryptanalysis techniques, the schemes they apply to, their relation to quantum computing, and what they mean for smart city devices.

Table 1. Overview of cryptanalysis techniques, applicable schemes, and their resistance to quantum attacks

Technique	Applicable To	Quantum Impact	Remarks	Impact on Smart City Devices
Brute Force	Symmetric, small-key PQC	Grover speeds search	Requires larger keys	Higher memory/energy demand
Differential Analysis	Symmetric algorithms	Minimal quantum effect	Needs large plaintext ciphertext sets	Stricter data handling needed
Linear Analysis	Block ciphers	Minimal quantum effect	Exploits weak S-boxes	IoT firmware must use stronger S-boxes
Algebraic/MitM Attacks	RSA, multivariate PQC	Shor breaks RSA; PQC mostly safe	Targets algebraic structures	Legacy servers need PQC upgrade
Lattice Reduction (BKZ)	Lattice-based PQC	Sub exponential algorithms exist	Major risk to lattice schemes	Parameter tuning critical; devices may struggle
Decoding Attacks	Code-based PQC	Moderate quantum speedups	Based on code decoding hardness	May exceed device compute limits
Isogeny Graph Traversal	SIDH/SIKE	Quantum impact unclear	Relies on graph path-finding	Hardware acceleration may be required

These metrics and techniques show that security is not just about mathematics, but also about how algorithms behave in the real world. For managers and practitioners, this means focusing on resilience under practical conditions — limited hardware, energy costs, and system constraints — rather than only theoretical strength. In practice, adopting PQC requires balancing security, cost, and feasibility, especially for smart city and IoT systems.

4. CRYPTANALYSIS OF LEADING PQC ALGORITHMS

4.1 Cryptanalysis of Lattice-Based Schemes

Lattice-based schemes such as Kyber, Dilithium, NTRU, and FrodoKEM have become central to post-quantum cryptography due to their efficiency and scalability. Their security is built on hard problems including Learning With Errors (LWE), Learning With Rounding (LWR), and the Shortest Vector Problem (SVP). Lattice-reduction algorithms, especially BKZ (Block Korkine-Zolotarev), and its versions, are most often targeted in attacks, and try to represent short vectors that can expose useful material.

Kyber is particularly analysed, and it has been noted that a smaller key size or degree of polynomials can enable the recovery of information by BKZ and sieving attacks with lower efficiency. The same applies to Dilithium, in which a leakage of partial secrets can be caused by mistakes in the parameters of the Gaussian sampling. Quantum-accelerated sieving provides sub-exponential speedups, and quantum versions of ISD further narrow margins, although complete breaks remain elusive. The sensitivity of parameterization is clear whereby the security is greatly compromised when the dimensions of lattices or the size of error is under-estimated. This fact was mirrored in the NIST PQC Round 3 decision, which further developed Kyber and Dilithium to draught standards, and terminated Rainbow because of its vulnerabilities.

4.2 Cryptanalysis of Code-Based Schemes

Code-based systems, represented by Classic McEliece, BIKE, and HQC, rely on the assumed hardness of decoding random linear codes. Their primary threat comes from Information-Set Decoding (ISD) algorithms, beginning with Prange and refined by Stern, MMT, and BJMM, which reduce complexity by exploiting error-free positions in codewords.

Structural weaknesses can further reduce security. Variants of McEliece that used Reed-Solomon or poorly chosen Goppa codes have been shown vulnerable to algebraic or Gröbner-basis attacks. In contrast, Classic McEliece with carefully selected Goppa codes has withstood decades of cryptanalytic effort. The main challenge remains parameter selection: code length and error weight must be sufficient to resist ISD and syndrome-based attacks, including quantum-assisted decoding strategies. Practical deployment in IoT and urban networks is constrained by large key sizes and high computational requirements, underscoring the need for balance between efficiency and resilience.

4.3 Cryptanalysis of Multivariate Schemes

Multivariate schemes such as Rainbow, Unbalanced Oil and Vinegar (UOV), and HFE are built on the NP-hardness of solving multivariate polynomial equations over finite fields. Despite this foundation, they have proven susceptible to algebraic attacks. MinRank exploits low-rank representations of public keys, while Gröbner basis algorithms (F4, F5, and hybrids) can eliminate variables efficiently when schemes are poorly parameterized.

Rainbow was withdrawn from the NIST process after its parameter sets were shown vulnerable to MinRank and direct algebraic attacks. UOV, though simpler in design, requires careful tuning of the Oil-to-Vinegar ratio; small imbalances allow Gröbner solvers to break instances rapidly. Research shows that even modest parameter changes can reduce security margins to hours or minutes on commodity hardware. To remain viable, multivariate schemes must employ high algebraic degree, strong randomness, and minimal structural leakage. While promising in principle, their reliance on fine-grained parameterization continues to raise concerns for long-term deployment.

4.4 Cryptanalysis of Hash-Based Schemes

Hash-based signatures such as SPHINCS+, XMSS, and LMS derive security from the one-wayness of hash functions. Their resilience depends largely on output length: Grover's algorithm halves effective strength, but a 256-bit hash still provides about 128-bit post-quantum security. Collisions and preimage attacks remain computationally infeasible with adequately chosen parameters.

The main risks arise from implementation. Stateful schemes like XMSS require strict one-time key usage; reusing a signing key can enable forgery. Stateless constructions such as SPHINCS+ mitigate this by employing hypertree structures and few-time signatures, though at the cost of larger signature sizes. So far, no practical cryptanalytic shortcuts have been demonstrated beyond these considerations. Ensuring security therefore relies on careful state management, correct key generation, and adherence to parameter guidelines.

4.5 Cryptanalysis of Isogeny-Based Schemes

Isogeny-based schemes such as SIDH and SIKE gained attention for their compact keys and strong theoretical foundations. However, cryptanalysis has exposed severe weaknesses. In 2022, Castryck and Decru exploited torsion-point information and isogeny graph properties to reduce secret-path recovery to polynomial time, effectively breaking SIDH/SIKE.

These results highlight a general vulnerability: elegant mathematical structures can create exploitable regularities. Even small leaks, such as auxiliary point data or bilinear maps, drastically lower complexity and compromise security. While isogeny-based cryptography remains of theoretical interest, its practical prospects as a post-quantum standard have been largely undermined.

4.6 Common Themes and Cross-Family Insights

Across PQC families, several recurring vulnerabilities emerge. Under-parameterization reduces security margins: insufficient lattice dimensions in Kyber, short codes in McEliece, or weak Oil–Vinegar ratios in UOV all enable sub-exponential attacks. Structural leakage also creates risks, as shown by MinRank exploits, improved lattice-reduction methods, and side-channel attacks. Even schemes based on NP-hard problems can fail when specific instantiations expose algebraic weaknesses.

To mitigate these issues, designers increasingly adopt layered defenses. Hybrid models combine classical and post-quantum primitives, side-channel protection is integrated into implementations, and parameters are chosen conservatively in line with the latest cryptanalytic results. Careful state management and cryptographic agility remain essential to ensuring long-term resilience. With continued refinement, these strategies can support the emergence of robust PQC suitable for critical infrastructure. Figure 1 illustrates the principal PQC families under consideration.

Figure 1. PQC Cryptographic Schemes

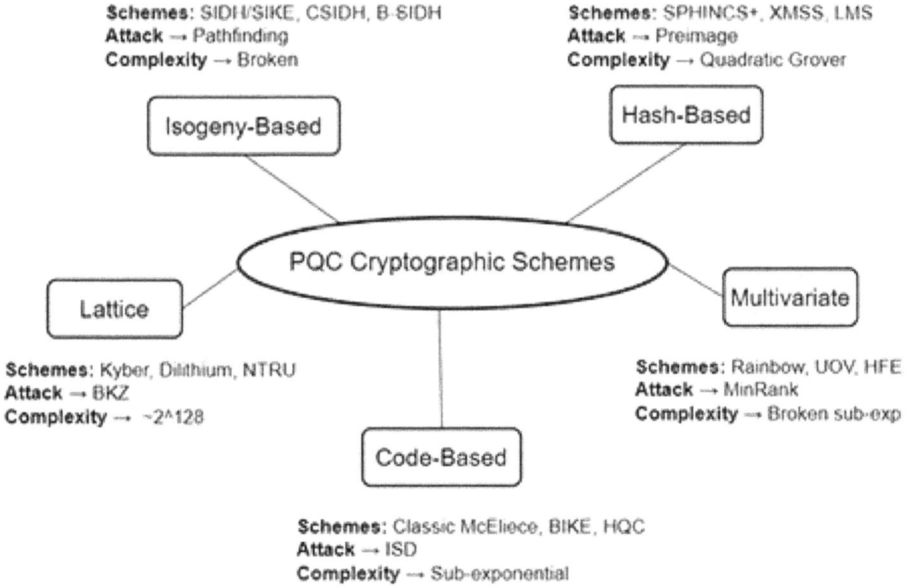

A comparison of lattice-, hash-, multivariate-, code-, and isogeny-based PQC schemes shows that none achieves dominance across security, efficiency, and practicality. Each family has distinct weaknesses: lattice schemes face parameter sensitivity, hash-based systems struggle with scalability, multivariate designs are vulnerable to algebraic attacks, and isogeny schemes remain immature. AI-assisted cryptanalysis further exposes hidden anomalies that traditional methods may miss. For managers and policymakers, these differences imply that no one-size-fits-all solution exists. Adoption must weigh algorithmic strength, hardware constraints, compliance demands, and standardization timelines. In smart city and IoT settings, forward-looking strategies—balancing cost, regulation, and cryptographic agility—are essential, making PQC not only a technical challenge but also a governance issue.

5. AI-ASSISTED CRYPTANALYSIS: USING MACHINE LEARNING FOR CRYPTOGRAPHIC WEAKNESS DETECTION

Machine learning (ML) is increasingly employed in modern cryptanalysis as a complement to traditional methods. While algebraic analysis, statistical techniques, and lattice-reduction remain fundamental, they may overlook subtle irregularities in complex cryptographic data. In contrast, ML can handle massive volumes of data, find latent correlations, and identify statistical outliers that can provide insight into a weakness, which is especially applicable with next-generation PQC algorithms.

The section outlines an AI-driven experimentation on PQC resilience. This is done by synthetically generating key material which is transformed into feature vectors and analysed with classifiers that are trained to detect non-random structures or statistical leakage. The implementation considerations, parameter tuning, scaling, and the general importance of the results are discussed.

5.1 Dataset Generation and Feature Extraction

5.1.1 PQClean Library

To perform AI-aided cryptanalysis, a vast set of public-secret keys would certainly be needed to create an underlying domain upon which to acquire features and learn to describe the objects. PQClean is an open-source C library providing verified versions of the PQC algorithms being considered in the NIST post-quantum standards process. It has been cross-platformed and its code base has received good reviews with support of schemes like Kyber (a lattice-based Key Encapsulation Mechanism) and Dilithium (a lattice-based signature scheme). The choice of these algorithms to be included in the study was based on the following considerations: These algorithms are state-of-the-art PQC, and are considered to be secure against classical adversaries as well as against quantum adversaries.

Using PQClean meant that the ensuing key material was parameterized according to best-practice parameterization and thus that no unnecessary vulnerabilities caused by bespoke or rushed parameterization would be present.

5.1.2 Key Pair Generation

To obtain a sufficiently large dataset, we generated thousands of public secret key pairs were generated, amounting to a dataset large enough to support machine learning experimentation with PQClean currently including the reference implementation of Kyber768. Every call to the key generation routine generated a single public key and a secret key. The outcome was a set of thousands of these key pairs, giving a statistically useful sample space for statistical learning and cryptanalytic experimentation. Importantly, by using only the standardized implementations in PQClean, the extractable keys were compliant with the candidate specifications in NIST and without any biases created by custom or ad-hoc implementations. (Detailed implementation code is provided in Appendix A.)

5.1.3 Transforming Raw Keys into Feature Vectors

After the pairing of the public keys is established, the explicit version of each of the key is to be transformed into a form that is applicable to the machine-learning classifiers in the supervised mode. The form of the public key is publicly shared in the majority of protocol frameworks, and thus may consist of constructs that can be abused by attackers. Every such public key will be in the form of an unsigned binary object with size which follows the Kyber768 parameterization (1,184 bytes). The raw bytes are projected on numeric features to allow the classification:

- **Byte value distributions:** The set can be enumerated by counting the number of each of the 256 possible byte-values, thus producing a 256-dimensional histogram.
- **Descriptive statistics:** Mean, variance, skewness, and kurtosis of the byte values.
- **Higher-order moments:** To capture non-linear structure, features like entropy and autocorrelation can also be computed.

Each public key is loaded into a Python script as a histogrammed set of unsigned integers (np.uint8), but a normalized histogram of 256 bins is constructed and summary statistics such as the mean, standard deviation, Shannon entropy and a proxy autocorrelation are calculated. The feature vectors thus obtained are combined into a CSV file (features.csv), where each key has its own line. This data will be the training data of the next step: to train the classifiers able to reveal which public keys differ with randomness significantly and which do not. The overall process can be summarized as a structured pipeline, linking key generation, feature extraction, and classification into a unified cryptanalytic workflow as depicted in Figure 2 .

Figure 2. Workflow of AI-assisted cryptanalysis showing the sequence from PQClean key generation through feature extraction, vectorization, machine learning classification, and final evaluation

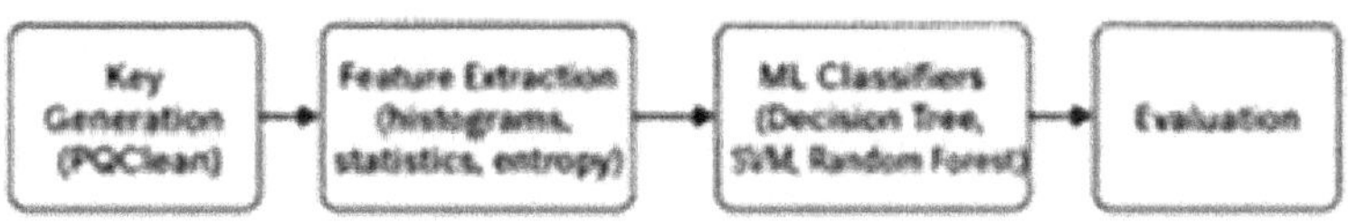

5.2 Training Machine Learning Models

5.2.1 Training and Test Sets

The data collection, which is collected in 5.1, was divided into a training and test set in a proportion of approximately 80:20. Every partition wanted to have a representative balance in terms of overall distribution.

5.2.2 Training Multiple Classifiers

To explore how different algorithms detect structure, we trained three classic classifiers that provide a balance of interpretability, capacity, and ensemble power:

- **Decision Tree:** Interpretable baseline classifier
- **Support Vector Machine (SVM):** A model that can separate classes with non-linear decision boundaries
- **Random Forest:** An ensemble that benefits from variance-reduction and can discover subtle feature interactions

All the models were tuned using 5-fold cross-validation, with the respective hyperparameters being maximised: max_depth in Decision Tree, C and kernel in SVM and n_estimators in Random Forest. Once training is complete, we evaluate the classifiers on the held-out test set to obtain metrics like accuracy, precision, recall, and F1-score. (Implementation scripts are provided in Appendix A.)

5.3 Performance Comparison and Insights

5.3.1 Evaluation Metrics

To evaluate the performance of the considered classifiers and establish it scientifically, standard statistics were calculated over the test set. In this case of binary classification, accuracy, precision, recall and F1-score grew to complement each other:

- **Accuracy** is the amount of correct predictions
- **Precision** measures the number of positive predictions labelled as positive, now including the ones that are really positive
- **Recall** represents the percentage of the actual positive instances which are recognized by the classifier
- **F1-score** balances the precision and recall

The results listed below are obtained after training each classifier on the Kyber768 key features:

Table 2. Different Models Results

Model	Accuracy (%)	Precision (%)	Recall (%)	F1-Score (%)
DecisionTree	85.2	84.1	86.3	85.2
SVM	89.7	90.5	88.7	89.6
RandomForest	91.3	91.0	91.5	91.2

RandomForest had the best cumulative results. RandomForest utilizes an ensemble voting approach to capture theoretically insignificant dependencies between features that cannot be picked up with single DecisionTrees and hyperplanes of SVMs.

5.3.2 Discussion of the Results

Results showed the experimental findings in which predictive performance of analytical classifiers, trained using relatively small statistical ramifications i.e. the histograms of bytes, and the mean frequency were stable. This result evidences machine-learning methods in detecting minor deviations that could be signs of non-randomness or some unknown problems with implementations. It is also possible that the structure of PQC schemes whose theoretical foundations are proven based on NP-hard computational problems is also susceptible to data-driven leakage detection. The significance of this empirical observation to embedded and resource-constrained systems that may be deployed in a smart-city or IoT architecture is significant. It could be the case that an attacker is interested in exploiting such structural hints to enhance key-recovery attacks, particularly in combination with the AI-based extensions present in this work, in case the seeding of PQC key generation on an IoT node is based on a low-entropy pseudorandom-number source, or some other subtle implementation bugs are causing key material to biases out of the uniform distribution.

5.4 Policy and Transition Challenges

In addition to technical tests, there are a number of policy and transition challenges that define the actual implementation of PQC. Although necessary, the NIST standardization process is associated with delays that bring uncertainty to those industries that need guidance urgently. National cybersecurity strategies are beginning to integrate PQC preparedness, often aligned with regulations such as GDPR, yet inconsistent regional policies hinder global adoption. At the industry level, smart cities and IoT systems face particular risks, as legacy devices often lack the resources to support PQC without costly upgrades. These challenges underscore the need for cryptographic agility designing systems capable of adapting to new algorithms without wholesale hardware replacement.

5.5 Discussion and Future Directions

This case study demonstrates the value of AI-assisted cryptanalysis as a complement to traditional methods, capable of detecting subtle patterns in key material and guiding further algebraic or lattice-based analysis. Future research should focus on richer feature engineering (e.g., N-gram sequences, autocorrelation, spectral features), integration of explainable AI tools such as SHAP or LIME to clarify classifier decisions, and adversarial testing methods like FGSM to simulate malicious bias in key generation. Broader evaluations across multiple PQC families (e.g., SIKE, Dilithium, Rainbow, McEliece) and scaling experiments involving larger key datasets are also needed to assess robustness under real-world conditions.

6. CASE STUDY: AI-ENHANCED SIDE-CHANNEL & LATTICE ATTACK ON CRYSTALS-KYBER

6.1 Introduction

Although post-quantum cryptographic schemes such as CRYSTALS-Kyber have been designed with mathematical hardness assumptions that resist quantum adversaries, real-world hardware implementations often introduce unintended vulnerabilities. One of the most striking examples is the emergence of adversarial machine learning techniques blended with side-channel analysis. This case study explores a successful hybrid attack conducted on Kyber key exchange, where carefully trained convolutional neural networks (CNNs) leveraged subtle variations in power consumption to reveal secret key material in practice.

6.2 Attack Methodology

Researchers conducted their experiments on a commonly used embedded platform equipped with an ARM Cortex-M4 microcontroller. The attacker began by gathering side-channel traces during Kyber decapsulation operations. In traditional settings, side-channel attacks like correlation power analysis would require hundreds or thousands of traces to extract partial information. However, this case leveraged an

AI-driven classifier trained on a small set of such power traces to discern patterns that reveal partial information about the secret key.

The training process focused on predicting byte-wise components of the secret key using a convolutional neural network. Classical statistics, including Pearson and Kendall correlations, were combined with the neural network's feature maps to reduce noise and highlight leakage points. This significantly reduced the number of traces required for a successful attack. In practice, the researchers showed that they could extract significant portions of the secret key with as few as fifteen traces, an order of magnitude fewer than traditional methods.

6.3 Combining Machine Learning with Lattice Reduction

Once partial key information was derived from these traces, the researchers bridged this leakage into a lattice-based recovery process. Lattice-reduction algorithms such as BKZ were adapted to reconstruct the full secret key, even under noisy and incomplete leakage. The AI-driven pre-processing gave the lattice algorithms a substantial "head start," allowing them to complete the recovery in mere minutes. The experiment was repeated across multiple parameter sets of Kyber—Kyber-512, Kyber-768, and Kyber-1024—and across different hardware platforms such as FPGAs and general-purpose CPUs. The successful recovery on a broad range of setups suggested the scalability and practicality of the hybrid AI-cryptanalysis attack.

6.4 Results and Impact

The researchers reported successful key recovery on a commodity PC (Xeon-class CPU) within approximately ten minutes of trace collection. The implications are profound: even a theoretically quantum-safe scheme can be rendered practically insecure if its implementation is susceptible to this style of AI-assisted leakage exploitation. Table 3 summarizes the key parameters of the attack.

Table 3. Aspect and Details

Aspect	Details
Target Scheme	CRYSTALS-Kyber (512/768/1024)
Hardware Platform	ARM Cortex-M4, also tested on FPGAs
Side-Channel Input	Power consumption traces (~15 per attack)
Machine Learning Model	CNN with hybrid correlation metrics
Lattice Recovery Method	BKZ-based solver
Time to Full Key Recovery	~9–10 minutes per instance

6.5 Discussion and Mitigation

This case underscores that PQC is not necessarily impervious when it is implemented on physical equipment. Even if the underlying algorithm is mathematically sound against Shor's or Grover's algorithm, real-world devices often emit exploitable side-channels. These leakages are further enhanced by AI-based classifiers, who mean that enemies can avoid the classical noise and recycle sensitive data with minimal data.

Mitigation is not a parameter that can be adjusted or an algorithm modification. The strategies should also include hardware countermeasures such as power-masking, constant-time operations and dynamic shuffling. It is important to note that the designers of PQC schemes must realise that security in the real-world is not only present in ensuring that an algorithm can withstand analysis by the attackers, but also in ensuring that the system is designed in a manner that is leakage-resistant. Besides this, XAI can also help in knowing the trends that these neural networks are following in order that the hardware designers can eliminate potential information flows by sealing them prior to release.

This case study demonstrates the evolving landscape of cryptanalysis is bringing the progressive computation and adversarial learning together. These two areas, machine learning and side-channel analysis, complicate the assumptions of post-quantum security. Even schemes that have a strong mathematical basis can be weak when they do not take into account the hardware level. Adversarial ML is certain to become a formidable weapon in the cryptanalyst arsenal in the future, and it has never been more critically important that cryptographic schemes are tested on such a multidisciplinary set of attack vectors, before they become constituent components of the smart city and IoT infrastructure.

7. IMPACT ON SMART CITIES & IOT SECURITY

7.1 PQC Vulnerabilities and Urban Infrastructure

PQC is the promise that is attracting architects of smart cities to believe in its importance to the safety of urban infrastructure. Smart cities are based on dynamic traffic lights, environmental sensors, smart grids, and emergency systems all of which need cryptography to keep them confidential, confidentiality, integrity, authentication and availability. However, the emergence of PQC creates dangers. In contrast to the time-tested traditional cryptosystems, PQC is novel and can widen attack space with difficult mathematics, hardware constraints and bugs. As an example, lattice-based schemes are powerful but may be susceptible to side-channel leaks of low-priced IoT devices. Cities that are getting ready to quantum attacks, therefore, can become exposed to novel vulnerabilities.

7.2 Threat Modeling for Critical Urban Systems

A detailed threat model is essential for understanding how vulnerabilities in PQC could impact the operational safety of smart city infrastructure. Below, we explore potential vectors of attack across key domains:

- **Traffic management networks** These systems depend on the integrity and authenticity of signals exchanged between traffic lights, sensors, and centralized controllers. A cryptanalytic break that compromises authentication protocols could allow an attacker to forge or alter commands, resulting in gridlock or even accidents at scale.
- **Smart energy and water grids** Modern urban utilities rely on encrypted telemetry and control commands to manage loads, detect faults, and coordinate distributed energy resources. A successful cryptanalytic attack on key exchange protocols could permit injection of unauthorized commands — for example, disabling parts of the power grid or falsifying water treatment telemetry.
- **Emergency response and public safety systems** These systems require highly reliable communication during crises. Cryptographic failures could allow adversaries to intercept, delay, or block communications between first responders, or worse, inject false information that hampers coordinated action.

Each of these domains illustrates that a compromise of cryptographic primitives — even at a single point in the network — can have disproportionate, city-wide consequences.

7.3 Scalability and Attack Amplification

One defining feature of smart city and IoT deployments is the sheer scale and uniformity of their devices and protocols. A typical smart city could have millions of devices from environmental sensors to public Wi-Fi routers all running similar firmware, built on identical hardware platforms, and using the same cryptographic configurations for ease of management.

In such an environment, the discovery of a cryptanalytic weakness, or a successful side-channel or AI-assisted attack on a particular PQC scheme, does not merely affect one device. Rather it is a force multiplier: attackers can immediately copy the exploit over the entire network. One attack on a major exchange mechanism might enable enemies to decrypt all communications over large parts of the city, scale sensor data, or send fake control instructions. This amplification effect is what causes a localized cryptanalytic success to become systemic risk, which strongly suggests that using cryptographic diversity and defense-in-depth methods in an urban IoT network.

7.4 Real-World Constraints on PQC Deployment

PQC is theoretically resilient, but practically very difficult to implement in smart cities.

- **Resource-constrained devices** Smart cities have many IoT devices with strict processing power, memory, and battery life limitations. Big key sizes or complicated calculations by use of the PQC scheme might not be unaffordable in terms of hardware modifications.
- **Long hardware lifecycles** The devices of urban infrastructure are typically left in the field over decades. It is both logistically and financially difficult to retrofit or swap cryptographic modules once deployed, particularly in locations that are difficult access such as underground utilities or rooftops in high-rise buildings.
- **Delayed patching and maintenance** The magnitude of IoT implementations implies that software updates are usually hard to synchronize on time. The vulnerabilities identified during post-deployment can have lifespan and the systems may remain vulnerable to newer cryptanalytic methods or vulnerabilities in their implementation.

These limitations require critical trade-offs between cryptography strength, ability of the device, and manageability of smart cities.

7.5 Case Study: Breaking a Post-Quantum IoT Network

Imagine a smart city with PQC-based lattice based scheme as sensors of traffic and to provide control systems. The side-channel analysis with the assistance of AI is performed on the small amount of available devices by an attacker, who extracts a piece of the key. The attacker retrieves complete secret keys using a small amount of power traces using lattice-reduction algorithms such as BKZ. When traffic messages are forged, with the use of these keys, the major intersections are left red during rush time, thus causing a traffic jam in the streets, and slowing down the emergency services. Impatient motorists make hazardous efforts to bypass the road and form accidents as well as flooding of neighborhoods streets with strains to dir命 other routes.

The attack scales because of using the same cryptographic settings being applied on city-wide basis. Digital boards are used to issue bogus notifications, public transport schedules are disrupted and traffic lights are impaired. The security failures have rippling effects on the community, affect the business operations, and pose political problems to the city governments. Recovery requires purchasing new hardware with flaky parts, and new credentials, as well as investing in more malware-resistant solutions, which is costly and time-consuming. The failure to protect at least some compromised machines can turn into a statewide crisis. This underscores the necessity of safe implementations, varied parameters, fast key change, and robust incident reaction. Cryptanalysis impacts the smart cities through transportation, security, economic stability, and trust of the citizens. Hence, resilient urban systems cannot only attain strong post-quantum security but also it becomes a critical issue of concern.

7.6 Implications for Smart City Governance and Policy

When it comes to smart city cryptography, it is more of a governance issue than a technical one. Cities, utility or procurement officers have to establish resilience as the significant procurement driver, verify PQC implementations against side-channel and AI-enhanced attacks independently, and make sure that the contractual terms of cryptographic agility are established in such a way that the systems are not bound to a fixed research direction. Regulatory agencies should also define minimum robustness illustrations and require the revelation of vulnerabilities to facilitate co-ordinated reply.

7.7 Recommendations for Future-Proofing Smart Cities

In light of the risks outlined above, urban planners and system architects should adopt several key strategies to secure smart city infrastructure in the post-quantum era:

- **Embrace hybrid cryptography:** During the transitional period, combine PQC with well-established classical schemes to hedge against unexpected breaks in either domain.
- **Ensure cryptographic diversity:** Avoid monocultures of cryptographic algorithms; diversify schemes and parameter sets across systems and vendors.
- **Prioritize hardware security:** Invest into IoT hardware that has side-channel-resistant design and also has hardware modules that are security oriented.

- **Bring in real-time monitoring:** Install intrusion detection systems and anomaly detector systems that can identify cryptanalytic attacks or behaviors of suspicious devices within real time.
- **Plan for cryptographic agility:** Design systems that support updates or replacements of cryptographic components without requiring wholesale hardware changes.

By adopting these measures, cities can not only prepare for quantum threats but also build a more resilient, adaptable, and trustworthy digital infrastructure that safeguards citizens and services alike.

8. FUTURE PROSPECTS & RESEARCH DIRECTIONS

8.1 Evolution Toward Hybrid Cryptography

With the practical use of quantum computers about to become a reality, hybrid cryptography is finding its way as a viable transition between traditional and post-quantum cryptology. In this architecture, post-quantum algorithms like Kyber or NTRU are combined with classical algorithms to ensure the security of the communications with allowing gradual migration to quantum-resistant cryptography, such as RSA and ECC. This mixed method allows the legacy systems to communicate with the new ones without the risk of discarding proven technologies too fast. In the case of smart cities, it implies that the security layers of IoT devices can be reinforced gradually without disruption or device incompatibility. Current studies are exploring the most efficient hybrid solutions that can be considered effective in terms of efficiency and security of PQC implementation in embedded systems and edge networks without affecting the safety-critical or time-sensitive processes of urban environment.

8.2 AI-Driven Advances in Cryptanalysis

Cryptanalysis and vulnerability discovery are shifting toward machine learning and AI. Methods like deep learning classifiers, generative adversarial networks (GANs), and reinforcement learning agents can reveal subtle statistical weaknesses that traditional tools might miss. AI models can quickly sift through high-dimensional keys or ciphertext to highlight patterns and anomalies that point to structural flaws. This automation speeds up the cryptanalytic process, but also raises scalability concerns: as AI techniques grow more powerful, researchers must develop countermeasures that assume adversaries could use similar AI tools. That shift means future cryptographic designs should include AI-aware testing in their security proofs and pre-deployment reviews.

8.3 Adaptive Cryptographic Protocols for Smart Cities

Smart city ecosystems must prepare for a dynamic threat landscape as quantum computing and AI mature. Adaptive protocols that adjust parameters, switch algorithms, or refresh keys in real time offer a promising solution. On the fly parameter tuning using environmental signals or threat intelligence could help urban IoT networks stay ahead of adversaries. For example, a traffic sensor network might increase key sizes or rotate keys more often if communication patterns suggest reconnaissance. Research into self healing protocols and distributed ledger methods for authenticating and revoking devices will further strengthen resilience and ensure that heterogeneous long lived devices remain protected.

8.4 Ethical and Privacy Considerations

The increasing use of AI in cryptanalysis and cybersecurity testing raises ethical concerns. Automated tools can find exploitable flaws faster than engineers can fix them, and if those findings are leaked or misused they become powerful weapons for attackers. Using AI to analyze network traffic or device communications also creates privacy risks, especially when personal data is captured unintentionally or inference techniques deanonymize people. Researchers and practitioners must adopt robust ethical guidelines, including responsible disclosure and strict data handling, and commit to transparent stakeholder communication, privacy by design, and strong legal safeguards to preserve public trust in urban digital systems.

8.5 Directions for Future Research

Future research on post quantum cryptography will require interdisciplinary collaboration across cryptography, computer science, hardware engineering, ethics, and policy. Priority areas include designing hardware countermeasures against side channel and fault attacks, developing explainable AI tools to reveal cryptanalytic weaknesses, and building collaborative security frameworks for coordinated incident response. Work should also refine international standards and certification for post quantum algorithms used in critical infrastructure while addressing long term sustainability through lightweight and energy efficient implementations and clear governance frameworks. Pursuing these directions will help secure smart city ecosystems against emerging quantum era threats while protecting their social and economic foundations.

9. CONCLUSION

This chapter has presented a detailed review of the field of PQC in a cryptanalysis perspective; in other words, it has examined the technical security summaries and the system-level implication of its usage. The performance of the various PQC families including lattice-based, hash-based, code-based, isogeny-based and multivariate forms have been compared and it was noted that each of the PQC families is effective and weak in its respective adversary (classical adversary or quantum adversary). Even though lattice based schemes such as CRYSTALS-Kyber, as well as Dilithium have both demonstrated performance as well as different practical applicability, there are still families of schemes that can be attacked, and it is worth noting that there are other schemes that have or continue to be subjected to cryptanalysis. The chapter has lingered on the three fundamental measurements of complexity time, space, and data when it comes to determining the success of cryptanalytic work. These are the most put into practice benchmarks in the field and they constitute a transparent framework of the PQC resilience evaluation.

Energy consumption, implementation cost, and hardware constraints should guide future evaluations of post quantum cryptography in smart city and Internet of Things real world deployments. Case studies suggest full integration can be impractical: larger key sizes, performance overheads, and deployment complexity strain constrained devices and networks. Although some algorithms are more efficient for low resource hardware, scalability remains a concern. Combining post quantum techniques with artificial intelligence offers paths to optimize performance and adaptivity, but it also opens new attack vectors. Overall, technological progress brings both opportunity and risk, so pragmatic, context aware assessments are essential for secure, sustainable adoption.

Lastly, this chapter highlighted managerial and policy implications of the post quantum cryptography transition. Standardization bottlenecks, regulatory compliance requirements, and the need for cryptographic agility are key determinants of adoption. In smart cities and IoT ecosystems, where cryptographic devices have long lifetimes and infrastructure is heterogeneous, these considerations can be as important as the technical strength of algorithms. Successful adoption will therefore require cryptanalytic rigor and practical deployment strategies combined with governance foresight and active ongoing stakeholder engagement. Treating post quantum cryptography as a socio technical challenge ensures that resilient and sustainable digital infrastructure is built for the quantum era.

REFERENCES

Alagic, G., Alperin-Sheriff, J., Apon, D., Cooper, D., Dang, Q., Liu, Y. K., & Miller, C. (2020). *Status report on the second round of the NIST post-quantum cryptography standardization process*. National Institute of Standards and Technology. DOI: 10.6028/NIST.IR.8309

Bavdekar, R., Chopde, E. J., Agrawal, A., Bhatia, A., & Tiwari, K. (2023). Post-quantum cryptography: A review of techniques, challenges, and standardizations. In *2023 International Conference on Information Networking (ICOIN)* (pp. 146–151). IEEE. DOI: 10.1109/ICOIN56518.2023.10048976

Chen, L., Jordan, S., Liu, Y. K., Moody, D., Peralta, R., Perlner, R., & Smith-Tone, D. (2016). *Report on post-quantum cryptography*. National Institute of Standards and Technology. DOI: 10.6028/NIST.IR.8105

Dam, D.-T., Tran, T.-H., Hoang, V.-P., Pham, C.-K., & Hoang, T.-T. (2023). A survey of post-quantum cryptography: Start of a new race. *Cryptography*, *7*(3), 40. DOI: 10.3390/cryptography7030040

Darzi, S., Yavuz, A. A., & Behnia, R. (2024). PQC meets ML or AI: Exploring the synergy of machine learning and post-quantum cryptography. *TechRxiv*. DOI: 10.36227/techrxiv.170785010.08081159.v

European Commission. (2018). *General Data Protection Regulation (GDPR). Official Journal of the European Union*. https://eur-lex.europa.eu/eli/reg/2016/679/oj

European Union Agency for Cybersecurity (ENISA). (2021). *Post-quantum cryptography: Current state and quantum mitigation*. https://www.enisa.europa.eu/publications/post-quantum-cryptography-current-state-and-quantum-mitigation

Gupta, A., & Mittal, S. (2025, July 10). *AI-driven quantum cryptography*. *SSRN*. DOI: 10.2139/ssrn.5348579

Gupta, H. (2025). AI/ML assisted cryptanalysis: A deep learning-based approach to cipher pattern detection. *SSRN*. DOI: 10.2139/ssrn.5268832

Hanafi, B., & Ali, M. (2025). Analyzing the research impact in post-quantum cryptography through scientometric evaluation. *Discover Computing*, *28*(1), 32. DOI: 10.1007/s10791-025-09507-3

Horpenyuk, A., Opirskyy, I., & Vorobets, P. (2023). Analysis of problems and prospects of implementation of post-quantum cryptographic algorithms. In Proceedings of the Workshop on Classic, Quantum, and Post-Quantum Cryptography (CQPC 2023). CEUR-WS.org. http://ceur-ws.org

Jumaa, S., Ali, Q. A., & Alshmmri, M. A. (2022). Review: Methods of cryptography. *Al-Salam Journal for Engineering and Technology, 1*(2), 30–34. DOI: 10.55145/ajest.2022.01.02.006

Kerimbayeva, A. (2023). Analysis of existing approaches and algorithms of post-quantum cryptography. *Revue d'Intelligence Artificielle, 37*(3), 655–664. DOI: 10.18280/ria.370314

Kumar, M. (2022). Post-quantum cryptography algorithms standardization and performance analysis. *arXiv Preprint*. https://arxiv.org/abs/2204.02571

Mmaduekwe, E. P., Osholake, F., Ederhion, J., & Iyanuoluwa, T. (2024). Using machine learning to enhance post-quantum cryptographic algorithms. *International Journal of Advances in Engineering and Management, 8*(5), 715–728. DOI: 10.35629/5252-0702715728

Mosca, M. (2018). Cybersecurity in an era with quantum computers: Will we be ready? *IEEE Security and Privacy, 16*(5), 38–41. DOI: 10.1109/MSP.2018.3761723

National Institute of Standards and Technology (NIST). (2023). *Post-quantum cryptography standardization process: Third round finalists*. U.S. Department of Commerce. https://csrc.nist.gov/projects/post-quantum-cryptography

National Security Agency (NSA). (2022). *Quantum-resistant cryptography timeline*. U.S. Department of Defense. https://www.nsa.gov

Nitaj, A., & Rachidi, T. (2023). Applications of neural network-based AI in cryptography. *Cryptography, 7*(3), 39. DOI: 10.3390/cryptography7030039

P. C. S., Jain, K., & Krishnan, P. (2022). Analysis of post-quantum cryptography for Internet of Things. In *2022 6th International Conference on Intelligent Computing and Control Systems (ICICCS)* (pp. 387–394). IEEE. DOI: 10.1109/ICICCS53718.2022.9787987

Quantum-safe networking for critical AI/ML infrastructure. (2025). *Journal of Data Analysis and Critical Management, 1*(3), 19–29. DOI: 10.64235/hv81xw26

Radanliev, P. (2024). Artificial intelligence and quantum cryptography. *Journal of Analytical Science and Technology, 15*(1), 4. DOI: 10.1186/s40543-024-00416-6

Ravi, P., Jap, D., Bhasin, S., & Chattopadhyay, A. (2023). Invited paper: Machine learning-based blind side-channel attacks on PQC-based KEMs—A case study of Kyber KEM. In *2023 IEEE/ACM International Conference on Computer Aided Design (ICCAD)* (pp. 1–7). IEEE. DOI: 10.1109/ICCAD57390.2023.10323721

Sarkar, A., & Jhamb, M. (2025). Artificial intelligence-based Lagrange interpolation patterned post-quantum cryptography for secure cyber-physical systems in Internet of Things. *International Journal of Information Technology : an Official Journal of Bharati Vidyapeeth's Institute of Computer Applications and Management*, *17*(7), 3445–3453. DOI: 10.1007/s41870-025-02524-x

Satrya, G. B., Agus, Y. M., & Mnaouer, A. B. (2023). A comparative study of post-quantum cryptographic algorithm implementations for secure and efficient energy systems monitoring. *Electronics (Basel)*, *12*(18), 3824. DOI: 10.3390/electronics12183824

Thomas, S. A., & Gharge, S. (2017). Review on various visual cryptography schemes. In *2017 International Conference on Current Trends in Computer, Electrical, Electronics and Communication (CTCEEC)* (pp. 1164–1167). IEEE. DOI: 10.1109/CTCEEC.2017.8455136

APPENDIX A: IMPLEMENTATION DETAILS

The present appendix will include details on the steps, scripts, and programs by which the dataset used in the research was generated along with the machine learning models used to train the classifiers. Most of the chapter consists of the description of methods and findings, but to reproduce them, these technical specifications are maintained here.

A.1 Key Pair Generation Using PQClean

The following minimal C program, generate_keys.c, calls the crypto_kem_keypair() API to output one public key and its corresponding secret key.

```
#include <stdio.h>
#include "api.h"
int main(void) {
unsigned char public_key[CRYPTO_PUBLICKEYBYTES];
unsigned char secret_key[CRYPTO_SECRETKEYBYTES];
if (crypto_kem_keypair(public_key, secret_key) != 0) {
fprintf(stderr, "Keypair generation failed.\n");
return 1;
}
FILE *pub = fopen("public_key.bin", "wb");
FILE *sec = fopen("secret_key.bin", "wb");
fwrite(public_key, 1, CRYPTO_PUBLICKEYBYTES, pub);
fwrite(secret_key, 1, CRYPTO_SECRETKEYBYTES, sec);
fclose(pub); fclose(sec);
return 0;
}
```

A.2 Compilation and Automation

The program was compiled using GCC with the PQClean sources.

```
gcc -I PQClean/crypto_kem/kyber768/clean/ \
PQClean/crypto_kem/kyber768/clean/*.c generate_keys.c -o generate_keys
```

To build a sufficiently large dataset, a Bash script automated repeated execution of the binary. The following script generated 1,000 public–secret key pairs, stored sequentially in a directory keys/.

```
#!/bin/bash
```

```
mkdir -p keys
for i in $(seq 1 1000); do
./generate_keys
mv public_key.bin keys/pub_${i}.bin
mv secret_key.bin keys/sec_${i}.bin
don
```

This process yielded 2,000 binary files (1,000 public keys and 1,000 secret keys), which formed the raw dataset.

A.3 Feature Extraction in Python

The binary public keys were transformed into feature vectors suitable for machine learning

```
import numpy as np
import os
import glob
import pandas as pd
from scipy.stats import skew, kurtosis, entropy
feature_vectors = []
for filename in glob.glob("keys/pub_*.bin"):
with open(filename, "rb") as f:
key_bytes = np.frombuffer(f.read(), dtype=np.uint8)
# Histogram
hist, _ = np.histogram(key_bytes, bins=256, range=(0, 255), density=True)
# Descriptive statistics
mean_val = np.mean(key_bytes)
var_val = np.var(key_bytes)
skew_val = skew(key_bytes)
kurt_val = kurtosis(key_bytes)
entropy_val = entropy(hist + 1e-12) # avoid log(0)
# Simple autocorrelation proxy
autocorr_val = np.corrcoef(key_bytes[:-1], key_bytes[1:])[0, 1]
features = np.concatenate((hist, [mean_val, var_val, skew_val, kurt_val, en-
tropy_val, autocorr_val]))
feature_vectors.append(features)
# Save dataset
df = pd.DataFrame(feature_vectors)
df.to_csv("features.csv", index=False)
```

A.4 Machine Learning Training

A general Pythonic version with the scikit-learn library is given below.

```
from sklearn.tree import DecisionTreeClassifier
from sklearn.svm import SVC
from sklearn.ensemble import RandomForestClassifier
dt = DecisionTreeClassifier(max_depth=10)
svm = SVC(C=1.0, kernel='rbf')
rf = RandomForestClassifier(n_estimators=100, max_depth=20)
dt.fit(X_train, y_train)
svm.fit(X_train, y_train)
rf.fit(X_train, y_train)
```

Chapter 8
Protecting Symmetric Cryptography From Quantum Attacks:
Challenges and Mitigation Strategies

Beslin Pajila
https://orcid.org/0000-0002-3905-2460
Vel Tech Rangarajan Dr. Sagunthala R&D Institute of Science and Technology, India

Anish T. P.
https://orcid.org/0000-0002-4308-9645
R.M.K. College of Engineering and Technology, India

B. Yamini
https://orcid.org/0000-0003-3531-108X
SRM Institute of Science and Technology, India

ABSTRACT

The emergence of quantum computing presents profound implications for classical cryptographic systems, including symmetric encryption. This chapter surveys the impact of quantum computing on symmetric cryptography, outlines key challenges such as reduced security margins and implementation vulnerabilities, and explores mitigation strategies including increased key sizes, quantum-resistant designs, hybrid encryption models, and algorithm agility. Future research directions are discussed, emphasizing the need for quantum-native symmetric primitives, efficient post-quantum

DOI: 10.4018/979-8-3373-3166-9.ch008

implementations, and secure key exchange through quantum key distribution. The chapter advocates for a proactive transition toward quantum-resilient cryptographic infrastructures to ensure long-term data security.

1. INTRODUCTION

1.1 Symmetric Cryptography in the Era of Quantum Threats

Symmetric cryptography forms the basis of the modern cryptographic system and is vital in the provision of data confidentiality, integrity and authenticity. In contrast to asymmetric cryptography, in which different keys are used to encrypt and decrypt, a symmetric cryptography utilizes a shared secret key to encrypt and decrypt. This has made it very efficient and is applicable in securing large amounts of data in different applications such as virtual private networks (VPNs), secure file storage, financial transactions, embedded systems among others. The use of algorithm like Advanced Encryption Standard (AES), Data Encryption Standard (DES), Triple DES (3DES) and lightweight ciphers has been widely spread because of their computational efficiency and good performance in limited settings (Subramanian, R. S et al., 2024). Symmetric key algorithms are also used in a number of hybrid encryption systems as they encrypt real data but the key exchange is done by means of public-key cryptography (Muthumanickam, K et al., 2023). The ongoing development of quantum computing presents significant threats to classical cryptographic systems. Whereas the public-key cryptosystems such as RSA and ECC are especially susceptible to the Shor algorithm whose efficient implementation can factor large integers and solve discrete logarithm problems, symmetric cryptographic systems are mostly at risk of the Grover algorithm. Grover algorithm provides a quadratic speed-up in brute-force search of keys effectively reducing the security level of symmetric key cryptography by a factor of two. As an illustration, a 128-bit symmetric key, thought to be secure in classical computing paradigm, would provide only 64 bits of security against an adversary having access to a powerful enough quantum computer. This diminishing security margin has been a matter of concern in the entire world of cybersecurity, and this has led to reconsideration by researchers, standardization organizations, and governments on the long-term sustainability of symmetric cryptographic systems (Sihare, S., & Khang, A 2023). Since symmetric cryptography is imperative in protecting the digital infrastructure and since quantum computing is expected to be advanced in the future, it is imperative to comprehend the level of quantum threats to symmetric algorithms and come up with mitigation strategies that can be effective. While the threat posed by Grover's algorithm is not as immediate or damaging as the one posed by Shor's algorithm to public-key systems, it remains significant, particularly for systems expected to remain secure in the long term. In addition, quantum attack models such as quantum chosen-plaintext attack and quantum memory attacks undermine the classically based assumptions of cryptographic security, and compel a fundamental rethink of cryptographic design and analysis in the quantum setting. Quantum cryptanalysis is an emerging field which is expanding the arena and the types of attacks that can be launched against symmetric cryptographic systems. In the meantime, some scientific effort is underway on new symmetric primitives that may provide more quantum-security to an adversary, e.g. more key-size, more complexity, or more quantum oracle queries. This dual breakthrough in the offensive and defensive fronts of quantum algorithms and quantum resilient design is what amplifies the dynamic and urgent threats to the security of symmetric cryptography in the quantum world.

1.2 Motivation, Objectives, and Structure of the Chapter

The primary motivating factor in conducting this survey chapter is that there has been growing urgency to ensure that symmetric cryptographic algorithms are immune to the latest threat of quantum computing. Though most of the recent discussion in the area of post-quantum cryptography (PQC) revolves around the topic of public-key schemes, the implications of the former to symmetric systems are not any less significant, only more subtle. As the technology behind quantum computing advances and the use of practical quantum computers is no more than a year away, one can clearly see that it is high time to estimate the vulnerability of the existing symmetric schemes and come up with foolproof measures that will ensure that cryptographic systems will not succumb to attacks in the far future. This chapter tries to explicitly examine the threat scenario of symmetric cryptography in quantum age. It is concerned with how quantum algorithms and Grover algorithm specifically affect the security of many popular symmetric primitives, and how key length and the complexity of an attack behave in a quantum world. Other forms of quantum attack models such as quantum oracle based attacks and side channel attacks which could be implemented in quantum environment are also discussed in the chapter. These models are also vital in effective risk assessment and formulation of more robust cryptographic requirements. The second objective of the chapter is to summarize and analyze the current and recommended mitigation strategies that could help protect the symmetric cryptography against quantum attacks. This includes a detailed discussion of key size increase, considering algorithm agility as potentially feasible in the future and the use of hybrid cryptography systems combining symmetric and post-quantum systems. In addition, the chapter discusses quantum resistant symmetric designs and their suitability to real world systems considering performance and scalability constraints as well as resource constraints.

To help in these purposes, the chapter outline will be as follows. Section 2 provides a background on the basics of symmetric cryptography and quantum computing and the quantum algorithms underpinning cryptographic systems. Section 3 discusses the quantum threat model in symmetric cryptography, the quantum threat to many symmetric primitives, and quantum attacks models. The main issues with symmetric cryptography security against the quantum threat are presented in Section 4 and they are problems with key management, vulnerabilities of implementation, and weaknesses of legacy systems. The section 5 provides an in-depth description of the mitigation steps, such as extending cryptographic keys, using algorithm agility and hybrid systems. In section 6 future research directions are discussed with quantum-native symmetric systems and more sophisticated quantum key distribution methods. Finally, Section 7 is the conclusion of the chapter that summarises the main findings and emphasizes the need to constantly innovate and actively defend the cryptographic community.

2. BACKGROUND CONCEPTS

To comprehend the effect that quantum computing will have on symmetric cryptography, it is important to have a good knowledge of the principles of the symmetric encryption and the main principles of quantum computing. This section presents the background information that is needed to understand the problems and threats presented by quantum algorithms and their impacts on the security assumptions of symmetric cryptographic systems.

2.1 Symmetric Cryptography Overview

Secret-key cryptography Symmetric cryptography is the classical cryptographic algorithm where the same key is employed both to encrypt and to decrypt. The main strength of symmetric encryption is that it is simple and computationally cheaper thus very appropriate in securing large amount of data and real time communication. Symmetric cryptographic algorithms are normally faster and less resource-intensive to compute than the public-key systems that have overheads because of their complex mathematical formulations. Symmetric encryption, in its essence, refers to a process of encrypting plaintext into ciphertext with the help of a secret key and a clear algorithm. This ciphertext cannot be decoded back to the original form without the same key and this guarantees confidentiality. Symmetric cryptography has an important key management. The key distribution and storage should be secured as both the sender and the receiver have to share the same secret key otherwise the integrity of the whole system is jeopardized. Symmetric keys In practice, symmetric keys are frequently deployed with the help of secure key exchange protocols, which can in turn be based on asymmetric cryptography, a property that is undesirable in the post-quantum world. A number of symmetric algorithms have been popularized in many sectors. The most common symmetric encryption algorithm is the Advanced encryption Standard (AES), nowadays. It has a key size of 128, 192 and 256 bits and it has been utilized in secure file storage, secure online transactions, VPNs and government communications. The older Data Encryption Standard (DES), 56-bit key, has been mostly superseded by brute-force attacks, although its enhanced version, Triple DES (3DES), which uses DES three times, has also been phased out, because of its small block size and inefficiencies. Newer stream ciphers have found popularity in response to the demand of high-speed and resource-efficient encryption in resource-constrained systems like mobile devices and IoT systems. Although these algorithms are quite strong in the classical setting, the current security is being reconsidered in view of the upcoming quantum technologies. Although symmetric encryption is usually more quantum-resistant than asymmetric cryptography, it is not quantum-proof. Quantum computing is growing more and more in importance and the necessity to reconsider key sizes, cipher structures, and operational parameters is becoming apparent.

2.2 Basics of Quantum Computing

Quantum computing is a new paradigm of computing, which uses concepts of quantum mechanics to process information in radically new ways. Quantum computers differ with classical computers in the sense that classical computers use binary bits to represent information in two states (0 or 1) whereas the quantum computers use quantum bits, also known as qubits, which can be in a superposition of both states at the same time. This is what makes quantum computers capable of performing a lot of calculations in parallel, which makes them have a massive potential in computing power in specific areas of problems (Brijwani, G. N et al., 2023). The other important concept of quantum mechanics is entanglement which is a phenomenon in which the states of two or more qubits are inseparably coupled. The state of each pair of entangled qubits will be instantaneously affected by the state of the other qubit irrespective of the distance between the two qubits. This is what enables quantum algorithms to organize themselves to perform operations on large numbers of qubits in a very efficient way (Chittem, M. B., & Pradhan, A. K. 2025).

Quantum gates are unitary transformations which acts on qubits and govern quantum computation. Quantum gates are reversible unlike classical logic gates whose operation is irreversible, that is, they do not lose information. Such reversibility is the basis of quantum coherence and the implementation of complex algorithms, such as Shor and Grover.

Two quantum algorithms have attained special significance in the cryptography context because they threaten to break or compromise classical cryptographic systems:

1.Shor Algorithm: This algorithm was proposed by Peter Shor in 1994 and is able to factor large integers, and to compute discrete logarithms in poly-time. This is disastrous to the popular asymmetric cryptosystems such as RSA, Diffie-Hellman and Elliptic Curve Cryptography (ECC) that are based on the computational complexity of these mathematical problems. Such crypto-systems can be made obsolete using Shor algorithm in a quantum computer powerful enough.

2.Grover Algorithm: Lov Grover proposed this algorithm in 1996 and it provides a quadratic speed up on the problem of unstructured search. Grover algorithm In symmetric cryptography, Grover algorithm can be used to search a key using brute-force with time complexity of $\sqrt{N}$, where N is the size of the key space. This reduces symmetric encryption algorithms security to half. Although Grover algorithm does not totally defeat symmetric cryptographic systems, it effectively lowers the effective strength of such systems requiring doubling thc kcy sizes or the development of new designs to maintain the same classical strength. In addition, Grover algorithm is the best algorithm to unstructured search and there is no known quantum algorithm that can give an exponential advantage to symmetric key attacks and this makes symmetric cryptography to have a comparative advantage over asymmetric ones in a post-quantum world.

2.3 Quantum Threats to Cryptography

The emergence of the quantum computing poses varying degrees of threats to the classical cryptographic systems, asymmetric and symmetric schemes being impacted differently. The public-key systems are at risk of extinction because of Shor algorithm, which can efficiently solve the mathematical problems that are the foundation of their security. Consequently, such algorithms as RSA and ECC will be completely insecure as soon as scalable quantum computers are implemented. Symmetric cryptography however is more resilient but not completely immune. The threat posed by Grover algorithm is the main one, a quantum adversary can search a key space in approximately the square root of the time needed by a brute-force search. This is in effect halving the strength of a symmetric cipher. As an example, AES-128, which is thought not to be vulnerable to classical attacks, would only provide 64-bit security to an adversary having access to Grover algorithm. In order to reach the security level of 128 bits, it is suggested to use AES-256 that would still need 2128 operations, which is impossible even to quantum computers. Moreover, the quantum threat model also proposes new attack models, such as quantum oracle access, where the adversary may query the encryption function in superposition. This has the effect of invalidating conventional expectations of adversarial models and the need to develop quantum-secure definitions and proofs of cryptographic primitives. As an example, a secure encryption algorithm under a classical chosen-plaintext attack (CPA) model fails to be secure under quantum CPA (qCPA) attack in which the adversary is allowed to make quantum queries. As quantum computing becomes a reality, it is becoming clear that besides revolutionizing the publicly-key-based cryptography, the transition to quantum-resilient cryptography will demand significant modifications to symmetric cryptography (Das, S., & Das, A 2023).

3. QUANTUM THREAT LANDSCAPE FOR SYMMETRIC CRYPTOGRAPHY

The introduction of quantum computing represents a paradigm shift in the computational resources that directly challenge the premises upon which current cryptographic security is premised. Although there is an impending and grave danger to the public-key cryptography by the likes of Shor, symmetric cryptography cannot be ignored owing to the efficiency that can be achieved courtesy of Grover. The quantum threat model of symmetric systems is subtle and needs an extensive knowledge of the characteristics of different primitives such as block ciphers, stream ciphers, and cryptographic hash functions when they are subjected to quantum adversarial models. Also, quantum computing brings new attack models, which are fundamentally different to classical assumptions.

3.1 Impact of Grover's Algorithm

Lov Grover (1996) proposed Grover algorithm, a quantum algorithm to the unstructured search problem. In classical computing, search of a given object within an unordered list of N objects takes O(N) operations. Grover algorithm achieves this in $O(\sqrt{N})$ operations, which is a quadratic speed up. Applied to symmetric cryptography this implies that a brute-force key search over a key space of size N, an operation that would classically require 2n operations, can be performed in about 2^(n/2) quantum operations. This has far reaching consequences to successful security of symmetric encryption schemes. An example is cipher such as AES-128 that offers 128 bits of protection against classical brute-force would only offer 64 bits of protection against a quantum opponent with Grover algorithm. Although this remains computationally infeasible with existing or near-term quantum computers, this is much less secure than the original level of security was intended. In order to offset such loss in effective security, cryptographers suggest doubling the key size. Therefore, AES-256, with its traditional 256-bit security is nonetheless secure with 128-bit security against Grover-based attacks, which is a sufficient degree of security in most practical cases. Notably, Grover algorithm is a universal quantum instrument. It does not take advantage of structural vulnerabilities in a cipher, instead it speeds up brute-force key search. It means that symmetric cryptographic algorithms, which would have been otherwise regarded as cryptographically sound in a classical setting, can be susceptible in case they do not use sufficiently long keys. Also, Grover's algorithm is considered the optimal quantum search algorithm for brute-force attacks, providing a quadratic speed-up. Nevertheless, Grover algorithm has a limited real-life applicability due to a number of practical factors. First, the practical application of Grover algorithm to a large scale problem needs many errors corrected qubits and long coherent run time which is still a big engineering problem. Second, every run of Grover algorithm involves the implementation of the cryptographic function a quantum circuit, which can be expensive in terms of the complexity and depth of quantum gates. Third, a large number of practical systems use key derivation functions (KDFs), password based key generation, or dynamic key rotation schemes that render direct brute-force infeasible. Nevertheless, even these caveats do not make the decrease in the effective key size a purely theoretical issue. It requires proactive modifications to security parameters, particularly in long-lived systems like embedded devices, secure archival systems and national infrastructure where post-deployment replacement of cryptographic standards with more recent ones is expensive or not possible. It is therefore important to know the implications of the algorithm developed by Grover in order to evaluate quantum threats and develop robust symmetric cryptographic systems.

3.2 Quantum Attacks on Symmetric Primitives

Although the main implication of Grover s algorithm to the key search in block ciphers, other symmetric primitives such as stream ciphers and hash functions are also threatened by the quantum computing. Depending on the structure and the context of its usage, each group of primitive is impacted in a different way.

BlockCiphers: AES and the DES are very popular block ciphers that are used in many cryptographic protocols and applications. In classical models of attack, their security is quantified by the effort required to recover the key or break the cipher through differential, linear or algebraic cryptanalysis. In Grover algorithm, the key space is more reachable and this in effect reduces the security level by half as explained earlier. But then there are more sophisticated quantum attacks on block ciphers as well. As an example, in theoretical models in which quantum adversaries are allowed to access encryption oracles in superposition (a so-called quantum oracle model), other attack vectors can be enabled which are not possible in the classical setting. Such models enable the adversaries to manipulate several plaintext-ciphertext pairs in parallel, and may allow non-trivial knowledge of the cipher structure or the use of superposition-based differential attacks, but most practical block ciphers such as AES are thought to be immune to these in realistic quantum models.

StreamCiphers: Another key family of symmetric cryptographic primitives are stream ciphers, which encrypt plaintext a bit or a byte at a time by XORing it with a pseudorandom keystream. Although these ciphers do not directly fall prey to Grover-style brute-force attacks (other than an attack on the key itself, or internal state), the keystream generation algorithm can be attacked in the case that the internal state or the key is small. Moreover, quantum protocols can be used to attack linear feedback shift registers (LFSRs) or nonlinear feedback circuits that some stream ciphers employ, in a quantum context; these quantum algorithms would attempt to analyze or invert the state transitions. Nevertheless, as opposed to key search, there is no general-purpose quantum algorithm to break well-designed modern stream ciphers much faster than with square-root speedup in brute-force search.

HashFunctions: Security of cryptographic hash functions which are applied in data integrity, digital signatures, message authentication codes (MACs), and password storage is also affected by quantum computing. Classical cryptanalysis A collision in a hash function, two inputs that give the same hash value, can usually be found in O(2^n/2) operations with an n-bit hash result (the birthday bound). Quantum computing makes this O(2^n/3) operations such as quantum collision- finding algorithm. This speed increase is not exponential, but still represents a large threat, especially to legacy systems that employ shorter hash output such as SHA-1 (160 bits) or MD5 (128 bits). In a quantum world, collision resistance of SHA-256 would fall to 2^128 to 2^85 to use longer or more powerful hash functions.

Some of the applications of hash functions include the use of hash functions in digital signatures due to the integrity and the non-repudiation that is provided by the functions. Quantum attacks can compromise such guarantees, possibly in a cascading way, to decentralized trust systems and cryptographic protocols.

3.3 Quantum Attack Models

In addition to Grover or BHT algorithm itself, quantum computing also offers qualitatively new models of attack that are not classical adversarial. An example of such models is the quantum chosen-plaintext attack (qCPA) in which an adversary is permitted to submit superposition queries to the encryption oracle. This is unlike the conventional chosen-plaintext attack in which the attacker provides plaintexts and monitors the respective ciphertexts in isolation. A qCPA model attacker can transmit a superposition of all the possible inputs and receives in return a superposition of all the possible outputs, enabling potentially more powerful analysis tools that cannot be modeled classically. There are known-plaintext attacks (KPA) and chosen-plaintext attacks (CPA), which also assume different forms in a quantum environment. An example to consider is the existence of a quantum-memory adversary capable of storing superposition states, or of re-creating or processing known plaintext-ciphertext pairs, in a manner that cannot be accomplished classically. This causes the necessity of new security proofs with quantum memory, quantum indistinguishability and adversarial learning. In brief, quantum attack models alter the cryptographic analysis game. They question the assumptions that most symmetric primitives are designed and experimented with, and theoretical and practical security guarantees need to be reevaluated. The models have a significant role in the design of future-proof symmetric systems, and in the formulation of meaningful mitigation strategies.

4. SECURITY CHALLENGES IN THE QUANTUM ERA

With quantum computing slowly but surely becoming a reality, the consequences that this technology will have on the area of symmetric cryptography is swiftly gaining topicality. Even though the symmetric algorithm is typically assumed to have fewer vulnerability to quantum attacks than the asymmetric algorithm, it is not immune to quantum-driving attacks. The quantum threat space poses new security margin, algorithm design, and implementation problem. In addition, the limitation of legacy systems is that the migration to quantum-resilient cryptography schemes is especially complicated. This section identifies and discusses the most important problems of symmetric cryptography in the post-quantum world, which are key length and security margins, algorithmic weaknesses and implementation limitations.

4.1 Key Length and Security Margin

Among the most notable challenges that quantum computing presented to us is the fact that Grover algorithm reduces effective security margins of symmetric key algorithms. As mentioned in previous sections, Grover quantum search algorithm enables brute-force attack to retrieve symmetric n-bit key in about 2n/2 steps which is a cut-down of symmetric systems security into half. An example is the AES-128 which has 128 bits of security against classical brute-force attacks; similarly in a quantum environment it has 64 bits of security. Such a degree of security is not deemed as sufficient in the long-term protection against future quantum attackers. The biggest threat to this threat is to increase the size of cryptographic keys. With AES-256 as an example, this would regain a good level of security of 128 bits against Grover algorithm. Even though this solution might sound as easy, there are several practical implications that come with it. First, the increase in the key sizes may cause the performance degradation, particularly in the platforms with limited resources, including embedded systems, IoT devices, and mobile platforms. The larger keys will likely consume additional processing resources, memory and bandwidth that such systems may not be readily able to sustain. Second, a longer key length increases the computation complexity of a key management operation, especially when a system employs a dynamic key exchange or key derivation protocol. Moving key exchange protocols to post-quantum key exchange protocols added further complexity and potential latency even in cases where the symmetric keys are produced by a public-key cryptographic scheme, which can be broken by the Shor algorithm. Moreover, the increase in the size of keys without the re-evaluation of the encryption protocol overall is not sufficient. The security margins also depend not only on the size of the key but also on other factors such as block size, round transformations and quantum models of attack.

As an example, using a key of adequate length, a cipher with a small block size might still be vulnerable to quantum-enhanced differential attacks or ciphertext block collisions during high throughput usage. The other issue is that security margins are overestimated because it lacks quantum costs in the real world. Theoretical models usually assume ideal quantum operations, though quantum error correction, decoherence and gate fidelity problems can result in overheads in real implementations. It is however wise to always expect the worst scenario when designing or choosing symmetric cryptographic systems which will be secure in the long run (Yamini, B et al., 2024). Overall, key length adjustment is not a sufficient but is a necessary prerequisite to the secure symmetric cryptography in the quantum age. Key size should be considered as part of an overall security strategy that should consider algorithm design, system performance and the increasing capabilities of quantum attackers.

Figure 1. Security Challenges in the Quantum Era

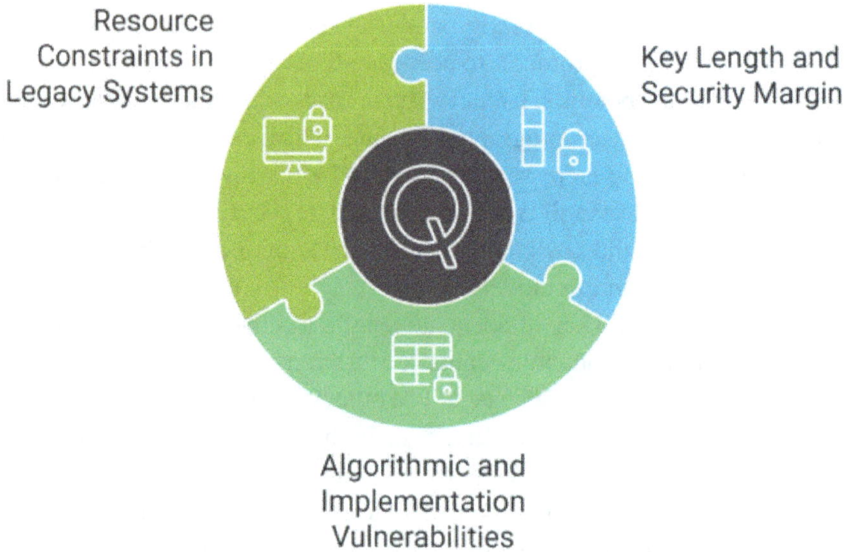

4.2 Algorithmic and Implementation Vulnerabilities

Although enlarging the key size provides a first line of defense, quantum computing also introduces novel avenues of cryptanalytic attacks on the flaws of the structure or implementation of symmetric algorithms. The attack vectors are unique to quantum and cannot be considered as only theoretical threats, which need to be considered to ensure that a system remains intact. An example of such a vector is the quantum-accessible memory attack that exploits the fact that quantum adversaries can be in superposition to cryptographic oracles or memory. In such cases, the attackers are able to issue queries in more than one state at a time and it might result in exponential data leakage in case the system is not well designed. Whereas classical oracles can only give one answer to each single query, quantum oracles can provide a superposition state that can contain the answers to different queries.

Such a capability questions the standard cryptographic assumptions and can undermine such security properties as indistinguishability under chosen-plaintext attacks (IND-CPA) or indistinguishability under chosen-ciphertext attacks (IND-CCA). Symmetric encryption schemes based on deterministic internal structures or predictable substitution-permutation layers, are examples of encryption schemes that might be vulnerable against quantum superposition queries. Enemies can use constructive interference between quantum states to enhance distinguishing characteristics, and may be able to infer regularities in cipher text. Although it is not suspected that existing symmetric ciphers such as AES are subject to these attacks in practice, the absence of formal proofs of quantum security mean that care is required and that further work is needed. Side-channel attacks constitute another type of vulnerabilities and are founded on the unintentional release of physical information by cryptographic devices. Such attacks are power analysis, electromagnetic radiation, timing analysis and even acoustic side-channels. Although side-channel attacks are well-known in the classical cryptography, quantum adversaries might have extra abilities in processing, storing, or analyzing side-channel information. The sensitivity with which side-channel emissions may be detected and analysed, or the amount of information that may be extracted based on a limited number of observations, might be increased by quantum-enabled signal processing. Also, when quantum computers are applied in conjunction with machine learning or pattern recognition models, they can potentially be able to recover secret keys faster than with conventional methods (Minu et al 2024; Paul, S., & Mitra, A 2022). The theoretical possibility of quantum-enhanced side-channel analysis is in its infancy, but could potentially re-define the risk model of hardware-based cryptographic systems. The weaknesses in implementation are of great concern when the implementation is large scale and cryptographic operations are being performed using low-end or obsolete hardware. In these situations side-channel attacks susceptibility can be inevitable because of design limitations. Besides, software cryptographic libraries can accidentally create timing or cache-based vulnerabilities that can be exploited by quantum-assisted attackers with more sophisticated measurement devices or predictive models. To overcome these threats, symmetric algorithms should be used carefully focusing on constant-time operations, power-analysis resistance and memory-based leakage protection. Also post quantum implementation guidelines ought to contain stress testing of hypothetical attacks with quantum attack and formal verification of hardware and software components with quantum-aware models.

4.3 Resource Constraints in Legacy Systems

One of the strongest obstacles to making symmetric cryptographic systems quantum-resistant is that so many legacy systems are in place. Numerous systems that are in use today such as industrial control systems, embedded medical devices, smart meters and consumer electronics are constructed with fixed cryptographic parameters and are not flexible enough to support increased key sizes or enhanced encryption protocols. Such systems are frequently intended to last many years and the identification of cryptographic weaknesses after deployment is very difficult to deal with. Another important limitation of legacy environments is the fact that key sizes or algorithms cannot be altered without significant hardware or firmware changes. As an example, a smart card or embedded processor that is hard-coded to use AES-128 will need to be replaced with an entirely new device to switch to AES-256, which is not cost-effective and unrealistic to do on a large scale. In the same way, in case the encryption algorithm is part of the system-on-chip (SoC) design, it might not be possible to update it without redesigning and recertifying the entire system. Backward compatibility is another big question, especially with large enterprise or government systems that have thousands or even millions of devices to interoperate securely. The shift to quantum-resistant symmetric settings threatens to lose compatibility with older devices, software platforms or communication protocols. The infrastructure in most of the cases has been developed based on the assumption that symmetric key cryptography would be safe throughout the life of the device an assumption that is currently facing a threat. This issue is made worse in other sectors such as healthcare and defense where data security needs to be on the long term basis. Government archives, medical records and classified documents can be required to be kept secret throughout decades. In the event that such data is encrypted through algorithms that can be decrypted by quantum algorithms then their privacy and national security might be compromised. Furthermore, the opponents can implement a strategy of storing today encrypted information with intention to decrypt it in the future when quantum computers will be available. The solution to the problem of resource limitation is a phased strategy. Systems where feasible must be algorithm agile, that is, they must be designed such that cryptography components can be replaced or upgraded without changing hardware. To enable smooth transitions, middleware and communication protocols ought to support several cryptography profiles. Security audit must be able to determine the high risk systems and rank order their upgrade path according to sensitivity, exposure and feasibility. Lastly, government, industry and academia must cooperate to design and standardize light and quantum-resistant symmetric algorithms that can be implemented on resource-limited devices. These endeavours may enable the transition between quantum security theory and practice, so that even the resource-poor systems may be resilient in the quantum world.

5. MITIGATION STRATEGIES

As the world of quantum computing is rapidly developing, our defensive measures against its disruptive potential have to be developed as well. Although symmetric cryptography is more resistant to quantum threats than an asymmetric scheme, it is vulnerable anyway, particularly to the complexity reduction of brute-force key search provided by Grover algorithm. In this section, the major mitigation techniques that can be used to strengthen symmetric cryptography are outlined and they include expanding key sizes, creating quantum-resistant symmetric solutions, using hybrid cryptographic methods, and designing systems with algorithm flexibility.

5.1 Increasing Key Sizes

The most short-term and feasible solution to defend quantum attacks on symmetric cryptography is to enlarge the encryption keys. The idea of this strategy is directly related to the implication of Grover algorithm that decreases the effective security of a symmetric key by half of its length (n bits to about *n/2* bits). Thus it would be possible to exploit a 128-bit key like that used in AES-128 simply by providing the adversary with a 64-bit key, which is usually considered insecure to high-security uses. It is a well-recommended response to upgrade to AES-256. AES-256 can provide 256-bit security classically and this is halved to 128 bits against Grover algorithm that is still within acceptable quantum-resistant security. Such transition is already possible in the majority of modern systems, because AES-256 is supported by practically all leading cryptographic libraries, such as OpenSSL, Bouncy Castle and Microsoft Cryptography API. But with the raising of key size, there are performance issues. The AES-256 contains a greater quantity of rounds (14) than the AES-128 (10), which results in the enhanced time of calculation and energy consumption. This could cause minimal latency in large- throughput networks like cloud servers and VPNs. More importantly, the increased processing burden might become an issue to the devices that have limited resources, e.g., embedded sensors, mobile IoT devices, and wearable technologies (Prajapat, M et al., 2024). Also there are interoperability and backward compatibility issues. Legacy systems can utilize pre-determined, AES-128 or earlier symmetric-based configurations and might not be able to utilize AES- 256 without firmware or hardware revision. Scaling up of such systems may be both expensive and challenging, particularly in the industrial automation, transportation infrastructure, and medical devices. Nonetheless, these disadvantages notwithstanding, the expansion of key sizes is one of the core mitigation measures. It has an immediate benefit in terms of post-quantum resilience without re-architecting. The quantum computing development will continue to make key length an important parameter of the cryptographic strength, particularly in long-term applications like secure data archiving and digital signature.

5.2 Quantum-Resistant Symmetric Designs

Although extending key lengths is a reactive measure to deal with Grover algorithm, proactive measure is to design symmetric algorithms that are inherently quantum resistant. These are quantum-resistant symmetric schemes with classical robustness and classical-informed quantum-aware models of attack, including quantum chosen-plaintext attacks (qCPA), quantum oracle access and superposition query resistance. Classical assumptions were used to design such traditional symmetric algorithms as AES. They seem to be safe against known quantum attacks, but they do not have any formal security proofs in quantum-accessible models. As a solution to this deficiency quantum-secure pseudorandom functions (QPRFs), message authentication codes (QMACs) and new block ciphers that can be analyzed formally in quantum models are under investigation. On the one hand, the increase of internal complexity and randomness in ciphers is resolved. The modern designs are directed to create nonlinearity more, diffusion amplification more and add major schedules that cannot be analyzed by quantum superposition. These properties make quantum adversaries inefficient to amplify specific computational events, or to take advantage of structural weaknesses in quantum interferences. Quantum-resistant symmetric designs are new, but represent a step toward cryptographic primitives that are not just quantum-resistant, but quantum-native. These designs (along with formal verification and real-world testing) can contribute to a potentially winning approach on the long-term security of cryptography.

5.3 Hybrid Cryptographic Approaches

Hybrid cryptography provides a feasible transition between traditional and post-quantum security paradigm. Symmetric encryption is adopted in hybrid systems together with the classical and the post-quantum public-key algorithms, providing layered and future-resistant protection. In this strategy, the fast and efficient symmetric encryption is used and the key exchange and authentication are based on quantum-resistant algorithms. In existing cryptographic systems, symmetric key agreement is frequently negotiated by an asymmetric key exchange algorithm, e.g. RSA or Elliptic Curve Diffie-Hellman (ECDH). These are extremely susceptible to Shor algorithm which is efficient in factoring in large integers and solving discrete logarithms. These functions are now being replaced with post-quantum key encapsulation mechanisms (KEMs), e.g. lattice-based KEMs. In a hybrid encryption system, symmetric algorithm such as AES-256 is applied to confidentiality of the data, whereas the symmetric key is exchanged by a classical and a post-quantum KEM. The recipient also checks the two outputs of the key derivation and only picks the shared key when the two key exchanges are successful. Such a two-layer design guarantees forward secrecy of the post-quantum algorithm even in case the classical key exchange can be broken in the future by a quantum computer.

The advantages of hybrid schemes are many:

Redundancy and safety net: In case of failure of one algorithm (because of classical or quantum attack), the system has a secure second channel upon which it can depend.

Gradual migration path: Hybrid systems enable the organization to adopt post-quantum cryptography without having to give up on the existing systems completely.

Regulatory compliance: The government agencies are likely soon to demand quantum-safe transitions, and hybrid cryptography offers a standards-compatible approach to such transitions.

Nevertheless, hybrid methods should not be overlooked as they are a realistic and intermediate measure that can be adopted by organizations now to start their post-quantum migration process.

5.4 Algorithm Agility

Algorithm agility is a fundamental architectural concept to use in cryptographic systems because quantum developments are unpredictable. The concept of algorithm agility is the capability of a system to easily replace cryptographic primitives, e.g. block ciphers, hash functions or key exchange protocols, without necessitating a central change of the overall system architecture. Such flexibility is particularly critical in the post-quantum world, in which new algorithms are continually being proposed, studied, and standardized. A cryptographic algorithm considered secure today can be discovered unsecure tomorrow because of unexpected breakthroughs in quantum computer or cryptanalysis. Agile systems are able to switch to more powerful primitives without much disturbance. The agility of algorithms should be built into the systems (software and hardware) with caution. Plug-and-play modules ought to be supported by cryptographic APIs, which enable the addition of new algorithms and sets of parameters to be easily added. Such protocols as TLS, SSH, and IPsec are expected to support a variety of cipher suites and allow dynamic negotiation of algorithms to be used, depending on the capabilities of the endpoints or the application of policy. In the case of hardware-based cryptographic modules (including HSMs, TPMs and smart cards), algorithm agility can take the form of modular firmware or reconfigurable logic. As an example, the FPGAs may be upgraded even after deployment to accommodate new cryptographic cores. These devices must have secure firmware update mechanisms because they can be patched with vulnerabilities and new quantum safe algorithms added. Algorithm agility is essential in the long-lifecycle systems that include satellites, military installations, and other critical infrastructures. These systems need to plan cryptographic change decades ahead of time, and they should be able to add the upgrade without the physical access or downtime. Agility can be used to future-proof, meet the changing standards, and zero-day vulnerabilities. Conclusively, algorithm agility forms the pillar of quantum-resilient design. It allows quick adjustment to new threats and cryptographic advances, thus keeping the systems safe as the cryptographic environment in which they have to operate changes in an unpredictable way.

6. FUTURE RESEARCH DIRECTIONS

Because quantum computing is gradually moving from being a theoretical possibility towards the reality of practical potential, symmetric cryptography will have to change to continue being secure and efficient. Although the existing mitigation measures like the use of larger key sizes and the hybrid schemes offer a short-term escape, the long-term security of the digital systems in a quantum world requires more innovation and revolution. The symmetric cryptographic research in the future cannot only expect to resist the power of quantum attackers, but also utilize the quantum principles in a favorable manner. The following are some of the major research directions in the future, with the advancement of quantum-native symmetric cryptography, the incorporation of quantum key distribution (QKD) to secure symmetric key exchange and the optimization of symmetric encryption algorithms to remain efficient in post-quantum settings.

6.1 Development of Quantum-Native Symmetric Cryptography

The idea of quantum-native symmetric cryptography is the radical rethinking of the cryptographic primitive design and implementation. The existing symmetric ciphers like AES are developed in a classical paradigm, but quantum-native cryptography are the algorithms that are explicitly developed to work reliably and effectively in a quantum-capable system. This is not just in the resistance to quantum attacks but also, perhaps, in depending upon quantum methods of computation to enhance any security properties. A major challenge in this field is to build symmetric primitives that are sound against quantum superposition queries, and quantum-oracle attacks. Most classical structures fail or erode in security when the adversary is able to supply super positioned inputs and when the adversary can read entangled outputs. Future symmetric algorithms will need to be defined based on formal models of quantum-accessible security, e.g. Quantum Indistinguishability under Chosen Plaintext Attack and be resistant to more general forms of adversarial interaction than previously assumed in a threat model.

Moreover, quantum-native cryptographic architecture gives an opportunity to investigate the potential of applying quantum phenomena such as entanglement and quantum noise to design cryptographic functions currently insecure or ineffective in the classical environment. An example is that with quantum randomness or collapse of measurement, you would be able to generate fundamentally unpredictable outputs and thus achieve the benefit of improving security in an unpredictable way. Symmetric encryption Quantum-based symmetric encryption schemes based on these principles can offer shorter ciphertext, higher entropy, or stronger privacy guarantees in some attack models. These innovations however are still in the conceptual or experimental stages. Substantial foundation research is required to define, model and test quantum-native symmetric systems in practice. These involve the design of simulation frameworks to test how algorithms behave against quantum adversaries, design of quantum hardware to prototype encryption and decryption and the formulation of standard security metrics to assess. Quantum-native cryptography is only in its infancy and as it advances, it is likely to not only prolong the life of symmetric systems but also change the face of cryptography altogether in a world where quantum computing capabilities are available to both the attacker and the defender.

6.2 Exploration of Quantum Key Distribution (QKD) for Symmetric Key Exchange

One more hot area of research in the post-quantum cryptography field is the combination of the Quantum Key Distribution (QKD) with symmetric encryption algorithms. QKD offers a basis of a secure means of creating and sharing symmetric keys with quantum mechanics. In contrast to the classical key exchange protocols, which are based on the assumptions of computational hardness (and can be broken using quantum algorithms such as Shor), QKD provides the confidentiality of keys by using the laws of quantum physics. An example of one of the first and the most famous QKD protocols is the BB84 protocol that illustrates the process of how two parties can distribute a secret key by exchanging qubits through a quantum channel. Any eavesdropping is interfering with the quantum state of the particles and acts as a warning of a potential attack to the legitimate parties. This guarantees the security of the key exchange process, even with the full computing power of an adversary, including the adversary who has a full-scale quantum computer. QKD and symmetric encryption provide a highly powerful communications security mechanism. After a symmetric key is securely generated with QKD, it may be used to encrypt data at high speed with standard symmetric ciphers such as AES or lightweight block ciphers. This hybrid system (hybrid of QKD and symmetric encryption) offers forward secrecy and even the performance can be scaled. Notwithstanding this promise, there are a number of research challenges facing QKD that would have to be overcome before it can be widely used. First, QKD now needs dedicated hardware to send and receive qubits such as photons sources, beam splitters, and single-photon detectors. This renders such elements expensive, sensitive and vulnerable to environmental factors and can be deployed only in a controlled or priority system such as the government or military network. Second, short-haul distance limitations imposed restrictions on the application of QKD systems because photons are lost in optical fibers and the channel is noisy. Despite the development of quantum repeaters or satellite-based QKD to increase the distance over which viable distances can be achieved, stability and scalability at large scale networks has been a critical concern. The idea of including QKD into the already-established communication systems is architecturally problematic. The research community is actively working toward developing standardized interfaces and interoperability layers that would allow keys generated through Quantum Key Distribution (QKD) to be seamlessly integrated with symmetric encryption algorithms, without compromising either performance or usability. However, for QKD to become practical on a larger scale, significant advancements are still required. Future work must focus on making QKD components smaller, more affordable, and fault-tolerant, while also enabling them to function over longer distances and at higher speeds. Another promising direction involves hybrid key management protocols, where QKD is combined with classical and post-quantum key exchange mechanisms. Such approaches provide flexibility, especially in cases where quantum communication infrastructure is only partially deployed. In summary, the secure exchange of symmetric keys via QKD represents one of the most promising avenues for achieving fully secure communication in a quantum era. Its theoretical development, coupled with the necessary engineering advancements, will be fundamental to its large-scale deployment.

6.3 Improving Efficiency of Symmetric Encryption Under Post-Quantum Constraints

Although a significant part of the current research has been devoted to enhancing the defensive strengths of symmetric cryptography against the threats related to quantization, the equal significance should be attached to preservation of efficiency and performance in the post-quantum world. The more complex cipher structures and longer keys are definitely more resistant to quantum attacks but usually require a lot of processing power, memory and communications bandwidth. This may be particularly difficult where there are resource constraints like IoT devices, smart cards, and mobile systems. An important direction of study is how to design lightweight symmetric algorithms with balance between security and efficiency. The aim is to provide security that is at quantum levels and with minimum implementation costs. Lightweight primitives, stream ciphers, reduced-round block ciphers, and permutation-based constructions that are environment-specific promise to be promising. Hardware efficiency is also an important consideration, and cipher designs are becoming more optimized to small footprint, high throughput, and low power consumption. Beyond algorithm design, protocol-level optimization is also being investigated. Other methods to reduce the cost without compromising the security include a reduction in the number of cipher rounds, minimization of padding overhead, or parallel encryption block. Authentication, such as GCM (Galois/Counter Mode) and OCB (Offset Codebook Mode) can also be set up in a way that it does not incur performance costs without post-quantum primitives (integrity and confidentiality). Also, memory efficiency is now a major issue of concern, and key-derivation functions and storage systems should be carefully optimized to fit within the finite capabilities of many platforms. Key hierarchies, ephemeral key reuse and secure bootstrapping strategies are emerging solutions and are intended to reduce the overhead of quantum-resistant systems. Finally, to develop useful post-quantum symmetric encryption, it is necessary to interdisciplinarily coordinate cryptographic theory with embedded systems engineering, microarchitecture design, and software optimization. Future studies need not only aim to achieve the theoretical quantum resistance, but also to achieve scalability, efficiency, and applicability in practice.

7. CONCLUSION

The fast development of quantum computing is becoming a significant threat to all existing cryptographic systems, such as symmetric cryptography. Symmetric algorithms are typically less susceptible to attacks by quantum systems than asymmetric systems, but they are still susceptible because of the effects of the Grover algorithm. This highlights the fact that existing cryptography techniques must be reevaluated and updated to maintain long term data confidentiality and integrity in a post-quantum era. This survey has examined quantum-related threats to symmetric cryptography, which include key strength erosion, design vulnerabilities in current algorithms, and system shortcomings of older systems. To address these problems, some promising solutions have been mentioned, such as larger key sizes, designing quantum-resistant symmetric primitives, using hybrid systems based on classical and post-quantum designs, and implementing algorithmic agility to make it easy to migrate to new designs in the future. Collectively these actions provide more than just short-term reinforcements, but long-term resilience. It is crucial that there is close coordination between researchers, industry stakeholders, and policymakers to achieve a successful transition to quantum-resilient infrastructures. The shaping of genuinely quantum-native symmetric systems will be dominated by key technologies, including QKD to exchange keys safely and performance analysis of cryptographic protocols executed in post-quantum settings. Because of the urgency, the construction of such strong systems will be critical in securing sensitive information against present and future attackers. It will take both technological innovation and strategic foresight and international cooperation to address the quantum threat. To fulfil the requirements of the quantum-based digital world, standardization, adaptive strategies, and long-term research are all needed. By combining these efforts, one can guarantee that the digital ecosystem of the globe will stay safe and stable even after the age of quantum is reached.

REFERENCES

Brijwani, G. N., Ajmire, P. E., & Thawani, P. V. (2023). Future of quantum computing in cyber security. In *Handbook of research on quantum computing for smart environments* (pp. 267–298). IGI Global. DOI: 10.4018/978-1-6684-6697-1.ch016

Chittem, M. B., & Pradhan, A. K. (2025, January). Hybrid Quantum-Classical Transfer Learning for Real-Time Data Processing. In *2025 17th International Conference on COMmunication Systems and NETworks (COMSNETS)* (pp. 84-89). IEEE. DOI: 10.1109/COMSNETS63942.2025.10885700

Das, S., & Das, A. (2023). Future Perspective of Quantum Cryptography for Smart Cities of the 21st Century. In *Handbook of Research on Quantum Computing for Smart Environments* (pp. 326-342). IGI Global.

Minu, R. I., Nagarajan, G., & Yamini, G. (2024, August). Quantum Machine Learning of Bigdata Set Using Randomized Measurements. In *2024 7th International Conference on Circuit Power and Computing Technologies (ICCPCT)* (Vol. 1, pp. 32-35). IEEE. DOI: 10.1109/ICCPCT61902.2024.10673223

Muthumanickam, K., Mahesh, P. S., & Ragab, M. (2023). A review on quantum computing and security. *Handbook of research on quantum computing for smart environments*, 84-102.

Paul, S., & Mitra, A. (2022). A review on applications of quantum computing in machine learning. *Technology Road Mapping for Quantum Computing and Engineering*, 57-80.

Prajapat, M., Choure, K. K., Qazi, G., Devi, P. P., Tiwari, M., & Singh, G. (2024, November). Quantum Sensors for Next-Generation Sensing: Techniques, Applications, and Recent Advancements. In *2024 4th International Conference on Technological Advancements in Computational Sciences (ICTACS)* (pp. 1748-1751). IEEE.

Sihare, S., & Khang, A. (2023). Effects of quantum technology on the metaverse. In *Handbook of Research on AI-Based Technologies and Applications in the Era of the Metaverse* (pp. 174–203). IGI Global Scientific Publishing. DOI: 10.4018/978-1-6684-8851-5.ch009

Subramanian, R. S., Maheswari, B., Nithya, T., Girija, P., Karthikeyan, M., & Saraswathi, T. (2024). Quantum Computing: Unveiling the Paradigm Shift and Diverse Applications. In *Applications and Principles of Quantum Computing* (pp. 95-112). IGI Global Scientific Publishing.

Yamini, B., Nithyanandhan, R., Sudha, K., Nithya, T., Vijayakumar, K., & Subramanian, R. S. (2024, April). Maximizing the Revolutionary Potential of Quantum Computing: Challenges, Opportunities, and Future Directions. In *2024 10th International Conference on Communication and Signal Processing (ICCSP)* (pp. 756-761). IEEE.

Chapter 9
Quantum Algorithms:
Principles, Challenges, and Future Prospects in Computational Paradigms

A. Jeyamurugan
https://orcid.org/0009-0003-7339-9649
Vel Tech Multi Tech Dr. Rangarajan Dr. Sakunthala Engineering College, India

M. Anita
https://orcid.org/0009-0009-0093-2928
SRM Institute of Science and Technology, India

A. Revathi
https://orcid.org/0009-0003-1640-777X
R.M.K. College of Engineering and Technology, India

ABSTRACT

Quantum algorithms have emerged as powerful computational tools that leverage the principles of quantum mechanics to address complex problems beyond the scope of classical computing. This chapter explores the foundational concepts, classifications, implementation challenges, and future prospects of quantum algorithms. Key breakthroughs such as Grover's and Shor's algorithms are explored alongside recent developments in quantum machine learning and optimization. The chapter also compares quantum and classical algorithmic complexity, highlighting areas of potential speedup. Practical limitations including hardware constraints, error correction, and resource estimation are critically analyzed. Finally, the chapter outlines emerging research directions and ethical considerations essential for responsible quantum computing development.

DOI: 10.4018/979-8-3373-3166-9.ch009

1. INTRODUCTION

1.1 Motivation for Quantum Computing in the Era of Classical Computational Limitations

Classical computing has developed over the last few decades at an unimaginable rate, enabling revolutionary achievements in all fields of science, engineering, and industry. This development has been largely driven by the tremendous growth in transistor density, where performance has doubled approximately every two years. But with the physical and economical constraints in miniaturization of silicon-based transistors, the conventional computing techniques are finding it difficult to keep up with the growing performance and efficiency requirements. The real world problem instances, especially those problems with combinatorial optimization, cryptographic analysis, and large-scale simulations, tend to be computationally intractable on classical machines. Issues like protein folding, simulating quantum systems and factoring large integers are beyond the reach of even the most powerful supercomputers because they require a number of computational resources that grow exponentially. In this context, quantum computing has come out as a paradigm shift that aims to use the rules of quantum mechanics to handle data in a completely different manner. Quantum bits (qubits), unlike classical bits, which exist only in one of two states (0 or 1), can exist in a superposition of states allowing large-scale parallel processing in quantum machines. Furthermore, qubits are able to take part in non-classical correlations due to the phenomenon of entanglement, which results in more computational power over some types of problems. Such properties can result in huge speedups in solving certain tasks compared to traditional methods, and thus stimulate an intense study of quantum-based methods that make use of such quantum effects to solve problems otherwise considered intractable.

1.2 Historical Evolution of Quantum Algorithms

The theoretical background behind quantum computing was formulated during the early 80s which indicated that imitating quantum systems on standard computers would demand exponential resources, but a quantum computer would be able to do so efficiently. This observation led to the thought of constructing quantum-mechanical computers. The model of quantum Turing machine was formalized in 1985, and it presented the idea of the general quantum computer as a computer that is able to simulate any physical process. The barrier to practical quantum-based algorithm design was notably overcome in the 1990s, when the first prominent quantum algorithms were developed. In 1994, Shor published a number factorization method that is significantly quicker than the best-known classical methods, and this threatened the security of many cryptographic systems, like RSA. This algorithm was a breakthrough since it demonstrated that quantum systems could be more powerful than traditional computers in solving real problems. About the same period, Lov Grover introduced an algorithm that searches unstructured databases and is quadratically faster than the traditional solutions. Since that time the research into quantum algorithms has grown substantially. In addition to the algorithms of Shor and Grover, quantum algorithms have been developed for tasks such as optimization, simulation, linear algebra, and machine learning. Even though most of these algorithms are now formulated under idealized conditions and fault-tolerant architectures, their theoretical input has laid a rich foundation on the quantum paradigms of computing. As quantum hardware and error-correction techniques have improved, such previously hypothetical algorithms are slowly becoming more feasible to implement experimentally, and useful in practice (Brijwani et al., 2023).

1.3 Purpose and Scope of the Chapter

The field of quantum algorithms is large and constantly developing, and disciplines such as physics, computer science, mathematics, and engineering are still contributing to it. This chapter aims to give an exhaustive summary of the concepts behind quantum algorithms, to group the most significant algorithmic advances, to analyze the issues limiting the practical implementation of quantum algorithms. Other than this, the chapter also aims to highlight the current trends, new applications, and future directions that quantum algorithm research will be inclined to take. This chapter is organized in such a way that it discusses basic and advanced topics. It begins by providing a theoretical overview of the concepts of quantum computing required to understand quantum algorithms, such as superposition, entanglement, and unitary operations. It then categorizes quantum algorithms by their primary functionality, which includes search and factorization, optimization and machine learning, and analyzes the speedup they offer over classical algorithms. Moreover, the chapter also focuses on the key challenges to quantum algorithm development, including hardware limitations, methodological complexity, and error management. It also compares the performance of quantum methods to the performance of classical algorithms in the context of computational complexity theory. Finally, the chapter looks at new paradigms, such as hybrid quantum-classical approaches, and the long-term impact of quantum computing on research, business, and security.

1.4 Structure of the Chapter

This section consists of eight subsections, each containing an important aspect of quantum algorithm research. Section 2 contains the background information on the fundamental basics of quantum computing, such as qubits, quantum gates, and measurements, to help those readers unfamiliar with the field. Section 3 groups large quantum-based methods, including Grover's search technique, Shor's factoring method, quantum simulation algorithms and machine learning algorithms, and discusses their design, complexity, and use. In section 4, the discussion of practical implementation issues, such as decoherence, gate errors, hardware limitations, fault tolerance, and noise reduction techniques is presented. In section 5, classical and quantum algorithms are compared, and the complexity categories like P, NP, and BQP are analyzed, and the point where quantum algorithms actually provide more computational power is evaluated. Section 6 looks at the future directions such as hybrid quantum-classical models, and the possible effects on industries. It also addresses the ethical concerns and the significance of post-quantum cryptography. The open research questions are presented in section 7, which include developing novel algorithms and analyzing the complexity. Finally, Section 8 concludes by briefly pointing out some of the highlights and why having an interdisciplinary approach is necessary to realize what is possible with quantum computing.

2. FOUNDATIONS OF QUANTUM COMPUTING

Quantum computing is a significant change in the way in which we can process data, and it is constructed on the principles of quantum mechanics which cannot be described with classical intuition. In order to understand the design of quantum algorithms and their functionality, it is necessary to first describe the theoretical background within which quantum computation is built. In this part, the key notions are introduced: superposition, entanglement, quantum gates and measurement that render quantum computing distinct to classical computing. A combination of these factors makes it possible to create a new generation of algorithms that can solve some problems more efficiently, than the classical ones.

2.1 Quantum Mechanics for Computing

Quantum computing is based on the fact that particles behave in a strange manner that is dictated by quantum physics. Quantum systems are probabilistic, unlike classical systems which are deterministic, in which particles in quantum states can be in multiple conditions until they are measured. This property is referred to as superposition. In classical computing, the smallest unit of data is the bit, which can only take the value 0 or 1. By contrast a quantum bit, or qubit, may be simultaneously in a linear superposition of both states, described mathematically as $|\psi\rangle = \alpha|0\rangle + \beta|1\rangle$, where α and β are complex numbers and $|\alpha|^2 + |\beta|^2 = 1$. The concomitant possession of many states allows quantum computers to access a vastly greater state space than classical systems. The other major tenet of quantum physics is entanglement, where two or more qubits are linked in such a way that the condition of one qubit cannot be defined without considering the other qubits. When entanglement occurs, the state of one qubit instantly affects the other, though the two qubits may be physically separated. The non-local correlation enables extremely efficient computation and data manipulation, so entanglement is a crucial element in numerous quantum-based techniques and systems of quantum communication (Biju, J et al., 2025). Another quantum effect that is necessary in computing is interference. Quantum interference helps quantum systems improve accuracy by cancelling out the wrong ones due to constructive and destructive interference. This process is essential in steering quantum algorithms into the correct answer as in the case of an algorithm such as the Grover's search where the interference is important in isolating the desired object within an unsorted database much faster than its classical counterparts. All of these properties combined, namely, superposition, entanglement, and interference, are the foundation of quantum computation. They allow a quantum computer to search through many paths of potential solutions parallel, coordinate between qubits, and optimize the probability distribution to settle on the right answer. This ability brings the possibility of solving problems which were considered to be unsolvable using classical approaches.

2.2 Quantum Gates and Circuits

Similarly to classical computers, which use logic gates to operate on bits, quantum computers operate on qubits using quantum gates. But the quantum gates unlike classical gates operate on probability amplitudes and must be unitary operations. A unitary operation is reversible, i.e. it conserves the total probability (norm) of a quantum state, and thus no information is destroyed in the course of a computation.

Quantum gates commonly used are:

Hadamard Gate (H): A superposition is created out of a basis state. Applied to $|0\rangle$, it yields $(|0\rangle + |1\rangle)/\sqrt{2}$, so the probability of measuring 0 or 1 becomes equal.

Pauli Gates (X, Y, Z): Similar to classical bit-flip (X) and phase-flip gates (Z). The Pauli gates are fundamental single-qubit gates. The X gate switches $|0\rangle$ to $|1\rangle$ and vice versa.

CNOT Gate: A two-qubit gate which flips the 2nd (target) qubit provided the 1st (control) qubit is $|1\rangle$, and leaves it unchanged otherwise. This gate is necessary to make an entanglement.

Phase Shift Gates (S, T): Add a relative phase between the quantum basis states and play an important role in quantum Fourier transform and phase estimation algorithms.

Quantum computation is normally described with quantum circuits, in which qubits are prepared and acted on by a series of quantum gates and ultimately measured. A quantum circuit diagrammatically depicts the chronological ordering of quantum transformations on a register of qubits in analogy with the flow of binary signals in classical logic circuits. The diagram is a representation of the wires and the qubits & the symbols on the wires represent the gates that are used at different time steps. Quantum circuits are built so that the researcher can design algorithms in a systematic and modular manner. To take one example, Shor algorithm to factor large integers uses modular exponentiation and quantum Fourier transform, both of which can be constructed with a combination of basic gates. Likewise, Grover's algorithm applies an oracle and a diffusion operator both of which are realized as sub-circuits in a bigger quantum circuit structure. Gate depth is another significant property of quantum gates and circuits, this metric is the sequence of consecutive gate operations that must be performed successfully in order to realize an algorithm. In practice, lower depth circuits are desirable because deeper circuits are more error-prone because of qubit decoherence and noise. Quantum circuit optimization is therefore a big field of current research aimed at improving algorithmic efficiency on the current, noisy, quantum processors (Chittem, M. B., & Pradhan, A. K. 2025).

2.3 Quantum Measurement and Decoherence

Once a quantum calculation is done, the information has to be retrieved in a process known as measurement. Quantum mechanics dictates that the quantum state reduces during a measurement because of an interaction with the measurement device, collapsing a superposed state into one of the basis states, resulting in a classical outcome. For a single qubit under superposition $|\psi\rangle = \alpha|0\rangle + \beta|1\rangle$, measuring it will yield 0 with likelihood $|\alpha|^2$ or 1 with likelihood $|\beta|^2$. This probabilistic character of measurement implies that quantum algorithms frequently have to be run many times to produce a meaningful distribution of results.

Measurement is also basis dependent (i.e. the result of a measurement will depend on the basis it is carried out). Although the typical measurement basis is the computational basis $\{|0\rangle, |1\rangle\}$, measurements in other bases may be attained by preceding a unitary basis transformation of the quantum system by measurement. Understanding and selecting the right basis of measurement is crucial in most algorithms with the quantum phase estimation method being one among them. Decoherence is one of the greatest obstacles to the construction of useful quantum computers, the loss of quantum properties of quantum systems and the start of classical behavior as a result of interaction with the environment. The superposition and entanglement are corrupted because superposition and entanglement collapse due to the effect of decoherence. Decoherence can be caused by even small changes in the environment e.g. temperature changes or electromagnetic radiation. One of the most closely related topics to decoherence is the problem of quantum noise, that adds random errors to the quantum computations. The mistakes can be made due to not ideal gate operations, inaccuracy in the readout when measuring, or physical instability of qubit systems. To overcome them, quantum error correction (QEC) methods have been invented, in which logical qubits are encoded in a number of physical qubits. Although QEC enhances the quantum computation resistance, it also needs more qubits and creates computation overhead. Since the development of quantum devices is in progress, one of the most important areas of concern is to minimize the impact of decoherence and noise. Modern systems also strive to maximize the coherence time, i.e. length of time during which qubits remain in their quantum state, and to minimize gate errors & increase fidelity. Such enhancements are needed to achieve successful implementation of large-scale quantum algorithms, which can need thousands or millions of operations(Eswaran, U et al., 2024).

3. CLASSIFICATION OF QUANTUM ALGORITHMS

Quantum algorithms can in principle be more powerful than classical algorithms, solving certain problems more efficiently using such properties of quantum systems as superposition, entanglement & interference. Within recent decades, a number of algorithmic models were built to show quantum advantage, especially in search, factorization, machine learning, and optimization. This part splits the most influential quantum algorithms into four large categories depending on their fundamental functionality and field of application. Both the categories not only give the theoretical contribution of such algorithms but also points out their practical importance both in the academic and industrial fields.

3.1 Algorithms for Quantum Search

Grover's algorithm, introduced by Lov Grover in 1996, is one of the earliest and the most popular quantum algorithms. The method provides a quadratic speedup in unstructured search. With a database of NN unordered items and a function capable of telling whether a given item is the target, Grover's algorithm has the potential of finding a marked element in time, compared to O(N) using conventional search methods. Although the improvement is not exponential, it is nonetheless remarkable, particularly in case of large-scale datasets. Grover's algorithm works by putting the system in a superposition over all candidate states, an oracle that identifies the correct solution and a series of operations called the Grover's iteration amplifies the likelihood amplitude of the correct result. The act of measuring the quantum register at some point in iterations will provide the correct answer with a high probability. Grover's algorithm has much more applications than the mere search of a database. It may be used to solve many NP-complete problems, including satisfiability (SAT), graph colouring, and subset-sum, by viewing them as search problems on huge solution spaces. Also, the technique underlying Grover's algorithm can be extended to other quantum algorithms to enhance subroutines that comprise search or decision making. It is simple in relative terms and general enough to be a building block in quantum algorithm design(Gayathri et al., 2024).

3.2 Algorithms for Factoring and Cryptography

One of the most popular quantum algorithms as far as its social implications are concerned is the Shor algorithm which was invented in 1994 by Peter Shor. The method addresses the problem of prime factorization within polynomial time, which is exponentially faster than the best-known classical techniques. Shor's algorithm operates by reducing a factoring problem into a period-finding task. It constructs a quantum subroutine that determines the period of a function by applying the Quantum Fourier Transform (QFT), which is a quantum analogue of the classical Fourier transform. When this period is determined, classical post-processing methods may then recover the prime factors of the original integer.

The primary consequence of the introduction of Shor's algorithm is that it threatens RSA encryption, which underpins most of the secure communications on the internet today. RSA relies on the assumption that factoring large integers is computationally hard. Should fault-tolerant large-scale quantum computers ever prove viable, Shor's algorithm may be used to crack RSA and other cryptographic algorithms like ECC (Elliptic Curve Cryptography), rendering them insecure. Consequently, the area of research that is most urgent now is the development of post-quantum cryptographic schemes that remain secure against quantum attacks. The algorithm of Shor has also had some impact in the creation of quantum algorithms to discrete logarithm, order finding, and other algebraic problems that many rely upon in cryptosystems that are public key. A combination of these algorithms shows how quantum computation can disrupt the sphere of cybersecurity and cryptanalysis.

3.3 Quantum Machine Learning Algorithms

Quantum computing and machine learning have in recent years formed a lively field of research called Quantum Machine Learning (QML). The domain seeks to speed up the ML processes by exploiting the computational strengths of quantum systems. Some quantum algorithms have been created or ported to achieve supervised, unsupervised and reinforcement learning faster than classical methods in some circumstances. The other potential solution is the QNN that tries to emulate the layered structure of classical neural networks with quantum gates and qubit interactions. In their early stages of development QNNs are being considered in applications such as pattern recognition, image classification and signal processing. Amplitude encoding of classical data, in which classical data is encoded into the amplitude of a quantum state, allows large sets of data to be encoded in exponentially fewer qubits, although the process of loading the data is also a large bottleneck.

Figure 1. Classification of Quantum Algorithms

One very useful research direction is hybrid quantum-classical methods, that take advantage of both classical and quantum computers. Such models as VQC and QAOA-based learners use parameterized quantum circuits and optimize the parameters of the circuit using classical algorithms. This method is suitable to quantum devices in the near future because it makes the circuit less deep and noise less harmful. On the whole, quantum machine learning has potential to speed up the data processing tasks, discover new patterns, solve problems intractable by classical approaches. Yet, most of the speedups are conditional, and further research is required to estimate its feasibility on real-life data(Khang, A 2024).

3.4 Quantum Walks and Optimization Algorithms

Quantum walks The quantum analog of classical random walks, quantum walks are a potent computational tool to construct quantum algorithms, particularly in graph-based search and optimization problems. Quantum walks are of both discrete-time and continuous-time variety and both take advantage of the probabilistic interference of quantum paths to increase exploration efficiency. The quantum walks were among the first applications to achieve success, namely in the design of search algorithms on graphs that beat their classical analogues. As an example, quantum walks can find a marked node on a graph within O(time in the spatial search problem, providing a quadratic speedup. Element distinctness problems, triangle finding in graphs and network traversal problems have also used quantum walk algorithms.

4. IMPLEMENTATION CHALLENGES

Although there is tremendous theoretical potential to quantum algorithms, in practice there are a no of daunting obstacles. The quantum computing systems are still in the infant stage with the existing systems being very sensitive, error prone and small in scale. The researcher should clear many technical hurdles in the fields of hardware development, error correction, resource optimization, and software standardization to fill the gap between theory and practice. This part delves into these difficulties and examines the following important limitations that now limit the large-scale implementation and real-world application of quantum algorithms.

4.1 Hardware Constraints

Among the most urgent issues in quantum computing, there is a demand to create scalable and stable hardware that will be able to perform complex algorithms. The quantum bits or qubits are very delicate. In contrast to classical bits, which can be kept in a stable 0 or 1 state, qubits must be kept in coherent quantum states, frequently superposition or entangled states, which are very sensitive both to environmental noise and to flaws in the operations. The problem of constructing a large scale quantum system comprising of high fidelity qubits that can be reliably interacted is an open problem. Quantum processors today can handle tens to a few hundred physical qubits, but even fairly simple algorithms can need thousands or millions of logical qubits, with error correction included. Scalability is also a problem, as it is not only about adding more qubits but about how well they are connected, controlled and decoupled of decoherence. The other important concern is the gate fidelity- a factor that determines the accuracy of a quantum gate executing a desired operation. The outcome of low fidelity is computational errors and these errors grow rapidly in deep circuits. The single-qubit gate fidelities in most current systems are above 99.9 percent and two-qubit gate fidelities are a bit lower, yet even these levels of errors are not suitable to scalable fault-tolerant quantum computation. The steps to reduce such errors are to develop material science, control electronics, and architectural design. Further, the coherence time – i.e., the duration for which a qubit can hold its quantum coherence, is short,, frequently to microseconds or milliseconds. This time frame is limited which limits the amount of operations that can be made before the loss of information. Therefore, quantum algorithms require not only logical efficiency but also realistic timing requirements of the hardware(Kathirvel, A et al., 2023).

4.2 Error Correction and Fault Tolerance

Due to the natural fragility of quantum information, any reasonably scalable quantum computer will need to use error-correction on a quantum scale (QEC). In contrast to classical error correction, where redundancy is achieved by copying of bits, QEC needs to maintain quantum states but without infringing the no-cloning theorem It is done by encoding one logical qubit across multiple physical qubits and creating quantum error-correcting codes. QEC schemes are designed to correct both bit-flip and phase-flip errors, which are the most common in quantum systems. There are, however, large overheads in implementing these codes. As an example, encoding a single logical qubit using surface codes might need 1,000 or more physical qubits, depending on the desired fault tolerance and the intended error rate.

In theory, fault-tolerant quantum computation has a theoretical foundation known as the threshold theorem, which states that if the probability of error per operation is sufficiently low, quantum computation can succeed with the assistance of QEC. But staying under this threshold is always a challenge for most existing hardware platforms. Moreover, error-correcting schemes require advanced methods including magic state distillation, logic gate synthesis and syndrome measurement cycles, all of which increase the complexity and time delay of quantum computations. Such correction and control layers should be done efficiently and in real time and challenge quantum control systems and classical feedback loops. Active research effort is aimed at minimizing the quantum error correction overhead, maximizing code efficiency and creating error-mitigation schemes that can be adapted to near-term quantum devices. Although full-fledged fault-tolerant quantum computing remains an ambitious long-term objective, small steps towards that direction are imperative to the execution of realistic quantum algorithms on noisy machines.

4.3 Algorithm Complexity and Resource Estimation

Although the hardware and error correcting systems will be enhanced, it is clear that a quantum algorithm cannot be run effectively without a thorough study of the complexity of algorithms and resource estimation. In contrast to classical computation, where time and space complexity are well defined, quantum algorithms require new measures of complexity, like the number of qubits, the depth of a circuit, and the width of a circuit to measure their practicality on current hardware. One of the issues is the number of qubits needed by most theoretically efficient quantum algorithms. Such algorithms as Shor or the QPE usually needs access to tens or even hundreds of clean and error-free qubits to work properly. Error correction can make physical qubits several orders of magnitude more than what is currently possible on current machines.

Also, most algorithms are deep, that is, they involve long chains of operations which have to be performed before the decoherence sets in. Such depth is undesirable because of low coherence times of existing hardware. Depth and width have a trade-off, one can employ more qubits to realize shorter circuits or the reverse, but in NISQ devices both resources are severely limited. Resource estimation also entails the knowledge of the requirements of the precision of different quantum subroutines. A typical example is that phase estimation algorithms should be able to measure phase differences that are small and this needs a precise gate sequence and a long calculation time. This once more results in high resource requirements which can hardly be achieved in practice. In a bid to overcome these challenges, there is a research into resource-efficient alternative versions of algorithms, approximate algorithms, and compilers capable of optimizing circuits to a particular hardware target. The tools are necessary in filling the gap between the high level algorithm design and the feasibility of low level implementation.

Figure 2. Implementation Challenges

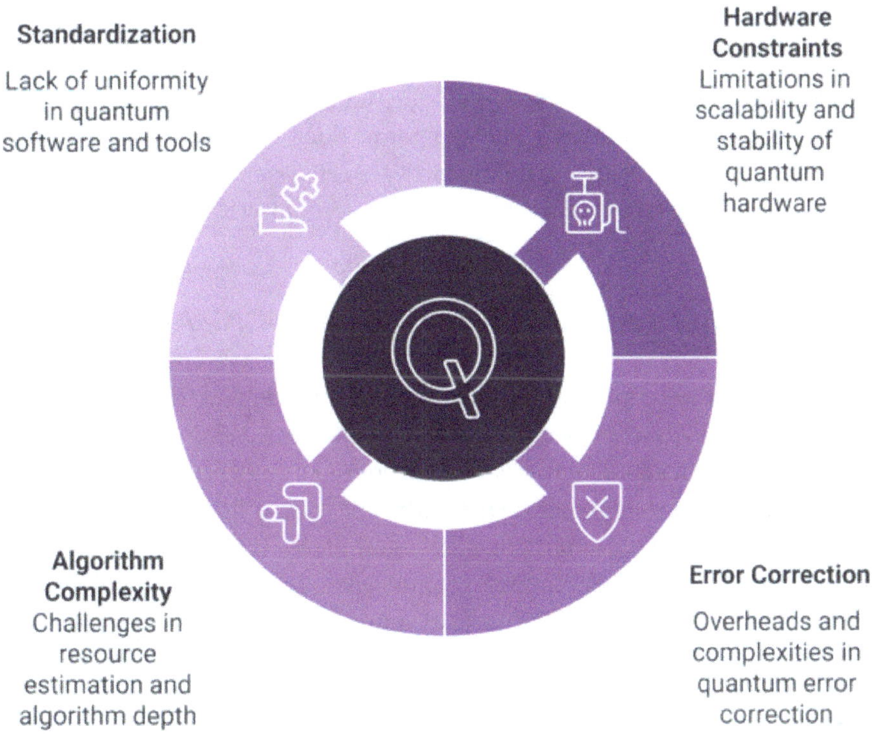

4.4 Lack of Standardization and Tooling

The other major obstacle to the deployment of quantum algorithms is that of standardization of quantum software tooling. The technology is now divided and there are numerous programming languages, hardware platforms and software development kits (SDKs) with various capabilities, interfaces and abstractions. The diversity results in a high learning curve of developers and inhibits the portability and reproducibility of quantum algorithms. Every quantum programming language has a different method of defining and simulating quantum circuits. Although such tools have come a long way in terms of accessibility, they tend to be lacking in the aspect of interoperability and also differ in terms of abstraction level. Often developers are required to select a platform early in the development process and making that choice may commit them to a particular hardware backend. In addition, quantum software has not yet acquired mature functionality that is found in classical computing, including debugging, performance profiler and automated testing frameworks. In absence of such tools, the creation of complex quantum applications is erroneous and time consuming. Moreover, quantum compilers do not yet have the complexity to achieve hardware-specific optimization (e.g. connectivity, noise profiles, gate durations). Standardization is currently being undertaken, and this would provide standard interfaces, benchmarks, and programs. Such initiatives will be critical to the development of a healthy quantum software ecosystem and the ability to work with more members of the quantum computing community(Kaushik, M et al., 2024).

5. COMPARATIVE ANALYSIS WITH CLASSICAL ALGORITHMS

The emergence of quantum algorithms tempts a more detailed comparison of them with classical algorithms in the aspects of computational efficiency and theoretical strength. Whereas in classical computing the known complexity classes, including P and NP, have been used to define the realms of tractability, quantum computing offers paradigms, including BQP, that are significantly more tractable than classical complexity classes. This section explains where quantum algorithms fit in the theory of computational complexity and examines what sorts of speedups quantum algorithms can give over classical algorithms, both quadratic and exponential.

5.1 Complexity Classes: P, NP, BQP

In order to comprehend the theoretical effects of quantum algorithms, we have to discuss their positioning in known classes of complexity. Class P is a collection of solvable problems in a classical deterministic Turing machine in polynomial time, and NP is a collection of problems, whose proposed solutions can be verified in polynomial time. Whether P is equal to NP is a major open question in theoretical computer science, and the question has not been solved. Quantum computing gives rise to the class BQP the set of decision problems that can be solved by a quantum computer in polynomial time with probability of error less than 1/3 on all instances. Notably, it is all the problems in P, because quantum computers can simulate classical ones. Nevertheless, it is not known whether BQP is equal to NP, although most people believe that BQP and NP are not comparable, so that each class has problems which cannot be solved by the other. Remarkably, certain issues which are thought to be unsolvable by classical polynomial-time algorithms are in BQP. As an example, factoring integers, the basis of RSA encryption, is not known to be in P, but can be efficiently solved by Shor algorithm, so is in BQP. Conversely, most NP-complete problems, including Boolean satisfiability (SAT) are not likely to have solutions in BQP, as no such solution has been found to be exponentially faster than brute force.

These class relations can serve to illuminate where quantum advantage can be achieved and where it fails to be achieved. Even though quantum computing does not address all hard problems, it resets new horizons of efficient computation of many tasks.

5.2 Speedup Analysis

Among the strongest arguments on why quantum algorithms are worth studying is the possibility that they can provide exponential speedups to classical methods. Such speedups are either of quadratic or exponential type. An example of quadratic speedup is Grover's algorithm that finds solutions to unstructured search problems in O(time instead of the classical O(N) time. Although this is not exponential, this is a fundamental change in the efficiency of algorithms of a broad range of problems, especially those involving exhaustive search or pattern matching. Instead, Shor algorithm provides an exponential speedup to problems such as integer factorization & discrete logarithm. These issues can be classically solved only in sub-exponential or exponential time but in quantum machines they fall in the region of polynomial time. Such a drastic change has a dire consequence in terms of cryptography and data protection. However, there are issues in which there is quantum-classical equivalence. As an example, the inversion of some matrices, or the solution of some linear equations, are exponentially faster in some data access models, but not when classical preprocessing, or data loading, is taken into consideration. This brings out the value of considering practical constraints in the analysis of quantum advantage.

Altogether, quantum algorithms aren't necessarily more powerful than classical ones, but they expand the range of what's computationally tractable to a small but growing number of problems: redefining the field of algorithmic theory and practice (Nagarajan, R et al., 2022).

6. FUTURE PROSPECTS AND EMERGING DIRECTIONS

The quantum computing has progressed over several decades and the development of quantum computing has been impressive - from theoretical ideas to working prototypes. But despite this development, the field has not yet matured and has not yet realized its transformative potential. The success of quantum algorithms and their potential for application depends entirely on the development of more scalable, fault-tolerant hardware, improved integration with the classical computing infrastructure, and success in applying the algorithms to real-world domains. Meanwhile, this technological revolution leaves a lot of ethical and security-related questions. The current section examines the future trends in quantum computing and provides the roadmap to the practical quantum advantage and discusses the implications of the field on the society and industry at large.

6.1 Scalability and Quantum Advantage

Practical quantum advantage, a quantum computer being more useful than a classical system at some real-world task, is one of the most important objectives of current quantum research. Although quantum supremacy, or the ability to prove that a quantum machine can solve a problem that a classical computer cannot is demonstrated by Google and other institutions on special-purpose contrived problems, quantum supremacy is not yet being used in a practical application. The second significant milestone is the realization of quantum advantage on practical applications that need tremendous progress in scaling, error rates, and fidelity of the execution. Scalability is a very daunting challenge. The majority of quantum algorithms of practical use, including Shor algorithm to factor or quantum approximate optimization algorithm (QAOA) to perform optimization tasks, need the number of logical qubits to satisfy their requirements that is by orders of magnitude more than is possible with the current NISQ devices. Moreover, to complicate matters, each logical qubit needs to be backed up with hundreds or thousands of physical qubits because of the requirement to perform error correction. Consequently, to achieve just hundreds or thousands of logical qubits, one will have to invent large-scale quantum processors using millions of highly coherent and low-error physical qubits, which remains many years, or even decades, away. In the future, numerous quantum computing roadmaps target the development of thousands of error-corrected qubit systems within the early 2030s. Such would be the opening to the operation of complex quantum algorithms. In the meantime, a lot of work is being invested in short term improvement with NISQ-friendly algorithms and enhanced quantum gate fidelity, error mitigation strategies, and modular architectures that allow parallelism and hybrid control.

6.2 Integration with Classical Systems

At this point due to the shortcomings of the existing quantum devices, the quantum and classical hybridization provides a well-grounded and feasible way forward. Hybrid models try to combine the benefits of both paradigms: the computational parallelism of quantum systems, and the control and storage capabilities of classical systems as well as their resilience to errors. Fruitful approaches have already been developed in this direction, in particular in optimization, simulation, and machine learning.

Among the most well-known frameworks in this area include the Variational Quantum Eigensolver (VQE) that finds its main application in quantum chemistry and materials science. VQE is a method to optimize quantum circuits by iteratively varying parameters to minimize an energy function, by constructing a parameterized quantum circuit and then tuning the parameters using a classical optimizer. In addition to quantum algorithms, quantum-inspired algorithms also have been discovered as a side product of quantum-inspired techniques. These are classical algorithms that adapt the principles of quantum computation (e.g. tensor networks, amplitude amplification, or quantum annealing heuristics) to solve problems more efficiently than the usual classical algorithms. As an example, quantum-inspired optimization solvers designed by such companies as Microsoft have demonstrated greater efficiency on some of the large-scale scheduling and routing problems with classical hardware. The next step to quantum-classical integration is probably the cloud-based quantum computing platforms, where the users will be able to remotely access the quantum processors and use them as the co-processors to address specific workloads. Such model resembles the initial years of GPUs whose use shifted from specific-purpose graphics processors to general-purpose accelerators applied in machine learning and scientific computation. The same transitions are anticipated in quantum computing as tooling and ecosystem develops.

6.3 Impact on Scientific and Industrial Domains

The possible use of quantum algorithms is broad and many fields will probably gain the advantage earlier than others depending on the level of maturity of quantum hardware and the form of the problems they are seeking to solve. Areas that are fundamentally quantum in character, e.g. quantum chemistry, molecular modeling or condensed matter physics are likely to get tremendous benefit of quantum simulation capability. As an example, to simulate molecular interactions, reaction mechanisms or material properties at the quantum level is computationally intractable on classical computers, but can be made tractable on quantum processors, providing breakthroughs in drug discovery, materials design and green energy technologies. Quantum algorithms can be used in finance to optimize portfolios, to simulate market behavior and to price complex derivatives. The nature of these tasks is frequently to solve high-dimensional linear algebra problems or to carry out stochastic simulations; quantum algorithms including HHL, amplitude estimation, and QAOA can offer speedups in these areas. Quantum-enhanced optimization can also be used in the logistics and transportation industry. Such problems as vehicle routing, warehouse scheduling, or supply chain network design belong to the family of combinatorial problems that are notoriously hard to solve in an efficient manner. The quantum walk algorithms, quantum annealing and QAOA are being considered in such tasks, particularly in conjunction with classical heuristics to control search strategies. Artificial intelligence (AI) is another direction that is promising; quantum machine learning (QML) is becoming a topic of interest. Most QML models remain theoretical or experimental, but quantum kernels and quantum-enhanced feature spaces as well as parameterized quantum circuits provide new opportunities in classification, clustering and generative modeling. Although it has not yet been proved that quantum advantage in AI is attainable, preliminary studies can indicate that quantum models could be more effective than classical models on certain structured data sets, especially in high-dimensional correlation or entanglement settings. Cybersecurity, telecommunications, aerospace and climate modelling industries are also investigating the potential of quantum computing. Its effects in the long run are going to be transformative as it will be able to carry out real-time modeling, secure communication, and optimization levels that are way beyond what we can do today(Mishra, B. K 2022).

6.4 Ethical and Security Implications

As the potential power of quantum computing is immense, so is the set of ethical and security issues that should be anticipated and resolved in advance. A possible quantum attack on classical cryptographic systems is one of the most imminent issues. Such algorithms as Shor are a direct threat to public-key cryptosystems, which are commonly used to secure internet communications, financial transactions and national defense systems, including RSA, DSA and ECC. To counter such threats, the international research community is already attempting to create PQC i.e. cryptographic algorithms that are thought to be immune to quantum attacks and can be run on classical hardware. Governments, companies and providers of infrastructure are being encouraged to start to plan quantum-safe transitions to ensure sensitive data is safe well into the future. More than security, the moral questions of quantum computing are also the responsible development and deployment of quantum computing. The issues of data privacy, algorithmic bias, and monopolies in the field of technology are even more relevant when computation becomes much more powerful and concentrated. In case the access to the advanced quantum systems is restricted to a small number of corporations or countries, global inequality will increase and cause unequal distribution of technology benefits. In addition, the application of quantum algorithms in sensitive fields like military, genetic studies, or financial fraud has ethical issues concerning the intent, control, and the implications of the application to the society. Similar to the case with AI, it is important to work out a framework of ethical quantum governance. This encompasses the establishment of principles of transparent benchmarking, open research and international collaboration in order to prevent the race-to-the-bottom scenario in which security and safety are sacrificed in order to achieve supremacy. Finally, the environmental impact of the large-scale quantum computing centers, in particular, with cryogenic cooling systems, should be addressed. The long-term viability of quantum computing technology will be partly determined by its sustainability and sustainability in design, i.e. low-energy materials used in quantum computing, efficient error correction protocols.

7. OPEN PROBLEMS AND RESEARCH OPPORTUNITIES

With quantum computing firmly moving on the path toward theory to early practice, there are many unsolved problems and unexplored directions. The challenges offer a rich field to researchers in many fields, including theoretical computer science and physics, engineering and software development. The next subsections describe some of the most important open problems which require additional research to realize the full computational power of quantum systems.

Figure 3. Open Problems and Research Opportunities

7.1 Developing New Quantum Algorithms

One of the most important research problems is finding new quantum algorithms which provide a substantial advantage over the corresponding classical ones. Only a few quantum algorithms have been demonstrated to have quantum speedups that are unambiguous. The first few algorithms are still used in most applications as adaptations. New algorithms which are suitable for real-life problems, optimizations, simulations, learning etc. are needed desperately. This includes exploring emerging paradigms such as quantum walk algorithms, variational approaches and problem-specific quantum heuristics.

7.2 Minimizing Qubit Requirement

The other important question is the resource-efficiency of quantum algorithms, particularly in terms of the minimum number of qubits. Theoretically powerful algorithms need hundreds or thousands of qubits to make a meaningful run, which is beyond what we can expect of current hardware. The research should be undertaken to demonstrate the realization of small-scale algorithmic circuits, reduce the number of ancillary qubits and explore compressed data representation in quantum systems. In the near term, resource-aware algorithm design will be needed to improve quantum device utility.

7.3 Improving Quantum Error Correction Efficiency

Scaling of quantum systems cannot be achieved without Quantum Error Correction (QEC), yet existing schemes require enormous overheads both in the number of qubits and in the latency of computations. One of the research areas is how to enhance the efficiency of QEC schemes, lessen the cost of fault-tolerant operations, and devise more scalable error-correcting codes such as surface and subsystem codes.

7.4 Verifying Quantum Computations

Quantum computations are more complex and the more complex they are the harder it is to be sure of its correctness and reliability. Large quantum processes are frequently not classical verifiable. Establishing quantum verification protocols, e.g. interactive proofs, zero knowledge schemes, or cross platform benchmarking, is essential to establish confidence in quantum results, particularly in cloud and multi-tenant quantum systems.

7.5 Bridging the Theory-Practice Gap

Lastly, one of the greatest research possibilities is to reduce the dichotomy between theoretical quantum algorithms and implementation. Most of the algorithms suggested are idealized whereas the devices in reality are noisy and constrained. It will be important to design practical abstractions, adaptive compilers and hardware-aware algorithm design strategies to bring quantum computing to the real world.

8. CONCLUSION

Quantum algorithms are among the most exciting areas of computational science, and have the potential to enable a class of problems to be solved exponentially faster than would be possible using any classical algorithm. This chapter has explored the principles of quantum computation on which it is founded: superposition, entanglement, quantum gate operations. Also discussed some of the most important algorithmic advances like the Grover and Shor algorithms, and emerging paradigms like quantum machine learning and optimization. These algorithms not only show theoretical speedups, but also spawn new methods of thinking about information processing in the quantum era. Meanwhile, quantum algorithm applications in the real world remain full of pitfalls. Scalability of qubits, high error rate, and a complex error correction process will continue to be a bottleneck in the use of quantum applications. As we have already observed in the discussion of the current classes of complexity, quantum computing does not solve every hard problem, but in some respects it radically changes the landscape of computation. The benefits and the drawbacks of quantum computing are also explained in comparison with the classical algorithms, especially the possible speedup and the position in the complexity class. In the future, the road to a ubiquitous quantum advantage will be paved by continued increases in hardware scale, by the entrapment of quantum systems into the classical world, and by the creation of hybrid systems, in which the benefits of both worlds could be exploited. The pharmaceutical, financial, artificial intelligence, logistical, and cryptography industries are highly likely to be revolutionized by quantum computing. However, the vision cannot be achieved only in consequence of scientific and engineering progress, but also the moral vision and the elaboration of international standards of security, interoperability and responsible use. Briefly, quantum algorithms are at the edge of theory and practice. Even though the majority of questions remain open, regarding the design of algorithms and optimization of resources, verification and tooling, active research is constantly closing the gap between what is conceivable and what can be implemented. Physicists, computer scientists, engineers and policy makers will in the future be required to work interdisciplinarity. We can unite the academic, industry and the government sector to help jumpstart the development of quantum technologies and make their effects positive, fair and secure. Quantum computing is not a myth, and the way to create this revolutionary paradigm need some time, imagination and will to open its potential.

REFERENCES

Biju, J. V., & Mallya, A. P., & P, K. (2025, February). Prediction of Cardiac Disease Using Quantum Enhanced Ensemble Learning Approach. In *2025 International Conference on Innovative Trends in Information Technology (ICITIIT)* (pp. 1-6). IEEE. DOI: 10.1109/ICITIIT64777.2025.11041018

Brijwani, G. N., Ajmire, P. E., & Thawani, P. V. (2023). Future of quantum computing in cyber security. In *Handbook of research on quantum computing for smart environments* (pp. 267–298). IGI Global. DOI: 10.4018/978-1-6684-6697-1.ch016

Chittem, M. B., & Pradhan, A. K. (2025, January). Hybrid Quantum-Classical Transfer Learning for Real-Time Data Processing. In *2025 17th International Conference on COMmunication Systems and NETworks (COMSNETS)* (pp. 84-89). IEEE. DOI: 10.1109/COMSNETS63942.2025.10885700

Eswaran, U., Khang, A., & Eswaran, V. (2024). Role of Quantum Computing in the Era of Artificial Intelligence (AI). In *Applications and Principles of Quantum Computing* (pp. 46–68). IGI Global Scientific Publishing. DOI: 10.4018/979-8-3693-1168-4.ch003

Gayathri, M., Karthik, P. C., Sandhia, G. K., Thilagavathy, R., & Pushpalatha, M. (2024). Quantum Computing Principles: Harnessing the Potential of Quantum Mechanics. In *Applications and Principles of Quantum Computing* (pp. 81-94). IGI Global Scientific Publishing.

Kathirvel, A., Maheswaran, C. P., Subramaniam, M., & Naren, A. K. (2023). Quantum Computers Based on Distributed Computing Systems for the Next Generation: Overview and Applications. *Handbook of Research on Quantum Computing for Smart Environments*, 474-494.

Kaushik, M., Sindhwani, N., & Saxena, K. (2024). Quantum Computing Security: Application of Quantum Computing in Computer Security. In *Applications and Principles of Quantum Computing* (pp. 399-417). IGI Global Scientific Publishing.

Khang, A. (Ed.). (2024). *Applications and principles of quantum computing*. IGI Global. DOI: 10.4018/979-8-3693-1168-4

Mishra, B. K. (Ed.). (2022). *Technology road mapping for quantum computing and engineering*. IGI Global. DOI: 10.4018/978-1-7998-9183-3

Nagarajan, R., Kannadhasan, S., & Venusamy, K. (2022). Recent developments in quantum computing and their challenges. *Technology Road Mapping for Quantum Computing and Engineering*, 24-35.

Chapter 10
Urban IoT and Quantum Computing:
Bridging Cryptographic Security and Sustainable Development

V. Saranya
https://orcid.org/0009-0007-7631-4371
Panimalar Engineering College, India

K. Vijayalakshmi
https://orcid.org/0000-0002-4827-3011
SRM Institute of Science and Technology, India

S. Udhayashankar
https://orcid.org/0009-0006-3781-8801
Vel Tech Multi Tech Dr. Rangarajan Dr. Sakunthala Engineering College, India

ABSTRACT

As quantum computing advances, existing cryptographic techniques used in smart city infrastructures face increasing vulnerability, especially within internet of things (IoT) networks. This chapter explores the critical role of post-quantum cryptography (PQC) in securing urban IoT ecosystems against quantum threats while addressing sustainability challenges. It covers PQC principles, algorithm families, integration with IoT communication protocols, and the protection of critical sectors such as energy, healthcare, and transportation. The chapter also explores quantum-specific network attacks, supply chain vulnerabilities, and the role of green cryptography and AI-assisted security. Emphasis is placed on balancing quantum resilience

DOI: 10.4018/979-8-3373-3166-9.ch010

with energy efficiency to ensure secure, scalable, and sustainable smart cities. The chapter concludes by identifying future research directions to guide the transition toward quantum-safe and eco-conscious urban infrastructure.

1. INTRODUCTION

1.1 Evolution of Smart Urban Environments

The rapid implementation of emerging technologies has been changing the urban environment on a massive scale over the past 20 years, primarily the Internet of Things (IoT). The need to create efficient, responsive and sustainable infrastructures has also caused the emergence of smart cities in response to overcrowding and increased resource demands of cities. Digital technology is connected to physical infrastructure in these smart cities, which enables them to gather information in real-time, make intelligent decisions, and improve the quality of life of the population. Examples of major uses are smart electrical management, intelligent transport system, smart medicine, environmental control and social security. This is not just a trend, but a necessity to solve the urgency of urbanization which includes pollution, traffic jam, energy crisis and health hazards to the population. The secret of such intelligent systems is the flawless interconnection of equipment and integrity, confidentiality, and availability of the large amounts of data that such equipment conveys.

1.2 Role of IoT in Urban Infrastructure

The intelligent urban infrastructure is based on the Internet of Things as it is applied to integrate physical items with sensors, applications, and communication ports. The IoT applications gather, transmit and process data and enable increased automation and real-time tracking of the different industries. Smart transport, e.g. IoT technology tracks the movement of cars, carbon footprint and pedestrians to provide the greatest freedom of movement and the least harm to the environment. Energy systems have smart meters and grid sensors that help in managing the usage patterns and faults to help optimize energy usage effectively and sustainably. Another instance of IoT assisting urban governance is that cities use real-time information to operate waste collection, water distribution, and safety. However, the security of the IoT devices becomes a significant challenge when the number of IoT devices grows exponentially. They are typically resource constrained, heterogeneous and installed within the possibly soft targets of cyber-attack. In that case, the success of the deployment of urban IoT infrastructure will be determined by the security of communications, data privacy, and operational integrity.

1.3 Emerging Threats from Quantum Computing

Although the classical computing systems are based on binary logic, quantum computing is based on the quantum mechanics instead, where the qubits can exist in the states of both 0 and 1 at the same time due to superposition. This radically new computing paradigm holds out the prospect of exponential increases in speed on some problems, and on problems of cryptographic importance in particular. Another potential threat to the security basis of existing cryptographic systems is quantum algorithms, e.g. Shor algorithm, which can efficiently factor large integers and solve discrete logarithm problems, on which many commonly used encryption schemes (e.g. RSA, ECC) are based. Consequently, the emergence of quantum computing will make most of the current public-key cryptography redundant. This has an imminent effect on intelligent urban ecosystems that rely heavily on safe communication between interconnected objects of the Internet of Things, central control systems, and cloud platforms. In case those systems are hacked with the help of quantum attacks, it may result in massive data leakage, infrastructure tampering and loss of popular credibility on smart technologies. Considering that the practical quantum computers are expected to be developed within the next few decades, it is necessary to make the proactive shift to quantum-resistant cryptographic systems (Brijwani et al., 2023).

1.4 Importance of Post-Quantum Cryptographic Security and Sustainability

The next step in the field is Post-Quantum Cryptography (PQC) that aims at protecting digital communication against quantum-capable adversaries. As opposed to conventional cryptography, PQC algorithms are resistant to classical and quantum computers. The National institute of Standards and Technology (NIST) has been forefront in working to standardize PQC schemes that can be used in the real world. In the IoT in city case, PQC needs to be lightweight, scalable and able to integrate with low-resource devices that are strong against future quantum attacks. But mass deployment of the PQC solution is challenging, especially in terms of energy consumption and the cost of computation. Most PQC algorithms are either limited in key size or require more processing power, which can be overloaded by resource-restricted IoT nodes and add extra resource overhead to smart infrastructures. That is why the sustainability of cryptographic solutions, as the security mixed with energy efficiency, long-term applicability, and sustainability, is highly required. Ensuring the sustainability of cryptography means that smart cities will be safe, sustainable and environmentally viable.

1.5 Objectives and Scope of the Chapter

The chapter is meant to give a detailed picture of the overlap of quantum computing and post-quantum cryptography and smart urban IoT systems, especially in terms of security and sustainability. It starts with the analysis of the structure and communication protocols of the urban IoT ecosystems and new threats of quantum algorithms. The chapter then explains the concepts of PQC and the various types of algorithms, their advantages and limitations and the way it could be implemented within the smart infrastructure. Of specific attention are quantum-specific threats to the IoT such as network attacks and supply chain attack vulnerabilities and symmetric cryptography protection in the quantum world. In addition, the chapter explains the relative power of probabilistic and quantum algorithms in relation to the real-world applications of cryptography. It also concerns the sustainability and the energy implication of the deployment of PQC within the urban space. Lastly, the chapter ends with a wrap-up of the required policy frameworks, standardization and future study plans that are needed in order to ensure smart cities become secure, scaled and sustainable in the post-quantum world. Through this holistic review, the chapter is geared towards giving recommendations to scientists, professionals and policy makers to develop resilient urban systems capable of withstanding the impact of a quantum future.

2. URBAN IOT ECOSYSTEMS: INFRASTRUCTURE AND SECURITY NEEDS

2.1 Overview of Urban IoT Applications

The UIoT ecosystems are making the cities smart places by embedding sensors, actuators, and communication devices in most of all the services offered in the city. Such applications will make life easier in the city, consume less and enhance living standards of citizens. The smart grids are, perhaps, the most critical application, but in this case, the IoT devices enable dynamical control and monitoring of electricity production, distribution, and consumption in real-time. Smart meters and distributed energy resources should allow utility companies to optimize energy flow, identify faults and integrate renewable sources such as solar and wind by gathering data at smart meter and distributed resource levels.

IoT is also an important part of traffic management systems. The sensors installed in the road, traffic lights and vehicles assist in observing the congestion level, accidents, and give real time route recommendations. Intelligent traffic lights can change dynamically according to the car traffic, minimizing the time spent at lights and emissions. In the same way, IoT is used in smart public transport where buses and trains are monitored, real-time information is available to passengers and schedules are optimised.

Urban IoT applications in healthcare are remote patient monitoring, the organization of emergency response, and hospital resources management. Wearable devices, connected medical devices and smart ambulances are all parts of a single integrated system that enhances the delivery and responsiveness of medical services.

The other critical sector is the safety and surveillance of the people, and here the IoT cameras, gunshot detectors, and environmental sensors will be employed in detecting crimes, controlling the crowd, and responding to disasters. The systems are usually connected to centralized command centers where data of a variety of sources is combined and processed to provide quick decisions.

IoT also serves the urban waste management and water systems. The use of smart bins with fill-level sensors and linked water meters allows effective resource management and decreases the cost of operations. In general, applications of IoT in urban areas are numerous, interrelated, and data-based, which is why they become an important part of contemporary smart cities.

2.2 Data Security and Privacy Requirements

Since urban IoT systems are responsible to process more sensitive and mission-critical data, data security and privacy have become a priority. Surveillance cameras, health monitors, smart meters, and location-tracking gadgets may generate data that can provide detailed insights into an individual and his or her behavior. The unlawful use or interference with such data can lead to critical cases of privacy invasion, legal consequences and mistrust among the population.

Data security of IoT in cities has many faces: confidentiality, integrity, availability and authenticity. Confidentiality will ensure that the confidential data is not disclosed to unauthorized parties and integrity will ensure that the data was not altered in the course of transmission or storage. Availability means that the data and systems are accessible and functional even in the event of an emergency or a hacker attack. Authenticity also implies the checking of identities of devices and users to avoid impersonation or spoofing.

Since the IoT networks are decentralized and distributed, it is difficult to provide end-to-end security. The vulnerabilities are different at each layer, including sensing and edge processing, network and cloud services. The devices that are placed in the public areas are particularly vulnerable to physical attacks, side-channel attacks, and rogue device insertions.

Encryption, digital signatures, access control, secure boot and firmware integrity checks are common ways to deal with these concerns. Nonetheless, such mechanisms usually demand some computational resources and even energy, which are not easily accessible in the IoT nodes.

2.3 Communication Protocols in Urban IoT

The main component to the urban IoT infrastructure is communication protocols, which allows data to be exchanged among sensors, gateways, cloud platforms, and user interfaces. These protocols have a huge difference depending on the range, bandwidth, latency and energy demands of the application.

Bluetooth Low Energy (BLE), Zigbee and Wi-Fi are typical technologies of short-range communication. BLE is appropriate in low power wearable devices whereas Zigbee is common in home and building automation. Wi-Fi has a greater bandwidth and it is applied in video surveillance and public access points, but it consumes more power.

Low Power Wide Area Network (LPWAN) technologies (LoRaWAN, Sigfox and NB-IoT) are suitable in long-range and low-power applications. LoRaWAN is also popular in smart water and waste applications because of its long range, low data rate. NB-IoT is cellular-supported, which means that it has a superior coverage in underground and indoor urban areas and can be used in smart metering and tracking applications.

Among the most used application layer protocols of the IoT is MQTT (Message Queuing Telemetry Transport) at the protocol level, which is lightweight and is meant to be used in constrained environments. The other protocol that is efficient and optimized in RESTful services based on UDP is CoAP (Constrained Application Protocol) and is applicable to low-power devices.

These protocols are prone to security risks even though they have their benefits. Most of them were initially created without much security in mind paying more attention to reliability and ease of use. Extensions to provide security, e.g. DTLS (Datagram Transport Layer Security) to CoAP or TLS (Transport Layer Security) to MQTT, are required to provide confidentiality and integrity that might have performance overheads.

2.4 Constraints: Bandwidth, Power, and Real-Time Demands

The urban Internet of Things devices possess quite a strict range of limitations defining their performance, scalability, and security. The main bottleneck is the bandwidth because the vast majority of individuals will be transferring information through thousands of devices in the crowded cities. The overloaded networks may lead to delays, loss and underperformance of packets. This is especially needed when the application involves real time data processing like traffic control, emergency response performance, population tracking and monitoring.

The other major constraint is the power consumption. Most IoT devices use batteries, and they are deployed in such a way that they cannot be serviced or frequently recharged. One can drain the power in a relatively short time by executing cryptographic algorithms, or by maintaining a constant connection, thereby reducing the longevity of devices. This implies that it imposes a huge burden on lightweight cryptography and energy-saving communication protocols.

Mission critical applications in the urban environment require latency and real time responsiveness. The delay in transmission of data or processing can affect both the safety and efficiency of the smart system. As an example, a delay of a few milliseconds will cause serious problems with an autonomous traffic controller or an emergency medical service. Such power and bandwidth limited operation is most suitable with the use of advanced networking methods which include edge computing, caching and dynamic bandwidth allocation to provide low-latency and reliable communications.

Scalability is also a problem when more urban IoT deployments are instituted. The network design will be required to accommodate additional and additional devices without significant losses in performance or security. It involves proper management of devices, seamless connection with cloud and edge, and consistent security policies.

3. QUANTUM COMPUTING: THREATS AND TRANSFORMATIONS

3.1 Fundamentals of Quantum Computing

Quantum computing is a paradigm shift in information processing, which utilises the laws of quantum mechanics to perform computation in entirely new ways compared with classical computing. As opposed to the classical bits that are in one of the two states (0 or 1), quantum bits or qubits can be in a superposition of 0 and 1 simultaneously. This and additional features of entanglement and quantum interference enable quantum computers to process large quantities of data in parallel, and to solve certain classes of problems exponentially faster than classical computers(Khang, A 2023).

Quantum circuits and quantum gates are the fundamental devices of quantum computing: they perform unitary operations on qubits. Algorithms Quantum algorithms are built out of sequences of such gates, and are intended to take advantage of quantum phenomena to compute efficiently. Such systems are very susceptible to noise and decoherence and this has led to large-scale practical quantum computing becoming a major engineering problem.

Areas where quantum computing holds the potential of being transformative include simulation of quantum systems, optimization, and machine learning. Nevertheless, cryptography can be considered as one of the most important spheres, in which quantum computing has disruptive potential, as it can break popular security protocols used in modern communication systems.

3.2 Quantum Capabilities in Breaking Classical Cryptosystems

Shor algorithm which factors large integers and discovers discrete logarithms, is one of the most famous and influential quantum algorithms, because it solves two problems, which are used as the basis of security of most classic public-key cryptographic algorithms like RSA, Diffie-Hellman, and elliptic curve cryptography (ECC). These cryptosystems are based in the computational difficulty of these mathematical problems, so they are secure against all known efficient classical algorithms to solve them in a reasonable amount of time. Given a powerful enough quantum computer, Shor algorithm can be used to break these schemes in a polynomial time and as such these schemes will be vulnerable and outdated in a post-quantum world.

Grover algorithm is another important algorithm which provides quadratic speedup on brute-force search problem. Although it is not as threatening as Shor algorithm is, it still undermines the practical security of symmetric key cryptography systems in that it decreases their resistance to brute-force attacks. An example would be that a 128-bit key with Grover would only be 64 bits effective, and so in the future we would have to use longer keys to be resistant.

In addition to these, new quantum algorithms keep being developed and even though they are not currently more powerful than classical methods in every area, their theoretical implications are dramatic. Quantum computing compromises the fundamental assumptions that most of the modern secure communication relies on such as email encryption, secure web browsing (TLS), software updates, and digital signature. In that regard, proactive mitigation measures by means of post-quantum cryptography are essential (Nagarajan, R et al 2022).

3.3 Impact on Public Key Infrastructure (PKI) and Symmetric Encryption

The most significant aspect of trust and safe communication in the online environment is Public Key Infrastructure (PKI). It is a process of issuance, administration and verifies digital certificates, which allows secure key exchange and authentication.

PKI is used to provide secure communication channels through protocols, including SSL/TLS, SSH, VPNs, and secure email services, via untrusted networks.

Quantum computing poses the greatest threat to PKI since it is susceptible to quantum attacks. In case an adversary obtains access to a powerful enough quantum computer, the adversary will be able to decrypt the intercepted messages that were encrypted with a quantum encryption algorithm, construct a digital signature, and masquerade as a user or a server. This does not only compromise the privacy but also compromises the integrity and originality of data on the internet.

Quantum computers cannot crack symmetric encryption algorithms like AES, or hash functions like SHA-2, but quantum-resistant cryptography is relatively more resistant to quantum attacks. The security of them is degraded by Grover algorithm, which offers a quadratic speed-up to brute-force attacks. Consequently, the symmetric key sizes and the hash sizes must be doubled to achieve similar post-quantum security (e.g. AES-256 instead of AES-128). Whereas symmetric cryptography can be used in the quantum age when properly enhanced, the PKI systems would have to be redesigned completely to be quantum-resistant.

The effect of this impact is that there is need to switch to quantum-safe cryptographic algorithms that can be adapted to the current PKI framework or be used to replace them. Organizations and governments need to start an evaluation of their cryptographic dependencies and plan a slow migration to post-quantum standards.

3.4 Timeline and Realism of Quantum Threats

The theoretical power of quantum computers is well understood, whereas it is still an open question how to actually build a large-scale, fault-tolerant quantum computer. The existing quantum hardware has constraints in the number of qubits, coherence time and gate fidelity, and the use of such powerful quantum algorithms as Shor is not feasible now. The experts say that it would take thousands to millions of error-corrected logical qubits to break RSA-2048, or equivalently millions of physical qubits in the current error rates and quantum error correction requirements.

It is estimated that cryptographically significant quantum computers will become available between 10 and 30 years, depending on technological innovation, investment and research development. The uncertainty of this time line is however not an excuse to be complacent. There is a significant threat of the so-called harvest now, decrypt later attacks where encrypted data is gathered today with a purpose of decryption on a later day when quantum computers become accessible. Data like government communications, healthcare records, financial transactions and intellectual property might require being kept secret over several decades. So, those organizations whose security needs are long-term must have started planning and migrating towards quantum safe cryptographic systems (Mishra, B. K 2022).

4. POST-QUANTUM CRYPTOGRAPHY (PQC): PRINCIPLES AND ALGORITHMS

4.1 Overview and Goals of PQC

Post-Quantum Cryptography (PQC) Cryptographic algorithms that are intended to be resistant to both classical and quantum computers are called Post-Quantum Cryptography (PQC). The classical cryptographic schemes, including those based on number-theoretic problems, such as integer factorization and discrete logarithms, are getting under threat as quantum computing approaches a practical level. The main aim of PQC is to come up with cryptographic systems that are resistant to quantum attacks e.g. Shor and Grover attacks which are threats to most of the protocols used by the majority e.g. RSA, DSA, and ECC. In contrast to quantum cryptography which would need quantum communication infrastructure, PQC algorithms are developed to run on classical systems, which makes them feasible to be employed in a short term and large scale (Kumar, A., & Garhwal, S. 2021).

The general goals of PQC are quantum resistance, practical efficiency, scalability and interoperability with current communication systems and hardware. As it happens, modern digital infrastructures such as the Internet, IoT systems, and financial networks are constructed on top of the traditional cryptographic schemes, which is why the shift to PQC requires the new algorithms to be as efficient and flexible as their classical counterparts. In addition, PQC has to cope with the variety of constraints of various computing environments, including high-performance servers and lightweight IoT devices.

Since the confidentiality, integrity, and authenticity of digital communications are at risk of being compromised by quantum computers, PQC is not some sort of an academic exercise but a strategic requirement. Authorities like National Institute of Standards and Technology (NIST) have started working around the world in order to assess, normalize and propose the post-quantum algorithms after conducting rigorous multi-round contests. The migration to PQC should be a slow but decisive process, one that will guarantee that the data that is encrypted today will be safe even decades later, even against quantum adversaries.

4.2 PQC Algorithm Families

The Post-Quantum Cryptographic algorithms are divided into a number of groups depending on the mathematical backgrounds used to give them security. The classes have different benefits, compromises and performance, key sizes and implementation complexities. The five most influencing families include:

1. Lattice-Based Cryptography: The area of lattice-based cryptography is now one of the most promising areas of PQC because the methods provide strong security guarantees and are relatively efficient. These schemes are based on the hardness of the problems like the learning with errors (LWE) and the shortest vector problem (SVP). Lattice-based algorithms have a reputation of being versatile and they have been applied to build encryption, digital signatures and even sophisticated primitives such as fully homomorphic encryption. Examples Kyber (selected by NIST to be standardized as a key encapsulation mechanism) and Dilithium (to be used with digital signatures). The lattice-based schemes tend to be highly efficient and comparatively simple to implement, but they can have a substantial key and ciphertext size, in comparison to the classical schemes.
2. Code-Based Cryptography: Code-based cryptography stands on the complexity of the problem of decoding linear error-correcting codes, which is believed to be a difficult problem even in the quantum computer context. McEliece cryptosystem is the most popular example that survived decades of cryptanalysis. Code-based schemes provide rapid encryption and decryption, and their ciphertexts are small, but the public keys are usually extremely large, so the use of code-based schemes in resource-limited systems such as IoT devices may be constrained. However, they can be a good choice in some applications since they have a long history of security and key size is not a major bottleneck.
3. Multivariate Cryptography: Multivariate cryptography is the use of the difficulty of solving systems of multivariate quadratic equations over finite fields, which is NP-hard. Such schemes are especially interesting to implement digital signatures. Some examples are Rainbow that was a finalist in NIST competition. But there are multivariate schemes that have been cracked or weakened practically raising questions concerning their security strength. Nonetheless, this has not stopped their potential to have small signature sizes and quick verification, which has been the motivation behind research on them.
4. Hash-Based Cryptography: Hash-based cryptography is based on security of cryptographic hash functions (which are considered quantum-resistant (with suitable output lengths)). Such schemes can be primarily applied to digital signatures and have stateful and stateless versions. Prominent examples include XMSS (extended Merkle Signature Scheme) and SPHINCS+, the latter of which is stateless and selected by NIST as the subject of standardization. Hash-based signatures are highly secure and very straightforward in their design, and may suffer limitations of large signature sizes, slow key generation, and signing operations.
5. Isogeny-Based Cryptography One of the newer fields of PQC is isogeny-based cryptography which is based on the difficulty of computing isogenies between

elliptic curves. The most popular one is SIKE (Supersingular Isogeny Key Encapsulation). The key sizes in these schemes are very small and thus they are attractive in bandwidth-sensitive applications. But the isogeny based systems are in the development stage and SIKE was broken recently using classical cryptanalysis, which points out the necessity of further research and careful implementation.

These families of algorithms represent a trade-off of security and efficiency and there is no single family that is best suited to all applications, the choice of a family will depend on the application requirements in terms of computational capacity, communication overhead and system lifetime (Subramanian, R. S et al 2024).

4.3 Performance Metrics: Security, Speed, Size, and Complexity

In order to analyze the appropriateness of PQC algorithms to become widely used, it is necessary to critically analyze a number of performance indicators:

Security

The goal of all PQC schemes is to offer classical and quantum security. The security levels are normally stated in relation to the bit-security of AES (e.g. Level 1 is 128-bit AES security). Security analysis is the process of examining the resistance to recognized attacks and the ability to remain strong in a number of operating situations. Cryptographic reliability requires formal proofs, limited parameter selection, and side-channel and fault attacks resistance.

Speed

One of the reasons why PQC is adopted is efficiency, in particular, real-time applications. The speed of key generation, encryption/decryption (or encapsulation/decapsulation) and signing/verification should achieve satisfactory performance levels. Scheme such as Kyber and Dilithium are lattice-based and they tend to score well on this parameter, therefore, they are applicable in web servers, IoT devices, and embedded systems.

Size

The size of key and signature have a great impact on storage, bandwidth and the performance of the system in general. Other schemes, such as code-based cryptography, possess extremely large keys (the order of hundreds of kilobytes), a factor that may be a barrier in a limited environment. As in the case of blockchain, where every byte increases the size and cost of the transaction, signature size is particularly important.

Complexity and Implementation Overhead

The complexity of implementation of a PQC algorithm takes into account such factors as the amount of memory that will be required, the computational requirements and the compatibility with the existing systems. Lesser schemes such as hash-based or certain lattice-based ones are more straightforward to realize securely. Others will need more specific arithmetic or complex structures that cause more chances of implementation errors (Yamini, B et al 2024).

5. SECURING URBAN IoT WITH PQC

5.1 Integrating PQC into IoT Communication Protocols

IoT systems in the urban environment depend much on the effective and safe communication protocols to deliver data between devices, gateways and cloud platforms. Nevertheless, the advent of quantum computing has brought in vulnerabilities in the conventional cryptography methods on which the protocols are based. Consequently, the incorporation of Post-Quantum Cryptography (PQC) into the current IoT communication standards is crucial in terms of the quantum-resilient security. Such protocols as MQTT (Message Queuing Telemetry Transport), CoAP (Constrained Application Protocol), and 6LoWPAN, which are popular in urban IoT environments, are already based on traditional cryptographic suites such as RSA, ECC, and AES (Kathirvel, N et al., 2024; Goel, P. K. 2024).

The integration relies on substituting weak key exchange protocols using quantum-safe Key Encapsulation Mechanisms (KEMs): Kyber, and the classical digital signatures using the schemes: Dilithium or SPHINCS+. To demonstrate this, the TLS protocol, used to secure the majority of internet communications, can be refactored to use post-quantum key exchange algorithms, with hybrid modes where both PQC and classical algorithms are run in parallel to allow backward compatibility and forward security. In the same manner, CoAP can be augmented to utilize post-quantum version of Datagram Transport Layer Security (DTLS).

The size of keys and ciphertexts increases as one of the primary issues of PQC in IoT protocols that may overload bandwidth-constrained IoT networks. Hence, protocol extensions should be very well designed so as to reduce overheads as well as interoperability. The NIST and other international organizations standardization activities, as well as industry cooperation, are important in the determination of secure and efficient integration frameworks that can be applied in different IoT urban applications. The latency, power consumption and throughput functions must be evaluated and pilot implementations and simulation studies should be done to ensure that PQC-enhanced protocols are viable in the real world smart city settings (Tightiz, L., & Yang, H 2020).

5.2 Lightweight PQC for Resource-Constrained Devices

Another reason is that a large number of IoT devices in urban infrastructure (e.g. environmental sensors, traffic monitors, wearable health devices) are resource-constrained, having limited computational power, memory, and energy supply. Such limitations present an obstacle of significant magnitude to the direct implementation of most PQC schemes, as the schemes tend to have larger key sizes and more complicated operations than their classical counterparts. Thus, one research and implementation priority is the creation and implementation of lightweight PQC optimized to such resource-limited settings.

Lightweight PQC targets the minimization of the algorithmic complexity, key size, ciphertext size and speed of execution without compromising the security of the system to the quantum attacks. Lattice-based cryptography Lattice-based cryptography, notably Kyber and Dilithium, has been promising on low-power microcontrollers and embedded systems. An example is the Kyber, which offers an efficient key encapsulation mechanism with moderate key sizes and fast performance, thus suitable to be used in the limited IoT context.

The computational overhead of PQC can also be minimized by optimization techniques including algorithmic pruning, pre-computation, and hardware acceleration. Efficient implementation of post-quantum schemes could be also supported by hardware implementations based on lightweight FPGA or ASIC designs, but at the expense of system complexity.

Moreover, the design of new PQC schemes that are specifically applied to the IoT settings is actively under research. Such schemes are compact, efficient and resistant to known quantum attacks. The final ambition is to guarantee that even the tiniest IoT devices can be able to sustain secure communications in a post-quantum world without compromising on usability, battery and performance.

5.3 PQC for Critical Urban Sectors

Various sectors in smart urban ecosystems can be tagged as critical infrastructure because they have implications on the safety of the people, economic stability and the overall daily operations. These are energy systems (smart grids), transport systems (smart traffic systems) and healthcare services (connected medical devices and eHealth platforms). To secure and make these sectors resilient to the quantum era, it is important to adopt PQC early and strategically.

In smart energy systems, communication between smart meters, grid controllers and data centers must be secure to prevent manipulation, theft of data or services interruption. PQC is able to secure firmware updates over long distances, demand-response signals and real-time monitoring information. The lattice based and code based schemes, due to their powerful encryption and authentication features fit well in ensuring integrity and confidentiality of grid communications.

Urban mobility is based on Vehicle-to-Everything (V2X) communication, traffic data in real time, and smart signalling in the transportation sector. Violation of these systems may result in congestions, accidents or even targeted attacks. Post-quantum digital signatures may be used to guarantee the authenticity of the messages between autonomous vehicles and infrastructure nodes thus avoiding spoofing and man-in-the-middle attacks.

In the medical field, PQC is necessary to secure sensitive information about patients, to guarantee secure connection between wearable health devices and the cloud, and secure work of medical equipment. Healthcare records have long-term confidentiality requirements, which makes PQC especially applicable to the industry, as the data might have to be kept secret over decades. Besides, the outcomes of a security violation in healthcare are not merely economic or image-related, they may have a direct impact on human lives.

In both of these areas, the implementation of PQC could be used to offer a future-proof and secure solution that conforms to regulatory practices and increases the trust of the population in smart city technologies.

5.4 Hybrid Cryptographic Models for Urban Systems

Hybrid cryptographic models present a convenient and flexible solution to the protection of urban IoT systems in the transition to PQC. The transition to PQC is gradual and complex, and therefore hybrid cryptographic models will be a realistic solution to the problem of protecting urban IoT systems in the interim period. Hybrid schemes Hybrid schemes are a combination of classical cryptographic schemes (e.g., RSA, ECC) with post-quantum schemes to provide both classical and quantum security. Such a two-layer approach allows maintaining compatibility with the current infrastructure and an extra layer of protection(.

Practically, hybrid models may be applied to TLS handshake, where a classical and a PQC key exchange can be performed in parallel, and the session key is derived out of the two exchanges. This has the effect that as long as at least one of the algorithms is unbroken (e.g. by some future quantum computer) then the session will be secure. The same can be done to digital signatures, a classical signature can be paired with a post-quantum signature to provide backward compatibility and forward secrecy.

Hybrid schemes also have utility in boosting firmware and security protocols of legacy devices that are not yet fully compatible with PQCs. Allowing a gradual implementation of quantum-safe algorithms, organizations may ensure the testing of PQC functionality and compatibility and reduce the risk of acting too soon or not completing the implementation.

Nonetheless, the hybrid cryptography has also posed some challenges such as the higher computational overhead, messages size, and security analysis. So, it is very important to select parameters carefully, test them and standardize them so that hybrid implementations do not accidentally compromise system security or efficiency.

6. QUANTUM-SPECIFIC THREATS IN URBAN IoT

6.1 Quantum Network Attacks in Smart Cities

Since smart cities are developing into highly integrated places with IoT devices everywhere, they are also becoming a target of advanced cyber threats. A new type of risks that have emerged with quantum computing can disrupt the cryptographic basis of the urban communication networks. Quantum network attacks use the computing abilities of quantum algorithms especially Shor and Grover algorithms to crack the old encryption and compromise insecure urban IoT systems. When applied in the setting of a smart city, such attacks may be used to intercept and decrypt the traffic data, remotely control the traffic signals, shut down surveillance systems, or obtain sensitive data of healthcare or utility services.

The possible vulnerability that may be of interest is the public key infrastructure (PKI) applied on smart city platforms to perform safe key exchange and digital authentication. With the development of quantum computers, ill-willed individuals can use them to create digital certificates or decipher the previously intercepted encrypted messages. It makes currently used cryptography protocols like RSA and ECC, which are the basis of TLS, VPNs, and firmware updates, extremely vulnerable. This weakness may be used by attackers to insert false data in systems, hijack remote updates or masquerade as trusted parties.

Quantum-enabled man-in-the-middle (MITM) attacks are another important threat. In this case, an enemy may use quantum computation to read encrypted messages, compromise the key exchange protocol and silently modify or redirect messages. This is particularly dangerous in latency-sensitive systems like emergency response or autonomous transport system where any minor latency variation or imprecision would cause a critical failure. The growing danger of quantum network attacks demands urgent and active migration to post-quantum safe protocols that would enable the maintenance of confidentiality, authenticity and integrity against quantum attackers.

6.2 Post-Quantum Supply Chain Vulnerabilities

Smart cities adjust their supply chains that are integrated with the IoT devices which are complex in nature and feature many manufacturers, vendors and integrators. This complication provides numerous points of vulnerability that are exploitable, particularly in a post-quantum environment. The presence of hacked devices or software at any point in the supply chain can serve as a backdoor through which the adversaries can access the urban infrastructure.

Within this type of quantum-enabled threat scenario, the threat is then made worse by the fact that the attackers can now retroactively decrypt supply chain communications and gain access to sensitive information such as firmware updates, digital certificates, or configuration keys. Using the example, attackers will be able to capture encrypted updates delivered today and decrypt them in the future using quantum computers and disclose secrets of the system level or install malicious firmware many years after the incident.

Hardware Trojan and firmware manipulation is another huge threat. The bad players may implant backdoors or any other undesirable capabilities within the IoT hardware during the manufacturing process, and this may be remotely invoked or through encrypted instructions. In post-quantum era, the traditional authentication mechanisms which was developed to provide assurance that the hardware and software is genuine can be compromised with a lot of ease thereby causing mass compromise.

In order to deal with such risks, quantum-resistant cryptographic techniques should be implemented throughout the supply chain during both development, deployment and maintenance. This involves secure boot operations via post-quantum signature, encrypted update procedures with quantum-safe key exchange and strong integrity verification protocols. Further, auditing systems of the supply chain based on blockchain and integrated into PQC can give a transparent and tamper-free record of component origin and lifecycle, improving the resilience against post-quantum attacks.

6.3 Protection of Symmetric Cryptography Against Quantum Attacks

Although a lot of attention to post-quantum threats is on public-key cryptography, symmetric cryptography is also not quantum-safe. Grover algorithm gives a quadratic speed-up to brute-force attacks on symmetric cryptographic algorithms, effectively reducing the strength of the symmetric cryptography by a factor of two. As an example, AES-128, already providing 128-bit of security, would provide only 64 bits of security against a quantum attacker, and thus would become susceptible to exhaustive search in a post-quantum world.

In response to this, doubling of key sizes of symmetric algorithms is suggested; AES-256 rather than AES-128, and SHA-384 or SHA-512 when used in place of SHA-256 in hashing applications. Such modifications will bring the effective security margin back even in a situation where quantum attackers exist. Symmetric cryptography such as the AES and hash-based message authentication codes (HMACs) is more quantum-resistant in general because of its design and because it does not depend on number-theoretic problems. Nevertheless, their further resilience should be guaranteed by setting more robust parameters and frequent cryptographic updates.

In an urban IoT, where symmetric encryption is widely employed to secure the communication between constrained devices, some further consideration should be given to performance trade-offs. Raising the size of key may be costly in terms of memory, processing and battery life, especially in wireless sensor networks and mobile devices. Hence, there is a need to have lightweight symmetric cryptographic variants that are longer in key length and have an optimized implementation that will be both secure and efficient.

In addition to that, the protection measure can be increased with the combination of symmetric cryptography and post-quantum key distribution schemes. It is through the exchange of symmetric keys using PQC algorithms followed by the transfer of information using symmetric encryption, which is fast. The hybrid schemes represent the most effective combination of the two: they are as fast as symmetric encryption and as resistant to PQC as the key exchange.

6.4 Role of Quantum-Resistant Authentication Protocols

Authentication is the key component of a secure IoT communication system, as it ensures that the devices, users, and systems are what they claim to be. The integrity and trustworthiness of such communications have the highest priority in the smart city where a number of interconnected devices are communicating in real-time. However, quantum computing is threatening to the standard digital signature scheme, on which digital authentication of the existing systems relies.

Post-quantum digital signature schemes being under standardization as an alternative to weak classical signatures include Dilithium, Falcon and SPHINCS+. The schemes are immune to quantum attacks and could be utilized to secure essential functions such as firmware signing, secure boot and device-to-device authentication. As a reference, SPHINCS+ is a hash-based stateless signature scheme, very high protection level, and computationally expensive, which would be suitable to sign software updates and important instructions during the IoT networks.

Quantum resistant authentication algorithms are particularly important in dynamic systems like intelligent transportation, in which vehicles, units and infrastructure on the roadside must authenticate each other within milliseconds. Failure to do so can cause impersonation attacks and even injuries. The urban systems have the ability to defend the communication lifecycle against identity-based threats by incorporating PQC signatures within authentication protocols, including EAP (Extensible Authentication Protocol) or IKE (Internet Key Exchange).

7. SUSTAINABILITY ASPECTS OF PQC IN SMART CITIES

7.1 Energy and Resource Challenges in Cryptographic Operations

With the growing reliance of smart cities on cryptographic security of their IoT systems in the urban environment, the energy requirements of the cryptographic operations that underlie them have been put into the limelight. Cryptography needs to provide confidentiality, integrity and authenticity of network data, but the computation load of cryptography can be prohibitive in situations where the networked devices number in the thousands or even millions. The computational cost of traditional and post-quantum cryptography should be evaluated in terms of smart cities whose ultimate goals are energy efficiency, sustainability, and environmental stewardship.

In general, Post-Quantum Cryptography (PQC) schemes have more resource-demanding requirements than classical algorithms due to larger key sizes, more complex to compute and require more memory. By way of example, lattice-based protocols such as Kyber or Dilithium may require considerable processing cycles to perform key generation and signature verification, particularly on resource-constrained devices. The energy requirements can be aggregated quickly throughout the vast sensor, meter, actuator and mobile node networks in the urban environment, thus causing more energy consumption, shorter device life and greater environmental expense.

Besides, a large number of IoT devices in urban areas run on battery, and are installed in places that cannot be easily accessed or visited regularly. When PQC schemes are not optimized, frequent cryptographic operations, e.g. secure boot processes, encrypted communication, and firmware updates, may drain battery life at an increased rate. Therefore, although PQC is a necessary means to protect the infrastructure of smart cities against the potential quantum attacks in the future, it should be implemented in the way that does not undermine the sustainability agenda of contemporary urban development.

7.2 Environmental Impact of PQC Algorithms

Environmental impact of the scale deployment of PQC is not restricted to the power consumption of a device. A growing impact of the PQC implementation on the urban networks leads to more workloads in data centers, energy consumption in clouds, and manufacturing need in more capacious hardware elements. As an example, the use of PQC in secure communication protocols will need more storage and computational resources in cloud platforms that handle public key infrastructure, identity services as well as device provisioning.

These cryptographic activities which are employed by the smart city structures contribute to the carbon footprint of the smart city structures especially where the source of energy is not renewable. Additionally, the hardware needs that the more complex cryptographic computations will need could be linked to increased production and e-waste, particularly as the older machines will fall out of use due to their inability to run PQC algorithms. It provokes the questions of the sustainability of the urban IoT systems related to the life-cycle, which, in its turn, must be resolved by the means of modernization of the cryptography in general.

The quantitative research suggests that at this point, PQC may introduce a critical increase in the size of messages being exchanged and the computational load, especially, in digital signature schemes and key exchange protocols. It is a fact that additional energy will be consumed at wireless relay and more information will be stored and processed and more frequently the equipment will have to be updated and that is adding to the cost of the environment. Therefore, despite the critical role of the introduction of PQC in relation to cybersecurity, environmental costs of this technology must be properly managed to ensure the sustainability vision of smart cities in the long-term outlook.

7.3 Designing Energy-Efficient Security Protocols

To ensure the as-strong-as-possible post-quantum security and still allow the sustainable computing, there is an urgent need to create energy-saving PQC protocols. They should be designed to achieve the best tradeoff between security and energy use, and in real-time and low-power IoT applications in particular. Energy-saving cryptographic design can be sought out as a kind of algorithmic simplification, software acceleration, and communication optimization.

At the algorithmic level, researchers are trying to design lightweight versions of PQC schemes which are also quantum resistant but with lower computational costs.

This is in the form of reducing key sizes, number of rounds in signature verification and compressing the structures of the public keys. As an example, schemes such as Kyber-512 and Dilithium Level 1 are still post-quantum secure, but are more efficient in limited environments compared with their more secure counterparts. Such schemes may be applied selectively to non-critical applications, to save energy at the cost of less protection against quantum threats.

Energy efficiency of PQC operations can also be improved dramatically, by offloading computationally-intensive tasks to cryptographic co-processors or field-programmable gate arrays (FPGAs). Post-quantum algorithms have been implemented in custom silicon, which can be orders of magnitude more power efficient than a software-only implementation, and thus well suited to low power urban IoT nodes.

Communications-wise, optimization of the exchange of PQC-related information, e.g. to minimize overhead by compressing data, or by employing efficient transport layers, can also save energy.

7.4 PQC for Resilient and Sustainable Smart City Infrastructure

In addition to environmental efficiency, PQC is also paramount as it applies to resiliency and long-term sustainability of the smart city systems. The resilience here is that the system resists, and remains functional despite the disruption, it is either the cyberattack, or the malfunction of the device or communication. Post-quantum cryptography builds on this resilience by ensuring that, in the future, communications and data are resistant to adversaries with quantum capability, as well as to protecting the critical infrastructure, such as the power grid, water systems, and emergency response networks.

Sustainability-wise, PQC will promote the sustainability of technology and thus systems and devices implemented now will be secure throughout their estimated lifetimes. The IoT systems in many cities are likely to serve tens of years, and the application of cryptographic algorithms susceptible to quantum attacks may make them obsolete or unsafe in a few years. By incorporating PQC, such systems will be able to resist new threats, and there will be a minimum of retrofitting such systems in the future, which is disruptive and costly.

In addition to that, secure systems are also trustful systems, and the public trust is one of the pillars of sustainable digital transformation. When citizens are assured of the security and privacy of the technologies that support the smart city services, there is a higher chance of their adoption. PQC will help to build this trust by providing security to the personal data, service availability, and city governance as the adversaries become more advanced.

8. PROBABILISTIC VS. QUANTUM ALGORITHMS: IMPLICATIONS FOR SECURITY

8.1 Comparative Overview

The probabilistic algorithms and the quantum algorithms both bring non-determinism to computing, but on entirely different grounds. Probabilistic algorithms provide a random approach to decision making when presented with a complex problem, and thus can provide a solution to a complex problem quicker than a deterministic approach. The algorithms are widely used in cryptography, primality testing and in optimization. In comparison, quantum algorithms apply quantum mechanics ideas (superposition, entanglement, and interference) to search solution spaces in radically different ways. This can even result in improvement of quantum algorithms in some fields compared to either deterministic or probabilistic algorithms.

Cryptographic protocols rely on probabilistic algorithms to achieve security (in particular, they are what is used to generate unpredictable keys, to encrypt and decrypt things in a randomized fashion, and to produce digital signatures). The random character of them makes them resistant to brute force and replay attacks. Nevertheless, quantum algorithms threaten the hypotheses of these cryptosystems, by resolving some of the difficult mathematical problems in a considerably shorter time, than any possible classical/probabilistic algorithm. This analogy is especially relevant in the case of smart cities and IoT systems where secure and real-time communication is paramount, and where devices usually have to use lightweight cryptographic primitives.

8.2 Grover's and Shor's Algorithms vs. Probabilistic Counterparts

Grover and Shor algorithms are two of the most influential quantum algorithms as far as security is concerned. Grover algorithm gives a quadratic speed up on the unstructured search problems. Whereas a classical or probabilistic brute-force search would have to use O(N) time to search a space of N items, Grover algorithm can be used to search the same space with $O(\sqrt{N})$ time, essentially compromising the security of symmetric encryption such as AES and hash functions. To give an example, AES-128, the security of which is thought to be resistant to classical attacks, can be reduced to 64 bits security by Grover algorithm. Probabilistic methods provide no such simplification, and they take expected time to exhaustive search.

An exponential breakthrough in computational power, however, is Shor algorithm. It effectively computes integer factorization and discrete logarithm problems, which are regarded, under classical and probabilistic algorithms, to be a hard problem and the foundation of such public-key systems as RSA, Diffie-Hellman, and ECC. Although some such problems can be speeded up using probabilistic algorithms such as the Pollard rho algorithm, these results are at best only a small speed-up, since they do not scale as well as Shor algorithm on a quantum computer, which has an expected running time of polynomial time. It is this gap that necessitates the development of quantum computing as a major threat to the classical public-key cryptography that should be replaced by post-quantum alternatives.

8.3 Implications for Real-Time IoT Security

Latency, speed, and energy efficiency is of great importance in real-time IoT systems and especially in smart urban environments. Probabilistic based security protocols have long been used to offer powerful protection without incurring much overhead. Nevertheless, quantum algorithms, once implemented, would break these protocols practically overnight, which would leave the existing IoT security systems outdated.

As an example, ECC or RSA-based public key exchanges, frequently applied in the establishment of secure sessions between IoT nodes, are susceptible to being broken with Shor algorithm. This weakness introduces an opportunity to man-in-the-middle attacks, data leakage and device impersonation on real-time systems like traffic control, smart healthcare or energy distribution. In spite of the fact that Grover algorithm is not as dangerous, the effect of it on symmetric encryption implies that the key lengths and hash outputs have to be extended to preserve the existing security rates.

8.4 Hybrid Models and Algorithmic Adaptation

Because the computational power and performance of a probabilistic and quantum algorithm are dramatically different, many security researchers believe in the concept of hybrid cryptographic schemes. They are classical and post-quantum hybrid models to provide defense as we transition to full quantum-resilient infrastructures. One such scheme is hybrid key exchange schemes, which may incorporate both RSA/ ECC and a post-quantum algorithm such as Kyber to generate a common secret. This will mean that once any of the elements is broken then the whole system is secured.

Gradual algorithmic adaptation can also be achieved by using hybrid models, in which protocols developed on probabilistic models are extended to quantum-safe functionality without the need to completely redesign them. The method is especially relevant to large and heterogeneous smart urban settings where various systems and devices are exposed to varying constraints and capabilities. In addition, adaptive algorithms can be used to optimise efficiency and resiliency, by dynamically updating cryptographic schemes based on real-time performance and threat-analysis.

9. FUTURE RESEARCH DIRECTIONS

9.1 Quantum-Resilient Edge and Fog Computing

Because edge and fog computing is becoming increasingly popular in smart cities, where it can reduce latency and improve the effectiveness of data processing and real-time decisions, there is a need to secure such a decentralized environment. Edge and fog nodes tend to handle the sensitive data (traffic patterns, energy usage and healthcare information) and would be the primary target of cyberattacks, including those enabled by quantum computing. The next steps should be the development of quantum-resilient security systems of edge and fog layers, where lightweight Post-Quantum Cryptographic (PQC) schemes can be used, and they can work within their resource limits.

The major issues are to optimize PQC algorithms to fit low-power, intermittently connected edge devices and developing secure distributed consensus and device authentication mechanisms in fog networks. There should also be research on the protocols that will dynamically change cryptographic parameters depending on the local computational capabilities and threat levels. Moreover, the ability to support interoperability between cloud, edge, and device layers within a post-quantum system will be critical to the data exchange between the smart urban ecosystems.

9.2 Blockchain and PQC Synergies for Urban Governance

Blockchain technology is being considered as an underlying technology to govern a smart city, with secure, transparent and tamper proof applications to support identity management, land records, energy trading and public contracts. However, blockchain uses classical cryptographic algorithms and is thus vulnerable to quantum attacks particularly in digital signatures that secure transaction integrity.

The further research must target the exploration of the synergistic integration of PQC and blockchain with the post-quantum digital signature schemes to supplant ECDSA and other null schemes. Even the resource-constrained urban networks require light weight quantum-secure consensus protocols. These involve the research of PQC-accepted proof-of-stake or proof-of-authority algorithms that are safe and energy-efficient.

Figure 1. Future Research Directions

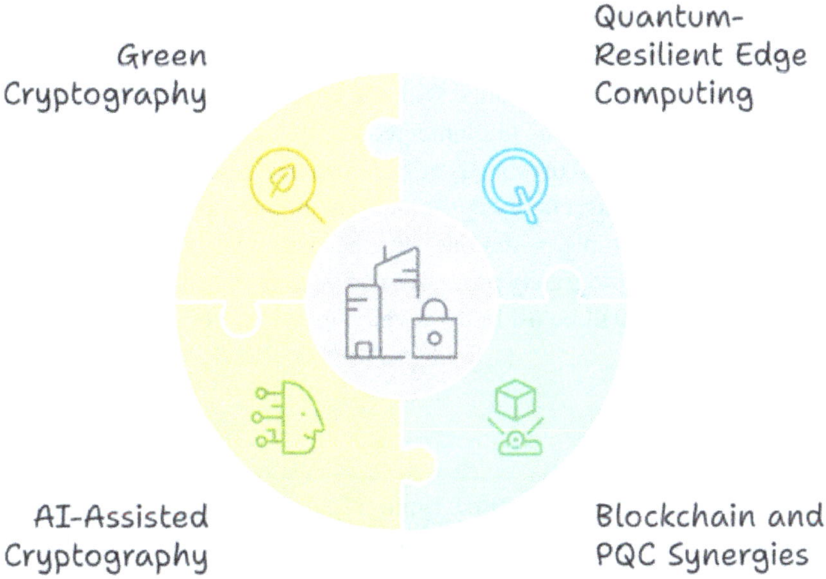

9.3 AI-Assisted Cryptography for Dynamic Threat Response

Artificial Intelligence (AI) has demonstrated an enormous ability to improve cybersecurity by detecting threats, examining actions, and automating response to threats. Within the framework of post-quantum security, AI can be used to dynamically evaluate the quantum threat environment, identify any deviations in encrypted traffic, and suggest cryptographic changes in real time due to the apparent vulnerabilities.

It should be taken into account in the future that the AI-aided cryptographic adaptation models will be utilized to ensure that the position of the maximum security of the IoT networks is calculated continuously, and the parameters of PQC are changed accordingly. This may include AI-assisted context-dependent cryptographic algorithm selection (e.g. data sensitivity, latency requirements or power supply), and the identification of side-channel attack vectors which may be exploited to attack post-quantum implementations.

9.4 Green Cryptography for Net-Zero Smart Cities

Sustainability of smart cities is among the most striking pillars in smart city development and as PQC joins the city landscape infrastructures, the environmental impact of this technology must be put under strict control. Green cryptography is the development and deployment of cryptographic systems with minimal energy costs and carbon footprint and high security assurances. This is especially significant in smart cities that want to follow the net-zero emissions agenda.

The future study will be connected with the evolution of energy-efficient post-quantum algorithms that may be implemented in constrained devices and green IoT systems. The computational overheads of PQC can be minimized through methods such as algorithmic pruning, energy-conscious scheduling and hardware acceleration (e.g. low-power FPGA implementations). Furthermore, the calculation of the environmental charge of cryptography processes and developing some universal metrics of green cryptography will be useful to develop green implementation methods.

10. CONCLUSION

The intersection of Post-Quantum Cryptography (PQC), urban IoT ecosystems, and sustainable smart city evolution has been thoroughly explored in this survey. Starting with the development of intelligent urban worlds and the essential role of the IoT in the transformation of city infrastructure, the research has highlighted the increasing threat of new quantum computing algorithms to the current cryptographic protocols. It discussed the concepts of PQC algorithms and their families, the issues of their implementation in urban IoT protocols, and their general effects on the security, performance, and sustainability. Defending against quantum-enabled network attacks and supply-chain security as well as redefining symmetric encryption and authentication protocols, PQC represents one of the most critical enablers of city-wide security in the future. PQC is not a mere technical answer to quantum threats- it is a necessary part of a robust and healthy urban future. It is relevant in the context of securing vital infrastructure such as energy, transportation and medical services, protecting long-term data confidentiality, and facilitating administrative tools such as blockchain. PQC needs to be effectively architected to work in low-power edge device and scalable cloud systems, to match the objectives of cybersecurity with energy efficiency and environmental sustainability. PQC represents the most important transition point between the existing security model and the one required to uphold the durability, integrity, and reliability of smart city systems as quantum computing matures. Regardless of its potential, there are major challenges associated with the adoption of PQC, such as the complexity of the algorithms, large key sizes, hardware limitations, and the absence of standardization in various IoT ecosystems. The ability to integrate PQC with real time, resource-constrained environments is an unsolved research problem. Nevertheless, such obstacles also lead to the possibility of new innovations in lightweight cryptography, green cryptographic design, AI-based security management, and quantum-resilient edge computing. In addition, cross-disciplinary teamwork of cryptographers, engineers, urban planners, and policymakers must be encouraged to develop scaled, secure, and sustainable implementations. With the dawn of a new era of quantum innovation and urbanized digital transformation, cryptographic resilience is now more than ever an imperative. Post-Quantum Cryptography is not only a reaction to new challenges, but also a move towards securing and maintaining sustainability in the upcoming cities. With the investment of PQC research, an adaptive and hybrid model, and embedding green and intelligent cryptographic systems in all levels of the smart city stack, we will be able to create a digital urban infrastructure not only safe against future attacks but also oriented towards the long-term ecological and societal objectives.

REFERENCES

Brijwani, G. N., Ajmire, P. E., & Thawani, P. V. (2023). Future of quantum computing in cyber security. In *Handbook of research on quantum computing for smart environments* (pp. 267–298). IGI Global. DOI: 10.4018/978-1-6684-6697-1.ch016

Kathirvel, N., Ayyaswamy, K., & Santhoshi, B. (2024). Critical Approaches to Data Engineering Systems Innovation and Industry Application Using IoT. In *Critical Approaches to Data Engineering Systems and Analysis* (pp. 64–89). IGI Global. DOI: 10.4018/979-8-3693-2260-4.ch005

Khang, A. (Ed.). (2024). *Applications and principles of quantum computing*. IGI Global. DOI: 10.4018/979-8-3693-1168-4

Kumar, A., & Garhwal, S. (2021). State-of-the-art survey of quantum cryptography. *Archives of Computational Methods in Engineering*, *28*(5), 3831–3868. DOI: 10.1007/s11831-021-09561-2

Mishra, B. K. (Ed.). (2022). *Technology road mapping for quantum computing and engineering*. IGI Global. DOI: 10.4018/978-1-7998-9183-3

Nagarajan, R., Kannadhasan, S., & Venusamy, K. (2022). Recent developments in quantum computing and their challenges. *Technology Road Mapping for Quantum Computing and Engineering*, 24-35.

Subramanian, R. S., Maheswari, B., Nithya, T., Girija, P., Karthikeyan, M., & Saraswathi, T. (2024). Quantum Computing: Unveiling the Paradigm Shift and Diverse Applications. In *Applications and Principles of Quantum Computing* (pp. 95-112). IGI Global Scientific Publishing.

Tightiz, L., & Yang, H. (2020). A comprehensive review on IoT protocols' features in smart grid communication. *Energies*, *13*(11), 2762. DOI: 10.3390/en13112762

Yamini, B., Nithyanandhan, R., Sudha, K., Nithya, T., Vijayakumar, K., & Subramanian, R. S. (2024, April). Maximizing the Revolutionary Potential of Quantum Computing: Challenges, Opportunities, and Future Directions. In *2024 10th International Conference on Communication and Signal Processing (ICCSP)* (pp. 756-761). IEEE.

Chapter 11
Internet of Things (IoT) in Urban Development: Applications, Challenges, and Future Research Directions

B. Maheswari
https://orcid.org/0000-0001-9711-7915
RMK Engineering College, India

S. Subha
https://orcid.org/0000-0001-8123-5941
SRM Institute of Science and Technology, India

T. Thilagam
https://orcid.org/0000-0002-7657-0726
Vel Tech Rangarajan Dr. Sagunthala R&D Institute of Science and Technology, India

ABSTRACT

The internet of things (IoT) is revolutionizing urban development by enabling real-time data collection, intelligent automation, and interconnected infrastructure across various sectors. This chapter explores the foundational concepts of IoT in the urban context; key application areas such as transportation, energy, waste management, public safety, and healthcare; and highlights current challenges including privacy, interoperability, and governance. It further discusses emerging trends like AI integration, digital twins, blockchain security, and sustainable IoT practices. The chapter also outlines future research directions focusing on interdisciplinary approaches, innovative business models, and ethical urban innovation. By examining both the potential and limitations of IoT, the chapter emphasizes its transformative role in building sustainable, inclusive, and resilient smart cities.

DOI: 10.4018/979-8-3373-3166-9.ch011

1. INTRODUCTION

1.1 Background and Motivation

One of the 21 st century traits is urbanization as over half the world population is already living in the urban areas which is bound to grow exponentially over the decades to come. Increased urban center population density and urbanization are leading to complex issues within the cities such as traffic congestion, pollution, inadequate infrastructure, resource management issues and a constantly growing demand of quality public services. These problems necessitate a radical shift in the way the city is planned and operated and the traditional methods are not sufficient to address the complicated nature of the modern urban experience. In this case, the emergence of the Internet of Things (IoT) is a new opportunity to change the urban development model. IoT is a physical devices communication system that is interconnected and includes sensors, software, and other technologies that enable the collection of data in real-time, its analysis, and transmission (Kuppusamy, P. 2019). The cities will be made smarter, efficient, responsive and sustainable through the potential of the IoT. The urgency to utilize the resources to optimum levels, to enhance the level of service offering, quality of life and sustainability of the urban development is the driving force behind the integration of the IoT in urban ecosystems (Solanki, A., & Nayyar, A. 2019). Such a blend of digital technologies, data analytics and pervasive connectivity is enabling the transition into an era where urban management becomes proactive, rather than reactive. The ability to view, scan, and act on real-time information generated by the IoT systems is redefining the way urban centers are operated and how the citizens are delivered such facilities (Kashyap, R. 2019). It is both a technical and strategic transformation, which endeavours to create resilient and adaptive inclusive urban environments.

1.2 Role of Technology in Urban Transformation

Technology has played a major part in the growth of the cities since the discovery of electricity and establishment of the transport system to the advent of the internet and mobile communication. Technology is currently becoming the heart of change in the urban world. The digital infrastructure, artificial intelligence (AI), big data, cloud computing, and IoT are becoming the key solutions to urban challenges and the overall functioning of cities by smart cities projects across the world (Jha, S. et al., 2024).

The concept of the smart city depends on the implementation of IoT in the urban development. Cities will be able to have unprecedented visibility to their operations by integrating sensors, connected devices into infrastructure like road, bridges, buildings, utility grid, transportation networks. This real time awareness allows predictive maintenance, dynamic resource allocation and responsive governance.

An example is the use of smart traffic with IoT sensors that can be used to track the flow of the vehicle and alter the signal timing to minimize traffic. Smart energy grids will enable the optimization of energy distribution and consumption depending on the demand in real time. Environmental monitoring systems are able to identify the pollution rates and warn the authorities to act in time. Urban resilience can be achieved through connected surveillance and emergency response systems that are used to run public safety systems (Boopathi, S. 2024).

Moreover, the implementation of edge computing and 5G connectivity foster the role of the IoT even more as it facilitates the processing of the data even quicker and minimizes the latency (Molakatala et al., 2024). This enables high-stakes applications like self-driving cars, real-time health monitoring and remote infrastructure operations. Thus, technology and IoT in particular is not something that comes as an appendage to the urban planning process but a transformative force that reinvents the urban life.

1.3 Importance of IoT in Urban Development

The role of IoT in urban development is the fact that it helps develop smarter, safer, and more sustainable cities. IoT allows cities to become living systems which constantly sense, learn, and adapt to the environment, and the requirements of its residents. Urban population is ever expanding and there are more and more needs of efficient public services, superior infrastructure and more environmental sustainability, which is where IoT can play a significant role (May, P. M. A et al., 2025).

One of the biggest strengths of IoT is potential to provide data-driven insights. The connected sensors used in the cities allow the city officials to obtain enormous amount of data on energy use, water supply, transport network, air pollution and garbage generation. This can be applied in policy formulation, to make urban processes work more efficiently and to prevent issues before they escalate to un manageable levels (Jaffrin, L. C et al., 2025).

IoT improves citizen participation and participatory governance as well. Using the mobile applications and smart services, citizens will be able to access the information on a real-time basis, report problems, and engage in the processes of decision-making. As an example, intelligent parking systems notify drivers about the available parking spaces, which decreases the duration of the search and decreases emissions. Solutions to waste management can alert the collection services when the bins are full and optimize routes and lower the cost of operations.

IoT helps to take action on climate and preserve the environment in the sphere of sustainability. Smart grids minimize energy losses, intelligent lighting systems adapt to the presence of people and to natural light and water monitoring systems contribute to saving water resources. Moreover, IoT is the key to creating resilient infrastructure able to resist natural disasters and urban stressors and react to them (Vujatović, M et al., 2022).

1.4 Objectives and Contributions of the Survey

The purpose of this survey is to provide a systematic and detailed description of the role of the IoT in the development of cities. It seeks to introduce the readers to the concepts of IoT, the technological aspects of the IoT, and how it can be applied in real-life urban planning and management. With a focus on the state-of-the-art trends, key use cases, technological trends, and the challenges associated with them, the chapter will explain how IoT will change urban environments.

Specifically, the proposed survey will be structured so that it: Characterizes the basics and the architecture of the IoT systems as applied to the urban infrastructure. Review some of the applications of IoT that involve transportation, energy, waste management, public safety, and healthcare. Highlight the most significant technologies employed to facilitate IoT including communication protocol, edge computing, and data analytics. Identify the most important issues and limitations which do not allow implementing and massifying IoT in urban development. Introduce new trends and future trends, such as AI-blockchain-digital twins. Disseminate cross-disciplinary research in this emerging field and explain research opportunities.

The chapter has many contributions. First, it compiles the existing knowledge on a very broad range of sources and creates a coherent account of IoT in urban development. Second, it classifies and contrasts different urban applications of IoT to disclose best practices and knowledge. Third, it offers a critical discussion of present challenges, which enables the policymakers, researchers, and practitioners to know the gaps and risks. Lastly, the chapter singles out future-oriented strategies that have the potential to guide sustainable and inclusive urban transformation with the help of IoT.

1.5 Structure of the Chapter

The rest of the chapter is divided into six major parts. It is in section 2 that the basic concepts of IoT in the urban environment are presented including its architecture, components, communication technologies, and computing paradigms like edge and cloud integration. Section 3 describes the major uses of IoT in some of the urban sectors, such as transportation, energy, buildings, environment, healthcare, and governance with illustration of the use of IoT in improving functionality and service delivery in each area.

Section 4 gives a detailed discussion of the issues and constraints of using IoT in the cities, including data privacy, standardization, infrastructure limitations and regulatory issues. Section 5 deals with some future directions and emerging trends, including the use of artificial intelligence, digital twins, green IoT, and citizen-centric design in the development of urban areas. The section 6 outlines the areas of research and interdisciplinary directions that may be used to expand the field of smart urbanism.

Lastly, Section 7 closes the survey with a summary of some of the most important findings and thoughts about the long-term potential of IoT in terms of the development of intelligent, inclusive, and sustainable urban futures.

2. FUNDAMENTALS OF IoT IN URBAN CONTEXT

2.1 Definition and Key Concepts of IoT

Internet of Things (IoT) is a vibrant network of physical objects connected by sensors, software, and connectivity that allows the objects to gather, transmit and respond to data. Such devices are commonly called smart objects, they may include ordinary household gadgets and mobile phones, as well as more sophisticated systems, e.g., traffic lights, energy meters, and industrial devices. The key concept of IoT is that a connection can be made between the physical and digital world and devices can interact with each other and with centralised platforms to enable the real-time monitoring, control and automation.

IoT plays a significant role in the city development scenario because it enables smart decision-making and efficiency in operations within the city systems. The concept encompasses the machine-to-machine (M2M) communication, real-time analytics, cloud integration, and automation that are integrated to support the functioning of the urban infrastructure. Scalability, interoperability, energy efficiency and context-awareness are the key characteristics of the IoT. These aspects allow the urban systems to become more responsive, adaptive and citizen oriented (Gómez et al., 2017). A smart traffic management system with IoT as an example can dynamically determine the signal timing of an individual vehicle based on the information regarding the traffic and aid in reducing emissions and congestion.

Also, cities do not just implement the IoT through technology, but the digital ecosystems of interconnecting people, data, and services. Urban IoT is thereby transforming the nature of urban design, management and experience. It makes it possible to proactively maintain the publicly owned infrastructure, to use the natural resources optimally, make the population safer, and provide services better. To that extent, one can state that a general overview of the key tenets of IoT will become the foundation of understanding the overall impact of the technology on the city environment.

2.2 Architecture and Components of IoT Systems

IoT architecture is the blueprint of structure that stipulates the interaction of different devices and systems within an IoT ecosystem and their functionality. The architecture of the IoT is usually designed into layered models in urban areas to handle the complexity of the large-scale deployment and smooth flow of data between the physical devices to the decision-making platforms. A typical model of architecture has four main levels namely the perception level, the network level, the data processing level and the application level.

The perception layer is made of sensors, actuators, RFID tags, etc. which read the environment. These tools are spread throughout the urban infrastructure including roads, buildings, water networks, and the street to get the real-time data about temperature, humidity, motion, pollution, sound, traffic, etc. As an example, a smart environment system contains temperature and air quality sensors that assist in monitoring the pollution and alert the city authorities of dangerous levels.

The network layer will be involved in the transmission of data acquired by the perception layer to distant servers, control rooms or cloud platforms with the help of different communication protocols. It has network gateways, routers and connective interfaces like Wi-Fi, Bluetooth, Zigbee and cellular networks.

The data processing layer is important in filtering, analysis and storage of data that is sent by the devices. The layer usually employs cloud computing, edge computing and data analytics platforms to convert raw data into actionable information. This layer in the smart cities can be able to forecast the electricity usage patterns or detect the traffic bottlenecks before they happen.

Last but not least, the application layer provides end-users with certain services, e.g. smart parking systems, intelligent lighting control, or waste management dashboards. This layer links urban administrators, utility providers and citizens by means of friendly user interfaces and decision support tools.

All these layers and the elements constituting them are the backbones of urban IoT systems, which allow them to be autonomous, intelligent, and secure in the process of operating cities.

2.3 Communication Technologies

The key technology to any IoT system is an effective communication technology specially in urban areas where the devices are scattered and must perform under different conditions. A number of communication technologies are developed to meet the particular needs of IoT: low power consumption, long-range transmission, scale ability, and reliability.

Low-Power Wide-Area Networks (LPWANs) are a type of technology, which is intended to offer long-range communication at low-power consumption, such as LoRa (Long Range) and Sigfox. They find specific application in devices that must periodically send small data over long distances e.g. environmental monitoring and utility metering.

Narrowband IoT (NB-IoT) is one more trendy technology that is specially adjusted to the IoT devices. It uses the current cellular networks and it has a high density of connections per cell, which means that it is applicable to massive IoT in urban centers. NB-IoT is very energy-efficient and has good indoor coverage and this makes it ideal in smart buildings and monitoring of underground infrastructure.

The fifth-generation (5G) mobile communication is the game changer of IoT in the urban environment. It provides ultra high-speed data transfer, low latency and an enormous number of connected devices. 5G is particularly essential to real-time applications like autonomous cars, smart surveillance and emergency response systems. It allows a high-bandwidth streaming of video CCTV cameras, quick reaction to a traffic accident, and smooth interaction between connected vehicles and infrastructure.

Short-range, indoor applications Wi-Fi, Bluetooth Low Energy (BLE) and Zigbee are typical of other wireless technologies, which are typically used in short-range indoor systems, including smart lighting, HVAC systems, and connected appliances in smart homes and offices.

The choice of communication technology is based on a number of factors which include the needs of data transmission, availability of power, area of coverage and cost. A hybrid communication infrastructure is usually implemented in most applications where performance, scalability, and cost-effectiveness of urban IoT projects need to be balanced.

2.4 Data Acquiring, Processing and Analysis

IoT systems run on data. This is initiated by data acquisition whereby sensors and gadgets are placed to constantly measure the urban characteristics including noise level, traffic, water pressure, and energy consumption. These raw data streams are further conveyed to centralized systems/distributed platforms to undergo further processing.

Data processing entails cleaning, validation and transformation of raw data into structured data that can be analyzed. Since processing the huge amount of data generated in cities is a huge task, this step may need edge computing devices or local gateways to process the data prior to sending it to the cloud. This decreases latency and saves network bandwidth. As an example, under a smart traffic system, edge devices deployed at the intersections can analyze camera images in real-time to detect congestion and change the traffic signal accordingly.

Another important layer is data analytics that transforms processed data to usable insights. Machine learning algorithms, statistical models, and AI tools can help urban administrators identify patterns, anticipate the future scenarios, and make informed decisions. As an example, the smart grids have predictive analytics that can be used to predict energy demand using past usage patterns and weather conditions to distribute energy efficiently.

Besides descriptive and predictive analytics, real-time analytics enables an emergency to be responded to in real-time. Such solutions are used in urban safety systems in a way that gunshot detection sensors and analytics platforms can communicate with law enforcement in real-time, decreasing the response time and potentially saving lives.

The success of IoT application in urban development directly depends on the extent to which data is gathered, processed, and analyzed. City management can be done through continuous improvement, optimization of performance and strategic planning through robust analytics.

2.5 Edge, Fog, and Cloud Computing Integration

Since the amount of data produced by IoT devices is increasing, there is a need to process this data cost-efficiently and effectively. The conventional models of cloud computing use the processes of sending all the data to the central data centers where they can be stored and analyzed. Although cloud platforms have an enormous amount of computational resources and scalability, their limitations are associated with latency, bandwidth, and data sovereignty, in particular, in time-sensitive urban applications (Bhuvanya, R et al., 2025).

To overcome these shortcomings, edge computing has come up as an alternative model where the processing of data takes place nearer to the data source. Smart gateways, embedded processors and intelligent sensors are edge devices that carry out real-time analysis and control processing at or near the edge of the network. This reduces the latency involved in transmission of data and increases responsiveness. As an example, edge computing can be used in an autonomous public transport to allow vehicles to make a split-second decision without communicating with remote servers.

Fog computing is a midway between the edge and cloud that enables distributed processing of data. Fog nodes, which can be found at network routers or base stations, collect data of several edge devices, conduct initial analytics, and send the corresponding data to the cloud. This model is hierarchical, minimises data traffic, increases scalability and allows hybrid processing environments. Fog computing is common in smart campuses and industrial parks that have the demand of localized IoT applications that need the coordination of several devices.

In the meantime, cloud services are a must-have in terms of storing data in the long term, running sophisticated analytics, and performing mass integration between city departments. It enables the application of AI models, historical data analysis, and visualization in the context of strategic planning. What emerges as a combination of edge, fog, and cloud computing is an improved infrastructure to facilitate real-time responsiveness, data-driven intelligence, and optimization of the entire systems within the urban IoT ecosystem.

3. APPLICATIONS OF IoT IN URBAN DEVELOPMENT

3.1 Smart Transportation and Traffic Management

Smart transportation and traffic management is one of the most vital IoT applications in the urban development (Pattani, K. A et al., 2024). The high rate of urbanization has contributed to the use of vehicles, congestion in the roads and air pollution which have become major problems to the sustainability and livability of the modern cities. IoT provides smart solutions because, through the monitoring in real-time, predictive analysis, and automated control systems, it will be possible to optimize the flow of traffic, make the use of public transport more efficient, and shorten the travel time.

Vehicles, traffic lights, and road infrastructure are installed with IoT-enabled sensors, GPS modules, and RFID tags to gather and relay real time data about vehicle speed, density, and road conditions. The traffic management platforms process this data and dynamically adjust signal timing, detect congestion points and recommend alternative routes. An example is the adaptive traffic signal control systems where live traffic information is used to optimize the light cycle and this minimise the time spent at an intersection doing nothing (Kaneti, V. R et al., 2025).

In the sphere of public transport, the IoT is used to increase the efficiency of the work of transport and the comfort of its users. Commuters are able to get the correct information on arrival and departure of buses and trains through the mobile applications in real time. IoT in fleet management systems allows monitoring vehicle performance, estimating the need of maintenance, and optimizing routes. Besides, smart parking systems with IoT sensors will lead drivers to vacant parking places, reducing the time they spend searching and emission levels.

Finally, IoT turns the transportation system into dynamic and data-driven, making the urban mobility safer, more efficient, and environmentally friendly.

3.2 Smart Energy and Utility Management

The rising needs of electricity, water and gas in the cities have prompted the need to have smarter and more sustainable systems of utility management. The use of IoT makes it possible to monitor and distribute resources intelligently, making cities optimize consumption and minimize wastage as well as guarantee service continuity (Ponmalar, A et al., 2025).

IoT is central in the smart grid operation in smart energy systems. Granular information is gathered in energy consumption in residential, commercial, and industrial sectors by smart meters and sensors. This information enables utility providers to identify anomalies, predict demand and real-time adjustment of supply. The consumers get the advantage of customized energy information so that they can control their consumption habits and minimize the utility bills.

IoT is also useful when integrating renewable energy sources (solar and wind) that should be provided with real-time data on generation and load balancing. IoT platforms are an effective way of coordinating distributed energy resources (DERs) such as rooftop solar panels and battery storage systems to stabilize the grid and minimize reliance on centralized power plants.

IoT is involved to detect the existence of leaks in the water management system, to monitor water quality, as well as to predictive maintain the pipeline. With smart water meters, one can get more data on water consumption, and cities will have an opportunity to understand where the water resources are used inefficiently, thus enabling cities to use that water more sustainably. Similarly, gas networks can be inspected on the basis of pressure anomalies and potential leakages and be safer and more effective.

IoT contributes to improving the reliability, maintainability, and engagement of city utility services through real-time monitoring and automation.

3.3 Waste Management and Environmental Monitoring

Good waste management and protection of the environment is part of urban sustainability. The conventional ways used to collect the garbage and control the pollution is usually reactive and ineffective. IoT presents active and data-driven solutions that add value to waste management, environmental quality, and resource conservation on a large scale.

Smart waste management systems are IoT sensors attached to bins and dumpsters to monitor fill level, temperature and location. The data are reported to central management systems and used to optimize collection routes and schedules that lower the operating costs and fuel usage. The waste segregation can also be increased by using containers which have sensors to detect the type of waste and inform the users or collectors about the same.

The other important use of IoT in urban development is environmental monitoring. The air quality, noise, humidity, temperature and radiation are measured across the city by the sensors that are installed. The data obtained is used to determine the pollution hotspots, changes over a certain period of time and to support environmental policy. As an example, air quality sensors may be used to issue warning in case of high pollution rates, thus, triggering traffic restrictions or health warnings by the authorities.

Moreover, IoT contributes to the resilience of the urban environment in the case of floods, heat waves, and preparedness of disasters. Through constant observation of the environmental parameters, cities will be able to address the risks early enough and protect the health of the people.

Environmental and waste solutions using IoT are the way to make cities cleaner, greener, and more sustainable.

3.4 Smart Buildings and Infrastructure

Smart buildings have to do with the integration of intelligence to structures so as to check and manage lighting, heating, ventilation, security and occupancy. IoT converts the existing buildings into the networked systems that dynamically react to the changing circumstances and requirements of the users, thus, enhancing energy efficiency, safety, and comfort.

Building IoT sensors and actuators gather information about temperature, humidity, occupancy and energy consumption. This information can be used to automate HVAC systems, use lighting schedules and minimize energy consumption that is not necessary through the building management systems (BMS). As an example, the lights automatically can be dimmed or switched off in the rooms which are not used, and the smart thermostats automatically can adjust the temperatures depending on the preferences of the user and the external conditions.

IoT is useful in the case of bridges, roads, tunnels, and water pipes when it comes to monitoring and maintaining them. SHMSs are based on the use of vibration sensors, strain gauges and thermal sensors to identify damage or stress early enough.

This will allow repairs to be done in time and minimize the chances of failure of the infrastructure.

Elevators, security cameras and access control systems are smart to increase building safety and functionality. Connection to fire alarms and emergency communications enhance occupant safety further.

Buildings that have the capability of IoT are not only energy efficient and cost effective but also more responsive to the changing needs of the occupants and city planners.

3.5 Urban Safety and Surveillance Systems

City security is a very important issue in the areas of high population. IoT offers powerful means to support the safety of the population and prevent crimes and emergency response by means of constant monitoring, data processing, and controlled response.

Smart surveillance systems are fitted with IoT cameras that have motion, face recognition, and AI-based behavior analysis capabilities. Such systems are able to detect the suspicious activities, abandoned items, or unauthorized access and inform the authorities in real time. Edge processing can be done on surveillance footage to reduce the time of response in case of emergency.

Such security systems as gunshot detection, panic buttons, and smart streetlights with sensors can help to detect the emergency faster and enhance situational awareness. As an illustration, in case of gunshot detection, the precision of its location is reported to law enforcement services, so that the response may be faster and the resources may be distributed more efficiently.

IoT is also used in disaster management and emergency. Wearables and mobile apps can monitor people in case of evacuation and organize the rescue process, as well as sensors installed in infrastructure can recognize earthquakes, fires, and floods.

Urban safety platforms can offer a comprehensive picture of the safety of the population, which makes cities safer and more resilient through the combination of data of different sources: video feeds, environmental sensors, and social media.

3.6 e-Governance and Citizen Services

IoT helps in transforming the conventional governance into e-governance in which services are efficiently delivered, and there is transparency and citizen engagement. IoT in governance introduces real-time information into administrative decision-making processes as well as increases citizen participation.

Kiosks providing public services on the basis of IoT, intelligent ticketing systems, interactive dashboards provide citizens with an opportunity to receive information, file complaints, and monitor the status of service requests. This digitalization eases the process of administration and minimizes redressal of grievances.

Centralized monitoring and management of municipal services like street lighting, traffic enforcement, water distribution, and sanitation can be undertaken by use of IoT dashboards. To take an example, sensors will automatically report the malfunctioning streetlights and maintenance will be done in time.

IoT-enabled smart city apps provide real-time traffic, weather, and public transportation and utility interruptions information. The mobile platforms also allow the citizens to give feedback and as a result they ensure that there is a two way communication between people and the administration.

IoT allows data-based decision-making and service optimization, which makes the urban administration more inclusive, transparent, and accountable.

3.7 Healthcare and Public Health Monitoring

The challenges that urban healthcare systems encounter are connected with the density of population, aging population, and a lack of healthcare resources. IoT provides the groundbreaking solutions to monitoring the health of the population, remote care, and emergency medical services, which makes healthcare more available and efficient.

The wearable and health sensors measure vital signs like the heart rate, blood pressure, oxygen level, and glucose level. This information can be shared with medical practitioners to monitor them continuously and detect any abnormalities in health. IoT promotes remote patient monitoring (RPM), which is less straining to the hospital and patients get to be taken care of in the comfort of their homes.

In the context of the field of public health, the IoT is used to monitor disease outbreaks, air and water quality, and the level of sanitation. During pandemics or natural disasters, there are thermometers, contact tracing devices, and quarantine monitoring devices that are linked and can track the infection spread and containment.

With ambulance tracking systems and connected emergency rooms, emergency response is quicker and well coordinated during critical situations. Intelligent hospitals also employ IoT to streamline bed occupancy, medical stock and patient flow.

IoT helps make populations and healthcare infrastructure healthier and more resistant by uniting health information and urban management systems.

4. CHALLENGES AND LIMITATIONS

4.1 Privacy and Data Security

With the introduction of IoT technologies in cities to gather and analyze huge amounts of data in the streets, infrastructure, and citizens, the issue of privacy and data protection have become the primary concern. The IoT devices collect and share sensitive data such as location, identity, health, and behavior related information, and in case of a breach of these data, it can cause severe breaches of personal privacy and public confidence. The risk is further increased by the fact that IoT systems are connected and a weakness in one device or system can possibly put a whole network at risk of cyberattacks.

Smart meters and health monitors are some examples of urban uses of the Internet of Things, and they can collect granular data on a continuous basis. Absence of strict control over protection of such data may result to misuse of such data, sales of such data or disclosure to third party. Besides this, processing is extremely limited and there is no security facility in the IoT equipment, thus it is prone to malware, spoofing or denial-of-service (DoS) attacks.

Encryption of the IoT system, authentication and updating the firmware are required but not all urban implementations have applied them equally. The concepts of privacy-by-design and data anonymization must be integrated into the project of smart cities at the initial steps. Moreover, cities are required to adhere to international and local data privacy laws or other similar systems. These issues need to be addressed in order to build confidence in the minds of the population and in order to guarantee the ethical use of the IoT technologies in cities.

4.2 Interoperability and Standardization

The interoperability and standardization that are critical in the development of harmonious and scalable urban IoT ecosystems is severely affected by the heterogeneity of IoT devices, platforms and protocols. Various manufacturers also use proprietary technologies, and this leads to fragmented systems which do not communicate or share information easily. These interoperability problems make cross-sector integration more difficult, more complex to implement, and limits the ability of cities to deploy integrated, city-wide smart services.

In this case, a smart transportation system manufactured by a particular vendor might not be compatible with the environmental monitoring system manufactured by another vendor. Similarly, operational silos can be created because the smart grid infrastructure may be built around a different communication protocol than smart building systems. The absence of a standard set of standards makes integrating such systems into a centralized smart city system expensive and ineffective.

International bodies are attempting to develop open IoT communication, data format and device certification standards. However, technological innovation and market competition is so rapid that such standards are formulated and implemented gradually. Governments and municipal agencies must take the initiative in mandating interoperability standards, open standards and developing vendor-to-vendor collaboration.

Not only will interoperability increase the efficiency of the system, but also allow innovations where developers can now develop applications that can run on various infrastructures not just to the benefit of the citizens but also the city managers.

4.3 Scalability and Network Congestion

Scalability is the inherent problem with urban IoT implementations, as the number of new connections is exponentially growing. Smart solutions demand that the cities interested in implementing them in large scale ensure that their network infrastructure is capable of delivering connections to millions of devices simultaneously and is reliable, low latency, and data integrity. As the number of applications associated with the internet of things grows beyond piloting projects to city-wide applications, the issue of scalability becomes more pronounced.

The congestion of the network occurs when many devices that are connected in the network are trying to send their data at the same time and this causes the loss of packets, high latency, and failure of the services. As an example, during rush hours in a smart transportation system, connected vehicles, cameras and sensors can be flooding available bandwidth, and this can affect real-time decision making processes. In a mission-critical system where delay or data loss may be very dangerous, like in emergency response or health monitoring, a failure of the system can be disastrous.

Application of the next generation communication technologies such as 5G and LPWAN (Low-Power Wide-Area Network) could be a solution since they are meant to support high density of devices with low power consumption and low latency. The local processing of data also helps in scalability as less data has to be transported in centralized networks.

Nonetheless, the scalability should not be planned only in terms of technology. It entails capacity planning, architecture design that is flexible and policies that foresee growth and technology changes. Cities cannot afford to leave these issues unattended as they will end up constructing a disjointed system that will not be able to support the needs of future cities.

4.4 Infrastructure Costs and Legacy Systems

Although the long-term advantages of IoT are evident, the preliminary expenditures (related to the development of infrastructure) are still a considerable obstacle, particularly in the cases of developing cities or regions with low budget. IoT systems deployment involves an outlay in sensors, communication systems, data centers, cybersecurity systems, and human resources. Besides, the cost of operation such as maintenance, upgrade, and energy demand may further pressure the public resources.

The other important challenge is the incorporation of the IoT technologies with the legacy systems, which is the old urban infrastructure not planned to be used with digital connectivity. A lot of cities use the old electrical, water, and public transportation networks, which are not compatible with modern IoT solutions. These systems cannot be retrofitted easily as it involves heavy engineering intervention and in many cases it is neither technically possible nor cost-effective.

As another example, the replacement of a water distribution system with an old system to install smart meters and leak detection sensors may require a lot of excavation and replacement of pipes, which leads to disruption of the services offered to the population and is costly. On the same note, the old analog CCTV network might require a total overhaul in order to incorporate smart surveillance.

Cities can break down the financial hurdle through public-private partnerships (PPPs), government grants and innovation funds. Upfront costs and risks can also be lessened by use of modular and scalable IoT systems that can be implemented in phases. However, the investments have to be planned and the stakeholders aligned so that the benefits of the investments can be sustainable and inclusive to the urban populations.

4.5 Governance, Policy, and Regulatory Issues

Technology is not the only prerequisite in the successful implementation of IoT in the development of urban areas; proper governance, good policy framework and future-oriented regulations are also important. The lack of a holistic approach to governance of smart technology implementation in most cities is a source of uncertainty, inefficiencies and risks associated with ownership of data, ethical use and accountability by the citizens.

Among the key issues is the definition of the roles and responsibilities of various stakeholders of the IoT ecosystem, including governments, private companies, citizens and service providers. Who is the owner of data produced by the sensors in the public? In case of system failure or data breaches who will be at fault? What is the way out of the conflict when several parties have to share infrastructure?

There are also policy gaps on the issue of surveillance ethics, AI transparency, and bias in automated decision-making. As an example, the application of facial recognition technologies in the street environment without any obvious regulatory control causes serious concerns regarding mass surveillance and human rights.

The regulations need to strike a balance between innovation and the interest of the people which means that the IoT technologies should be used in a manner that would not violate the rights of people, would be inclusive, and would be more transparent. The international cooperation may assist in aligning the standards and regulatory practices especially because the urban IoT solutions tend to involve international vendors and cross-border data flows.

5. EMERGING TRENDS AND FUTURE DIRECTIONS

5.1 AI and Machine Learning in Smart Cities

The AI and ML are progressively being applied to the IoT systems to introduce more intelligence, responsiveness, and automation to the smart cities. Although the IoT can bring cities access to colossal amounts of real-time data about their surroundings, AI and ML enable cities to access useful information, make conclusions, and make unbiased decisions based on it. Smart and dynamic cities that can handle the challenges that continue to evolve with minimal human interferences will be possible with the convergence.

To provide an example, AI algorithms in the context of smart transportation would use traffic information gathered through IoT-enabled cameras and sensors to predict traffic patterns and improve the order in which the traffic lights are run. Machine learning models could be used in public safety to analyze the data collected with the help of surveillance cameras to identify abnormal behavior, recognize the possible threat, and prompt law enforcement in real-time. These apps are very useful to improve the level of efficiency and speed of urban responses.

In addition, IoT systems that are AI-driven aid in predictive maintenance in cities. As an example, one can apply ML models to the data obtained by bridges, water pipelines, or electrical grids to detect the first signs of wear and prevent expensive failure. On the same note, AI is applied to predict energy demand, balance the load, and optimize energy consumption in buildings and neighbourhoods in energy management.

The future trend is the building of completely autonomous subsystems of a city in which AI can be found in the collaboration with IoT to control transportation, utilities, waste, and emergency response. Nevertheless, the further development of AI will be associated with the need to ensure the transparency of algorithms, their fairness, and accountability, which will be essential to the maintenance of the level of trust and ethics in the functioning of smart cities.

5.2 Digital Twins and Simulation Models

Digital twins are a very recent development in the sphere of smart urban planning, which became possible due to the combination of IoT and real-time simulation technologies. Digital twin is a computerized representation of a physical object, a building, a road, a utility network or even a whole city that is constantly updated with the real world data measured by IoT devices. This digital model enables urban planners and administrators to see the present situation, predict the future scenario, and take evidence-based decisions with little risk.

The main benefit of digital twins is that they can give dynamic and detailed picture of urban systems. Digital twins allow authorities to track how the infrastructure components are used, identify anomalies, and proactively react to problems because they reflect the real-time behavior and status of the components. To illustrate, water distribution network digital twin can be utilized to forecast and identify possible leakages, model the effect of repairs, and maximize the water consumption in the case of drought.

Digital twins of traffic networks can be used in transportation to model the impacts of road closures, new infrastructure schemes, or emergency evacuations. This predictive capability allows the cities to test the solutions in a virtual environment and then implement the same in the real environment thereby saving money and reducing the inconvenience. Conversely, digital twins have the potential to allow building managers to optimize energy performance, indoor air quality, and occupancy in real-time.

The integrated use of digital twins and immersive technologies augmented reality (AR) and virtual reality (VR) will enable the stakeholders to possess intuitive and interactive collaborative planning tools in future.

5.3 Blockchain for Secure IoT Ecosystems

The IoT gadgets being distributed in cities raise a myriad of questions on the security, integrity and trust of data. Blockchain technology is one of the most recent technologies able to provide a solution to all of these issues; it possesses an immutable and decentralized ledger system that can provide a secure infrastructure capable of storing, verifying, and distributing the data generated by the IoT to the parties involved.

Urban IoT can be deployed on blockchain to check authenticity of device, encryption of communication, and history of data transfer. This is particularly useful within the multi-vendor environment where different devices and systems are supposed to interact with each other without any problem and within a secure environment. Indicatively, blockchain can facilitate secure peer-to-peer energy interactions between households in a smart energy grid, which could enable the reduction of reliance on central authorities and democratization of energy.

The blockchain enhances visibility and responsibility in the area of government. Smart contracts are computer code that automatically completes agreements and could be applied to automate processes such as public procurements, land registry, and permit applications, and thereby reduce bureaucratic bottlenecks and corruption. Blockchain enables patients to share and store patient data across hospitals and clinics safely and provides high privacy constraints in healthcare.

The other application that is emerging is in the supply chain where blockchain and IoT sensors are used to guarantee the provenance and condition of supply chain goods like food, pharmaceuticals and construction materials. This is boosted in increasing trust and reliability in the urban services and industries.

Although blockchain integration with IoT is a relatively new concept, currently, there are researches and pilot projects that indicate that cities will be able to use blockchain to develop decentralized, transparent, and secure urban platforms. To achieve mainstream adoption, scalability, energy, and the regulatory frameworks will be key in smart city ecosystems.

5.4 Sustainable and Green IoT Solutions

The issue of sustainability is in the spotlight of urban development due to the current climate change, resource shortage, and the worldwide movement to net-zero emissions. The IoT technologies are also becoming central in facilitating green urban projects by making the available resources more efficient, minimising the impact on the environment, and enhancing the development of circular economics.

Smart energy systems are one of the most noticeable uses of green IoT. IoT sensors, analytics platforms can assist in monitoring and regulating energy consumption in buildings and optimize renewable energy sources, as well as minimize carbon emissions. Smart grids combine with the distributed energy resources like solar panels and battery storage to facilitate efficient distribution of energy in accordance with the real-time energy demand and supply trends.

The IoT also helps in conservation of water by the use of intelligent irrigation systems which regulate irrigation schedules depending on weather reports and soil moisture. Sensor enabled bins and route optimization software in waste management decrease the consumption of fuel and enhance the efficiency of collection. Intelligent air quality monitoring systems assist cities to monitor the sources of pollution and use specific mitigation measures.

Green IoT is not only limited to applications but also design and manufacturing of the IoT devices. The energy-efficient hardware, low-power communication protocols (such as LPWAN), and biodegradable or recyclable hardware are being given more and more importance to reduce the environmental impact of the IoT infrastructure.

In the future, sustainable IoT will be important in meeting the climate objectives in cities and contributing to international sustainability plans, including the Sustainable Development Goals (SDGs) by the United Nations. Cities can make a step toward more environmentally friendly and sustainable futures, incorporating sustainability in all levels of urban IoT systems.

5.5 Citizen-Centric Smart Urban Design

One of the main trends that will define the future of smart cities is the direction of citizen-centric design where people, not only technology, are the centers of urban innovation. Instead of considering residents as the passive users of services, it focuses on active participation of citizens, transparency, inclusivity, and human-oriented solutions.

IoT allows the cities to receive feedback directly by citizens using mobile applications, wearable devices, and community platforms. Such participatory data can be used to make policies, better services and also to be more responsive to local needs. As an example, the user-generated information on transportation systems could be used to streamline the routes and enhance safety in a public transport.

The accessibility, affordability, and digital inclusion are also the concerns of the citizen-centric design. The smart city solutions should be such that they are able to serve every part of the society and even the marginalized and underserved communities. Inclusive design means that services like e-governance portal, public health tracking, emergency alerts will reach the people with disabilities, people with low literacy or not having access to technology.

In addition, it is necessary to establish trust by being open. Cities have to be transparent about the processes of gathering, storing and utilizing data. IoT-powered open data projects can offer residents with the means of analyzing and visualizing urban statistics, thus allowing them to engage in decision-making and urban planning (Jha et al.,2021).

Citizen-led innovations can be observed through environmental monitoring in a community, participatory budgeting platforms and local alert systems. Co-creation of IoT solutions with a local context on a collaborative innovation model involving urban labs, startups, academia, and residents is something that we would see more of in the future.

Finally, smart urban development cannot be successful only due to technological progress but also due to the active, educated, and empowered urban community.

A citizen-focused approach of the IoT guarantees that technological advancement meets the values of the population, justice, and health.

6. RESEARCH OPPORTUNITIES

6.1 Interdisciplinary Approaches

The creation and implementation of IoT in the urban setting demand studies that cannot be limited to the disciplinary areas. Although the source of IoT is engineering and computer science, it affects cities, and this requires different fields of expertise, such as urban planning, environmental science, public health, sociology, economics, and law. The research in the future has to adopt the interdisciplinary approach to developing systems that are not only technologically viable, but also responsive socially, environmentally and culturally.

A potential avenue is the combination of urban informatics and behavioral sciences so that people can be better understood to interact with the smart city technologies. An example here is that the sensors can provide real-time information about the traffic congestion, but it is also necessary to learn how the commuters behave, how they make their decisions, what socio-economic factors influence their actions, and so on to develop adequate transportation solutions.

The interdisciplinary study also plays a vital role in the climate change process through urban IoT. The environmental scientists working with the engineers can develop sensor networks that monitor the emission of greenhouse gases, and the economists and policy analysts can model tradeoffs of costs and benefits of mitigation options. In the sphere of governance, cooperation of data scientists and legal scholars may be useful to overcome the problem of surveillance, data privacy, and algorithmic accountability.

Learning institutions, research institutes and urban governments should hence establish collaborative research systems and innovation ecosystems where multidisciplinary teams join hands in solving real urban issues. More comprehensive, effective and equitable solutions to urban IoT can be set in motion by encouraging joint publications, cross-departmental projects, and integrated curricula.

6.2 Innovative Business Models

Urban IoT solutions should be sustainable and scalable and their sustainability and scalability are strongly associated with the process of the development of the innovative business models that are viable both in economic and social terms. The old models of conducting public procurement and building infrastructure are not always able to keep the fast-changing, capital-intensive environment of smart city technologies in pace. The need to research on new economic and financial models that aid in the design, implementation and support of urban IoT systems is increasing.

Another very popular model is the Public-Private Partnerships (PPPs), which means that governments partner with the private industry to co-develop and co-finance smart infrastructure. But there is the need to study the details of risk-sharing, long-run value creation, and citizen participation in such arrangements in the future. What can be done to make sure PPPs are within the interest of the people? What are the governance mechanisms that are required to be transparent and fair in allocation of profits?

Other methods of delivering certain services in the city are subscription-based and pay-per-use models that can be used in smart parking, waste collection, or energy management. These models are flexible and responsive yet they create doubts over inclusivity and affordability. The strategies of pricing, subsidy systems, and access models of the services should be researched to make sure that such business models are applied to all urban populations equally.

In addition to that, the concept of data monetization is also becoming increasingly relevant. Cities and business organizations are discussing how to create economic value by extracting the large amounts of data produced by IoT systems. But this raises ethical and legal issues of ownership of data, consent and privacy. It needs to conduct research on how to create value with the just, secure, and legal urban data.

Innovation hubs and startup ecosystems also hold the solution to the future of the business model. The study should be guided by how the cities can empower entrepreneurship, pilot programs, and scale-up innovations which are proven to work and help in competition and empowerment of the citizens. In general, reconsideration of the business model of urban IoT will be prior to the release of the latter.

6.3 Long-Term Impact Assessment Studies

With cities already investing heavily in their IoT infrastructure, it is urgently required to conduct long-term impact assessment research beyond the short-term efficiency gains and examine the overall social, economic, and environmental impacts. Most of the existing tests concentrate on the short-term outcome measures like energy conservation or traffic patterns, or sensor accurateness. These are practical, however, they do not reflect the systemic, long-term impact of deployments of the IoT on the life of the city.

Studies should in future come up with good constructs and strategies that can help to identify the long term effects of projects in smart cities. The measurements should be quantitative as well as qualitative in terms of social equity, quality of life, citizen satisfaction and resilience of the community. Using the example, how will smart public transportation impact the access to jobs and healthcare of low-income residents in the long run? Are intelligent surveillance systems altering the sense of security and trust in the ruling?

The real ecological footprint of IoT technologies can be identified by monitoring the changes in the air and water quality, noise pollution, and energy usage over several years with the help of environmental assessments. In the same manner, the health impact studies can be conducted to determine the contribution of digital health monitoring towards the better population-level outcomes, lower healthcare expenses, and management of chronic diseases.

Longitudinal studies are also required to examine IoT devices and system lifecycle. How much does it cost in the long term to maintain, upgrade and decommission smart infrastructure? What is the sustainability of the sensors and devices material? What are the implications of e-wastes?

To facilitate meaningful assessment, cities must make an investment in baseline data collection, real-time monitoring and open-data platforms.

6.4 Ethical and Inclusive Urban Technology Development

As technologies of the IoT are being integrated into the city infrastructure and everyday routine, ethical concerns must be prioritized at the very top of the research and development agendas. In order to have a fair and equitable city that is also intelligent, it is important to ensure that innovations in smart cities will also bring equity, inclusiveness, and human rights.

Another ethical concern is the risk of digital marginalisation. Most IoT applications rely on smartphones, internet or digital literacy which may not be accessible to all classes of people such as the elderly population, low-income individuals, individuals with disabilities or migrants. It is desirable that the research should focus on identifying these gaps and bridging them through the application of the principles of inclusive design, universal accessibility requirements, and special outreach programs.

Other ethical considerations of immediate concern are privacy and surveillance. The security enforced by sensors, cameras, and wearable devices can positively impact service provision, but infringe upon the independence and civil rights of the targeted individuals unless it is managed in a reasonable way. The research on how to apply ethical data collection, informed consent, and data minimization models should be conducted in the future. Data governance Community-based approaches to data governance, including cooperative data governance or data trusts, can give citizens more control over the use of data.

The other potential issue is algorithmic fairness. As cities implement AI-powered IoT solutions to conduct such tasks as policing, social services, and housing distribution, the study of how such algorithms are trained, whether they are biased, and how their results can impact different groups is needed. The study must be on the development of explainable AI, audit system and accountability and redress mechanisms in automated urban system.

Another role of participatory research approaches may be the ethical maturation of urban technologies. Co-design, testing and evaluation of IoT solutions defined by engagement of the community will help to leave the technologies non-conflicting with values, needs and aspirations of local populations. Not only does it make the process of innovation more democratic, it also enhances the degree of trust with the population.

Lastly, the green sustainability ethical issues should also be brought up. A study will be carried out to identify the impact of the IoT systems on the ecological balance, energy consumption, and material consumption. An IoT approach to a circular economy can make urban technology ecosystems more sustainable, with the equipment being designed to be recycled, reused, and produce as little waste as possible.

7. CONCLUSION

This survey has addressed the multifaceted nature of Internet of Things (IoT) in the definition of future of urban development. It started with the context and the reason why the IoT technologies need to be more prevalent in urban planning, followed by the fundamentals of the IoT, architecture, communication technology, data processing models, and computing paradigms, including edge, fog, and cloud computing. It was understood that the IoT plays a role in urban development in different areas, such as smart transportation, energy management, environmental monitoring, waste systems, smart buildings, public safety, governance, and healthcare, and a focus on how real-time data and automation can enhance the effectiveness of operations and citizen welfare was made. It was then supplemented with the discussion of some of the primary challenges that comprise data privacy, incompatibility, network capacity, cost of infrastructure, limitations in policies, that should be addressed in order to fully realize the potential of smart cities with the assistance of IoT. The integration of AI and ML, the use of digital twins, the security of blockchain, sustainable design of IoT, and citizen-oriented innovation were discussed as the tendencies that will shape the future. Further, the research opportunities were outlined in interdisciplinary collaboration, new business models, long-term impacts assessment, ethical technology development, and the value of incorporating, resilient, and sustainable research models.

Urbanization, a shortage of resources, climate-induced changes, and social inequalities are issues that are yet to be tackled by cities, yet the IoT is not only becoming a technological answer to them but the key to transformation in a city. Its capability to generate actionable insights, automation of sophisticated systems, and data-driven governance is invaluable in the creation of future-proof cities. The responsible plannedness, moral anticipation, and the non-discriminatory engagement should also support the possibility of the IoT, though. Urban development of the future will not be solely reliant on technological innovation, but will be determined by whether or not we will be able to control, evaluate and adjust the tools to the better good of the larger population. And, at any rate, it means that IoT will be forced to become the tool of transforming cities into greener, fairer, and smarter, the tool that will enable to transform cities into the place, where people and technology will be able to live in a symbiotic relationship.

REFERENCES

Bhuvanya, R., Yamini, B., Sivakumar, K., VM, G., Sathya, V., & Subramanian, R. S. (2025). Data Analytics in Management Empowering Decision-Making Through Insights. In *Pioneering Approaches in Data Management* (pp. 1-30). IGI Global Scientific Publishing.

Boopathi, S. (2024). Sustainable Development Using IoT and AI Techniques for Water Utilization in Agriculture. In *Sustainable Development in AI, Blockchain, and E-Governance Applications* (pp. 204-228). IGI Global Scientific Publishing. DOI: 10.4018/979-8-3693-1722-8.ch012

Gómez, J. E., Marcillo, F. R., Triana, F. L., Gallo, V. T., Oviedo, B. W., & Hernández, V. L. (2017). IoT for environmental variables in urban areas. *Procedia Computer Science, 109*, 67–74. DOI: 10.1016/j.procs.2017.05.296

Jaffrin, L. C., Nithya, T., & Divya, J. (2025, April). IoT for Sustainable Development: Enhancing Environmental Efficiency and Resource Optimization. In *2025 5th International Conference on Trends in Material Science and Inventive Materials (ICTMIM)* (pp. 1224-1230). IEEE.

Jha, A. K., Ghimire, A., Thapa, S., Jha, A. M., & Raj, R. (2021, January). A review of AI for urban planning: Towards building sustainable smart cities. In *2021 6th International Conference on Inventive Computation Technologies (ICICT)* (pp. 937-944). IEEE.

Jha, S. K., Beevi, S. J., Babitha, M. N., Chinnusamy, S., & Boopathi, S. (2024). Artificial Intelligence-Infused Urban Connectivity for Smart Cities and the Evolution of IoT Communication Networks. In *Blockchain-Based Solutions for Accessibility in Smart Cities* (pp. 113–146). IGI Global. DOI: 10.4018/979-8-3693-3402-7.ch005

Kaneti, V. R., Yamini, B., Nagarajan, S., Adaikkammai, A., Gracious, L. A., Subramanian, R. S., & Girija, P. (2025). Smart Transportation Systems and Sustainable Urban Mobility. In *Revolutionizing Urban Development and Governance With Emerging Technologies* (pp. 261–288). IGI Global Scientific Publishing. DOI: 10.4018/979-8-3373-1375-7.ch009

Kashyap, R. (2019). Machine learning for internet of things. In *Next-generation wireless networks meet advanced machine learning applications* (pp. 57–83). IGI Global. DOI: 10.4018/978-1-5225-7458-3.ch003

Kuppusamy, P. (2019). Smart education using internet of things technology. In *Emerging Technologies and Applications in Data Processing and Management* (pp. 385–412). IGI Global. DOI: 10.4018/978-1-5225-8446-9.ch017

May, P. M. A., Savitha, V., Gayathri, S., & Mahalakshmi, S. (2025, April). Exploring Sustainable Computing: IoT, Big Data, and Energy-Efficient Solutions. In *2025 5th International Conference on Trends in Material Science and Inventive Materials (ICTMIM)* (pp. 1218-1223). IEEE.

Molakatala, N., Kumar, A., Patil, U., Mhatre, P. J., Sambathkumar, M., & Boopathi, S. (2024). Integrating 5G and IoT Technologies in Developing Smart City Communication Networks. In *Blockchain-Based Solutions for Accessibility in Smart Cities* (pp. 147-170). IGI Global Scientific Publishing.

Pattani, K. A., Gautam, S., & Rizvi, A. (2024). Emerging Horizons: IoT, 5G, and the Evolution of Smart Cities. In *Secure and Intelligent IoT-Enabled Smart Cities* (pp. 1-21). IGI Global.

Ponmalar, A., Muthuram, A., Therasa, M., Priya, V., Sathya, V., Subha, S., & Subramanian, R. S. (2025). Convergence of Advanced Technologies for Sustainable Development and Smart Cities. In *AI and Green Technology Applications in Society* (pp. 189–218). IGI Global Scientific Publishing.

Solanki, A., & Nayyar, A. (2019). Green internet of things (G-IoT): ICT technologies, principles, applications, projects, and challenges. In *Handbook of research on big data and the IoT* (pp. 379-405). IGI Global.

Vujatović, M. J., Milanović, S., & Janjić, I. (2022). Natural Disasters and Risk Management: A Theoretical Overview. *Prevention and Management of Soil Erosion and Torrential Floods*, 21-41.

About the Contributors

Baghavathi Priya S. is an Associate Professor of Computer Science and Engineering at Amrita Vishwa Vidyapeetham, Chennai. She received gold medal in M.Tech degree. She received Ph.D. from Jawaharlal Nehru Technological University Hyderabad. She has 26 years of experience in teaching and 14 years of experience in research. She has successfully supervised 09 research scholars. She has published around 68 research papers in various conferences and journals. She is the author of the book titled as Operating Systems. She has published 7 book chapters in IGI Global, CRC Press and Wiley Publications. She received best paper award in ICTIS 2015 at Ahmedabad and in CAASR International conference 2017 at Dubai. She received the award of Top 20 influential women educators in Tamil Nadu from the Academic Council of uLektz. She received Active participation woman award from CSI. She is a Life time member in CSI and IAENG.

Subha S. is currently working as Assistant Professor in the Department of Computing Technologies, SRM Institute of Science and Technology, Kattankulathur, Chennai. Previously she has served as Senior Assistant Professor for over 13 years and acted as Head in the Department of Computer Science and Business Systems (CSBS) at Rajalakshmi Institute of Technology, Chennai, India. She has done her undergraduate and postgraduate in Computer Science and Engineering and she pursued her Ph.D. in Information and Communication Engineering in Anna University, Chennai. She has 19 years of academic experience. She has presented many papers in National and International Conferences and published few papers in reputed Scopus indexed and SCI journals. She has published a book chapter in Wiley publications in the domain of Transfer Learning and published two patents. She has acted as resource person for online STTPs and FDPs during the pandemic period and handled offline sessions also in other colleges. Her area of interests includes Data Mining, Machine Learning and Deep Learning. She has done NPTEL certifications in machine learning, deep learning and data science. She is a member of

Computer Society of India (CSI). She has organized many guest lectures and Faculty Development Programs in her college in association with CSI. Besides academics, she held the role of Coordinator for the Women Empowerment Cell of Rajalakshmi Institute of Technology.

S.Sountharrajan is an Associate Professor, Amrita School of Computing, Amrita Vishwa Vidyapeetham, Chennai Campus, where he also serves as the Chairperson, Department of Computer Science and Engineering. His academic and research contributions are extensive: he has published over 84 High quality journal papers which includes conference articles, and book chapters. Additionally, he has Edited 3 books covering a wide range of emerging technologies. He earned his Bachelor's, Master's, and Ph.D. degrees from premier institutions in India. He has received research grants totaling 38 lakhs from renowned funding agencies such as the DST, AICTE, and ICMR. He is also a frequent keynote speaker and has delivered over 40+ invited talks at various academic and industry forums. He holds certifications from leading technology firms such as IBM and Dell EMC. His core areas of expertise include Artificial Intelligence, Quantum Computing and Cloud Computing.

Balamurugan Balusamy is currently working as Professor and Chairperson ,School of Engineering and IT, Manipal Academy of Higher Education, Dubai Campus, Dubai, UAE. Prior to this assignment he was Professor, School of Computing Sciences & Engineering and Director International Relations at Galgotias University, Greater Noida, India. His contributions focus on Engineering Education, Block chain and Data Sciences. His Academic degrees and twelve years of experience working as a faculty in a global University like VIT University, Vellore has made him more receptive and prominent in his domain. He does have 200 plus high impact factor papers in Springer, Elsevier, and IEEE. He has done more than 80 Edited and authored books and collaborated with eminent professors across the world from top QS ranked university. Prof. Balamurugan Balusamy has served up to the position of Associate Professor in his stint of 12 years of experience with VIT University, Vellore. He had completed his Bachelors, master's, and PhD Degrees from Top premier institutions from India. His passion is teaching and adapting different design thinking principles while delivering his lectures. He has published 80+ books on various technologies and visited 15 plus countries for his technical course. He has several top-notch conferences in his resume and has published over 200 quality journal, conference and book chapters combined. He serves on the advisory committee for several startups and forums and does consultancy work for industry on Industrial IOT. He has given over 195 talks in various events and symposium.

Suganya E. is an Assistant Professor with specialization in Data Science and Artificial Intelligence, currently serving at Department of Information Technology, Sri Sivasubramaniya Nadar College of Engineering, Chennai. She has authored over 42 research publications, including 33 international journal articles in reputed publishers such as Springer, Elsevier, IEEE, and Nature Scientific Reports. She is a Lifetime member of ISTE professional society. She has presented at 8 international conferences, edited 5 Books, authored 6 book chapters. She has also contributed to edited volumes on cybersecurity, IoT in agriculture, and green energy harvesting. She has successfully organized and coordinated numerous workshops, technical symposiums, hackathons, and outreach programs, inspiring students to engage in emerging technologies, innovation, and social impact projects. She also serves as the Coordinator of the IEEE WIE Affinity Group at SSN College of Engineering.

***

Jeyamurugan A. is a highly experienced Assistant Professor in the Department of Artificial Intelligence and Data Science at Vel Tech Multi Tech Engineering College in Avadi, Chennai. With a distinguished career spanning 16 years in academia, he is a dedicated educator, mentor, and researcher. His core expertise lies at the intersection of hardware and advanced computing, specializing in Embedded Systems, the Internet of Things (IoT), Artificial Intelligence (AI), and Data Science. He is deeply committed to mentoring and guiding students in emerging technologies. He actively contributes to academic growth through dedicated research, scholarly publications, and the implementation of innovative teaching methodologies aimed at finding and developing innovative solutions.

Revathi A. is a faculty member in the Department of Computer Science and Engineering (Cyber Security) at RMK College of Engineering and Technology. She is committed to nurturing students in the field of cybersecurity and advanced computing. Her areas of interest include network security, ethical hacking, and emerging cyber defense technologies. She contributes to academic excellence through teaching, mentoring, and research initiatives.

Maheswari B. is a faculty member at RMK Engineering College, Tamil Nadu, India. Her teaching and research interests span areas of computer science and engineering. She is actively involved in academic guidance and scholarly contributions in her field.

Yamini B. is a faculty member in the Department of Networking and Communications at SRM Institute of Science and Technology, Kattankulathur.

She has expertise in networking technologies, communication systems, and related research domains. Her academic contributions focus on blending technical knowledge with practical applications for students. She is actively involved in research and scholarly activities within the institution. Through her dedication, she continues to motivate and guide students in the field of Networking and Communications.

Yuvasri B. is a faculty member in the Department of Computer Science and Engineering at R.M.K. College of Engineering and Technology, Puduvoyal. She has expertise in core areas of computer science with a keen interest in emerging technologies and applications. Her teaching methodology blends strong theoretical foundations with practical, hands-on learning. She is actively engaged in academic activities, research contributions, and student mentoring. Through her commitment and passion, she continues to inspire students to excel in the field of computer science and engineering.

Veda Chatiyode is an undergraduate student pursuing a Bachelor's degree in Computer Science and Engineering with a specialization in Artificial Intelligence at Amrita Vishwa Vidyapeetham, Chennai, India. She has interned at Fidelity Investments as a full-stack developer and at Indium Software, working on deep learning projects with PyTorch. She has co-authored research papers in machine learning and deep learning and contributed to a book chapter on AI in higher education. Her interests include artificial intelligence, deep learning, and cloud-based software engineering.

Monica G. K. is a faculty member in the Department of Computer Science and Engineering (Cyber Security) at R.M.K. College of Engineering and Technology, Puduvoyal. She specializes in the field of cyber security, focusing on secure systems and emerging technologies. Her teaching emphasizes both theoretical knowledge and practical applications in real-world scenarios. She actively contributes to academic development, research activities, and student mentoring. With her dedication, she continues to inspire students to excel in the dynamic field of cyber security.

Viji Gripsy J. is an accomplished Associate Professor in the Department of Computer Science with Cognitive Systems at PSGR Krishnammal College for Women, Coimbatore. With academic credentials including M.Sc., M.Phil., Ph.D., and postdoctoral research, she specializes in mobile and ad-hoc wireless sensor networks. She has authored 24 UGC-recognized research articles, with 23 indexed in SCOPUS, and has published 11 books along with numerous book chapters. Her research focuses on energy-efficient routing protocols for MANETs and secure data transmission in IoT environments. A committed research supervisor, she has guided one Ph.D. scholar and is currently mentoring three more. In addition to her teaching and research responsibilities, Dr. Gripsy actively contributes to curriculum development as a member of various Boards of Studies and regularly participates in academic seminars, workshops, and conferences.

Kennady K. is currently working as an Assistant Professor in the Department of Artificial Intelligence and Data Science at Rajalakshmi Institute of Technology, Chennai. He holds expertise in the areas of Artificial Intelligence, Machine Learning, and Data Analytics. His research interests include developing intelligent systems for real-world problem solving and data-driven applications. He has been actively involved in guiding students and contributing to academic and research activities of the department. With a strong passion for teaching and research, he continues to publish and participate in conferences and workshops

Vijayalakshmi K. is an Assistant Professor at SRM Institute of Science and Technology, Kattankulathur. Her academic and research interests include Machine learning, intelligent systems, and emerging technologies. She is dedicated to teaching, mentoring students, and contributing to the advancement of her department. She actively engages in research and academic development to promote innovation in higher education.

M. Sasi Kala is the Head of the Department of Data Science at PSGR Krishnammal College for Women. A distinguished academician and dedicated leader, she brings a wealth of knowledge and expertise to the rapidly evolving field of data science. Under her guidance, the department has flourished, fostering innovation, research, and industry-relevant skills among students. Dr. Sasikala is known for her commitment to academic excellence, mentorship, and continuous upskilling, making her a pivotal force in shaping the next generation of data science professionals.

Anita M. is a faculty member at the SRM Institute of Science and Technology, Tamil Nadu, India. Her academic and research interests include emerging domains in computer science and engineering. She has been actively engaged in teaching, research, and scholarly publications.

Nalini M. is an Associate Professor in the Department of Computer Science and Engineering, S.A. Engineering College, Chennai, India. She received her B.E. in Computer Science and Engineering from Anna University, Chennai in 2010 and M.Tech. in Computer Science and Engineering from B.S. Abdur Rahman Crescent Institute of Science & Technology, Chennai, India in 2012. She was awarded Ph.D. in Computer Science and Engineering from St. Peter's Institute of Higher Education and Research, Chennai, India in 2018. She has 10 years teaching experience. Her research interests include Data Mining, Big Data Analytics and Networking. She has published many articles in reputed journals.

Usha M., Dean of the School of Computational Sciences at KG College of Arts and Science, is a highly respected academician with a strong track record in research and higher education leadership. She has played a pivotal role in strengthening the academic framework and curriculum design in computational sciences, ensuring alignment with industry trends and technological advancements. Dr. Usha has contributed extensively to scholarly research, with numerous publications in reputed national and international journals. Her research interests span across data analytics, artificial intelligence, and emerging technologies in computer science. She has also presented papers at prestigious conferences and has guided several student and faculty research projects. Her dedication to promoting a research-driven culture has significantly elevated the institution's academic profile and fostered a spirit of inquiry and innovation among students and faculty.

Dhanalakshmi P. serves as an Assistant Professor at Sri Ramakrishna College of Arts & Science for Women. With a strong academic background and a passion for teaching, she is committed to empowering young minds through quality education. Her dedication to academic excellence and student development has made her a respected faculty member within the institution. Dr. Dhanalakshmi actively engages in research and contributes to the academic community through seminars, workshops, and scholarly publications, fostering a dynamic and enriching learning environment for her students.

Beslin Pajila is a faculty member at Vel Tech Rangarajan Dr. Sagunthala R&D Institute of Science and Technology, Chennai, India. Her academic and research interests focus on emerging trends in computer science and engineering. She has contributed to teaching, research, and scholarly publications in her field.

Annamalai R. currently serves as an Assistant Professor, in the Department of Computer Science and Engineering, Amrita School of Engineering, Amrita Vishwa Vidyapeetham, Chennai. He has 20 years of experience in teaching and industry. His areas of interest include Machine Learning Programming languages, optimization algorithms. Dr. R. Annamalai is currently guiding 7 PhD research scholars and has guided 10 M.E projects and is Doctoral Committee Member for 2 Ph.D. Research Scholars. He has delivered many guest Lectures and acted as resource person in Faculty development programs. He has also acted as program committee member and session chair in national and international conferences.

Madhu Annam R. is a dedicated second-year student pursuing a Bachelor of Technology (B.Tech) degree in Information Technology. With a strong interest in technology and problem-solving, she is building a solid foundation in programming, data structures, databases, and emerging technologies. As an enthusiastic learner, she actively explores opportunities to enhance knowledge in areas such as software development, web technologies, and artificial intelligence. Passionate about innovation and continuous learning, she is focused on developing both technical and analytical skills to excel in the IT field. With a commitment to growth, she aims to contribute to impactful technology-driven solutions.

Siva Subramanian R. is a faculty member in the Department of Computer Science at SRM Institute of Science and Technology. He has extensive experience in teaching and research in advanced computing technologies. His work focuses on developing innovative solutions and contributing to academic research and student development.

Rajesh Kanna Rajendran is an accomplished academic with over 16 years of experience in the field of computer science and information technology. He holds a Ph.D. from Bharathiar University, Coimbatore, and an M.Phil from Vinayaka Missions University, Salem. He also earned his MCA from Periyar University, Salem. Currently, Dr. Rajeshkanna serves as an Assistant Professor in the Department of Computer Science at CHRIST (Deemed to be University), Bangalore, a position he has held since July 2022. Prior to this, he was the Professor and Head of the Department of Information Technology at Dr. N.G.P Arts & Science College (Autonomous), Coimbatore. His tenure at this institution, spanning from January 2020 to June 2022, followed a series of progressive roles, including Associate Professor and Head of the Department, and earlier, as an Assistant Professor. Dr. Rajeshkanna has made significant academic contributions through his research and scholarly activities. He has published 35 papers in reputed international journals with high impact factors and has contributed 16 book chapters through IGI Global Publications.

Ahamed Johnsha Ali S. is an Assistant Professor in the MCA department at Sri Krishna Aditya College of Arts and Science. He is dedicated to fostering a strong academic environment and guiding students in advanced computing concepts, programming, and research. With a focus on practical applications and emerging technologies, he actively engages in curriculum development, workshops, and mentorship to enhance student learning and professional growth. His passion for education and technology drives him to contribute to both scholarly and institutional advancement in the field of computer science.

Krithikha Sanju S. is an Assistant Professor in the Department of Information Technology at Sri Sivasubramaniya Nadar College of Engineering, Chennai, India. She received her B.E. degree in Electronics and Communication Engineering from Sethu Institute of Technology in 2015. Following graduation, she worked at IBM as a Technical Associate from July 2015 to June 2016. She pursued her M.E. in Computer Science and Engineering with a specialization in Big Data Analytics at CEG, Anna University, graduating in 2018. In February 2025, she obtained her Ph.D. in Information and Communication Engineering from CEG, Anna University. Her primary research interests include Natural Language Processing, Image Processing, and Social Network Analysis, with a focus on advanced computational techniques for real-world applications.

Saravanan S. is a faculty member in the Department of Computer Science and Engineering at Vel Tech Rangarajan Dr. Sagunthala R&D Institute of Science and Technology. His academic and research contributions focus on advancing knowledge in computer science, with a particular interest in exploring innovative technologies and their applications. He is actively involved in teaching, mentoring students, and guiding them towards achieving academic excellence. Through his work, he aims to bridge the gap between theoretical concepts and practical implementations, fostering a strong research culture within the department.

Udhayashankar S. is a distinguished member of Vel Tech Multi Tech Dr. Rangarajan Dr. Sakunthala Engineering College. Known for his dedication to advancing academic and technical knowledge, he plays a pivotal role at the institution

Janani Srinivasan Anusha is pursuing her Bachelor of Technology in Computer Science and Engineering with a specialization in Artificial Intelligence at Amrita Vishwa Vidyapeetham, Chennai. She has interned as a Full Stack Engineer at Fidelity Investments, contributing to scalable logging solutions and automation pipelines with LLM, and as a Data Science Intern at Elite Digital Logistics, developing OCR- and NLP-based systems for enterprise applications. Her research interests include artificial intelligence, machine learning, data science, and cloud-based software engineering. She has co-authored research articles and book chapters in data science, health informatics, and AI-driven learning technologies.

Thilagam T. is a faculty member in the Department of Computer Science and Engineering at Vel Tech Rangarajan Dr. Sagunthala R&D Institute of Science and Technology, Chennai. She specializes in core areas of computer science with a strong interest in emerging research domains. Her teaching emphasizes blending theoretical knowledge with practical applications to enhance learning outcomes. She actively contributes to academic development, research initiatives, and student mentoring.

Through her dedication and expertise, she continues to inspire students to pursue excellence in computer science and engineering.

Anish T. P. is an Assistant Professor in the Department of Computer Science and Engineering at R.M.K. College of Engineering and Technology, Puduvoyal. He specializes in computer science domains with a focus on emerging technologies and research applications. His teaching approach integrates theoretical foundations with practical insights to enhance student learning. He actively contributes to research, publications, and academic development within the institution. Residing in Tamil Nadu, he continues to inspire students in pursuing excellence in computer science and engineering.

Saranya V. is an Assistant Professor in the Department of Artificial Intelligence and Machine Learning at Panimalar Engineering College. Her teaching and research interests focus on artificial intelligence, machine learning, and emerging data-driven technologies. She is actively involved in guiding students and contributing to academic development in the field of AIML. She continues to pursue innovative approaches in research and education to enhance learning outcomes.

Index

A

C

D

G

I

K

L

M

P

Q

S

U

www.ingramcontent.com/pod-product-compliance
Lightning Source LLC
LaVergne TN
LVHW060003031026
849161LV00025B/1343